RETURNS

RETURNS

❖

Becoming Indigenous
in the Twenty-First
Century

JAMES CLIFFORD

HARVARD UNIVERSITY PRESS
Cambridge, Massachusetts
London, England
2013

Library of Congress Cataloging-in-Publication Data
Clifford, James, 1945–
    Returns : becoming indigenous in the twenty-first century / James Clifford.
       pages ; cm
    Includes index.
    ISBN 978-0-674-72492-1
    1. Indigenous peoples.   2. Indigenous peoples—Ethnic identity.   3. Indigenous
peoples—Social life and customs.   4. Cultural fusion.   I. Title.
GN380.C59 2013
305.8—dc23   2013012423

For my students, 1978–2013

Contents

RETURNS

Prologue

Returns is the third volume in a series beginning in 1988 with *The Predicament of Culture* and followed in 1997 by *Routes*. Like the others, it collects work written over roughly a decade. Ideas begun in one book are reworked in the others. All the important questions remain open. *Returns* is thus not a conclusion, the completion of a trilogy. It belongs to a continuing series of reflections, responses to changing times. In retrospect, how can these times be understood? What larger historical developments, shifting pressures and limits, have shaped this course of thinking and writing?

Situating one's own work historically, with limited hindsight, is a risky exercise. One is sure to be proven wrong, or at least out of date. Rereading my words in *The Predicament of Culture*, I feel most acutely their distance. They belong to another world. There is no "globalization" in the book's index, no "Internet," no "postcolonial." Searching for a historical narrative to make sense of what has changed, I now recognize a profound shift of power relations and discursive locations. Call this change, for short, the decentering of the West. I hasten to add that "decentering" doesn't mean the abolition, disappearance, or transcendence of that still potent zone of power. But a change, uneven and incomplete, has been going on. The ground has moved.

A conversation from the early 1970s comes to mind. I was a doctoral student conducting research in the Malinowski papers at the London School of Economics. One afternoon outside the library I found myself discussing the history of anthropology with Raymond Firth, the great anthropologist of Tikopia. Firth had been a student and colleague of Malinowski. He wondered about attempts to link cross-cultural research with colonial power, in particular the important book edited by Talal Asad, *Anthropology and the Colonial Encounter*. Without minimizing

1

the issue, Firth thought the relations between anthropology and empire were more complex than some of the critics were suggesting. He shook his head in a mixture of pretended and real confusion. What happened? Not so long ago we were radicals. We thought of ourselves as critical intellectuals, advocates for the value of indigenous cultures, defenders of our people. Now, all of a sudden, we're handmaidens of empire!

That is what it is like to feel "historical." The marking of colonialism as a period, a span of time with a possible ending, came suddenly to Euro-American liberal scholars. Who would have predicted in the early 1950s that within a decade most of the colonies ruled by France and Britain would be formally independent? Feeling historical can be like a rug pulled out: a gestalt change, perhaps, or a sense of sudden relocation, of exposure to some previously hidden gaze. For Euro-American anthropology, the experience of being identified as a "Western" science, a purveyor of partial truths, has been alienating, a difficult but ultimately enriching process. The same kind of challenge and learning experience would engage many scholars of my generation with respect to gender, race, and sexuality. For of course more than "the West" has been decentered during the past fifty years.

In retrospect, I locate my work within a postwar narrative of political and cultural shifts. Like Firth, I have come to feel historical.

Born in 1945, I grew up in New York City and Vermont. This was the peace of the victors: the Cold War standoff and a sustained, American-led, economic expansion. My fundamental sense of reality—what actually existed and was possible—would be formed in circumstances of unprecedented material prosperity and security. Of course my generation experienced recurring fears of nuclear annihilation. But since disarmament was not around the corner, we learned, on a daily basis, to live with "the balance of terror." In other respects the world seemed stable and expansive, at least for white, middle-class North Americans. We would never lack resources. Wars were fought elsewhere. The lines of geopolitical antagonism were clearly drawn and, most of the time, manageable.

New York City during the 1950s felt like the center of the world. North American power and influence was concentrated in downtown Manhattan. A subway ride took you to Wall Street, the United Nations, the Museum of Modern Art, or avant-garde Greenwich Village. The decolonizing movements of the postwar period arrived belatedly in the form of civil rights, the Vietnam debacle, and a growing receptiveness to cultural alternatives. My critical thinking was nurtured by radical art and the politics of diversity. Its sources were Dada and surrealism, cross-cultural anthropology, music, and popular culture. New historical actors—women, excluded racial and social groups—were making claims for justice and recognition.

Like many of my generation, I saw academic work as inseparable from these wider challenges to societal norms and cultural authority. The moment brought a new openness in intellectual, political, and cultural life. Established canons and institutional structures were challenged. The ferment also produced exclusivist identity politics, hedonistic subcultures, and forms of managed multiculturalism. The language of diversity could mask persistent inequalities. Most academic writing, including my own, never questioned the liberal privilege of "making space" for marginal perspectives. One should not overestimate the changes associated with "the sixties." Many apparent accomplishments— antipoverty initiatives, affirmative action, women's rights—are now embattled or in retreat. Yet something important happened. Things changed, unevenly, incompletely, but decisively. To mention only American universities: the blithely Eurocentric, male-dominated English department of the 1950s now seems like a bad dream.

When I was thirty-three, I moved from the North Atlantic to the edge of the Pacific, from one global ocean and world center to another. For a time, I lived as a New Yorker in diaspora, out on a periphery, the "West Coast." But little by little the presence of Asia, the long history of north/ south movements in the Americas, and influences from culturally rich Island Pacific worlds made themselves felt. In a decentered, dynamic world of contacts, the whole idea of the West, as a kind of historical headquarters, stopped making sense.

In Northern California it soon became clear that the decentering I had begun to feel was not just an outcome of postwar decolonizing energies and the contestations of the global sixties. These forces had made, and were still making, a difference. But the shift was also the work of newly flexible and mobile forms of capitalism. I was caught up in the double history of two unfinished, postwar forces working in tension and synergy: decolonization and globalization.

Santa Cruz, California, my home after 1978, epitomized this doubleness. A university town and enclave of countercultural, sixties visionaries, the town was also a bedroom community for the new high-tech

world of Silicon Valley. This was the "Pacific Rim" of massive capital
flows, Asian Tigers, and labor migrations. I also lived on a *frontera*, a
place in the uncontrolled, expanding borderland linking Latin America
with the United States and Canada. In the northern half of Santa Cruz
County: a university and town government that strongly identified with
multicultural, feminist, environmentalist, anti-imperial agendas. In the
southern part of the county: a changing population of Mexican/Latino
workers and the growing power of agribusiness. I began to think of the
present historical moment as a contradictory, inescapably ambivalent,
conjuncture: simultaneously post- and neocolonial.

Driving along the cliff tops to San Francisco I could contemplate a
line from Charles Olson: "Where we run out of continent." We?
California was coming to feel less like the "West Coast" of a United
States of America and more like a crossing of multiple histories. The
essays in *Routes* would reflect this complex sense of location and mobility.
And the final essay, "Fort Ross Meditation," would point me north to
Alaska, a different *frontera*. Fort Ross, now reconstructed just up the
coast from San Francisco, was an early nineteenth-century outpost of
the Russian fur-trading empire. Among the several populations gathered
there, the most numerous were maritime Alaska Natives (Alutiiq or
Sugpiaq as they now call themselves), a coerced labor force of sea otter
hunters. In my subsequent research, Part Three of *Returns,* I followed
the tracks of these mobile Natives to Kodiak Island, where today their
descendants are renewing a damaged heritage. The Fort Ross contact
zone also led me to a deeper interest in native California, and especially
to the changing story of Ishi, the state's most famous Indian. Today, the
"last wild Indian" is making a comeback in contexts unimaginable a
century ago. The many versions of Ishi's story are explored in *Returns,*
Part Two: a meditation on terror and healing, repatriation and renewal.

Teaching at the University of California, Santa Cruz, also opened
contacts with South Asia and the Island Pacific through the graduate
students who studied in UCSC's interdisciplinary History of Consciousness program. Academic voyagers, they identified themselves as
"postcolonial" and/or "indigenous." Some would remain to teach in the
United States; others went home. These younger scholars' clear sense of
working within, while looking beyond, a Euro-American world of ideas
and institutions intensified my own sense of being at the edge or the end
of something. I realized I had a part to play in the history they were constructing.

The essays in *Returns,* like their predecessors, are rooted in the 1980s and 1990s. As the sixties waned and a globalizing neoliberalism took hold, visions of revolution were replaced by cultural and intellectual tactics of transgression and critique. By the 1980s, frontal resistance to a mobile hegemony seemed useless. We were in a Gramscian "war of position," a series of small resistances and subversions. What could not be defeated might at least be undermined, transgressed, opened up. For many intellectuals working inside Euro-American centers of power this meant supporting "diversity" in both epistemological and sociocultural registers. Space could be cleared for discrepant senses of the real; positions could be staked out for future struggles; dominant forms of authority and common sense could be criticized and theoretically disassembled. Much of my writing in *The Predicament of Culture,* with its rejection of monological authority and its commitment to multiplicity and experimentation, made sense in this conjuncture. *Routes,* too, belongs in this world of critique, though its receptivity to emergent forms, both diasporic and indigenous, hints at something more. The current book, *Returns,* though still marked by the 1990s, begins to register a new historical conjuncture.

Developments after 2000 are less susceptible to narration than the post-sixties decades. A few things seem probable: the United States, newly vulnerable, is no longer an uncontested global leader. Its military surge following 9/11 proved unsustainable—a spasmodic reaction to secular, irreversible changes. There will doubtless be further adventures, but American global hegemony is no longer a credible project. It is countered by new centers of economic power, by Islam as only the most visible among non-Western globalizing ideologies, by forms of authoritarian capitalism in Asia. The signs of systemic crisis and transition are everywhere: financial instability and uncontrollable markets, rising inequality and scarcity, deepening ecological limits and competition for resources, the internal fragmentation and fiscal emergency of many nation-states. Crisis without resolution, transition without destination. In the 1980s Margaret Thatcher could famously declare: "TINA: There Is No Alternative." Today, a statement like this makes no sense: everyone knows there are alternatives, for better and for worse.

From my perch in the new millennium, I understand the last half-century as the interaction of two linked historical energies: decolonization and globalization. Neither process is linear or guaranteed. Neither can subsume the other. Both are contradictory and open ended. And both have worked to decenter the West, to "provincialize Europe," in Dipesh Chakrabarty's words. This is an unfinished but irreversible project.

"Globalization" is not, or not simply, "the capitalist world system." It is of course capitalist, and more. Globalization is a name for the evolving world of connections we know, but can't adequately represent. It is a sign of excess. This is obviously not the nineties version: "the end of history," "the flat earth." Nor is this the familiar enemy: Jose Bové tilting against McDonald's, the "Battle of Seattle." Globalization is the multidirectional, unrepresentable sum of material and cultural relationships linking places and people, distant and nearby. It is not just a continuation of empire, dominion by other, more flexible, means, as critics on the Left tend to argue. You can't say imperialism from below, but you can say globalization from below, or from the edge. "Globalization" is a placeholder, *in medias res*. The essays in *Returns* begin to explore this articulated, polycentric totality. Multiple Zeitgeists. A bush, or tangle, of histories.

Similarly, "decolonization" is an unfinished, excessive historical process. More than the national liberations of the 1950s and 1960s that were initially successful and then co-opted, decolonization names a recurring agency, a blocked, diverted, continually reinvented historical force. The energies once bundled in phrases like the "Third World" or "national liberation" are still with us. They reemerge in unexpected places and forms: "indigeneity" (all those people once destined to disappear . . .), the "Arab Spring" (whatever it turns out to be . . .), and even that universal adversary, the "terrorist."

There is certainly something hopeful in the surprises that an openended history can be counted on to deliver. Some of us, at least, can take heart from the failures of the dominant systems we resisted (and came, in the process, to depend on). The inability of neoliberal ideology to subsume alternatives, to round up and account for everyone, makes it easier to imagine new identities, social struggles, and kinds of conviviality. But this exciting sense of historical possibility is inseparable, at least for me, from another feeling, something I didn't experience twenty-five years ago: fear, the visceral awareness of a given world suddenly gone. Feeling historical: the ground shifting.

Suddenly there are serious questions about our grandchildren's future. And this sense of insecurity, no doubt related to cyclical processes of political-economic decline, is intensified by long-term ecological threats that can no longer be managed or exported. Historicity at a different scale: that of a species among other species, the past and future of a whole planet and its ability to sustain life. What happens when population growth reaches its limits, when the supplies run out, when the resource wars get really desperate? These instabilities are deep and world changing. Of course this feeling of exposure is something like what most people in the world have always known.

The certainty of having lived in a bubble, a "First World" security that is no more. Goodbye to all that. And now?

Returns follows just one emergent strand: the indigenous histories of survival, struggle, and renewal that became widely visible during the 1980s and 1990s. Tribal, aboriginal, or First Nations societies had long been destined to disappear in the progressive violence of Western civilization and economic development. Most well-informed people assumed that genocide (tragic) and acculturation (inevitable) would do history's work. But by the end of the twentieth century it became clear that something different was going on. Many native people were indeed killed; languages were lost, societies disrupted. But many have held on, adapting and recombining the remnants of an interrupted way of life. They reach back selectively to deeply rooted, adaptive traditions: creating new pathways in a complex postmodernity. Cultural endurance is a process of becoming.

In *Returns* I explore this becoming, as it works its way through pragmatic engagements with globalizing powers, with diverse capitalisms, and with particular national hegemonies. To account for indigenous life in these powerful force fields I grapple with issues of political-economic determination. And I revisit questions about cultural wholeness and historical continuity that were raised in the concluding chapter of *The Predicament of Culture*, "Identity in Mashpee." Twenty-five years later, the processes of indigenous persistence and revival suggested by these questions are more than just occasions for loosening Western categories. Now, at a time of systemic crisis and uncertain transition, I see them as real, alternative paths forward.

In *Returns* I argue for an ethnographic and historical realism—recognizing that ideas of history and the real are currently contested and also inventively translated in power-charged sites from land-claims courtrooms to museums and universities. All such conjunctures are contingent and composed of discrepant strands. Thus an adequate realism must juxtapose—connect and keep apart—consequential, partial stories. I work with three narratives, active in the last half-century: decolonization, globalization, and indigenous becoming. They represent distinct historical energies, scales of action, and politics of the possible. They cannot be reduced to a single determining structure or history. Nor can they be held apart for long. The three histories construct, reinforce, and trouble each other. "Big-enough" histories like these need to be held in dialectical tension, simultaneous but not synchronous. *Returns* thus offers a lumpy verisimilitude in which political, economic, social, and cultural forces intersect but do not form a whole. If the book is unable to wrap things up, to master the changing times, this failure, consciously engaged, underlies its claim to realism.

Returns is organized in three loosely connected sections.

Part One is general and theoretical in scope. It explores various ways of understanding the indigenous today, and it argues that ideas of historical destiny and developing time need to be revised to account for these cultural renewals and social movements. Tools for analyzing historical transformation and political agency are introduced: articulation, performance, and translation. Theories of cultural materialism, hegemony, and diaspora drawn from cultural studies in the tradition of Raymond Williams, Stuart Hall, and Paul Gilroy are linked with ethnographic-historical approaches from cultural anthropology. The three essays gathered in Part One begin to imagine a displaced, "post-Western" perspective, a place of translations through which to understand indigenous agency. Subsequent discussions develop these ideas in particular contemporary contexts.

Part Two tracks an exemplary story of indigenous disappearance that has become one of renewal. "Ishi" was famous in 1911 when he turned up in a settler-California town and was understood to be "the last wild Indian in America." He was famous again after 1960, when his biography, by Theodora Kroeber, became a best seller. And around 2000, Ishi could again be found in the newspapers as California Indians finally buried his physical remains and in the process reopened a legacy of settler-colonial violence. I followed the repatriation process with interest, attending public gatherings and talking with participants. Once a symbol for the disappearance of the state's original people, Ishi has come to represent their survival. His experience, enigmatic and productive, in life and in death, is meaningful to many people in many different ways. Ishi's story addresses the continuing legacy of colonial violence, the history of anthropology, the efficacy of healing, the prospects for postcolonial reconciliation, and much else.

Part Three, after a comparative glance at the Island Pacific, focuses on central Alaska, specifically the Kodiak archipelago. My discussion of Alutiiq/Sugpiaq cultural renewal is based on research over the last decade that could be described as academic visiting (or perhaps journalism with theoretical characteristics). The results are gathered in two linked essays. The first discusses collaborative heritage work, especially a major exhibition and multiply authored book of 2001, *Looking Both Ways*. The second centers on the Alutiiq Museum and Archaeological Repository, a Native-administered cultural center in Kodiak. It describes the return of nineteenth-century masks, loaned from their present home in France, and the new meanings these ancestral artifacts can evoke in a changing world. The masks' translated "second life" unfolds in tangled contexts of local history, transnational indigeneity, and state policies of corporate multiculturalism.

If Parts One and Three of *Returns* are conceived under the sign of realism, Part Two unfolds in a different analytic and imaginative way. It traces the collapse of a settler-colonial history but does not seek to replace it with a new, more adequate narrative. Instead it adopts an ironic, "meta" perspective that leaves space for plural, contradictory, and utopian outcomes. The stories surrounding the name "Ishi" proliferate, opening new possibilities. Other kinds of progress become imaginable: utopias that may be already here, ways forward that are not about progressing, but rather involve turning and returning. The challenge is to imagine different directions and movements in history, developments taking place together and apart. Here, *Returns* runs out of language.

The book's architecture requires some explanation. Like its two predecessors it is a collage of essays, written at different times and in distinct styles, or voices. I have not smoothed over the bumpy transitions. Rhetorical diversity keeps visible the contexts and audiences that have shaped the book's research and thinking. It suggests a process, not a final product. Familiar genres—the monograph, the essay collection—are currently in flux. In the years since *The Predicament of Culture* appeared a quarter-century ago, reading practices have changed. Fewer people consume books continuously, starting at the beginning and proceeding to the end. They copy, scan, and download parts. *Predicament* and *Routes,* after a period of existence as "books," have enjoyed a second life in the form of photocopies and PDF files. Some of this "publication" has occurred within the rules of copyright, some not. Knowledge transmitted this way cannot, nor should it, be legally contained. In any event, it has become all too clear that the academic book, as a physical object, does not travel very well. Disassembled and modular, the text gets around.

Returns is constructed with the new forms of distribution in mind. While it is more than the sum of its parts, the three sections are separable. Each is an extended essay that can be read independently and in any order. For lack of a better name, I have thought of them as academic "novellas"—intermediate forms of writing that can sustain complexity and development without sacrificing readability. I imagine that three short books can be read with more pleasure, at different times and in different moods, than a single long one. Moreover, within the three parts of *Returns* each chapter is a stand-alone essay.

A book organized in this way will contain a certain amount of redundancy. Important contexts need to be established more than once, and essential ideas recur. *Returns* does not proceed in a straight line: its "argument" loops and starts over. I have tried, however, to keep blatant repetitions to a minimum, and each chapter introduces a new context for exploring the work's central concerns. It should also be noted that some inconsistencies of usage remain. For example, in Alaska contexts I adopt the local convention of capitalizing Native and Elder, but not elsewhere.

A final word on changing names. Indigenous societies everywhere are in the process of removing colonial names and reviving, sometimes inventing, old/new ones. This is an essential part of the decolonizing process. Kwakwak'awakw replaces Kwakiutl; Tohono O'odham, Papago; Inuit, Eskimo: Aotearoa, New Zealand. In *Returns* I respect the changed names and use them. There are times, however, when it is appropriate to include both the colonial and postcolonial versions. This may reflect unsettled local usage, or a desire to avoid anachronism in historical contexts, or the need to be clear for uninitiated readers.

For my central subject, there is no universally satisfactory name: indigenous, native, aboriginal, tribal, Indian, Native American, First Nation (to mention only words in English). Depending on where one is and who is paying attention, one risks giving offense, or sounding tone deaf.

Part I

Jean-Marie Tjibaou, Kanak independence leader, in the Hienghène Valley, New Caledonia, 1978. Behind him is an ancestral habitat to which his tribe has returned after many years of colonial dispossession. (See Chapter 2.) (Photo by James Clifford.)

1

❖

Among Histories

Indian agency has often been read as a demand to return to a utopian
past that never was. Another emendation would suggest that we know
very well such a return is impossible: instead the conversation is about
a different kind of today, where we are present in the world like anyone
else. We always have been trying to be part of the world.
  —Paul Chaat Smith, *Everything You Know about Indians Is Wrong*

Indigenous people have emerged from history's blind spot. No longer
pathetic victims or noble messengers from lost worlds, they are visible
actors in local, national, and global arenas. On every continent, survi-
vors of colonial invasions and forced assimilation renew their cultural
heritage and reconnect with lost lands. They struggle within dominant
regimes that continue to belittle and misunderstand them, their very survival a form of resistance.

To take seriously the current resurgence of native, tribal, or aboriginal
societies we need to avoid both romantic celebration and knowing critique. An attitude of critical openness is required, a way of engaging with
complex historical transformations and intersecting paths in the contemporary world. I call this attitude realism. Its sources, primarily historical
and ethnographic, will emerge in this and subsequent chapters. Realism
is never a simple description. It is a narrative process assembling "big-
enough histories"—big enough to matter but not too big. Indigeneity
today is such a story. It unfolds, in Stuart Hall's words, on "the contradictory, stony ground of the present conjuncture" (1989: 151).

Today the word "indigenous" describes a work in progress. Derived
from old Latin, it means "born or produced from within," with primary
definitions suggesting nativeness; originating or growing in a country;

13

not exotic. Forty years ago, "indigenous" would most frequently have been applied to plants or animals. Now, paradoxically, this word featuring extreme localism has come to denote a global array. It is a general name for human societies throughout the world that were often called "primitive," "native," "tribal," or "aboriginal." A protean word, "indigenous" is evoked today by groups of differing shapes and sizes in a variety of social contexts. What is always at stake is an assertion of temporal priority, of relatively deep roots in a place. Relatively deep roots—because people who claim indigeneity have often come to their present home from elsewhere. The arrival may, however, be lost in the mists of time, with the claim of anteriority expressed as a story of autochthonous origins: we are born of the land, its original, chosen people.

Casting oneself as indigenous, and others alien, is never an innocent act. The violence potentially done by invoking "native" priority is stressed by Mahmood Mamdani (2002), writing about Hutu constructions of Tutsi in Rwanda. Mamdani argues trenchantly that the racial/ethnic opposition of native and outsider has been a particularly damaging legacy of colonialism in Africa. In a similar vein, Francis Nyamnjoh (2007) and Peter Geschiere (2009) criticize the ambiguous and often mischievous uses of tribal anteriority in African contexts of competition for power and resources. And Amita Baviskar (2007) provides a cautionary view from India, where Hindu nationalism can co-opt the politics of indigeneity. These examples reflect specific national situations, colonial legacies, and current struggles for advantage. They remind us that assertions of priority and ownership, in a world of movement and exchange, are always claims to power.

This does not mean, of course, that such assertions are never justified, especially in response to imperial invasion or state dominance. Some critics have suggested that contemporary indigenous assertions are inherently exclusivist, even potentially fascist. No doubt claims based on blood and land can trigger ugly associations. But one should not be too quick to draw negative conclusions. Communal aspirations and claims to sovereignty take diverse forms; and nationalist aspirations by the disempowered seeking liberation and autonomy are obviously different from the systematic policing and cultural assimilation imposed by states. Moreover, if the essences and traditions invoked by indigenous activists sometimes seem to repeat older colonial primitivisms, as dismissive critics like Adam Kuper (2003) have argued, they do so at another moment and for new purposes. Indigenous movements need to be located in shifting power relations (Friedman 2007), particular histories of conquest, hegemony, and inventive survival that interact with new regimes of freedom and control.

The term "indigenous" typically refers to societies that are relatively small-scale, people who sustain deep connections with a place. Applied to diverse communities, the name does not presume cultural similarity or essence but rather refers to comparable experiences of invasion, dispossession, resistance, and survival. Indigenous, in this definition, makes most sense in places like the Americas, Australia, the Island Pacific, and the Arctic. It is less relevant for most of Africa and much of Asia. Where settler-colonial histories are not sharply defined, it is difficult to identify unambiguous "first peoples." But elsewhere one finds clear examples of the indigenous as I use the term: Aborigines in Australia, Maori in Aotearoa/New Zealand, the Ainu of Hokkaido/Sakhalin, and the "Indian" tribes of North and South America. It would not be difficult to list hundreds more. Indeed, the United Nations now supports a permanent forum that maintains just such a list. A growing number of nongovernmental organizations are agitating for the rights of these embattled, small populations struggling for living space within, and sometimes across, nation-state borders. None of the societies in question is without internal frictions, discrepant elements, and disputes over authenticity and belonging. In this they resemble every other mobilized social group.

This chapter pursues two interconnected historical and ethnographic agendas. It raises the question of how we understand a complex historical emergence—that of indigenous cultural politics during the 1980s and 1990s. In particular, it asks how this development is related to contemporary forms of identity and multiculturalism—phenomena too quickly subsumed by labels such as "postmodernity" or "neoliberalism." And as this exercise in near-term historicizing proceeds, the very idea of history is kept in quotation marks, suspended in relations of translation. The chapter introduces several examples of indigenous "historical practice," ways of giving shape to time that question and expand conventional assumptions. The two agendas, one historicizing, the other metahistorical, are codependent. I let them alternate, complementing and troubling each other.

Indigènitude

During the 1980s and 1990s, a new public persona and globalizing voice made itself felt: a *présence indigene*. The reference, of course, is to another dramatic emergence into wide arenas of cultural performance and political influence: the *négritide* movement of the early 1950s with its famous journal, *Présence Africaine.* Negritude was an alliance of black activists—Léopold Senghor, Aimé Césaire, Leon Damas, Suzanne Césaire, and others—who recognized commonalities of culture, history, and political potential. A half-century later we might speak of *indigèni- tude,* reflecting a similar process of rearticulation. Traditions are recov- ered and connections made in relation to shared colonial, postcolonial, globalizing histories. Like negritude, *indigènitude* is a vision of liberation and cultural difference that challenges, or at least redirects, the modern- izing agendas of nation-states and transnational capitalism. *Indigènitude* is performed at the United Nations and the International Labor Organiza- tion, at arts and cultural festivals, at political events, and in many informal travels and contacts. *Indigènitude* is less a coherent ideology than a con- catenation of sources and projects. It operates at multiple scales: local traditions (kinship, language renewal, subsistence hunting, protection of sacred sites); national agendas and symbols (Hawai'ian sovereignty, Mayan politics in Guatemala, Maori mobilizations in Aotearoa/New Zealand); and transnational activism ("Red Power" from the global six- ties, or today's social movements around cultural values, the environment, and identity, movements often allied with NGOs). *Indigènitude* is sus- tained through media-disseminated images, including a shared symbolic repertoire ("the sacred," "Mother Earth," "shamanism," "sovereignty," the wisdom of "elders," stewardship of "the land"). The images can lapse into self-stereotyping. And they express a transformative renewal of attachments to culture and place. It is difficult to know, sometimes even for participants, how much of the performance of identity reflects deep belief, how much a tactical presentation of self.

Indigenous presence and globalizing neoliberalism both emerge in the 1980s and 1990s, and they are evidently linked in important ways. This coincidence troubles any inclination toward simple celebration. And it raises important questions of historical determination. I argue below that the convergence cannot be rounded up with periodizing terms like "late capitalism" or "postmodernity." Nor can we draw a simple link between political-economic structures and sociocultural expressions, claiming that one element (in this case, indigenous resurgence) is a result, or a production, of the other (neoliberal hegemony). We will see how ethnographic perspectives complicate this kind of causal account, making space for local agencies and contributing to a nonreductive, dia- lectical realism. In contemporary systems of government, wide latitudes of freedom to be different are allowed, indeed encouraged, but within limits imposed by national projects and the protection of capitalist accumulation (Hale 2002). These limits are not the same everywhere and take "variegated" forms (Ong 2006). New and revived orders of difference are supported in zones of exception, niche markets, and commodified cultural exchanges. Indigenous cultural resurgence and political self-determination can find room for maneuver in these relatively autonomous sites. Indian gaming in the United States is an obvious example. And there are other quasi-independent zones of tribal sovereignty: special accommodations for resource extraction, hunting, and fishing, and for the control of "cultural property" in museums, art markets, and other public performance sites.

In contemporary globalizing worlds, loosened imperial and national hegemonies offer opportunities for indigenous communities. People who for generations have been struggling to reclaim land, gain recognition, and preserve their heritage now participate in wider political contexts, and they profit from markets in art, culture, and natural resources. In many places indigenous populations are expanding rapidly as people rediscover lost roots (Sturm 2011; Forte 2006). But the new expansiveness does not occur in a space outside of power. Indigenous vitality requires a degree of tactical conformity with external expectations and at least a partial acceptance of multicultural roles and institutions (Conklin 1997; Povinelli 2002).

Economic success—tribal gaming, resource development, or commerce in art and culture—can bring significant increases in wealth. But it also encourages new hierarchies, communal divisions, and dependency on external markets and capital resources (Dombrowski 2002). Whatever material progress has been made over the past few decades is unevenly distributed. Indigenous populations in most contemporary nation-states remain poor, lacking adequate health and education, at the mercy of predatory national and transnational agents of "development." The modest, but real, gains in control over land and resources achieved by native groups in recent years are fragile, always susceptible to reversal by overwhelmingly more powerful majority populations. Intractable double binds—for example, an assumed contradiction between material wealth and cultural authenticity—are imposed on tribal people aspiring to something more than bare survival in settler-colonial states (Cattelino 2009).

None of this is unprecedented. Today's indigenous movements build pragmatically on older experiences of resistance and cultural survival.

Deep histories, grounded in place and kinship, take new forms in political mobilizations and in the creative "second lives" of heritage. The challenge facing realist accounts of indigenous cultural politics is to acknowledge the new command performances and commodifications of identity politics while simultaneously tracing the persistence of older practices: oral transmission, forms of social continuity and intercultural negotiation, and embodied experiences of place. A tension, a lucid ambivalence, needs to be maintained. Something is always being gained, something lost.

During the 1980s and 1990s, for example, native assertions of cultural property rights created new conditions for the possession and display of valued artifacts in museums and private collections. Michael Brown (2003) weighs the potential, and especially the danger, of claiming culture as property. This way of "having a culture" was lucidly explored in Richard Handler's (1988) critical ethnography of Quebecois nationalism. But owning culture is always a matter of both giving and holding back. This becomes very clear in Nicholas Thomas's (1999) incisive recoding of artistic/cultural "possessions" in a Native Pacific idiom of gifts and exchanges. Kimberly Christen (2005) and Jennifer Kramer (2006) explore specific modes of possession and sharing, the pragmatics of secrecy and revelation in the circulation of heritage and art. In their different contexts, one Australian Aboriginal and the other First Nation Canadian, these scholars show how struggles over culture become central to the changing terms of tribal autonomy and interdependence. Cooptation coexists with transgression, governance with transformative potential. Here, as elsewhere in the contemporary spaces of recognition and multiculturalism, ambivalence becomes a kind of method.

Obviously the present conjuncture of neoliberal hegemony—like all hegemonies, incomplete and contested—holds both opportunities and dangers. This is nothing new for the many indigenous people who are accustomed to maneuvering in the crosscurrents of colonial and neocolonial power. Their transformative survival has required selective assimilation, resistance, transgression, and concealment. They have always had to reckon with diverse audiences. Today these range from ancestors and family members to state agencies and NGOs, from the spirits that inhabit sacred places to business partners in boardrooms, from anthropologists to tourists. The indigenous presence of the 1980s and 1990s thus extends many particular histories of survival while it achieves unprecedented visibility on national and global stages. Here are some of the better-known public manifestations:

- *1969.* A group called Indians of All Tribes occupies the former prison of Alcatraz, an island in the San Francisco Bay, declaring it liberated Indian Country. The "Red Power" movement, inspired in part by "Black Power," initiates a new image-conscious tribal politics.

- *1971.* In response to concerted indigenous pressure and the corporate need to construct an oil pipeline, the Alaska Native Claims Settlement Act, a controversial law, creates powerful Native-owned development corporations.

- *1975.* Mélanésia 2000, the first Melanesian cultural festival, is held in New Caledonia. Two thousand indigenous people participate, and fifty thousand individuals from other ethnicities attend this celebration of Kanak identity. Cultural festivals will henceforth become regular occurrences in the Pacific, bringing together performers from many islands.

- *1982. I, Rigoberta Menchú* is published, quickly becoming a classic of international multiculturalism. Over the next decade Rigoberta Menchú Tum's image undergoes rearticulation from a symbol of Guatemala's poor peasants to a figure of pan-Mayan and increasingly pan-indigenous identity.

- *1992.* Hemispheric protests against the Columbian Quincentennary reject Eurocentric, expansionist history with its rights of "discovery." In this year, Menchú Tum is awarded the Nobel Peace Prize.

- *1992.* In Mabo vs. Queensland, the High Court of Australia rejects the *terra nullius* doctrine underlying settler-colonial sovereignty, affirming the continued existence of Aboriginal and Torres Straits Islander land tenure based on traditional occupancy.

- *1994.* The United Nations General Assembly declares 1995–2004 the International Decade of the World's Indigenous Peoples. The Permanent Forum on Indigenous Issues, in existence since 1982, gathers momentum.

- *The 1990s.* Indian tribes in the United States extend their gaming operations, bringing new wealth, political influence, and controversy. More indigenous groups are active in economic development projects. Markets in Aboriginal, Northwest Coast, and other "tribal arts" expand dramatically. Demands for repatriation of human remains and collected artifacts are increasingly common.

- *1997.* In Delgamuukw vs. British Columbia, the Supreme Court of Canada recognizes the specific nature of aboriginal land title and makes increased space for tribal oral histories in court proceedings.
- *1999.* The vast Inuit-governed region of Nunavut is created in Northeast Canada.
- *2000.* Striking images from the Sydney Summer Olympics circulate around the globe. Indigenous presence is performed simultaneously in dances within and protests outside Stadium Australia. The world cheers an Aboriginal athlete, Kathy Freeman.
- *2005.* Evo Morales, a publicly identified Aymara Indian, is elected president of Bolivia. There and elsewhere in Latin America, popular social movements unite under the sign of the indigenous. Journalists working in Latin America begin to speak of "the poor and indigenous," where a decade previously they would have said "the poor" or "the peasants."

These are only some of the more public manifestations of a strengthening presence. Ronald Niezen (2003) has written an excellent historical account of "international indigenism," formerly an oxymoronic expression, now a political reality. He describes the relatively recent emergence of loosely connected movements and their relations with international institutions such as the United Nations and the International Labor Organization, human rights and environmental NGOs, art markets, heritage productions, and many local and national arenas of identity performance. Since the 1970s, publications such as *Cultural Survival Quarterly* and the yearbook *Indigenous World* have surveyed an extraordinary range of social, ecological, religious, and artistic struggles—on six continents and three oceans. Being indigenous today is an aspiration supported by international institutions and NGOs. Indeed, the discourses of indigeneity seem to have attained a modular, highly mobile form. A close association of identity, culture, and ancestral land now undergirds communal resistance to invasive state and transnational forces from the Americas to Africa and China. The discourse also supports intercommunal struggles over priority as well as government-approved regional and touristic development. In the Caribbean, whose original inhabitants were widely thought to have been eliminated, Caribs and other resurgent Indian groups are claiming attention (Forte 2006).

Afro-Caribbean people with established local roots are adopting indigenous rhetoric, along with American hip-hop and consumer culture (Anderson 2009).

The fact of global *indigènitude* is inescapable. But in affirming this public presence we cannot forget the culture enacted around campfires and kitchen tables rather than at festivals or rallies. Native life unfolds in multiple contexts whose relations are not always harmonious. For example, clan-based groups or people with long-established tribal governments may reject the new "indigenous" label, finding it irrelevant to their lives, meaningful only for university programs, transnational activists, and uprooted urbanites. Any attempt to survey the social landscape of indigeneity confronts diversity and contradiction. In the United States, Australia, and Canada, a majority of indigenous-identified people now live in cities. There, as we will see in Chapters 2 and 3, older forms of social solidarity and cultural transmission are being rearticulated, performed in new contexts for different audiences. Inventive practices of urban indigenous life rely on circular migration to homelands and diaspora networking across distances. Facebook is now a site of tribal mobilization, as the successful "Idle No More" campaign of 2013 demonstrated. Heritage renewal and artistic creation use new technologies to reroute cultural connections. In her probing ethnography of urban Indians, Renya Ramirez (2007) writes of native "transnationals," evoking the ways people actively link two nations, one tribal and the other majoritarian.

It is premature, and no doubt ethnocentric, to ask what all these processes of pragmatic survival and cultural renewal amount to as a historical force. Where would one stand to make such a final judgment? For the moment, we can recognize the presence—the transformative survival and growing vitality—of tribal, aboriginal, or First Nations societies. Their very existence challenges narrative assumptions that have long authorized Western projections of civilization, modernity, or progress.

Alter Histories 1

For centuries the world was conceived, from a Euro-American vantage point, as divided into two kinds of societies. These were distinguished with terms such as "traditional" and "modern," "oral" and "literate," "cold" and "hot." The latter was Lévi-Strauss's famous distinction between small, tribal groups and the more change-oriented modern West

(1991: 125). Binary pairs such as these, once simply realistic descriptions, now seem clumsy simplifications, efficient mechanisms for distinguishing "us" from "them" and sorting everyone in time and space. This was the common sense of people who thought of themselves as embodying the future, for better and for worse. Revolutions in science, industrial production, and technology justified their worldview: a progressive, developmental history with Europe as its driving force. The worldview reached its apogee in the late nineteenth century with the rise of European nation-states, empires, and industry.

This "tunnel vision" of history (Blaut 1993) has persisted through the twentieth century: a developmental common sense in which some people are on history's cutting edge, others consigned to the past (Fabian 1983). The progressive ideology would be shaken by twentieth-century wars, economic depression, and by the racial violence, abroad and at home, perpetrated by those claiming the mantle of civilization (Lindqvist 1997). But after the Second World War, a sustained economic boom supported a renewed imperial vision, now dividing the planet into "developed" and "underdeveloped" sectors. Both the capitalist "First" and the socialist "Second" worlds saw themselves as agents of modernization in contrast to backward "Third World" societies. But when the postwar armed peace collapsed, as economic expansion faltered, and as globalizing connectivities became more ungovernable, the assumption of a linear path of development, with clear stages, epochal breaks, and transitions, would be harder to sustain. As the twentieth century ended, other histories, hidden by progressive visions of modernity, emerged from the shadows.

Not so long ago, the diverse people we now call indigenous were almost universally thought to have no futures. They were "people without history," destined to disappear. Progressive history was destiny: the all-too-efficient, destructive, and reconstructive mechanisms of trade, empire, missions, contagion, schooling, capitalism, Americanization, and now globalization would finish the job. This was just the way things were. But a contradictory reality, the fact that small-scale, tribal peoples do have futures, has been a surprise of the late twentieth century, a source of "anthropological enlightenment," in Marshall Sahlins's phrase (2000: ch. 15). Unexpected outcomes like this show that history isn't herding us all the same way. And they provide a reminder of what may be the one inescapable fact of history: its continually revised open-endedness.

No well-informed person now believes what was, for so long, taught in school: that Columbus "discovered America." The hemisphere was discovered more than once, and from more than one direction. There are now serious doubts about the peopling of the two American continents exclusively by populations crossing the Bering land bridge at the end of the last great ice age. Among the candidates for early arrival in the Americas being studied by physical anthropologists today are people whose bodily features resemble most closely the Ainu. These pioneers probably came from the vicinity of Sakhalin Island along the coastline, on foot and by boat. None of this was part of recognized historical reality even fifteen years ago. And can anyone imagine that there will be no further surprises from archaeology, genetics, or historical linguistics? The arrival of ships, armies, missionaries, and microbes in the sixteenth century was certainly of epochal significance. But the way this meeting of worlds is framed has been transformed by both science and native activism. Today, the very idea of a "New World" makes little sense. For if one takes seriously the deep and ongoing indigenous histories of the Americas—the complexity of cultures and languages, of migrations and exchanges, the empires, wars, and urban life of the Inca, the Maya, the Aztecs—then teleological narratives of a civilizing modernity (triumphant or tragic) seem blatantly ethnocentric.

Such historical narratives have been "provincialized" (Chakrabarty 2000). Since 1950, uneven and unfinished processes of decolonization have decentered the West and its epistemological assumptions, including the idea of a determined historical direction. There is no longer a place from which to tell the whole story (there never was). At the same time, connectivity in diverse idioms and media, and at many scales, has increased dramatically. This is the good and the bad news of globalization. We search for a realism that can engage a paradoxical world of simultaneous connection and divergence. Stuart Hall (1998) reminds us that a discursive linking of pasts and futures is integral to the positioning of collective subjects. Thus, to imagine a coherent future, people must selectively mobilize past resources—historical practices that take diverse forms and are expressed in unfamiliar idioms. To engage with these histories requires representational tact, a patient, self-reflexive openness that might be thought of as a kind of historical "negative capability." The phrase derives, of course, from John Keats's definition of the poetic attitude, an alert receptivity and willingness not to press for conclusions. A constant awareness of our own partial access to other experiences is required—tracking interference patterns and sites of emergence, piecing together more-than-local patterns. "Listening for histories" is now more important than "telling it like it is."

In this spirit, let us explore several indigenous ways of thinking historically, sites of translation where Western ontologies are challenged and potentially expanded. We are entering a broad comparative landscape that has yet to be studied systematically, although the work has been admirably begun by Peter Nabokov in *A Forest of Time: American Indian Ways of History* (2002). And we can draw from a growing ethnographic literature on particular ways of historicizing, from the pioneering work of Renato Rosaldo (1980, 1989) and Marshall Sahlins (1981, 1985) to David Shorter's remarkable study of Yoeme/Yaqui historicity, *We Will Dance Our Truth* (2009) and the collaborative website, *Vachiam Eecha/Planting the Seeds.* How far we still have to go is indicated by a recent collection of essays, *The Many Faces of Clio: Cross-Cultural Approaches to Historiography* (Wang and Fillaffer 2007). Virtually all of the twenty-five contributors are historians, and there is no mention of the growing anthropological literature on indigenous ways of narrating, remembering, and inscribing history. The impressive volume's "cross-cultural approach" is centered in Europe, with limited discussion of East and South Asia. "The people without history" are still missing.

Listen, then, to the Hawai'ian historian Lilikala Kame'eleihiwa, from her book *Native Land and Foreign Desires:*

> It is interesting to note that in Hawaiian, the past is referred to as *Ka wa mamua,* or "the time in front or before." Whereas the future, when thought of at all, is *Ka wa mahope,* or "the time which comes after or behind." It is as if the Hawaiian stands firmly in the present, with his back to the future, and his eyes fixed upon the past, seeking historical answers for present-day dilemmas. Such an orientation is to the Hawaiian an eminently practical one, for the future is always unknown, whereas the past is rich in glory and knowledge. (1992: 22–23)

This image of going backward into the future is reminiscent of Walter Benjamin's famous "Angel of History," from his "Theses on the Philosophy of History" (1969). Benjamin's angel is blown into the future, while facing the past. But the differences are telling. Kame'eleihiwa's Hawai'ian does not, like Benjamin's angel, confront the past as a ruin, a heap of broken scraps. Rather, she engages a generative, sociomythic tradition, "rich in glory and knowledge." Most significantly, perhaps, there is no relentless "wind" of "progress" blowing the indigenous Hawai'ian backward into the future. Time has no single, violent direction, but tacks resourcefully between present dilemmas and remembered answers: a pragmatic, not a teleological or a messianic orientation. The past, materialized in land and ancestors, is always a source of the new.

The Hawai'ian is comparable to—but not the same as—Benjamin's materialist historian, for whom the junk heap of the past contains possible other stories, prefigurations of outcomes different from the apparently inevitable reality of "what actually happened." Both look to the past to find a way, a path: one historical process is pragmatic and genealogical, the other critical and messianic. Neither is about aligning past, present, and future in a series. The future is always unwritten. Let us be clear that Kame'eleihiwa is not invoking repetition or cycles of recurrence. This temporality is not the opposite of a linear historical progression. It might be better, instead, to think of looping lines of recollection, and specific paths forward. We find a different way of acting historically but no essential clash of epistemologies, no either-or choice: tradition or modernity, myth or history. For Kame'eleihiwa, the Hawai'ian past is about generativity, not recurrence.

The Hawai'ian sovereignty movement, of which Lilikala Kame'eleihiwa is a leader, mobilizes cultural and political traditions with deep, spliced, and tangled roots. It has attained new momentum and visibility during the past several decades as part of the post-sixties indigenous context I have been evoking. Along with its more explicitly political activities, a dynamic process of remembering is under way. This movement has many dimensions: intensifying taro cultivation in rural enclaves, reviving and adapting hula dances and rituals, renewing native knowledge and language in schools, mobilizing media for political actions, asserting a space for indigenous epistemologies in the secular university, and connecting reggae rhythms with sovereignty lyrics. A renewed Hawai'ian tradition does not, of course, simply repeat past ways. It is a practical selection and critical reweaving of roots. New gender roles show this clearly, as do engagements with Christianity, state politics, and transnational indigenous coalitions. The diverse strategies are connected through appeals to a common genealogy, and they are all grounded by attachments to a homeland. In a living tradition, some elements will be actively remembered, others forgotten, and some appropriated from foreign influences or trans-

lated from analogous histories elsewhere. Differences of region, generation, class, gender, urban/rural location, and political strategy are sites of
tension and mediation. What is at stake in this selective and inventive
cultural politics is the power—always an incomplete power—to define
identity, to control culture, and to influence the unequal political, social,
and economic relationships that constitute modern native Hawai'ian life.

Kame'eleihiwa concludes that "the future is always unknown, whereas
the past is rich in glory and knowledge." A comparable perspective can
be found in Australian Aboriginal orientations to the "Dreaming," a
process by which ancestral beings create the known world: a landscape
of totemic sites that present generations renew through onsite rituals
and the observance of customary "Law." Deborah Bird Rose calls this
the "source," constantly renewed and renewing. She goes on to say that
the "temporal orientation" can be summarized as a sequence: "First the
earth, then Dreamings, then the ancestors. We [Aboriginal people] follow
along behind them, and our descendents follow along behind us" (2004:
152). Rose provides an absorbing account of how conquest and Christianity attempt to impose a different historical temporality, a "180-
degree shift," reorienting Aboriginal consciousness toward a "future" of
progress and salvation. This shift, when successful, transforms a "source"
into a "past," something left behind, perhaps eventually remembered in
a museum. Rose details Aborigines' resistance to the change, their continuing attachment to "country," the spatial matrix in which the Dreaming and ancestral Law are lived.

It is worth emphasizing that the temporal movement toward ancestors, totemic Dreaming, and the earth is not a return to the past. The
Dreaming is generative, and thus the traditionalism of Rose's more eloquent Aboriginal interlocutors does not resist all change. Elders, men
and women, are glad to use Toyota Land Cruisers, when available, for
ritual visits to sacred sites. Kim Christen (2008), following Merlan's
(1998) lead, provides an excellent account of ongoing relations with
"country" by town-based Warumungu women. Perhaps Rose's most
hopeful chapter evokes the legacies of Aboriginal labor in cattle stations,
what she calls a "non-linear twist" to the oppressive story of colonization (2004: 94). She explores the arts of cowboy life, especially interspe-
cies relationships and practices cultivated by both Aboriginals and
settlers. These crossover capacities are not external to an Aboriginal way
of living, but are part of an embodied cosmology that opens new routes
in a transforming myth-historical landscape.

For both Rose and Kame'eleihiwa, returning to a "source" is not a matter of going back in time. Turning—turning and returning—in an expanded present might be better. Yet "present" is not quite right, for it misses an important sense of drawing from something prior, or primal, a past that is never past, gone forever. It is difficult to avoid terms like past, present, and future, concepts embedded in a Western historical ontology. But we need to use them, like Kame'eleihiwa, as words in translation, bridges to something else. The Hawai'ian's turn "back" is a way to move "forward," or perhaps in some different direction for which we need another language. In any event, the genealogical turn is not a process of reversing time or of simply repeating what has already happened. Kame'eleihiwa's looping path forward is obviously not the "arrow of time" familiar to Western metahistorians. Nor is it a "mythic" alternative. Indigenous historical idioms reveal that nonrepeating developments can be expressed in a variety of shapes, scales, and uses. Listening for histories thus means deconstructing the opposition of linear and cyclical times.

Disarticulating Postmodernity

We return to the mundane tasks of historicizing. I have already raised the question of how the indigenous "presence" of the 1980s and 1990s can be related to the emergence of neoliberal hegemonies. In this context it is impossible to separate indigenous mobilizations from broader patterns of identity politics. To be sure, the social struggles and inventive processes at work often have deep precolonial, precapitalist roots: they retrieve and activate traditions that are grounded in particular ancestral places. Indigenous performative energies and countercultural visions precede, and potentially exceed, national and transnational systems of regulation. But native cultural traditions and social movements do not exist in isolation, however much they may at times assert their sovereignty and independence. Like other identity-based social movements they are enmeshed in powerful national and transnational regimes of coercion and opportunity. We need, therefore, to sustain a tension around issues of determination. This involves an ability to entertain complexity and ambivalence. It also means holding a place for transformative potential, what Kum Kum Sangari (2002) has called "the politics of the possible." Ethnographic-historical realism works to represent material constraints, intersecting histories, and emerging social forms without imposing structural closure or developmental destiny.

In an influential discussion, Raymond Williams (1977) argues against direct, or mechanical, forms of political-economic determinism, proposing instead a more supple "determination" of pressures and limits, of material-cultural forces articulated contingently at multiple levels. He also distinguishes "epochal" and "historical" kinds of analysis. In the former, "a cultural process is seized as a cultural system, with determinate dominant features." The latter "recognizes the complex interrelations between movements and tendencies both within and beyond a specific and effective dominance" (121). Epochal thinking subsumes layered and contradictory components of economic, social, and cultural existence within systematic wholes that are stages in a developmental narrative. In contrast, historical thinking is always grappling with the specific interactions of what Williams calls "dominant, residual, and emergent" (121) elements in any conjuncture. These factors do not necessarily form a coherent narrative in which the residual indexes the past, and the emergent the future. Williams notes that in modernizing, secular versions of epochal thinking, religion was long assumed to be of waning significance. Yet many forms of religious practice today—the global reach of Pentecostalism comes to mind—can be considered both residual and emergent. The same can be said of indigenous social and cultural movements that reach "backward" in order to move "ahead." When these "ancient" traditions are understood to be effectively "modern," the whole direction of Western historical development wavers. And when the analysis leaves Europe for the variegated and contradictory zones of colonial and postcolonial contact and struggle, Williams's sense of the "historical" is further complicated—thrown into dialogical relations of translation.

I have suggested that "history" belongs, significantly, to others. Its discourses and temporal shapes are idiomatic and varied. A concept of "historical practice" can help expand our range of attention, allowing us to take seriously the claims of oral transmission, genealogy, and ritual processes. These embodied, practical ways of representing the past have not been considered fully, realistically, historical by modern ideologies that privilege literacy and chronology. Historical practice can act as a translation tool for rethinking "tradition," a central process of indigenous survival and renewal. For example, native claims for recognition, land, cultural rights, and sovereignty always assume a continuity rooted in kinship and place. It is easy to understand this sense of belonging as essentially backward looking—tradition as inheritance, as a "residual"

element in the contemporary mix. However, when conceived as historical practice, tradition is freed from a primary association with the past
and grasped as a way of actively connecting different times: a source of
transformation (Phillips 2004). A vision of unified history thus yields to
entangled historical practices. Tradition and its many near synonyms
(heritage, *patrimoine, costumbre, coutume, kastom, adat*) denote interactive, creative, and adaptive processes.

The challenge for ethnographic (Williams's "historical") realism is
more than the task of creating multiscaled, nonreductive accounts of
changing social, cultural, and economic formations. It also grapples
with questions of pragmatic, sometimes utopic, possibility. Realism must
be attuned to what is emerging, what exceeds the familiar. The politics
of identity, or better, of identifications, has been difficult to contain.
What possibilities does identity open up? How are these energies channeled by specific powers in particular conjunctures? In the early twenty-
first century we confront a proliferation of cultures and identities. People
claim membership and distinguish themselves by a seemingly endless
array of markers that are both crosscutting and productive. They locate
themselves by place, nationality, culture, race, gender, sexuality, generation, or disability. The list can, in principle, be infinitely extended. The
phenomenon is so widespread it invites systemic explanation. Can the
proliferating claims be understood as products of a global historical
moment and a political-economic structure?

Two seminal works, by Fredric Jameson ("Postmodernism" [1984])
and David Harvey (*The Condition of Postmodernity* [1990]), represent
a powerful analytic tradition that shows no signs of waning. Rey Chow's
The Protestant Ethnic and the Spirit of Capitalism (2002) and John
Comaroff and Jean Comaroff's *Ethnicity, Inc.* (2009) are two recent
examples. Gathering evidence from diverse global sites, these scholars
link the performance and commodification of identity to a historical
moment: a global, systemic change that brings with it newly flexible and
decisive restructurings of local worlds. While accounts vary as to where,
when, and how comprehensively the change occurs, most agree that the
broad economic crisis of the 1970s marked a turning point: the down-
turn of an unusually long postwar expansion. By the 1980s, a restructured "neoliberal" hegemony would be consolidated based on increasingly
transnational markets and flexible methods of accumulation. A new
regime of cultural production and reception accompanied the shift: postmodernism (Jameson) or postmodernity (Harvey). In this perspective,

the invention and reinvention of identities is part of a late capitalist, or "postmodern," world system of cultural forms and regimes of recognition. Capitalist globalization allows and indeed encourages differences, as long as these differences do not threaten a dominant political-economic order. Distinctive cultural traditions are sustained, re-created, performed, and marketed in a theatre of identities.

In postmodernity, according to the analysis, local communities are pressured and enticed to reconstitute themselves within a kind of global shopping mall of identities. When "culture" and "place" are reasserted politically, it will tend to be in nostalgic, commodified forms. Tradition persists as simulacrum, lived custom as frozen heritage, folklore as fakelore. We increasingly confront what Dean MacCannell calls "reconstructed ethnicity . . . new and more highly deterministic ethnic forms . . . ethnicity-for-tourism in which exotic cultures figure as key attractions" (1992: 158). There is no dearth of self-stereotyping, more or less kitschy examples. And there is, certainly, a proliferating tendency to objectify, commodify, and perform identities—forms of cultural production enabled by the coalescence of multicultural pluralism with neoliberal marketing. The title of the Comaroffs' book, *Ethnicity, Inc.*, sums it up. All-too-neatly. For as we will see, the critique leaves little room for contingent articulations or contradictory trends; and it can fall into a complacent tough-mindedness that sees everything as an effect of systemic power. Globalization's production of differences through interconnection, a productive paradox first highlighted by Harvey, is explained away. And a genuinely dialectical analysis of hegemonic forms and countercurrents, anticipated by Jameson, is narrowed to a symptomatic critique (Clifford 2000).

In 1994, four years after *The Condition of Postmodernity* was published, the Zapatista uprising in Chiapas went public. Masked men and women, who seemed to appear from nowhere, declared war on global neoliberalism, challenging its logics at virtually every level. The Zapatistas would quickly become famous, thanks to a charismatic (anti-) leader, Subcomandante Marcos, a clear democratic message, and an ability to make connections at national and global scales. In the years since the uprising, the movement has articulated "indigenous" localism with class politics, gender equality, Christian liberation theology, and Mexican nationalist populism. It clearly represents a new kind of social mobilization. But how new? And how deeply "Mayan"? Are these agrarian rebels *indigenas* or *campesinos*? Or both? Some observers see merely a new twist for an older Marxist guerilla practice. Others announce a truly "postmodern" movement.

I cannot engage, here, with the many complex and ongoing arguments about the social composition, local history, and political significance of the uprising. I mention the Zapatistas because they are a social movement importantly based on claims of locality and identity that overflow narrow identifications. They evidently partake of "the condition of postmodernity." Savvy communicators and image managers, the Zapatistas brand their movement with recognizable images and symbols, and they encourage what has been called solidarity tourism. Moreover, in this instance indigenous localism is the result of migrations by diverse native groups into a relatively unpopulated frontier region. Settlers from the highlands and elsewhere in Mexico cobble together a multiethnic, "Mayan" tradition in a new place, adapting traditional practices to contemporary socialist and feminist ideals. At the same time, guerilla tactics and progressive ideologies are "indigenized." In a subtle analysis that extends back to New Spain, José Rabasa associates the historical practice of *Zapatismo* not with an essential indigenous culture or a politics of resistance but rather with a long established subaltern capacity for sustaining "plural noncontradictory worlds" (2010: 68).

While the movement acts with an eye to national and international recognition, it also sustains a commitment to democratic transformation at the village level—the so-called "autonomous communities." This collaborative, locally based process is obviously different from the marketing of place and difference described by Harvey in sites like Boston's Quincy Market. Yet the Zapatistas do not inhabit a radically different world, and it can sometimes be hard to decide whether they represent globalization's dialectical negation, a niche within its landscape of governed diversities, or something else. At the present time their resistance to neoliberal policies of coercive free trade and their expansive national populism appear to have been contained. A remarkable, ongoing experiment with indigenous socialism is limited to specific villages in Chiapas. Yet these are potentially the seeds of transformation, and the Zapatista movement has resonated with other traditions of locally based radicalism throughout Mexico and beyond (Stephen 2002).

The rebellion in Chiapas is just one, if dramatic, example that complicates epochal narratives of neoliberal globalization or of postmodernity as the latest stage of capitalism. Indeed, the whole language of "stages" now appears suspiciously unidirectional and Eurocentric. Many cross-cutting, countercultural histories disrupt the narrative. For example, Paul Gilroy (1993) traces alternate forms of modernity in the diasporic "Black Atlantic," challenging premature, Eurocentric visions of totality while also rejecting primordial claims of ethnic or racial absolutism. Similar alternatives emerge from the tangled local, regional, and global histories called "indigenous" today: Australian Aboriginal art production or Andean mobilizations around water rights, tribal museums in Alaska or land and language reclamations in Canada. To grasp the specific dialectics of innovation and constraint in these countercultures, a Gramscian analysis of changing hegemonies and struggles for relative power is far more historically concrete than before-after narratives of cultural loss, social assimilation, or inevitable economic subsumption. Hegemony is not domination, but rather a historical process: unfinished struggles, contingent alliances, and accommodations in an evolving field of unequal forces.

Alter Histories 2

Listening for other ways of thinking and doing history we turn to a provocative example provided by the anthropologist Nelson Graburn (1998). It was published in the journal *Museum Anthropology* among several papers on "indigenous curating."

Graburn is well known for his long ethnographic research with the Inuit of Northeast Canada. The region has been named and renamed, reflecting altered relations of power: from Rupertsland/Ungava, to Nouveau Quebec, to Nunavik. There are also a great many local names of varying antiquity. The protagonist of Graburn's article, Tamusi Qumak Nuvalinga, was raised in igloos and tents and died in 1993. Monolingual in Inuktitut, he devoted many years to constructing a dictionary that he hoped would preserve the native language and support its use in schools. He also created a local museum, which he called "Saputik" or "The Weir." It opened in 1978.

A weir is not exactly a "dam," which blocks a stream. More like a strainer, a weir as Tamusi knew it was a barrier of stones that could trap fish without completely holding back the river's flow. Many fish could thus be speared and dried for fall and winter subsistence. This technology of capture for purposes of survival provided an image of collecting and remembering. Tamusi's "weir" was a two-story faux igloo, made of wood. The structure contained clothes and possessions of loved ones, dogsleds (but not snowmobiles), soapstone carvings (a relatively new art form that has become a source of Inuit pride), 1950s and 1960s photographs of Inuit people, and upstairs, a re-created igloo interior with old and newly commissioned furnishings. A traditional world was gathered, but not a re-created "precontact" life. Things from the recent historical past filled the space, objects of cultural value that needed to be saved. According to Graburn, the Weir reflected a new historical awareness: "Tamusi envisaged time as a river carrying everything irrevocably out to sea to be lost forever" (1998: 26).

We should be clear that this is not a first-contact story, a sudden impact or a "fall" into modernity. Tamusi's epiphany, carefully historicized by Graburn, is a response to accelerated change in the 1960s and 1970s. Before that, Inuit had experienced an extended period of relations with explorers, traders, missionaries, anthropologists, and Canadian government officers. For much of the twentieth century the Inuit regions had enjoyed relative prosperity (trade in furs, especially white fox pelts), plus the elimination of starvation and some diseases. Technological changes (guns, wood houses) proved to be compatible with traditional subsistence patterns and social structures. For Tamusi, traditional life was something like the negotiated "middle ground" described by the historian Richard White (1991) in his influential book on early frontier relations. A relative balance of power could be sustained, with Inuit drawing on Canadian resources selectively and to a significant extent on their own terms. This balance would be disrupted in the 1960s, a time of declining trade, increased government and missionary intervention, wider schooling for the young, and language loss.

Tamusi's response to the changing situation was a local history museum. The Weir preserved personal or familial objects of value, in the process helping to establish them as "cultural" treasures or collective "heritage." Graburn links the museum to Tamusi's Inuktitut dictionary (another kind of "weir"). And the work is also inseparable from his leadership in a cooperative movement to resist a Hudson's Bay Company trade monopoly and to hold off a giant Quebec hydroelectric project in the 1960s. Graburn describes "a long struggle [by Inuit] to keep the economy under their control in the Cooperative and to ensure the education of their children in Inuktitut" (1998: 25). This was not the last-gasp movement of a doomed culture, but a continuing struggle within and against potent structural forces, national and capitalist. Thus Tamusi's gathering of Inuit heritage must not be thought of as a native version of "salvage" collecting (in the manner of early twentieth-century anthropology) where cultural disappearance and political defeat were taken for granted. The Weir actively reconstitutes a "selective tradition" (Williams 1977: ch. 7), identifying, retaining, and retranslating critical sources of identity, in the midst of change.

Graburn has much to say about subsequent developments—particularly the spread of indigenous curating practices in museums and cultural centers throughout Nouveau Quebec/Nunavut. He traces a general tendency toward articulating wider "ethnic" cultures, performed for diverse audiences: native, national, and touristic. Tamusi's project thus prefigures the identity politics that are integral to indigeneity today: new forms of autonomy and dependence, renewed traditions and capitalist development. The ultimate outcomes of these engagements, I have been arguing, cannot be read off in advance. They are specific articulations, historically open ended. Thus any presumption of a singular line of development needs to be held in suspension to make conceptual space for a world of intersecting historicities,

In many indigenous societies, autochthonous origin stories coexist with historical narratives of a past that came before and was different from the present. For example, Island Pacific cultures remember emerging from the land while also recalling the heroic landfalls of ocean-going ancestors (Bonnemaison 1994). Inuit oral traditions tell about entering their present homeland and displacing its prior inhabitants, the Dorset People (a migration seven to nine hundred years ago, as estimated by archaeologists). More recent changes are also grasped through a genealogical sense of "coming from but not going to" (Graburn personal communication). Such stories narrate the changes brought by trappers, whalers, and explorers, foreigners who came and left. These "middle-ground" histories register the new—the arrival of guns, commerce, houses, diseases—but without the sense of a qualitative break, a feeling of cultural loss. Genealogical histories confirm and explain a present: how we got here from somewhere different; what from the past defines us now. And while there is a direction to history it is one that keeps us who we are, as we change. Genealogy is thus not a story of abandoning the past for a whole new future: Westernized, Christian, capitalist, or modern.

In Tamusi's figuration of time, the river's destination is the ocean, a place of no return, where everything loses form. One thinks of the entropy

Lévi-Strauss so poignantly portrayed in *Tristes Tropiques* (1955). Here, world history takes the form of a Fall, from difference into sameness. Everywhere the future is convergence, undifferentiated homogeneity. Whether told as a lament for vanishing cultures or as a celebration of progress, the story is familiar. The new inexorably displaces the old. But does it? What else is going on? Tamusi's "ocean" is clearly an image for lost difference. But is it one of historical destiny? If the river and the weir mark, as Graburn says, "the advent of a new consciousness that we may label modernity" (1998: 18), are we speaking of some whole new modern consciousness and sense of the real? An epochal replacement? Or rather, as I think Graburn's contextual account allows, a process of rearticulation and translation? To posit too sharp a break is premature. It may also be ethnocentric. All-or-nothing, before-after transformations into modernity tend to assume that people change only to become like us. An ethnographic-historical realism grapples with a less determined process of transformation, occurring within specific social, economic, and political fields of force. It attends to the ways newness is articulated in practice, how difference and identity are translated, performed for different audiences. This can make it hard to say with certainty that one sense of time is emergent, another residual. Indigenous cultural politics often express the new, the way forward, in terms of the old. Tamusi, after all, called his technology of temporal capture a "weir" not a "museum." Changing is a process of "looking both ways" (see Chapter 6). Whatever development or sense of direction history may exhibit, it is composed of overlays, loops, and intersecting temporal paths.

Considered in this light, Tamusi's "Weir" project is not elegiac, nor is it museological in the familiar Western sense. It is linked to local cooperative movements, to land and language reclamation initiatives, to the emergence of "Inuit" identities, creative arts, and heritage projects. Its work of cultural salvage is part of a transformative continuity: the future-oriented traditionalism of First Nations, linked to new assertions of sovereignty. In Northeast Canada, Inuit activism has led to the creation of the large, semiautonomous region of Nunavut, along with a proliferation of neotraditional institutions, discourses, art forms, and social movements. This is no longer the "middle-ground" context of igloos, tents, dogsleds, hunting rifles, traded furs, and Inuktitut monolingualism, the world Tamusi's generation grew up in. But it is not an undifferentiated modernity either—all of us flowing the same way, down the same river.

Ethnographic Realism

Two recent research projects, one from southern Mexico, the other from Guatemala, offer examples of a historically and politically attuned ethnographic realism. With different mixes of optimism and pessimism they provide grounded alternatives to system-centered, top-down conceptions of power and cultural process. *Histories and Stories from Chiapas: Border Identities in Southern Mexico* (2001), by Rosalva Aida Hernández Castillo, is based on fieldwork in and around the Zapatista frontier zone. It follows the twists and turns of a small Mayan group's survival and reidentification during the last half of the twentieth century. Charles Hale, in a series of critical essays (2002, 2005) leading to a complex ethnography (2006) probes indigenous and Ladino responses to neoliberalism and the politics of identity in Guatemala.

On the Mexican side of the border, Hernández Castillo worked with people who increasingly think of themselves as "Mam," Mayan Indians. Erosion of the Mam language has been severe, and until recently individuals tended to blend into the Spanish-speaking "mestizo" populace, their social and cultural assimilation seemingly assured. A finer-grained ethnographic lens reveals a history of negotiated adaptation with communal distinction sustained through changing political climates. Hernández Castillo describes cultural renewal and Mam identity assertions that were under way well before the indigenous-identified Zapatistas went public in 1994. The Mam populations she frequented, in the Lacandon forest and also in the Chiapas highlands, are not active rebels. Many are Jehovah's Witnesses. A key interlocutor and an advocate of Mam cultural revival is also a longtime Presbyterian church activist and supporter of the Institutional Revolutionary Party, or PRI (for many decades Mexico's ruling party). Women's movements are relatively autonomous elements in the identity mix.

Hernández Castillo tracks a persistent, contradictory, and inventive politics of survival. Focusing on changing religious affiliations and women's activism, she shows how Mam people have both resisted and accommodated government models of modernization. This is a history of becoming "modern," but not, or not only, on terms dictated by the state. During the 1930s, if one were to benefit from the land redistributions of revolutionary Mexico, it was necessary to suppress local culture and speak Spanish. State policy forced incorporation on these terms, and compliance was both substantial and strategic. Several decades later,

Mam groups—who were displaced by land shortages in the highlands to lowland plains and then to frontier regions in the Lacandon rain forest— adopted Protestant religions as a way to change, to be modern. In the process they were also able to maintain a distance from the assimilationist state, a distance that would later find new forms of expression in revivals of cultural tradition and indigenous rights. People who had lived as "mestizo" would reemerge as "Mam."

State policy remained part of the process, as the ideal of a mestizo Mexico gave way to a policy of multiculturalism. In the 1980s, government organizations arrived in Chiapas actively encouraging peasants to recover their identity, especially their indigenous traditions and languages (political autonomy or sovereignty were not, of course, part of the message). Culture, and the respect that comes with identity, were now seen as integral to a balanced social and economic "development." Incorporation in the nation would be achieved through a managed diversity. But, as before, while government policy and institutions promoted and directed change, they did not control it. The strong diversity (autonomía) claimed by the Zapatistas and echoed by indigenous militants elsewhere in Mexico was certainly not part of the official program. And more subtly, in the Jehovah's Witness Mam community of the Lacandon Forest where Hernández Castillo did fieldwork, distinction would be articulated through Christian millenarianism, through links with religious centers in New York City, and through a growing interest in revived native traditions. Mam language radio broadcasts began to reconnect dispersed populations. Traditions, selectively remembered, could be consistent with Protestant norms. Ethnic crafts were revived, in part, with the idea of encouraging eco- and cultural tourism.

The emergence of Mam identity politics, as described by Hernández Castillo, is emphatically not a revivalist story of people returning to origins, rediscovering who they really are. Her book traces a hegemonic process, a history of communities working pragmatically for survival and distinction within and against shifting terms of national incorporation. The account is also not one of recruitment by contemporary multiculturalism, a system managed by the neoliberal state or by transnational markets. Global capital and the state are active forces but not determining structures. One could, of course, view the growing interest in Mam cultural performances, and especially the prospect of cultural tourism in the Lacandon rainforest, as commodifications of identity and place, processes integral to the "postmodern condition." They could be understood

in the context of the global neoliberal market for diversity recently surveyed by John and Jean Comaroff (2009). There are certainly anecdotes
that could be cherry-picked to fit the diagnosis. But Hernández Castillo's
historically detailed ethnography makes abundantly clear how reductive
such accounts would be, how many local roots and routes, how much
entangled, dialectical agency would vanish from sight.

Hernández Castillo shows that Mam survival (always a process of
change and transformation) has been engaged with state projects through
most of the twentieth century. In the neo-Gramscian language of Stuart
Hall (1986b), it is a politics of shifting articulations (disconnections and
reconnections). Based in Guatemala, Charles Hale also uses Gramscian
tools to trace the historical convergences and tensions of indigenous
mobilization and neoliberal governance during the 1980s and 1990s in
Latin America. His long-term ethnographic work is focused on Ladinos
in Guatemala, but his theoretical and comparative range is broad. In his
interventionist essays, particularly, he tracks the consequences of neoliberal reforms for mobilized Mayans as well as other indigenous groups in
Latin America. Hale shows how policies of rights and recognition open
spaces for cultural revival and identity-based social movements. These
offer opportunities for previously marginalized populations to mobilize,
to establish a cultural and political presence. But neoliberalism also cir-
cumscribes possibilities, attempting to control and incorporate the new
forces. In Guatemala, Hale tracks the efficacy of distinctions between
"good" and "bad" *Indios*: rights-based, cultural expressions of indigeneity versus radical, political claims to sovereignty or autonomy. Liberal
policies and institutions, both national and transnational, channel indigenous mobilizations into the former category, thus limiting their transformative potential. The analysis is widely relevant. Similar critiques of
human-rights regimes and the politics of cultural recognition come from
Africa (Englund 2006; Geschiere 2009) and Australia (Povinelli 2002).
We recognize local versions of Harvey's globalizing "condition of
postmodernity"—flexible, multicultural, market-driven. But Hale's ethnographic sensibility keeps him attuned to something more.

In a situation where Marxist revolution is not a realistic possibility
and "cultural rights" are a focus of hegemonic struggle, Hale poses a
fundamental question:

> In the present resolutely postrevolutionary era, cultural rights
> organisations are likely to occupy an exceedingly ambiguous

space: attempting to exercise rights granted by the neoliberal state, while at the same time eluding the constraints and dictates of those very concessions. The Gramscian notion of articulation, in these cases, becomes the analytical watchword: *will the subjugated knowledge and practices be articulated with the dominant, and neutralised? Or will they occupy the space opened from above while resisting its built-in logic, connect with others, toward "transformative" cultural-political alternatives that still cannot even be fully imagined?* Especially on a terrain as volatile and dynamic as indigenous politics in Latin America, it would be imprudent to allow theory to run out ahead of grounded analysis in response to these questions. (2002: 499, emphasis added)

The good and bad news are inextricable. Neoliberalism opens possibilities for identity-based social movements while also powerfully channeling diversity and transformation. But Hale goes further, leaving room for an excessive politics of the possible, for " 'transformative' cultural-political alternatives that still cannot even be fully imagined."

The "grounded analysis" Hale recommends is simultaneously ethnographic, historical, and political. In his richly detailed, probing ethnography of Ladino neoracism (which I cannot do justice to here) he also evokes psychic dispositions and habits that exist in tension with social categories. Like Hernández Castillo, Hale recognizes that sociocultural survival and identity (re)formation are active, relational processes, and that "spaces opened from above" are also being created from below. Interpellations and articulations occur simultaneously, in specific relations of power. Moreover, the future is indeterminate, because postmodernity isn't the end of history or neoliberalism the last hegemonic settlement. To say this is not to deny structural inequality and capitalist determination. In Guatemala and elsewhere in Latin America, new forms of social, economic, and cultural power are being imposed, negotiated, resisted, and appropriated. Hale sees limited room for maneuver by subaltern groups. But while throwing cold water on romantic notions that indigenous cultural renewals are necessarily counterhegemonic, Hale also sees the possibilities opened by neoliberal regimes of rights and multiculturalism. He looks and listens for emergent phenomena—potential sites of radical rearticulation.

For example, if the racialized opposition of "Ladino" and "Maya" in Guatemala could be broken down in the name of a pluralist democracy,

new possibilities for alliance would be created. Could "mestizo" identity
be reinvented, embraced by those willing to cross ethnic and racial
divides? Hale explores the emergent possibility of a "mestizaje from
below," no longer an assimilationist national norm and now a subversion of the divisive ethnoracial categories of neoliberal multiculturalism.
In urban settings, large numbers of poor people and youth refuse the
identity categories offered by the state, often acknowledging indigenous
ancestry but searching for a place "between." Some ladinos seeking
coalitional connections with Mayans could think of themselves as "new-
mestizos." Another hopeful trend: in Nicaragua and Honduras, territorial units or *bloques* have been formed by coalitions of indigenous and
black groups. These locally controlled regions, zones of relative autonomy,
exist in complex tension with norms imposed by the state and by development agencies such as the World Bank (Hale 2005). Hale detects these
nascent possibilities throughout Central America, but he recognizes that
they carry no guarantee of radical change or a progressive outcome. He
concludes that the old political maps—Marxist, nationalist, developmental, or liberal—are of limited value, and often a hindrance, in today's
"uncharted territory" (Hale 2002: 524).

   Ethnography like that of Hale and Hernández Castillo cannot rely on
a determining structural map. Multiple, intersecting maps are needed. In
this conjunctural perspective, "identities" are relational, social processes
of identification. But if there is nothing primordial or permanent about
being indigenous or ladino, black or white, Indian or settler, this does
not mean these social positions are illusions, or without power. It means
that social and cultural groups exist in historical change and contingency, constantly reckoning themselves among others. Mam identity,
like the *autonomía* of the Zapatistas, is a relative status, sustained in
embattled conditions. In this it resembles the diverse forms of sovereignty increasingly claimed by native groups in the Americas (Biolsi
2005). The best ethnographic-historical research, such as that by Jessica
Cattelino (2008) on Seminole gaming or Circe Sturm (2002) on Cherokee
blood politics and tribal identification, tracks specific continuities, tensions, and contradictions through Gramscian fields of force. Keeping
conjunctures open and complexly determined is not a product of post-
structuralist methodology, a theoretically driven deconstruction of historical or explanatory orders. It is a decentered realism, multiscaled and
nonreductive, working among determinations without determinism.

   Realism—after poststructuralism and decolonization—presupposes a fractured, contestable narrative perspective. There is no longer a stand-point from which to definitively map particular, local stories in an over-arching sequence, no narrative of human history, of enlightened progress, of economic development, or of a disseminating global system. In the early twenty-first century the grand, explanatory narratives have been decisively decentered. This is a familiar observation. But it does not leave us with the "postmodernist" predicament my late colleague John Schaar characterized as "all power to the fragments"—nothing but small histo-ries, local visions. For "the local" has never been anything but the oppo-site of "the global," both ideas equally abstract and ideological. We can, more concretely, explore everything in between. I have argued that realism works with "big-enough," more-than-local, narratives: histories that travel and translate, but without cumulating in a coherent destiny, progressive or apocalyptic. We thus rely on processes of juxtaposition and mediation, generalizing but never general. "The whole," Adorno famously wrote, "is the false" (1974: 50). And so is the fragment. Realism works self-consciously with partial histories, alert to their constitutive tensions. Ethnographic-historical studies like those of Hernández Castillo and Hale offer ways to critically engage, not explain away, the contradictions and paradoxes of postmodernity.

Alter Histories 3

Let us listen to one more resonant example of indigenous historical thinking (Pullar and Knecht 1995). It is a quotation I stumbled on about fifteen years ago, using it to conclude an essay about history that prefig-ures my present speculations (Clifford 1997a). The quotation has stayed with me. I asked then, and I still wonder, what kind of a "big-enough history" it could be telling.

Barbara Shangin, an Alutiiq Elder, is speaking sometime in the 1970s, on the Alaska Peninsula, near Kodiak Island:

> Our people have made it through lots of storms and disasters for thousands of years. All the troubles since the Russians are like one long stretch of bad weather. Like everything else, this storm will pass over some day.

We can, without too much difficulty, read these words as narrating a recognizable history: the colonization of Alaska and its consequences. I don't think Barbara Shangin is saying that Alutiiq people will eventually go back to what they were before capitalist modernity, in the form of Russian fur traders, began to integrate Alaska in the late eighteenth century. At least as I interpret her, she assumes that the bad weather brings irreversible changes, some of which, like the Russian Orthodoxy that has taken root as a genuine native religion, are of enduring value. The image of recurring weather suggests a kind of return without going backward in time. The cycles Barbara Shangin evokes are thus not unhistorical repetitions, but structuring patterns—for transformation, for continuity through change. Temporally deep stories such as hers narrate an indigenous *longue durée* reaching before and after colonization. This "reach," anachronistic and prophetic, is fundamental to contemporary native ways of telling history. We listen to Barbara Shangin's words as more than wishful thinking: she is making realist claims in a distinct historical idiom.

But perhaps it would be better to speak of a distinct "historical ecology." The Tongan writer, anthropologist, and visionary Epeli Hau'ofa (see Chapter 5) suggests as much in a luminous meditation on Island Pacific forms of memory. At times he seems to be extending Barbara Shangin's vision. Hau'ofa affirms that indigenous histories have deep roots in oral traditions and in place, in the inhabited land and ocean. Real history, history that matters, does not suddenly begin with, colonization, missionaries, literacy, and global development. The scope of history is more encompassing. Oral, place-based modes of recalling and moving in historical time work through cycles. Barbara Shangin's "weather" is always different and the same, always returning, always innovating. Hau'ofa refers to Kame'eleihiwa's evocation, discussed earlier, of the Hawai'ian past "in front," and the future "behind." And he asks, with characteristic humor: "Is this, then, the case of the dog chasing its tail?"

He answers in the affirmative, continuing in a passage that could be a commentary on Shangin's vision of change:

> Where time is circular, it does not exist independently of the natural surroundings and society. It is important for our historical reconstructions to know that the Oceanian emphasis on circular time is tied to the regularity of seasons marked by natural phenomena such as cyclical appearances of certain flowers, birds and marine creatures, shedding of certain leaves, phases of the moon,

changes in prevailing winds, and weather patterns, which themselves mark the commencement of and set the course for cycles of
human activity such as those related to agriculture, terrestrial and
marine foraging, trade and exchange, and voyaging, all with their
associated rituals, ceremonies, and festivities. This is a universal
phenomenon stressed variously by different cultures. (Hau'ofa
2008: 67)

Embodied, emplaced, ritually performed senses of time are present,
Hau'ofa affirms, in every society. But technologically advanced, urbanized worlds make it difficult to stay connected to homelands and their
rhythms. In Island Pacific societies, "Most of us who are urbanized and
living in accordance with the demands of the contemporary global culture still maintain relationships with our nonurban relatives and are
therefore entangled in the tussle between tradition and modernity, however defined." To represent this tussle, with its changing historical processes of attachment and distance, "we could use the notion of the spiral,
which connotes both cyclic and linear movement" (69). At issue is not
just a way of remembering, but a historical practice, a way of surviving,
continuing to live: "We could go further and incorporate this notion [the
spiral] in the formulation of an Oceanian ecological ideology, tying
linear development to natural cycles, with a view of guiding the applica-
tion of modern technologies on our environment. Our long-term survival within Oceania may well depend on some such guidance" (72).

Hau'ofa's "spiral" is a figure for indigenous thriving, for transformations and returns in endless, genealogical development—a profoundly
relational process. And the resonance of his image is wide. We have never
lived in an "arrow-of-time" history with a clear direction. I have suggested that we live in swirls of contemporary, coeval times: histories
going somewhere, separately and together. The concatenation cannot be
mapped on a single plane. Barbara Shangin's historical "weather" is
always different and the same, an image perhaps of indigenous historical
epistemology and practice. Like Hau'ofa's "spiral" it gives a shape to
transformations and returns in developing time. In their visions of history swirling, moving in more than one direction, the two narrative
forms are profoundly realistic. Moreover, their "ecological" sensibilities
are of obvious importance in more-than-local contexts. Given the crises
facing an unequal, overpopulated, environmentally ravaged planet today,
the survival of small societies that maintain, or at least aspire to, some

degree of social balance and responsible local attachment is, in itself, an achievement. But is this a "big-enough history"—big enough, that is, to matter? What difference does it make for all those crowding into cities? Will indigenous projects, in new contexts of articulation, somehow aggregate, becoming a more-than-local, globalizing force? And why would one want to ask such a question? Is not local survival enough?

Hau'ofa (1993, 2008) has eloquently argued that remaining local and small is not now, and has never been, a strategic option. People will connect with one another through travel, trade, technology, kinship, migration, invasion, and conflict. (He stresses that, paradoxically, this is especially true of island societies.) While it may be necessary, at times, to look inward, to build defensive walls, to cultivate one's garden, this has never been a long-term survival strategy. Interdependence and movement are historical realities that indigenous societies inflect, and partly control. They do this through interactive social processes of articulation, performance, and translation.

Articulation, Performance, Translation

Historicizing with Harvey and Jameson we imagine a changing capitalist world system that works through differences, that rewards and governs cultures and identities. Indigenous social movements unfold within these flexible structures. But I have argued that this cannot be the only, or the final, moment of analysis. And indeed, both of the thinkers just mentioned reserve a crucial place for "utopian," radically transformative visions (Harvey 2000; Jameson 2005). No doubt all global-systemic approaches run the risk of functionalist reductionism, where difference appears derivative of, or "produced" by, structural power. Conversely, ethnographic approaches too easily slip into nominalism. Devotion to specificity and detail can become a mantra-like objection to all generalizing analyses: "It's more complex than that . . ."

A combined approach synthesizing structure and process, "macro" and "micro" levels, the localized "thick description" of Clifford Geertz with the world historical "cognitive mapping" of Fredric Jameson, is the holy grail of sociocultural analysis today. It confronts serious methodological obstacles and epistemological antinomies. Synthetic accounts tend to reduce one "level" or "scale" to another, creating wholes from selected parts, or setting up artificial foregrounds and backgrounds. As I argued some time ago, these rhetorical/analytic strategies can only produce contingent syntheses, "partial truths" subject to refutation and revision by their constitutive exclusions. (Clifford 1986). Observations such as this were part of a radical critique of ethnography during the 1980s. Since then, variegated forms of holism and assemblage have been self-consciously pursued in ethnographic research governed by new assumptions and terms of engagement (Ong and Collier 2005; Otto and Bubandt 2010). I have myself experimented with an antisynthetic realism, essays made up of juxtaposed representational styles and narratives (Clifford 1997b). No sovereign method is available, only experiments working outside the frozen alternatives of local and global, structure and process, macro and micro, material and cultural.

It is widely recognized that global-systemic approaches simultaneously explain, and are cut down to size by, historical-ethnographic particulars. Conversely, microanalyses are subject to larger, world-making energies and forces that open up the local and subvert any discrete "field" of analytic attention (Gupta and Ferguson 1997a). We work among irreconcilable antinomies, entering the paradoxes and tensions of our historical moment with agendas that are positioned and relational, pushing against, while drawing on, partial perspectives. The result is a more realistic, because multiscaled, dialogical and unfinished, understanding of contemporary sociocultural worlds. This, at least, is my wager.

Approaching the complex terrain of contemporary indigeneity, I rely on three analytic terms: articulation, performance, and translation. They make up a portable toolkit for thinking nonreductively about social and cultural change. All are terms of process. The three tools—or perhaps better, theoretical metaphors—complement and complicate each other. They are used pragmatically and do not lend themselves to systematization. Let me dwell for a moment on each.

Articulation denotes a broad range of connections and disconnections—political, social, economic, and cultural (see Chapter 2). To see the concept at work, consider more closely Charles Hale's essential question, cited above:

Will the subjugated knowledge and practices be articulated with the dominant, and neutralized? Or will they occupy the space opened from above while resisting its built-in logic, connect with others, toward "transformative" cultural-political alternatives that still cannot even be fully imagined? (2002: 499)

The passage begins with the possibility that subaltern knowledges and practices will become tied to the dominant, neoliberal/state program and thus can no longer contribute to significant change. Hale's use of the word "articulation" indicates, not a necessary assimilation or loss of social or cultural identity, but rather an alliance of popular aspirations for recognition and autonomy with the agendas of state and transnational institutions: human rights regimes, NGOs, multicultural programs. Difference would not therefore be erased through articulation, but supported, even intensified, in forms that channel and contain it. This is hegemony at work: interactive and negotiated, but ultimately on terms dictated by the more powerful.

Hale goes on, however, to suggest a counterhegemonic range of possibilities. These too depend on processes of articulation. Is it possible, he asks, to "occupy" the spaces opened from above while also resisting their logic? Resistance, here, does not imply total rejection, for it is simultaneous with the activity of moving onto the new spaces. The word "occupy" also suggests a tactic rather than a necessary outcome. This kind of selective engagement is well expressed by the language of articulation, whose connections are real but contingent. Articulation always includes the possibility of disarticulation, a process suggested by the phrase "while resisting." Moreover, Hale also makes space for rearticulation, as in the final clauses of the quotation where subordinate groups "connect with others" in unprecedented alliances, in relations directed neither from "above" nor "below."

The fundamental question posed by the passage, inherent to the process of hegemony, is arguably constitutive of the present historical moment in many parts of the world. It is an antinomy that defines the real and should not be resolved too quickly. Hale's quotation marks around "transformative" sustain a critical uncertainty about what will count as significant, that is, structural, change. The language of articulation helps us focus on forms of power and conditions of maneuver, on specific material and semiotic connections, without foreclosing possibilities of delinking and reconnecting. It understands the world of cultural politics, its antagonisms and alliances, interpellations and resistances, as both materially constrained and open to invention.

Performance is another key term that helps us grasp the ambivalent complexity of contemporary social and cultural processes. In much recent work identity politics is understood as self-recognition, a kind of self-marketing in systems of neoliberal tolerance. Performance is reduced to interpellation. Persons or groups are "called" or "hailed" to perform themselves as authentic cultural subjects. This recognition occurs in situations of empowerment that are circumscribed by state and transnational regimes of governmentality. The latter term derives from Foucault, and the most sophisticated versions of this analysis, by authors such as Elizabeth Povinelli (2002) and Rey Chow (2002), are a concatenation of Marxist and Foucauldian perspectives. Cultural subjects discover themselves and make themselves legible for powerful audiences that dispose of attractive resources and coercive power. In this perspective, the staged authenticity of ethnic identification, the display of heritage, the branded localism of development projects, and the more or less calculated "acts" of cultural tourism are command performances. However, when Foucault is added to Marx it becomes more difficult to contain these performances within a specific hegemonic regime or economic system.

Foucault's mobile and decentered conception of power works through processes of subjectification—experiences of wholeness, empowerment, fulfillment, freedom. Viewed as social performances these subjective processes are excessive, both confirming and exceeding social or economic orders. Their political valence cannot be read off in advance. Freedom can be associated with either consumption or rebellion. Empowerment can be a matter of feeling good or of overturning a social order. Moreover, interpellation itself is performative. Cultural subjects "play themselves" for multiple audiences: the police, state agencies, schools, churches, NGOs, tourists; they also perform for family, friends, generations, ancestors, the tribe, animals, and a personal God. Subjectivity is plural and not simply a matter of turning toward power, as in Althusser's famous fable (1972). It can also involve turning away, falling silent, keeping secrets, using more than one name, being different in changing situations.

Attention to performance keeps us attuned to the specificity of acts and the role of discrepant audiences in sustaining identities. As we will see, particularly in Part Three, indigenous cultural expressions include all manner of arts and ceremonies, relations of "showing and telling" (Strang 2000) that are fundamental to claiming power and resources: dances, emblems, pow-wows, cultural festivals, museum displays, Zapatista bus caravans. And these public manifestations can make us forget the more private celebrations: family potlatches, initiations and life transitions, curings, memorials, and exchanges. Myths and histories of clan and tribe are passed on quietly, when the time is right. Cultural knowledge is always both revealed and held back, shared and kept secret through specific roles and protocols. For example, Australian Aboriginal clan authorities decide what to circulate—in traditional exchanges as well as in modern paintings, websites, or tribal museums—and what to keep to themselves. Men and women control and ritually enact knowledge differently, managing the performances of initiation, of teaching across generations. These are forms of subject formation that take place significantly, though probably never completely, outside the reach of capitalist markets and ideological hegemony. Indigenous identities today are performative, enacted for different audiences at different times, with varying latitudes of discipline and freedom. In Part Two we will follow in detail the anticipated roles and subversive silences of "the last wild Indian in America," "Ishi"—a man of many performances.

Translation is not transmission. For example, to see the spread of global ("American") culture as a series of translations recasts its apparent diffusion as a partial, imperfect, and productive process. Something is brought across, but in altered forms, with local differences. *Traditore tradutore.* There is always a loss or misunderstanding along the way. And something is gained, mixed into the message. As Ezra Pound said, translation is "making it new." Returning briefly to the Zapatista movement: Marxism was translated into Mayan terms and thus made new, now with women in the conversation (Hernández Castillo 1997). Subcomandante Marcos inventively translated a "politics of the possible" for the Mexican nation and for wider worlds. Out of sight, behind the masks, conversations have been taking place between different "Mayans" as well as among other displaced *campesinos* in the Lacandon frontier. In the "autonomous zones," discussions are ongoing across languages, between generations, and among men and women. Translation is a term for cultural processes that are profoundly dialogic and, like articulation, without closure or guarantee.

The concept of translation, better than transmission, communication, or mediation, brings out the bumps, losses, and makeshift solutions of social life. The theory/metaphor of translation keeps us focused on cultural truths that are continuously "carried across," transformed and reinvented in practice. We are less inclined to reify a correct or completed ideology: take it or leave it. And it is harder to naturalize a racial essence or an authentic cultural tradition: you belong or you don't. Cultural translation is always uneven, always betrayed. But this very interference and lack of smoothness is a source of new meanings, of historical traction, as Anna Tsing's seminal concept of intercultural "friction" (2005) and Donna Haraway's "diffraction" and "interference" (1997) make clear. The challenge, as we have seen, is to recognize overlapping but discrepant histories that struggle for room to maneuver in a paradoxically systematic and chaotic contemporary world.

Do "indigenous" historical practices matter, at local, national, even global scales? How important are they . . . really? The question—reductive and ethnocentric—cannot be avoided. It will be asked, often as a way to make tribal societies once again insignificant, residual, and disappearing. An adequate response, I've argued, must not replace one vision of unified history with another. We need to work at multiple scales and among discrepant histories, engaging with multiplicity and contradiction, inhabiting paradox. This alert uncertainty is realism. At the very least, to make a difference historically means to be going somewhere, claiming an original future. For small societies, flourishing is not a matter of catching up with purportedly more advanced economies and civilizations, but rather of multiplying the modalities of transformation, of continuity, of development. If historical time is not a single, directional flow, where are contemporary indigenous people going in an interconnected world? What difference does their global "presence" make? The question is newly important, and newly uncertain.

2

❖

INDIGENOUS ARTICULATIONS

L'indépendence, c'est de bien calculer les interdependences. (Independence is the good management of interdependence.)
—Jean-Marie Tjibaou, *La présence Kanak*

New Caledonia is a rather long island, about three hundred miles end to
end, and never more than fifty wide. Its spine is mountainous, with trans-
verse valleys running to the sea. In 1850 about thirty distinct language
groups occupied these separate valleys—a classic Western Pacific social
ecology. A century and a half later much has changed. New Caledonia is
a settler colony, once the site of a French penitentiary, now a nickel-
mining center, with a long history of violent displacements of the indigenous people. Since the sixties, there has been an intensification of
resistance to French rule, in the name of a more or less unified aboriginal
population who have appropriated the colonizers' name for generic
natives, canaques. (But capitalized, with a new spelling: Kanak.) The surviving language groups and custom areas on the island engage in a complex politics of alliance and competition within and outside this new
political identity. French is the lingua franca. The Kanak movement, since
the seventies, has made real trouble, both for the relatively liberal French
authorities, and for the more entrenched whites in the island. The result
is a growing economic and political autonomy for the overwhelmingly
indigenous northern province, and a very slow return of expropriated

This chapter was originally delivered at the symposium "Native Pacific Cultural
Studies at the Edge." The conference was organized by Vicente M. Diaz and J.
Kehaulani Kauanui at the Center for Cultural Studies, University of California, Santa
Cruz, 11–12 February, 2000. I have edited the talk, while preserving a sense of the
occasion: a gathering of indigenous scholars from Oceania.

lands. I can't go into the countercurrents and future uncertainties of this simultaneously post- and neocolonial situation. I only want to bring up one aspect of the modus vivendi, which I'm tempted to call "indigenous commuting." (The older meanings of the word "commute," by the way, have to do with exchanging, bartering, changing, mitigating . . .)

Most of New Caledonia's white and Pacific-mix populations live in and around the capital city, Noumea, near the rather barren southern end of the island. Most indigenous life is located elsewhere, to the north and east in fertile mountain valleys. When I was in New Caledonia in the late 1970s, I was taken around one of these northern habitats, Hienghène, by Jean-Marie Tjibaou, who was then in the process of becoming the Kanak movement's most prominent spokesman. Tjibaou was mayor of Hienghène, and he was involved in the return of his clan to ancestral lands that had for more than a half-century been forcibly alienated by colonial cattle ranchers. Tjibaou lived in Noumea, where he had political work to do, but he was able to travel regularly to Hienghène for meetings, ceremonies, and family business, using the road system put in place by the French. It was about a six-hour drive. Tjibaou, who had spent most of the last twenty years away from the valley of his birth, was comfortable in more than one place. And yet there was no doubt in his mind where he belonged. He deeply believed that a continuous relationship with a place—its ancestors, history, and ecology—was necessary if Kanak people were to feel *à l'aise,* if they were to find breathing room in the contemporary world (Tjibaou 1996). The restoration of lost lands has always been a crucial goal of Kanak insurgency.

Among New Caledonia's Melanesians there is no mass tendency to exodus from rural villages into swelling cities, either on or off the island. A significant Kanak urban population resides in and around Noumea, the political and commercial capital. But there's a lot of coming and going. And recent studies have confirmed that older patterns of mobility persist in the migrations and circulation linking tribe and town (Hamelin 2000; Naepels 2000). When I first noticed this mobility, I was struck by a homology of scale between pre- and postcolonial lifeways. People used to walk from village to village, from one end of a valley to the other, on various social, economic, and political errands. It took a day or two. Today, using the automotive infrastructure, it takes a day or two to traverse the length of the island, to visit and return. People still travel, circulate, and manage to be home when it matters. *Plus ça change.*

All of this raises some key issues for our discussions today:

1. How is "indigeneity" both rooted in and routed through particular places? How shall we begin to think about a complex dynamic of local landedness and expansive social spaces? Should we think of a continuum of indigenous and diasporic situations? Or is there a specifically indigenous kind of diasporism? A lived dialectic of urban *and* rural? Life on and off the reservation? Island *and* mainland native experiences? There are real tensions, to be sure, along the indigenous continuum of locations. But as Murray Chapman's (1978, 1991) extensive research on "circulation" in the Solomon Islands and beyond suggests, we should be wary of binary oppositions between home and away, or a before/after progress from village life to cosmopolitan modernity. As we try to grasp the full range of indigenous ways to be "modern," it's crucial to recognize patterns of visiting and return, of desire and nostalgia, of lived connections across distances and differences.

2. Relations between "edge" and "center." How should we conceive of an expansive indigenous region: a "Native Pacific"? What traditions and practices allow one to feel rooted without being localized, kept small? I always think of Black Elk, the Sioux shaman and Catholic catechist, traveling as a young man with Buffalo Bill in Paris (a stop Tjibaou would later make on a different indigenous detour). Black Elk says something like: "Harney Peak (in the North Dakota Badlands) is the center of the world. And wherever you are can be the center of the world." How do moving people take their roots with them, as "rooted cosmopolitans," in Kwame Anthony Appiah's (1998: 91) phrase? And are there specifically indigenous kinds of homes away from home?

3. Which raises the question: just how expansive can notions of indigenous or native affiliation become before they begin to lose specificity, falling into more generalized "postcolonial" discourses of displacement? In this conference we find ourselves occupying the sometimes fraught borderland (not, I will argue, a sharp line) between "indigenous" and "diasporic" affiliations and identities. I hope we will actively inhabit and explore, not flee from, the mutually constitutive tension of indigenous and diasporist visions and experiences. We will need to wrestle both with the seductions of a premature, postmodern pluralism and with the inescapable dangers of exclusivist self/other definitions.

Considering a "Native Pacific Cultural Studies on the Edge," we necessarily turn our attention to indigenous dynamism, interaction, dwelling-in-travel. But it will be equally important to remember that being "native" in a more-than-local sense does not mean sacrificing attachments to a place, or places—the grounding that helps one feel at home in a world of complex interdependences. Black Elk took Harney Peak along when he went to Paris. Moreover, the example of "Kanak commuting" I began with may also help remind us that the "edge" of a Native Pacific isn't always "out there" thousands of miles from the island centers. In New Caledonia, Noumea marks the powerful "edge" of a particular Native Pacific. The city has long been a white enclave. But it's an edge that has come to be in contact, back and forth, with "*la tribu*" (landed sites of *la coutume*, customary life). For Tjibaou and many of his compatriots it has never been a matter of choosing one *or* the other, tradition or modernity, but of sustaining a livable interaction while struggling for power.

Being *à l'aise* with the contemporary world, *as a Kanak,* meant living and working both in villages and cities. The indigenous cultural politics Tjibaou espoused took shape in landmark events like the 1975 festival Mélanésia 2000—whose name invoked a dynamic *future*. The festival operated at many levels: a revival and public intertribal exchange of traditional stories, dances, alliances; an emerging articulation of "Kanak" identity at the level of New Caledonia and the Loyalty Islands; a manifestation of an expansive "Melanesian" culture for European New Caledonia, for neocolonial France, for other Pacific nations, and for international bodies like the United Nations. Tjibaou insisted that the cultural center he envisaged (now, after his tragic assassination, named after him) needed to be located in the hostile settler-colonial city of Noumea. The politics of cultural and political identity, as he saw it, always worked the boundaries. And as Alban Bensa (2000) has shown, the Centre Culturel Jean-Marie Tjibaou is, in its spatial design, an articulated ensemble, juxtaposing and connecting, not without tensions, *la coutume* with the transnational world of art and culture.

So as we consider Native Pacific lives on the "edge," in places like Auckland, Oakland, or Los Angeles, we can remember that the edges, the traversed and guarded frontiers of a dynamic native life, are not just to be found out here in places like California (riding the rim of the Pacific plate, as Vince Diaz always reminds us). Edges and borders crosscut the region, defining different conjunctures: local, national, and regional; urban, rural, and in between; colonial, neocolonial, postcolonial.

This brings me to my central point about "indigeneity" today—its "articulated" nature. I'll be exploring some of the advantages and limits of articulation theory for an emergent "Native Pacific Cultural Studies," weighing the possibilities of translating notions like articulation and diaspora from their North Atlantic locations into the spaces and histories of the Pacific. During the conference others will certainly have more to say about the specific paths, pitfalls, and detours of cultural studies in the Pacific, unfinished routes of what, following Edward Said (1983), we can call "traveling theories."

For clarity's sake at the outset let me make some rather sharp distinctions, oppositions I'll need to blur later on. The notion of articulated sites of indigeneity rejects two claims often made about today's tribal movements. On the one hand, articulation approaches question the assumption that indigeneity is essentially about primordial, transhistorical attachments (ancestral "laws," continuous traditions, spirituality, respect for Mother Earth, etc.). Such understandings miss the pragmatic, entangled, contemporary forms of indigenous cultural politics. On the other hand, articulation theory finds it equally reductive to see indigenous or First Nations claims as the result of a post-sixties, "postmodern" identity politics (appeals to ethnicity and "heritage" by fragmented groups functioning as "invented traditions" within a late-capitalist, commodified multiculturalism). This viewpoint brushes aside long histories of indigenous resistance and transformative links with roots prior to and outside the world system. We must, I think, firmly reject these simplistic explanations—while weighing the partial truth each one contains.

To think of indigeneity as "articulated" is to recognize the *diversity* of cultures and histories that currently make claims under this banner. What exactly unites Hawai'ians (whose history includes a monarchic state) and much smaller Amazonian or New Guinean groups? What connects pan-Mayan activists with U.S. tribal gaming operations? What allies the new Inuit autonomous province of Nunavut with Aboriginal and Torres Straits Islander land claims (rather than with, say, the similar strong regionalisms of Catalonia, or perhaps what's emerging in Scotland or Wales)? What do "tribal" peoples in India have in common with the Fijian Great Council of Chiefs?

I do not think we can arrive at a core list of essential "indigenous" features. The commonality is more historically contingent, though no less real for all that. Indigenous movements are positioned, and potentially but not necessarily connected, by overlapping histories and struggles with respect to Euro-American, Russian, Japanese, and other imperialisms. They all contest the power of assimilationist nation-states, making strong claims for autonomy, or for various forms of sovereignty.

In recent decades, positive discourses of indigenous commonality have emerged, drawing together this range of historical predicaments. I'm thinking of the various pan-Indian, pan-Aboriginal, pan-Mayan, indigenous "Arctic" movements, as well as an expanding network of Fourth World coalitions. The discourses are also propagated through United Nations, NGO, and tourist networks. Thus, today, a number of expansive ideologies express positive notions of "indigenousness," ideas that in turn feed back into local traditions.

To see such chains of equivalence (which must always downplay or silence salient differences) as articulated phenomena is not to view them as inauthentic or "merely" political—invented or opportunistic. Articulation as I understand it evokes a deeper sense of the "political"—productive processes of consensus, exclusion, alliance, and antagonism that are inherent in the transformative life of all societies.

I will take up the strengths and limits of articulation theory a bit later. But first I want to raise some broad historical issues, identifying features that distinguish Island Pacific contexts from those in which North Atlantic cultural studies tools have been hammered out. And I hasten to add that I'm not pleading "Pacific exceptionalism" but highlighting salient differences within a connected, open-ended history of the late twentieth century. The point is to locate Pacific histories in relation to global forces, not outside them, and not in a predetermined condition that must forever play catch-up to linear progress.

The timing of decolonization (an uneven, unfinished process) in the region is critical. Changes in formal political sovereignty generally came to the Pacific in the 1970s and the 1980s—a couple of decades after the clustered postwar experiences of African or South Asian independence. Decolonization is, of course, not an all-or-nothing, once-and-for-all transition; and long, ongoing histories of resistance and accommodation, of unlinking and relinking with imperial forces, need to be kept in view. But the national independence movements of the 1950s and 1960s represent an epochal moment in this process and as such retain a certain normative status. Pacific decolonizations encounter a rather different historical situation, with altered constraints and possibilities (Firth 2000). Since the 1960s, for example, the notion that political independence under the leadership of nationalizing elites would lead to liberation and social justice has been pretty definitively exploded, particularly for local or tribal peoples. In many parts of the world today nation-state affiliations no longer seem so unambiguously the royal road to a better future.

Moreover, the capitalist world system has been going through important mutations since the early 1970s, emerging as what's variously called flexible accumulation, late capitalism, post-Fordism, or postmodernity (Jameson 1984; Harvey 1990; Ong 1999). As a result, the very idea, the rallying cry, of independence seems increasingly to have quotation marks placed around it. For Jean-Marie Tjibaou "independence" and "interdependence" were inseparable. Thus sovereignty could never be separatist, an end in itself: "It's sovereignty that gives us the right and the power to negotiate interdependencies. For a small country like ours, independence is the good management of interdependence" (Tjibaou 1996: 179). The notion of sovereignty, control over borders, over culture, over economy, is complicated by the fact that today no nation, not even the most powerful, efficiently governs its economy, frontiers, and cultural symbols. You can't keep out illegal immigrants, drugs, Coke, and Michael Jordan. Or Bob Marley: the articulation of reggae with indigenous projects in the Pacific and elsewhere is a resonant, if unorganized, form of "globalization from below" (Brecher, Costello, and Smith 2000). Moreover, since movements of people across borders are dramatic and often nonlinear, experiences of identity and citizenship are complexly parceled out. Families may be organized in long-distance patterns. Indeed, one can be born and live in Los Angeles, Salt Lake City, or Auckland and yet be deeply connected to Hawai'i, to Tonga, to Samoa, or to the Cook Islands (Small 1997; Kauanui 1999). Such diasporic predicaments, the remittance economies they often reflect, and the "commuting" (exchanging, changing, mitigating) they entail, are facilitated by technologies of air travel, the Internet, videos, cell phones, and all the rest. If people in the Pacific have occupied large spaces with canoes, why can't they dwell with airplanes and the Web?

Of course, transnational dynamics have long existed. But their salience for the cultural politics of decolonization was not at all clear in the 1950s and 1960s. Then, a modernist vision of nationhood held sway, a vision of drawing lines around particular territories and building imagined communities inside. Nation building—making "Nigerians" or "Indonesians," for example—in ethnically complex territories, involved reducing or opposing retrograde "tribalisms." The nation-state alone could be progressive. Nation-state projects are, of course, far from dead, but things are inescapably more ambiguous today. Revived, newly configured projects of the indigenous and the local pull against such modernizing attitudes. (As I write, the multiethnic nation-state edifice seems especially rickety in places like Fiji, the Solomon Islands, and Indonesia.)

These developments reflect old and new "ethnic" antagonisms, traditional regional differences, as well as the pressures and opportunities of a capitalist world system. Theorists of globalization and postmodernity tend to see a newly "flexible" system actively making room for, and to a degree commodifying, the politics of localism, identity, and culture. I would insist, however, on the phrase "to a degree." The partial entanglements of indigenous and local societies in global structures are not simply the world system's unfinished business. They have their own dynamism. As much historically minded ethnography in the Pacific has shown, the contemporary movements around identity, *kastom*, and sovereignty continue and transform long histories of conflict and interaction (for example: Dening 1980; G. White 1991; Finney 1994; Jolly 1994; Sahlins 1994; Bensa 1995; Thomas 1997).

This work converges with that of indigenous scholars (for example: Diaz 1993; Helu 1999; Hereniko 1995, 2000; Teaiwa 2001a) to trace sustained experiences of cultural survival, resistance, and innovation in changing contexts of performance and alliance. Traditions articulate—selectively remember and connect—pasts and presents. Indeed, as both Roy Wagner (1979) and Lilikala Kame'eleihiwa (1992) in their different ways affirm, the "past" in indigenous epistemologies is where one looks for the "future." The quotation marks suggest how a Western commonsense view of historical development, based on the opposition of tradition and modernity, is deconstructed in translation. Moreover, as Jonathan Friedman (1994) has argued, such dynamic traditions now find expanded room for political expression in the "ethnic" and "racial" spaces of a decentered West—sites of mobilization too quickly rounded up under the rubrics "multiculturalism" or "identity politics" (Clifford 2000). The increasingly strong tribal sovereignty movements of the 1980s and 1990s show, at least, that the current hegemony—call it neo-colonialism, postmodernity, globalization, Americanization, or neoliberalism—is fractured, significantly open ended. Very old cultural dispositions—historically rerouted by religious conversion, formations of race/ethnicity, communication technologies, new gender roles, capitalist pressures—are being actively remade.

Pacific decolonization struggles thus have their own temporalities

and traditions. And because political decolonization comes to the Pacific
when sovereignty is an increasingly compromised reality, we see the
emergence of different forms of national identity, new sorts of negotiations among the local, the regional, the national, and the global. Compare
the current process of "nation building" in Papua New Guinea with that
in sixties Africa. Consider new forms of federalism, of indigenous
autonomy within partially liberalized settler regimes (New Caledonia,
Aotearoa/New Zealand). Consider the two Samoas. Or think of the different agendas proposed by advocates of Hawai'ian sovereignty. Given a
general loosening of the hyphen in the nation-state norm, it's revealing
to compare questions of regionalism and nationalism in the Pacific with
similar issues being worked out elsewhere, for example in the European
Union. Comparisons of this sort can now be made without recourse to
notions of margin and center, backward and advanced, notions that
have, in the Western imaginary, long kept the Pacific "out there" and
"back then."

Of course, today's mobile capital and labor regimes can work through
regions as well as—sometimes better than—nations. But region making
is not only a top-down process. Catalonia may make sense economically
in the New Europe, but it responds also to long-standing cultural, linguistic, and political aspirations for autonomy, within and separate from
Spain. There's often a bottom-up or ex-centric element to regional aspirations, a history deeper than postmodern spatial structures and financial networks. We're all familiar with Epeli Hau'ofa's resonant hope:
that Pacific Islanders see themselves, and the spaces between their homelands, not as dots in a vast ocean but as relays in a sea of islands that they
themselves create through old and new practices of travel, visiting, trade,
and migration (Hau'ofa 1993). Hau'ofa connects old stories with modern
situations, recognizing temporal overlays in a complexly contemporary
space. Hau'ofa's sea of islands is not, of course, the "Pacific Rim," a
regionalization based on capital flows, with an empty center (Connery
1994). It's a region cobbled together, articulated, from the inside out,
based on everyday practices that link islands with each other and with
mainland diasporas. Hau'ofa reaches back to voyaging canoes and, at
the same time, tells stories about jumbo jets—about Tongans, Samoans,
and Hawai'ians going back and forth to Los Angeles, Auckland, and Salt
Lake City. Like Paul Gilroy's "Black Atlantic" or emerging indigenous
connections across the "Arctic," the Pacific "sea of islands" helps us
conceptualize practices of subaltern region making, realities invisible

to more world-systemic, center-periphery, models of globalization and locality.

Hau'ofa's Pacific mobilities reveal, unmistakably, a kind of indigenous cosmopolitanism (see also Thaman 1985). Yet there's a paradox, a rich and sometimes difficult tension, here. For to recognize a specifically indigenous dialectic of dwelling and traveling requires more than simply unmaking the exoticist/colonialist concept of the homebody native, always firmly at home, in his or her place. I've learned a lot from island-savvy graduate students at the University of California, Santa Cruz— Teresia Teaiwa, Vince Diaz, Kehaulani Kauanui, Pam Kido, Noelani Goodyear-Kaopua, Heather Waldroup, and April Henderson—about different lived experiences of roots and routes. To do justice to complex strategies of dwelling and traveling in the Native Pacific, and across its multiple edges, we need something rather different from the influential perspectives of Appadurai (1990) or Gupta and Ferguson (1992), crucial though their critiques of naturalized places, "cultures," and "natives" have been. (For an engaged counterpoint, see Teaiwa 2001b.) The contrast between colonial fixity and post-colonial mobility, between indigenous roots and diasporic routes, can't be allowed to harden into an opposition or a before-after scenario in which cosmopolitan equals modern. When reckoning with traveling natives, if I can call them that, in the Pacific, this sort of categorization breaks down. We are left with a range of attachments to land and place—articulated, old/new traditions of indigenous dwelling and traveling.

Let me now focus more directly on how articulation theory helps us understand all this. What are its limits? Where does it need to be adapted, customized? The politics of articulation for Stuart Hall is, of course, an updating of Gramsci (Hall 1986a, 1986b; Slack 1996). It understands frontier effects, the lining up of friends and enemies, us and them, insiders and outsiders, on one side or another of a line, as tactical. Instead of rigid confrontations—civilized and primitive, bourgeois and proletarian, white and black, men and women, West and Third World, Christian and pagan—one sees continuing struggles across a terrain, portions of which are captured by different alliances, hooking up and unhooking particular elements. There's a lot of middle ground. Many political and cultural positions are not firmly anchored on one side or the other but are contested and up for grabs.

The term "articulation," of course, suggests discourse or speech—but
never a self-present, "expressive" voice and subject. Meaningful discourse is a cutting up and combining of linguistic elements, always a
selection from a vastly greater repertoire of semiotic possibilities. So an
articulated tradition is a kind of collective "voice" but always in this
constructed, contingent sense. In another register—outside the domain
of language with its orders of grammar and speech, structure and
performance—articulation refers to concrete connections, joints. Stuart
Hall's favorite example is an "articulated lorry" (something that to us
U.S. Americans sounds very exotic!). Something that's articulated or
hooked together (like a truck's cab and trailer, or a sentence's constituent
parts) can also be unhooked and recombined. So when you understand
a social or cultural formation as an articulated ensemble it does not
allow you to prefigure it on an organic model, as a living, persistent,
"growing" body, continuous and developing through time. An articulated ensemble is more like a political coalition or, in its ability to con-
join disparate elements, a cyborg. While the possible elements and
positions of a sociocultural ensemble are historically imposed, constraints that can be quite persistent over time, there is no eternal or natural shape to their configuration.

Articulation offers a nonreductive way to think about cultural transformation and the apparent coming and going of "traditional" forms.
All-or-nothing, fatal-impact notions of change tend to assume that cultures are living bodies with organic structures. So, for example, indigenous languages, traditional religions, or kinship arrangements may
appear to be critical organs that if lost, transformed, or combined in
novel structures should logically imply the organism's death. You can't
live without a heart or lungs. But indigenous societies have, in fact, persisted with few, or no, native-language speakers, as fervent Christians,
and with "modern" family structures, involvement in capitalist economies, and new social roles for women and men. "Inner" elements have,
historically, been connected with "exterior" forms in processes of selective, syncretic transformation. When Jean-Marie Tjibaou (1996: 303),
speaking both as a former priest and as an advocate of Kanak *coutume*,
says that the Bible does not belong to Westerners (who seized it "passing
through"), he is detaching and rearticulating European and Melanesian
religious traditions.

The creation of unexpected political/religious ensembles, often in
moments of colonial stress, is what first fascinated me about the Pacific

when I worked on the linked "conversion" experiences of the missionary-ethnographer Maurice Leenhardt and Melanesian Protestants (Clifford 1982). Across the Pacific, people have attached themselves and their societies to parts of Christianity while rejecting or thoroughly transforming other elements. (The essays collected by John Barker [1990] provide abundant examples.) To a degree, it has been a matter of processing the new through dynamic traditional structures. This is the part of the story that Marshall Sahlins's seminal work (for example, 1985) has featured and made inescapable. But it cannot be the whole story: arguments for cultural continuity through structural transformation are most persuasive in earlier periods of commercial contact and need to be supplemented by other, more politically contingent processes, especially once regimes of colonial and now neocolonial governmentality are in place. (Carrier [1992: 140] suggests a similar reservation.) The "cultural" continuity of indigenous societies has frequently been uneven, not guaranteed by a persistent, transformative structure. Since local traditions during the past two centuries have been violently disrupted, and inasmuch as new modes of individualism, universalism, exchange, and communication have restructured bodies, societies, and spaces, the traditions that indeed persist need to be seen as particular combinations of heterogeneous elements, old and new, indigenous and foreign. James Carrier's (1992) explicit use of articulation to describe the historical relation of gift and commodity forms in Ponam Island society is exemplary in this regard. (See also Errington and Gewertz [1991] on colonial, evangelical, and capitalist interactions in New Britain; and Tsing [1999] on "articulations" of environmentalism in Malaysia and Indonesia.) Indigenous women's movements weave together traditional and Christian roles, deploying the languages of *kastom* and anticolonialism to grapple with patriarchal power at local, national, and international levels (Molisa 1987; Jolly 1994). What emerges is a quite different picture from that of an authentic, ancient tradition holding out over the centuries by selectively integrating and rejecting external pressures and temptations. (Diane Nelson's [1999] use of articulation theory in an analysis of large-scale indigenous mobilization in Guatemala offers a rich comparison, as does Alcida Ramos's [1998] account of entangled indigenous and national agendas in Brazil.)

In articulation theory, the whole question of authenticity is secondary, and the process of social and cultural persistence is political all the way back. It's assumed that cultural forms will always be made, unmade, and

remade. Communities can and must reconfigure themselves, drawing
selectively on remembered pasts. The relevant question is whether, and
how, they convince and coerce insiders and outsiders, often in power-
charged, unequal situations, to accept the autonomy of a "we." This
seems to me a more realistic way of talking about what has been called
cultural "invention." I don't need to remind this audience that the invention of tradition is much disputed in the Pacific. The storm around Allan
Hanson's (1989) article on Maori traditions and Haunani-Kay Trask's
(1991) categorical rejection of anthropological authority in works by
Roger Keesing (1991) and Jocelyn Linnekin (1991) are the best-known
cases. The debate often came down to drawing lines between "insider"
and "outsider" representations of indigenous cultures. And in this it
expressed an appropriate decentering (not necessarily a refutation) of
nonnative expertise—a strong claim for the value of local historical
accounts and oral traditions. But decolonizing struggles pitting anthropological against native authority have, at least in the short run, tended
to obscure substantive historical issues.

    How should differently positioned authorities (academic and nonaca-
demic, native and nonnative) represent a living tradition's combined and
uneven processes of continuity, rupture, transformation, and revival?
My suggestions today about articulation contribute to an ongoing argument (and, I hope, a conversation) on these critical issues. I am not per-
suaded that "the invention of tradition" approach in the Pacific was
essentially a matter of anthropologists, faced by new indigenous challenges, clinging to their professional authority to represent cultures and
adjudicate authenticity (Friedman 1993; for a more nuanced account of
struggles over "authenticity" see Wittersheim 1999). That is certainly
part of the story. But the notion of "invention" was also getting at something important, albeit in a clumsy way. The thinking of Roy Wagner
(1975), deeply influenced in its structure by New Guinean poetics and
politics, is a better source for the term's nonreductive meanings than the
usual reference, Hobsbawm and Ranger (1983). This prescient recognition of inventive cultural *process* has tended to be lost in the flood of
analyses that demystify nationalist fictions and manipulations.

    Recognizing this tendency, it seems to me that the notion of invention
can be usefully rethought as a politics of articulation. We are on more
concrete, because more dynamic, historical grounds. The whole notion
of custom looks quite different when seen this way, when what Margaret
Jolly (1992) has pointedly called "specters of inauthenticity" are laid to

rest. The question of what is borrowed from here or there, what is lost and rediscovered in new situations, can be discussed within the realm of normal political/cultural activity.

Articulation theory cannot account for everything. Pushed to extremes it can take you to a point where every cultural form, every structure or restructuration, every connection and disconnection, has a radical contingency as if, at any moment, anything were possible. That is, in fact, a misreading of Stuart Hall on articulation. He is quite clear that the possible connections and disconnections are constrained at any historical moment. And indeed, certain forms and structural antagonisms persist over long periods. Yet these enduring forces—whether they be Christianity and capitalism or traditional cosmology and kinship—can be understood concretely only as they work through specific cultural symbols and political blocs. These are never guaranteed, but are actively produced and potentially challenged.

When thinking of differently articulated sites of indigeneity, however, one of the enduring constraints in the changing mix will always be landedness, or the power of place. This is a fundamental component of all tribal, First Nations identifications. Not everyone is equally on the move. Many people live where they have always lived, even as the habitat around them goes through sometimes violent transformations. And as the scale of "tribal" and "national" existence alters dramatically, people living exiled from ancestral places often sustain and revive a yearning, an active memory of land. This grounding, however tenuous, offers a sense of depth and continuity running through all the ruptures and attachments, the effects of religious conversion, state control, new technologies, commodities, schooling, tourism, and so on. Indigenous forms of dwelling cover a range of sites and intensities: there are "native" homebodies, commuters, travelers, and exiles. The desire called "the land," is differently, persistently active. Epeli Hau'ofa captures this desire in the vision of a displaced Tongan, raised in New Guinea, living in Fiji.

> To deny human beings the sense of a homeland is to deny them a deep spot on Earth to anchor their roots. Most East Oceanians have Havaiki, a shared ancestral homeland that exists hazily in primordial memory. Every so often in the hills of Suva, when moon and red wine play tricks on an aging mind, I scan the

horizon beyond Laucala Bay, the Rewa Plain, and the Reefs by
Nukulau Island, for Vaihi, Havaiki, homeland. It is there, far into
the past ahead, leading on to other memories, other realities, other
homelands. (2000: 470)

Land (*ples* in Vanuatu, country in Australia, *la tribu* in New
Caledonia, etc.) signifies the past in the future, a continuous, changing
base of political and cultural operations. Articulation theory, which sees
everything as potentially realigned, cut and mixed, has difficulty with
this material nexus of continuity. When a community has been living on
an island for more than a thousand years, it's not enough to say that its
members' claims to identity with a place are strategies of opposition or
coalition in struggles with neighbors, or reactions to colonizing or world-
systemic forces. It may be true and useful to say these things. But it's not
enough. (See Thomas [1997: 11–15] for a discussion of these emphases
and their appropriate tension.) People aren't, of course, always attached
to a habitat in the same old ways, consistent over the centuries. Communities change. The land alters. Men and women speak and act differently, in new ways, on behalf of tradition and place. Senses of locale are
expressed and felt through continuously renegotiated insides and outsides. And yet . . . this historical sense of entangled, changing places
doesn't capture the identity of ancestors with a mountain, for as long as
anyone remembers and plausibly far beyond that. Old myths and genealogies change, connect, and reach out, but always in relation to an
enduring spatial nexus. This is the indigenous *longue durée,* the precolonial that tends to be lost in postcolonial projections. Thus indigenous
claims always transcend colonial disruptions (including the posts and
the neos): we were here before all that; we are still here; we will make a
future here. (See too the exemplary statement by Alutiiq Elder Barbara
Shangin, quoted in Clifford [1997a: 343] and [2000: 107].)

While recognizing this fundamental claim to a distinctly rooted history, I want to argue against rigid oppositions in defining the current
array of indigenous experiences. We need to distinguish, and also (carefully, partially) to connect "diasporism" and "indigenism." What's at
stake is the articulation, the cobbling together, of "big-enough" worlds:
concrete lives led in specific circuits *between* the global and the local. We
cannot lose sight of ordinary people sustaining relational communities
and cosmologies: composite "worlds" that share the planet with others,
overlapping and translating. An absolutist indigenism, where each dis-

tinct "people" strives to occupy an original bit of ground, is a frightening utopia. It would entail relocation and ethnic cleansing on an unimaginable scale: a denial of all the deep histories of movement, urbanization, habitation, reindigenization, sinking roots, moving on, invading, mixing—the very stuff of human history. There must be, and in practice there are, many ways to conceive of "nativeness" in less absolute terms.

Nativism, the xenophobic shadow of indigeneity, values wholeness and separation, pure blood and autochthonous land. It denies the messy, pragmatic politics of articulation. Of course there's no shortage of violent examples in today's ethnically divided world to remind us of this ever-present tendency. But nationalist chauvinism, while a constant tendency, is not a necessary outcome of the new indigenisms. The articulated, rooted, *and* cosmopolitan practices I've been trying to sketch today register more complex, emergent possibilities (see also Childs 1993, 1998). Indeed, our conference is well positioned to bring into view an extended range of ways to be "native," an expansion evident in the work of its organizers (Diaz 1993, 1994; Kauanui 1999). The movements of Native Pacific people suggest newly inventive struggles for breathing space, for relational sovereignty, in post-/neocolonial conditions of complex connectivity. They are about finding ways to exist *in* a multiplex modernity, but with a difference, a difference located in cultural tradition, in landedness, and in ongoing histories of displacement, travel, and circulation. As Hau'ofa suggests, an element of "diasporism," of movement between places, is part of escaping belittlement—of becoming big, global, enough. But he also stresses that this must not mean losing contact with specific ecologies, places, and "pasts to remember" (Hau'ofa 1993, 2000). Since indigenism and diasporism aren't one-size-fits-all categories, we need to work toward a more nuanced vocabulary, finding concrete ways to represent dispersed *and* connected populations.

Native Pacific conditions are importantly different from those generating North Atlantic cultural studies, a difference registered by this conference's oxymoronic coupling of indigenous and diasporic agendas. In my own work, I've found that when importing Stuart Hall or Paul Gilroy, Avtar Brah or Doreen Massey into the Pacific I've been made sharply aware of the Caribbean, South Asian, and British histories that lie behind their "worldings" (as Gayatri Spivak might put it). In these histories the "indigenous"—particularly in its stronger, autochthonous, First Nations

version—makes no persistent claim. But if Black Atlantic and South
Asian diaspora theory is to travel well in the Pacific, there needs to be a
significant adaptation to a different map and history. Obviously I think
such a theoretical translation can only be good for the unfinished project
called "cultural studies." (Indeed, as it's developing in Australia,
Aotearoa/New Zealand, and Canada, often under indigenous pressures,
we can see new forms already emerging.) The provincialization of theory
as a condition for its travel is crucial for a really cross-cultural, rooted
and routed, cultural studies.

This will suggest, perhaps, my personal excitement at this conference—
feeling myself simultaneously displaced and recruited by an emerging
Native Pacific Cultural Studies.

In closing, let me return briefly to New Caledonia and Jean-Marie
Tjibaou for a glimpse of an articulated, rooted and mobile, indigenous
world. I've said that Tjibaou took me around Hienghène, his home in the
north of the island. He had left for more than twenty years, to be trained
as a Catholic priest. Now that he had quit the church and that his clan
was moving to occupy expropriated ancestral lands, he returned as a
Kanak activist.

Northeast New Caledonia has steep green valleys, with mountainous
outcroppings—every cliff and stone holding ancestral significance. The
Kanak villages often occupy rising ground, with symbolic trees, palms,
and special plants laid out in a very beautiful, orderly way.

We were in one of these villages near Hienghène, reclining on the
lawn, talking and just feeling comfortable looking out through the trees.
Earlier I had been inside several of the village houses, concrete structures
that seemed empty with perhaps a few newspaper clippings stuck hap-
hazardly on the walls. I was puzzled and asked Tjibaou: "Look at this
village, beautifully set in this valley, everything so aesthetically arranged.
Yet inside the houses it's bare . . ."

We talked it over, agreeing that here, after all, people don't spend a
lot of time indoors. Then suddenly my guide made a sweep with his hand
that took in the village, the valley, and the mountains: "Mais, c'est ça la
maison." But that's the house.

Tjibaou's sweep of the hand—including so much within his Kanak
house—expressed a deep sense of being centered in a village and a valley.
This feeling of belonging, of being in scale with the world, was funda-

mental to Tjibaou's hope that his people might find ways to feel *à l'aise,* at home, in the twenty-first century.

And in the intervening years, as I've read more of Tjibaou's political, ethnographic, and personal writings—now collected in a superb volume, *La présence Kanak* (1996)—I've come to think his gesture was taking in even more. Beyond the Hienghène Valley he certainly included New Caledonia and the Loyalty Islands, where a composite "Kanak" identity was emerging in political struggle. But didn't he also embrace the Pacific sea of islands—a wider world of cultural exchanges and alliances that were always critical for Tjibaou's thinking about independence as interdependence? And neocolonial France—whose religion and civilization, for better and worse, still contribute to the Kanak house? And . . . in a new indigenous articulation, the world?

3

❖

Varieties of Indigenous Experience

We shall visit our people who have gone to the lands of diaspora and tell them that we have built something, a new home for all of us. And taking a cue from the ocean's ever-flowing and encircling nature, we will travel far and wide to connect with oceanic and maritime peoples elsewhere, and swap stories of voyages that we have taken and those yet to be embarked on.
 —Epeli Hau'ofa, on the Oceania Centre for Arts and Culture

Home is where the navel cord was cut.
 —A Melanesian saying

What contradictory people we are!
 —Linda Tuhiwai Smith, Wenner-Gren conference, "Indigenous Experience Today"

"Indigenous experience" is difficult to contain: the senses of belonging evoked by the phrase are integral to many, and diverse, localisms and nationalisms. Sometimes it comes down to a minimal claim, relational and strategic: "We were here before *you*." Feeling indigenous may crystallize around hostility to outsiders, to invaders or immigrants. Many forms of nativism sustain these sorts of borders, reflecting immediate political agendas, self-defense, or aggression. The anteriority claimed can be relatively shallow and fundamentally contested: all sorts of people, these days, claim "indigeneity" vis-à-vis someone else. There are, nonetheless, many social groups with undeniably deep roots in a familiar place, and they are the subjects of this essay. The peoples in question are called Aboriginal, tribal, First Nations, Native, autochthonous, or a range of more particular, local names. They may or may not (or may only sometimes) claim the identity "indigenous." Whatever names these people take or are given, they are defined by long attachment to a locale and by violent histories of occupation, expropriation, and marginalization. A diverse range of experiences falls within this loose grouping, and its boundaries are fuzzy, despite attempts at the International Labor Organization and United Nations to formally define indigenous peoples (Niezen 2003; Brown 2003).

This fuzziness suggests a certain open-ended historical dynamism. People are improvising new ways to be native: articulations, performances, and translations of old and new cultures and projects. The increase of indigenous movements at different scales—local, national, regional, and international—has been one of the surprises of the late twentieth century. Tribal ("archaic" or "primitive") peoples were, after all, destined to wither in the relentless wind of modernization. This was a historical fact, understood by everyone—except the people in question, busy with difficult and inventive survival struggles. This "survival" has been an interactive, dynamic process of shifting scales and affiliations, uprooting and rerooting, the waxing and waning of identities. In the current moment these processes take shape as a complex emergence, a *présence indigène* or a performative indigenous "voice" (Tsing 2007). What experiences of loss and renewal, what shifting past and present attachments, what social, cultural, and political strategies are active in these rearticulations? A growing body of scholarship grapples with these questions: for example, the programmatic overview of Sahlins (1999) and the complex Native American histories of Harmon (1998) and Sturm (2002).

To grasp the active, unfinished processes at work in various articulated sites of indigeneity it helps to open up, or at least "loosen" (Teaiwa 2001a), common understandings of key terms like native, autochthonous, and sovereign. The definitional closures built into these words, the cultural and political practices they authorize, are both necessary and dangerous. The strong claims they express contribute centrally to indigenous social movements. They also close down possibilities, and are, in practice, supplemented and crosscut by less absolute experiences and tactics. There are various ways to be "native" in relation to a place; assumptions of firstness or "autochthony" often obscure important histories of movement; and "sovereign" control is always compromised and relative. More happens under the sign of the indigenous than being born, or belonging, in a bounded land or nation.

This essay works to make space for contradiction and excess across a broad spectrum of indigenous experiences today by loosening the common opposition of "indigenous" and "diasporic" forms of life. The goal is a richer and more contingent realism, a fuller sense of what has happened, is happening, and may be emerging. The argument does not deny claims for landed, rooted, or local identities, asserting that they really are, or ought to be, diasporic. Nor does it assume that cosmopolitan experiences are historically more progressive—even though new scales and dimensions of indigenous life are proliferating in a globally interconnected, locally inflected postmodernity. Questioning an essential opposition does not eliminate the historical differences or tensions expressed by the contrast. Native or tribal peoples claim, often with strong historical justification, to belong in a place, a densely familiar and deeply inhabited landscape. Australian Aborigines, for example, have been living in and with their "country" for an extremely long time—long enough to persuade even skeptics committed to a linear historical ontology that it makes sense to say they have been there "forever," or "from the beginning." Such quintessentially "mythic" assertions of ancient origins evoke a "historical" continuity. With varying degrees of archaeological support, Inuit, Pacific Islanders, the various native peoples of North and South America; Sami in Norway, Sweden, Finland, and Russia; the Dayaks of West Kalimantan all make credible claims, if not to autochthony, at least to deep local roots: an indigenous *longue durée*. Such historical experiences begin and end with lives grounded, profoundly, in one place. What could be more distant from diasporic identifications, experiences that originate in, are constituted by, physical displacements, uprootings?

Yet many of the experiences made visible and intelligible by diaspora theorists such as Hall (1990), Gilroy (1993), Mishra (1996a, 1996b), or Brah (1996); the transmigrant circuits revealed by Roger Rouse (1991) and Nina Glick-Schiller (1995); and the historical pressures and structures analyzed by comparative sociologists like Robin Cohen (1997) have their equivalents, or near equivalents, in contemporary indigenous life. In everyday practices of mobility and dwelling, the line separating the diasporic from the indigenous thickens; a complex borderland opens up. Contested lines of indigenous autonomy and sovereignty are drawn across it, such as the fraught relationship of "off-island" Hawai'ians to movements of native nationalism (Kauanui 1999), or tensions between urban-dwelling Aboriginals or Indians with those living close to ancestral lands. Indigenous attachments to place are complexly mediated and do not necessarily entail continuous residence, especially in contexts such as the United States, Canada, Australia, and Aotearoa/New Zealand, where a majority of native people now live in cities. Thus it makes some sense to speak of "indigenous diasporas."

What kind of sense? Translation is continually at issue. One cannot simply import a concept that is associated with, say, the North Atlantic slave trade's aftermath (Gilroy 1993) or with postcolonial migrations to former imperial centers (Brah 1996) into situations of profound, ongoing connection with land and country, experiences associated with Australian Aborigines, with Pacific Islanders, with Arctic Inuit, or with Mayan Indians. We need to explore the specificity of indigenous diasporas, or perhaps better, diasporic *dimensions* or *conjunctures* in contemporary native lives. To bring the language of diaspora into indigenous contexts is to confront its built-in difficulties. Among recent critiques of diasporic/postcolonial theorizing, native scholars (e.g., Teaiwa 2001b) observe that when traveling, displacement, and migration are seen as normative, or at least characteristic of the contemporary world, the focus tends to relegate native peoples, yet again, to the past or to the margins. For example, when cultural studies diaspora theorists reject "nativism" in its racist, little England, Thatcherite forms, they can make all deeply rooted attachments seem illegitimate, bad essentialisms. Genuinely complex indigenous histories, which involve mobility as well as staying put, and which have always been based on transformative, potentially expansive interactions, become invisible. The native is thrown out with the bathwater of nativism. (For correctives, see the essays in Diaz and Kauanui [2001].)

The result is to obscure specifically indigenous forms of interactive cosmopolitanism: genealogical inclusion of outsiders, trading relations, circular migration, vernacular discourses of "development," or mission, maritime, and military travel (Swain 1993; Sahlins 2000; Phillips 1998; Gidwani and Sivaramakrishnan 2003; Gegeo 1998; Chappell 1997). Exclusivist nativism is, of course, prominent in political indigenism: for example, the nationalist rhetoric of "Red Power," of Hawai'ian sovereignty movements, and of Native Fijian attacks on diasporic Indians. However, such claims are not sustainable in all, or even in most, lived circumstances. Across the current range of indigenous experiences, identifications are seldom exclusively local or inward looking but rather work at multiple scales of interaction. The language of diaspora can be useful in bringing something of this complexity into view. It cannot transcend the tension between the material interests and normative visions of natives and newcomers, particularly in structurally unequal settler-colonial situations (Fujikane and Okamura 2000). But when diasporic displacements, memories, networks, and reidentifications are recognized as integral to tribal, aboriginal, native survival and dynamism, a lived, historical landscape of ruptures and affiliations becomes more visible.

"Diaspora theory" may have enjoyed its fifteen minutes of academic fame. Aihwa Ong (1999) and others writing about overseas Chinese have questioned its extension. Some cultural studies writers—like Ien Ang in her recent collection, *On Not Speaking Chinese* (2001)—have backed away from an earlier positive embrace of diasporic self-location, now grappling with the absolutist dimensions of what Benedict Anderson (1998) calls "long-distance nationalisms." In his accounts of Indian diaspora cultures, Vijay Mishra avoids celebration, always keeping the constitutive tension between essentialism and hybridity clearly in view, showing the "interrelated conditions" of what he calls diasporas of "exclusivism" and of "the border," the former focused on return, the other on interaction and crossover (Mishra 1996a, 1996b). Celebratory visions of diaspora, whether they take nationalist or antinationalist form, are permanently troubled by their opposites. This dialectical instability, however, can be an analytic strength: the opposed tendencies of diasporic experience, exclusivism and border-crossing, are good to think with. Indeed, a contradictory complexity with respect to belonging— both inside and outside national structures in contemporary multisited social worlds—may turn out to be diaspora's most productive "theoretical" contribution. The last section of this essay argues that indigenous claims to "sovereignty" contain analogous contradictions, as well as possibilities.

Colin Calloway (1990), an ethnohistorian of the Abenaki Indians in the U.S. state of Vermont, uses the term diaspora to describe the dispersal of local Indian groups in the face of settler encroachments during the nineteenth century. The apparent melting away of the Abenaki, which was interpreted as a disappearance (there were of course the usual military pressures and epidemiological disasters), was, according to Calloway, in part at least a movement to different, safer, places in the neighboring state of Maine and in Canada (see also Ghere 1993). According to this account, diaspora was a means of survival for the Abenaki, who did not entirely lose contact with each other and are still around, reconstituting elements of their culture in new circumstances. For relatively mobile native groups, the experience of moving away from homelands under pressure may not be adequately captured by the notion of "exile."

"Diaspora" gets somewhat closer to a sociospatial reality of connectedness-in-dispersion.

"Exile" denotes a condition of enforced absence, with the sustained expectation of returning home as soon as the conditions of expulsion can be corrected. The term thus applies to a broad range of displaced native peoples, even to those still living on their ancestral lands in reduced reservations or enclaves without the ability to freely hunt, fish, gather, travel, or conduct ceremonies in appropriate sites. The goal of an actual return remains alive, and it takes concrete political form in land claims and repatriations. At the same time, many people give up the idea of a physical return to traditional communities, and land, focusing instead on ceremonial observations, seasonal visits to reservations or "country," and symbolic tokens or performances of tradition. To the extent that later generations, forced or drawn into towns or cities, have no realistic intention of actually living continuously in traditional places, then the connection to lost homelands comes closer to a diasporic relation, with its characteristic forms of longing, long-distance nationalism, and displaced performances of "heritage." Diaspora classically presupposes distance from the place of origin and deferred returns. This distinguishes it from the "circuits of migration" and "borderlands" experiences of many Mexicanos in the United States or Caribbeans in New York City, where coming and going is frequent. Yet modern communications can shrink distances and make many diasporas more like borderlands in the frequency and intimacy of possible contacts (Clifford 1994).

Indigenous populations actively sustain these sorts of diasporic borderlands, as we will see in an Alaskan example discussed in detail below. It will be no surprise to anyone who studies labor migrations that many native populations are spatially far-flung. Indians from Michoacan inhabit Mexico City and do farm work in California. There are many thousands of Samoans in Auckland, Tongans in Salt Lake City, and Hawai'ians in Los Angeles. Significant Navajo populations can be found in the San Francisco area (the result of government relocation programs in the 1960s). Examples could be multiplied: the classic portrayal by Mitchell (1960) of Mohawk steelworkers; Gossen's early account of Chamulan migration as expansive cosmology (1999); the Kabre diaspora and travel circuits integral to Piot's recent ethnography, *Remotely Global* (1999); Darnell's (1998) grounded "accordion model of nomadic Native American social organization."

When addressing the lived spectrum of indigenous separations from, and orientations to, homeland, village, or reservation, we need to complicate diasporic assumptions of "loss" and "distance." Likewise, urbanization should not be conceived as a one-way trip from village to city. Gidwani and Sivaramakrishnan (2003) provide a sophisticated critique of both Marxist and liberal modernisms in an ethnographically persuasive account of "circular migration" by "tribals" and "dalits" in India. Embodied practices of work and desire are portrayed in Gramscian terms as entangled counterhegemonic projects opening up "rural cosmopolitan" possibilities for identity and cultural assertion. The same can be said of much contemporary "indigenous" migration—coerced, voluntary, or specific combinations of the two. Avoiding a modernist teleology of urbanization as the simple abandonment of rural life, ethnographic accounts now follow the "routes" of multisited communities. (Lambert [2002] provides a rich West African case study.) The focus shifts to particular connections and translations, intermediate stopping places and circuits of return. For example, in Merlan's finely detailed ethnography, Australian Aboriginal "mobs" have clustered on the outskirts of towns, and at cattle stations, while orienting these settlements in the direction of traditional "country" and making regular journeys "out bush" in groups to gather traditional foods and to dance and sing at sacred sites (Merlan 1998; see also Christen 2004). Relations of kinship with country can, in practice, be sustained, even when the land is legally owned by non-Aboriginals. Of course there are struggles over multiple "uses," and access is not always negotiable. (The same goes for hunting, fishing, and gathering rights in North America.) But the essential fact of pragmatic, if not legally recognized, sovereignty is that concrete ties to ancestral places have not been severed. "Diasporic" distance is specific and relational.

These partially displaced, sustained relations to "country" need to be compared, along a continuum, with the seasonal, or deferred, "returns" of more distant city dwellers. Recent scholarship in Australia has invoked the language of diaspora when addressing differential attachments to land in the "Native Title Era" (Rigsby 1995; Smith 2000; Weiner 2002; see also Lilley's archaeological interventions: 2004, 2006). Without reducing Aboriginal identity to a single nexus of struggle, it is worth dwelling on how key issues of articulated continuity are being debated in the emerging land-claims context. Benjamin Richard Smith (2000), drawing on Rigsby, questions a rigid distinction, prevalent in both scholarship and law, between "traditional" and "historical" people. The former live in proximate relationships with ancient lands and customs and express this in "mythic" claims to have "been here forever"; the latter trace their "Aboriginal" heritage through colonial histories of displacement and recovered genealogies. Native title law has tended to recognize the claims of locally based groups while denying those of Aboriginals whose physical distance from country is viewed as an index of lost authenticity. Smith makes clear that many of the people he calls "diasporic," living in towns and cities, do not fall readily into either historical or traditional categories. He sees negotiable differences, not an essential opposition. City dwellers tend to subscribe to a more homogenous "tribal" model of Aboriginality than local people whose sense of belonging and ownership is based on specific clans and responsibilities to sites. This difference of perspective may lead to incomprehension and mutual suspicion. But in the process of making land claims, the two groups can overcome initial suspicions and work together. One group learns to defer, at least some of the time, to the local knowledge of elders; the other, at least pragmatically, comes to embrace a wider "Aboriginal" mobilization and future. Of course there is no guarantee of unity in these contingent alliances. Drawing on what Merlan (1997) observes is an "epistemological openness" in Aboriginal connections to country, and on a common, underlying sociocultural structure, diasporic and local people fashion new coalitions and scales of identification. Rather than embodying the "mythic" past and the "historical" future, local and diasporic groups represent "two trajectories of cultural continuity articulating with changing contexts" (Smith 2000: 8; see also Sutton 1988 for practical fusions of myth and history).

James Weiner (2002) challenges legal and anthropological notions of "continuity" that see specific traits (such as physical proximity to country, language fluency, religious observance, etc.) as make-or-break conditions of identity. He recognizes a more polythetic and dynamic ensemble through time (see also Clifford 1988a, 2001). The reproduction of social life is always a matter of recurring "loss" and "recovery," of selective transmission and reconstructed history in changing circumstances. Urban Aboriginals who reconnect identities and affiliations are doing nothing fundamentally new. Drawing on Jewish diaspora experiences, Weiner lends support to land rights for displaced Aboriginals: "The idea or image of a homeland, such as has sustained diasporic populations throughout the world in countless examples through the centuries, would be sufficient to maintain something that the legal profession would have to call proprietary rights to country." This rather strong culturalist position is kept in tension with a materialist criterion deployed by Australian courts (and more than a few hard-nosed Marxists) that would require native title to be based on continuing use, "a system of economic and adaptational relations to a particular territory." Accepting the tension, and properly rejecting any ideational/materialist dichotomy, Weiner concludes: "Somewhere between these two poles—as imaginary as they are unrealistic in Australian terms—lie *all* of the native title claims in Australia" (10, original emphases). Between these poles, too, lies an uneven continuum of ideational, embodied, structural, and material practices that needs to be understood as both complexly rooted and diasporic.

Confronting the actual diversity of indigenous societies, one works with a series of contexts and scales, new terms of political mobilization and expanded social maps. Collective terms such as Native American, Native Alaskan, First Peoples (in Canada), Kanak (in New Caledonia), Mayan (in Guatemala), Aboriginal (in Australia), or Masyarakat Adat (in Indonesia) represent articulated identities—alliances of particular "tribes," language groups, villages, or clans. They include people sustaining different spatial and social relations with ancestral places, a range of distances from "land." For all who identify as "native," "tribal," or "indigenous, a feeling of connectedness to a homeland and to kin, a feeling of grounded peoplehood, is basic. How this feeling is practiced, in discursive, embodied, emplaced ways, can be quite varied. Urban populations may or may not return to rural places for family gatherings, ceremonial events, subsistence activities, dance festivals, and pow-wows. For some it is a matter of frequent visits; others go once a year, for summer or midwinter social activities; some return rarely or never.

The varieties of indigenous experience proliferate between the poles of autochthony (we are here and have been here forever) and diaspora (we yearn for a homeland: "Next year in the Black Hills!"). Seeing an articulated continuum, a complex range of affiliations, offers a fresh perspective on both ends of the spectrum. If there are diasporic aspects of indigenous life, the reverse is also true. For something like an indigenous desire animates diasporic consciousness: the search for somewhere to belong that is outside the imagined community of the dominant nation-state. In diaspora, the authentic home is found in another imagined place (simultaneously past and future, lost and desired) as well as in concrete social networks of linked places. This whole range of felt attachments is crucially a part of what Avtar Brah has called "a homing desire"

(1996: 180). Diasporic dwelling practices (as distinct from the absolutist ideologies of return that often accompany them) avoid the either/or of exile or assimilation. People make a place here by keeping alive a strong feeling of attachment elsewhere. The all or nothing of naturalization, of proper citizenship, is sidestepped, but without condemning oneself to a condition of permanent marginality. This, at least, is the project of diasporic belonging: to be black *and* British, Muslim *and* French, Latino *and* U.S. American. In this lived practice, various strong forms of "cultural citizenship" emerge and become battlegrounds, as the hyphen in "nation-state" loosens (Flores and Benmayor 1997; Ramirez 2007).

Analogues from indigenous experience are not hard to find: it is common, for example, to be a tribally enrolled American Indian, to love baseball and be proud of one's service in the United States Army. Such "double belonging" (a phrase applied to Turks in Germany by Riva Kastoriano [2003]) requires a portable sense of the indigenous. It is why claims to ethnic identity or peoplehood can be profound yet not nationalist in a bounded, territorial sense (Hall 1989). In lived practice, then, indigenous and diasporic multiple attachments are not mutually exclusive. And although there are certainly situations of political struggle in which the ideological opposition indigenous/diasporic is activated, there are also a great many relatively invisible intermediate, pragmatic experiences where the two kinds of belonging interpenetrate and coexist. The purpose of opening up the borderland between diasporic and indigenous paradigms is to recognize an uneven terrain of spatial scales, cultural affiliations, and social projects. (Tsing [2000] offers a lucid and complex map.) A realistic account of "indigenous experience" engages with actual life overflowing the definitions, the political programs, and all the museums of archaism and authenticity—self-created and externally imposed.

Let us now turn to a particular case, drawn from the work of Ann Fienup-Riordan (1990, 2000), an anthropologist who has worked closely for nearly thirty years with the Nelson Island Yup'ik of western Alaska. Fienup-Riordan and her Native collaborators have described Yup'ik society, colonial and postcolonial, in considerable detail. What follows are the broad outlines.

Before the arrival of the Russians in the late eighteenth century, the inhabitants of the Kuskokwim and Yukon deltas lived a life of settled mobility, "nomadic" within discrete territories. Hunting, gathering, and fishing (freshwater and ocean) provided a relatively rich livelihood. Long classified as "Eskimos" (based on linguistic and social similarities to Inupiaq and Inuit), Yup'ik have never lived in igloos or speared seals through the ice. In many ways they defy common stereotypes (Fienup-Riordan 1990). The colonial impact of the Russians was relatively light, since there were no sea otters to hunt along the Bering Sea coast. The aboriginal inhabitants of western Alaska did not suffer the harsh conquest and forced-labor regimes imposed on their neighbors to the south, "Aleuts"—a Russian catchall term now distinguished as Onangan (Aleutian Islanders) and Alutiiq (former Pacific Eskimos). Later, the absence of gold in Yup'ik territories spared them the heavy disruptions experienced by other Native populations in Alaska. Yup'ik did suffer from contact diseases, and their societies underwent disruptive changes.

If Russian influence was more gradual than elsewhere, it did result in widespread conversion to Russian Orthodoxy (albeit with syncretic indigenous components), the presence of Creole kinship (Russian colonization encouraged intermarriage), and new trade and commercial relationships. After the Americans took control of Alaska in the 1870s, fresh missionaries arrived, and new indigenized Christianities took hold, particularly Catholic and Moravian. Over these years, Native kinship structures, village affiliations, subsistence food consumption, and language use, while undergoing transformations, remained viable. In recent decades, with the renewal of Native land claims in Alaska, heritage displays, development activities, and identity politics, Yupiit have sustained their reputation as a locally rooted people, confident in their sense of identity, still connected with traditional affiliations while pragmatically asserting new ways to be Native.

There is no need to paint a romantic picture of sociocultural survival. Many Yupiit continue to suffer the pernicious effects of colonial disruption, economic marginalization, and blocked futures. As elsewhere in Native Alaska, alcoholism and high suicide rates take their toll. Welfare dependency coexists with independent subsistence hunting and fishing. The sweeping land settlements of 1971 (the Alaska Native Claims Settlement Act, or ANCSA) were a mixed blessing. ANCSA stabilized landholdings in a state where indigenous populations, while dispossessed of much territory, had never been subjected to the forced localization of a reservation system. And while it brought considerable new resources to tribal communities, ANCSA capped indigenous title to land and introduced property boundaries between Native communities and Native corporations. The settlement subsidized new forms of economic activity and the emergence of corporate elites. It also supported a broad range of heritage projects, the articulation, translation, and performance of what Fienup-Riordan calls "conscious culture" (2000: 167). In Yup'ik country this involved the revival of mask making and dancing, once banned, now encouraged, by Christian authorities—part of a more general context of Native resurgence, alliance, and entanglement with state structures. (Dombrowski [2002] and Clifford [2004a] offer contrasting assessments of these developments.) In this ongoing period of Native Alaskan socio-cultural realignments, tribal governments and liberal state structures can neither be separated nor melded in a functioning hegemony. Fienup-Riordan documents a generally hopeful story of Yup'ik continuity: a dynamic local tradition is sustained, refocused, and in certain respects strengthened by experiences of mobility and diaspora.

In *Hunting Tradition in a Changing World* (2000) Fienup-Riordan shows that movement out of traditional Yup'ik villages into regional towns and state urban centers has markedly increased. And while the story she tells may have a class bias, focused as it is on Yupiit who have the means to create extended networks, to travel and distribute food in the city (279n13), the phenomena she traces are far from limited to a narrow elite. Most importantly, this migration does not conform to the one-way "urbanization" of modernization models. There is considerable circulation between traditional Yup'ik country and new centers of Native life in Anchorage, Alaska's largest city. Fienup-Riordan portrays these movements as part of an emerging Yup'ik "worldwide web": multi-centered Native life at new social and spatial scales. In 1970, 4,800 Alaska Natives were living in Anchorage more or less permanently ("more or less" is an important qualification). By 1990 the number had risen to 14,500, and by 2000 it was approaching 19,000. In Fienup-Riordan's assessment, the trend reflects not so much an emptying of Yup'ik country as its extension.

Yup'ik circulation between village and city adapts and transforms traditional exchanges and seasonal rhythms. Formerly, the summer was a time of mobile hunting and gathering in small family units, the winter a time for coming together in large social groupings, intense ritual life, festivals, and exchanges. For urban-based Yupiit, similar social activities are performed in new ways and sometimes at different times. This is the result of many factors, including employment patterns and vacations as well as transportation possibilities. Yup'ik community is stitched together today with snow machines, telephones, and especially airplanes, large and small. Yupiit living in Anchorage regularly return to villages around Nelson Island and the Kuskwokwim delta to engage in fishing, hunting, and gathering of seasonal foods. "Subsistence" activities (widely identified in Alaska with Native identity and "tradition") can be combined with commercial projects. In winter, recently revived dance festivals, Catholic and Moravian holidays, and the Orthodox Christmas and New Year draw return visitors. During an especially intense period in early and mid-January, old midwinter traditions of social gathering and exchanges meld with Christian rituals brought by the Russians two centuries ago (Fienup-Riordan 1990).

Yupiit who dwell in regional villages and towns visit Anchorage for a variety of reasons, including marriages, births, deaths, and shopping, as well as dropping off frozen and recently gathered "Native foods." They also travel to the Alaska Native Medical Center. (ANMC is something more than a medical establishment; it is specifically designed for Native Alaskan health needs and organized with local cultures in mind. Its gift shop offers an important outlet for arts and crafts.) Political and educational gatherings are also a draw, for example the convention of Alaskan bilingual teachers that annually draws more than one thousand participants from all over the state. Heritage performances and sharing of Native foods play a central role in all such encounters.

Patterns of visiting and circulation between village and city are driven by interlocking social, economic, political, and cultural forces. Clearly many of the pressures and opportunities that are familiar from modernization theories, forces that work to "dis-embed" local societies (Giddens 1990), are responsible for the movement out of villages and into cities. These forces include poverty and an erosion of rural subsistence, as well as a search for employment and loosened social constraints around gender, religion, or age. What emerges from Fienup-Riordan's account, however, is a recognizably "indigenous" form of modernity, or at least its entangled possibility. Traditional hunting, fishing, and gathering, while they are threatened and regulated, have not been wiped out by capitalist modes of production and distribution. They take new forms alongside, and in conjunction with, modern economies. Communal (familial, village-level) affiliations and exchanges are extended by movements into and out of cities. Rather than a linear process of disembedding (or deterritorializing), one observes a transformation and extension of culturally distinctive spatial and social practices: reembedding, extending territories, dwelling with airplanes.

Fienup-Riordan sees strategies of survival and "development," individual and communitarian, that are pursued to significant degrees on Native terms. (Compare work on indigenous conceptions of development in Melanesia by Gegeo [1998]; Sahlins [2000]; Curtis [2003]; and in Africa by Peel [1978].) This agency is not free or unconstrained. Nor is it simply coerced. For example, more young women than young men from Yup'ik country are going to Anchorage—both in search of education and to escape village restrictions. Such "modernizing" strategies are not experienced as a loss of Native identity—quite the contrary. In Anchorage, Yupiit enter extended networks of economic exchange, politics, and culture—connections at state, national, and international levels. In these networks they come to feel "Yup'ik," rather than primarily rooted in specific kin groups or villages. This tribal or national ethnonym, which only began to be widely used after the 1960s, now marks distinction in multiethnic neighborhoods, in pan-Alaskan Native settings, in Fourth World contacts, in relations with non-Natives, in a variety of cultural performances, exhibits, websites, and the like.

Clearly, an increase of traveling and dwelling beyond local villages and regional centers has contributed to an expanded articulation of "Yup'ik" identity. The experience is far from unique. David Gegeo evokes a comparable, though differently compelled, Solomon Island experience, in which Malitans migrating away from their homeland "will see their movement as *an expansion of place,* and attendant on it will be a strengthening of the sense of indigeneity" (2001: 499, original emphasis). Indeed, many nationalisms have first been articulated by exiles or students in foreign capitals. (See, for example, Vicente Rafael [1989] on José Rizal and the Filipino "ilustrados.") Indigenous "tribal," as opposed to place-based or clan, affiliations, tend to be more characteristic of displaced populations living in urban settings where language, extended kinship, and consumable symbols of objectified "heritage" predominate over specific local ties with land and family. It would be wrong, however, to turn a contrast into an opposition. In practice, identifications are plural and situated: one is from a village, from Nelson Island, from the Kuskokwim region, a Yup'ik, or an Alaska Native, depending on the situation. Local affiliations are not replaced by wider "indigenous" formations in a zero-sum relation. Linda Tuhiwai Smith suggested a similar complexity at the 2005 Wenner-Gren conference referenced in the epigraph to this chapter, saying she grew up thinking that being bicultural was being a Maori person (since women's roles were so different in her mother's and father's tribes). Being "indigenous," she observed, has been a way of working through the different layers of her identity: "What contradictory people we are!"

In Alaska, the emergence of larger-scale "tribal" and "Native Alaskan" social formations is bound up with liberal multiculturalism and governmentality: ANCSA, Native art markets, heritage venues, tourism, UN forums, environmental NGOs, and human rights organizations. *Présence indigène* comes at a price (Hale 2002; Clifford 2004a). As we saw in Chapter 2, the new scales and performances of identity are "called out" by hegemonic structures of managed multiculturalism. Yet the new identifications also transform and translate deep, if not always continuous, local roots (Friedman 1993). The range of phenomena sometimes lumped together as "identity politics" includes processes of interpellation, performativity, translation, and political strategy. When associating new tribal identifications with displaced populations it is critical to recognize the specificity and flexibility of Native landedness, the expansive senses of "place" evoked by Gegeo. Large-scale tribal identities can remain in close articulation with other levels of affiliation and with homelands, both geographically and socially defined.

At a time when men and women go from and come back to their home villages in greater numbers for longer periods of time, the villages themselves take on special importance. Personhood and "placehood" are closely intertwined in contemporary Yup'ik life. Although a person does not need uninterrupted residence on the land for that relationship to continue, the existence of the homeland is at the core of contemporary Yup'ik identity (Fienup-Riordan 2000: 156). This perspective is echoed in the final sentences of "Yup'iks in the City," an essay by radio journalist John Active that is included in Fienup-Riordan's *Hunting Tradition*. Active suggests something of the performativity of Native identity in urban settings: "All in all, Anchorage is a fun place to visit, but I wouldn't want to live there. Besides, the pavement is too hard on my ankles, and I always have to prove my Yup'icity to the kass'aqs [white people]" (Active 2000: 182).

As this view of the city and "Yup'icity" suggests, different kinds of performance are required in specific relational sites. For John Active, the city is a nice place to visit, but also a place of uncomfortable encounters and coerced performances. For other Yupiit it feels like an extension of home. For others (or at different times) it is an exciting new place in which to branch out. Fienup-Riordan clearly insists that "the existence of the homeland is at the core of contemporary Yup'ik identity," but she also rejects any linear progression between rural and urban, old and new, performative sites. Tribal diaspora is not a condition of exile, of obstructed return; it is more multiplex, relational, and productive. (Compare Darnell's account of traditional Algonquian "semi-nomadic" social structure, "a process of subsistence-motivated expansion and contraction," sustained and translated in new historical contexts [1998: 91].) Fienup-Riordan offers concrete examples of ways that contacts with villages (kin ties) and land (subsistence activities) are sustained by urban Yup'iks from a connected distance that is not that of an émigré or an exile. (Research on Indian communities in the San Francisco Bay area by Native American scholars Kurt Peters [1995] and Renya Ramirez [2007] echoes this complex experience of networking and multiattachment.) The language of "diaspora" (in its recent versions overlapping with paradigms of extended borderlands and migrant cycles) renders something of these mobile, multipolar practices of belonging. "Transmigrants," who create and sustain very particular "transnational communities," might seem a more exact analogue (e.g., Levitt 2001). But while there is considerable overlap, the newly articulated sense of tribal identification at something like a national scale, combined with renewed yearnings for a return to tradition and land, is more suggestive of diaspora.

No single analytic language can exhaust what is at stake in these complexly rooted and routed experiences. Diaspora discourse is good at keeping multisited, multiscaled predicaments in view and resisting teleological narratives of transformation. It acknowledges but does not adequately analyze the political, economic, and social forces at work in contemporary displacements: histories of violent dispossession, the material push/pull of labor mobility, collective strategies of circular migration, individual flights from oppressive social conditions, consumerist desires, and the lure of the modern. And obviously, the sociocultural connections sustained in diaspora networks cannot compensate for, though they may make more livable, the poverty and racial exclusions typically suffered by indigenous people. Moreover, there is an "indigenous" specificity that eludes diaspora's central emphasis on displacement, loss, and deferred desire for the homeland. People who identify as First Nations, aboriginal, or tribal share histories of having been invaded and dispossessed within fairly recent memory. Many currently dwell either on reduced parcels of their former territory or nearby. The feeling that one has never left one's deep ancestral home is strong, both as a lived reality and as a redemptive political myth. This affects the ways space and time are experienced, distances and connections lived. Urban-based Yup'it, as understood by Fienup-Riordan, are not so much displaced from a homeland as extensions of it. She points to similar patterns for other Alaska Native groups. Thus it is not a question of the center holding or not, but rather one of open-ended social networks sustaining transformed connections to land and kin. The tribal home—its animals, plants, social gatherings, shared foods, ancestors, and spiritual powers—is not imagined from a distance. It is activated, "practiced" (de Certeau 1984), made meaningful in a range of sites by seasonal rituals, social gatherings, visits, and subsistence activities. "Diasporic" natives are more like offshoots than broken branches.

No doubt this is an idealization. Negative experiences of exile, poverty, alienation from family, despair, loss of language and tradition, endlessly deferred returns, nostalgia and yearning are certainly part of the varied experiences of native peoples living in settings removed from their homelands. The physical separation and different knowledge bases of "diaspora" and "local" peoples cannot always be bridged by kin ties, exchanges, and political alliances. The politics of culture and identity at new "tribal," regional, and international scales cannot avoid failed, or very partial, translation between sites and generations, social exclusions, tests for racial purity and cultural authenticity. New leaders, culture brokers, and economic elites, new dependencies on governmental, corporate, academic, and philanthropic resources are inextricably part of the processes by which extended indigenous connections are being made. Fienup-Riordan's Yup'ik "worldwide web" is both a description and a hope that cannot be automatically generalized. Yup'ik, who enjoy relatively strong ongoing connections with language, land, and tradition, are able to sustain social ties across an enlarged space. And in this rooted experience of routes, they represent one example from a spectrum of decentered indigenous stories. Yet if the locally grounded "worldwide web" in Fienup-Riordan's account is an idealization, it is not a delusion. For it describes established native practices and aspirations in many parts of the world today. The rather bright Yup'ik picture will always be shadowed by other realities of poverty, racial subjugation, inferior health care and limited education. Diasporic consciousness expresses contradictory experiences of loss and hope, despair and messianism (Clifford

1994). Thus, in thinking about indigenous diasporas, one necessarily confronts the disastrous histories of oppression that have created them, while simultaneously recognizing the sociocultural connections that sustain a sense of peoplehood and, in tangled political-economic situations, project a rooted, expansive future.

While this essay has suggested some of the characteristic features of "indigenous diasporas," it has not drawn a sharp contrast with the experiences of other migrants and transnational dwellers. What has emerged is an uneven, overlapping range of experiences, constraints, and possibilities. In practice, for those many self-identified natives who dwell in, and circulate through, urban and semiurban settings, there can be no essential, privative opposition between "indigenous" and "diasporic" experiences. The terms break down in the compromises and inconsistencies of everyday life. We struggle for languages to represent the layered, faceted realities of the "indigenous" today, without imposing reductive, backward-looking criteria of authenticity. What's at stake in this representational struggle is an adequate *realism* in our ways of thinking comparatively about a range of old and emergent histories.

Realism is a term that needs to be used carefully. Here it is evoked in both its descriptive/historicist and pragmatic/political senses. The main problem with much descriptive realism is that it projects its vision of what's really there and what's really possible from an unacknowledged vantage point in time and space. Sooner or later, "full," "realistic" accounts of historical development, modernity, progress, Westernization, or national liberation will be situated (Haraway 1988) or provincialized (Chakrabarty 2000) by the emergence of new historical subjects. Of course, some of these "new" subjects, whose interventions trouble formerly settled projections of the real, are not new (recently invented) but formerly silenced, marginalized peoples who, in specific conditions, attain a widely recognized presence or voice. The continuity (Friedman 1993) and ethnogenesis (Hill 1996) at work in these processes of survival/emergence include political *articulations,* conjunctural *performances,* and partial *translations* (Clifford 2004a). New historical subjects (in the present context, those loosely labeled "indigenous") are seen and heard in translocal circuits, exerting enough political pressure to make them more than marginal actors in a broad historical field of forces.

We have already seen that historical (historicized and translated) realism does not project one synthetic big story. It works with open-ended (because linear historical time is ontologically unfinished) "big-enough stories," sites of contact, struggle, and dialogue (Clifford 2002). What counts as a big-enough story—representing a force, happening, or presence that "matters"—is not something that can be finally decided by scholarly expertise or by cultural or political authority. Every projection of "the real," however diverse, contested or polythetic, presupposes exclusion and forgetting: constitutive outsides, silences, or specters from unburied pasts that can reemerge as "realistic" in conjunctures or emergencies either currently unimaginable or utopian (Benjamin 1968). The current persistence and renaissance of so many different small-scale tribal and native societies rearticulated under the sign of the "indigenous" is just such a critique and expansion of the historically real. Real refers here, simultaneously, to something that actually exists and that has a future in a nonteleological postmodernity.

In this perspective, the present essay questions a conceptual opposition (diaspora vs. indigenous) that has impeded understanding of how native peoples have reacted to experiences of genocide, material dispossession, forced assimilation; how they have reckoned with political, cultural, racial, and economic marginality, as well as with opportunities for change and reidentification. (Marisol de la Cadena [2000] does similar work by opening up of the opposition *indio/mestizo*.) This kind of realism foregrounds complex histories: the syncretic experiences of diverse native Christians; "travels" with Buffalo Bill, on whaling ships, or as coerced and contract laborers; the work of Aboriginals on cattle stations, Mayans in coffee plantations, or Indians on high steel; and the broad range of "urban indigenous" experiences. This perspective struggles for a lucid ambivalence with respect to tribal engagements with tourism, with capitalist development, with museums and art markets. It views these activities as "historical practices" integral to "traditional futures" (Clifford 2004b). This, like any realism, is deployed at a particular moment and from a specific location.

Recognizing one's own standpoint is, of course, difficult. Others can be counted on to help, not always generously. The present essay may be criticized as overly invested in the interactive, spliced, spatially dispersed aspects of tribal or native lives at the expense of continuities in place, kinship, language, and tradition. And this emphasis may be read as unfriendly to the necessary essentialist claims of nationalist movements for independence and sovereignty. There is warrant for this reading. The essay does argue that indigenous historical experiences are layered and fundamentally relational, that ethnically or racially absolute assertions foreshorten lived reality and foreclose crucial possibilities. Diaspora has not, however, been proposed as an alternative or cure for strong identity claims. Diasporic *dimensions* are understood as aspects of an uneven continuum of attachments. Strong alternate claims to autochthony, localism, and cultural/racial essence are equally part of the process. Indeed, groups and individuals migrate between these apparently contradictory positions depending on situation, audience, or pragmatic goals. An adequate realism needs to grasp specific interactions of diasporic/cosmopolitan and autochthonous/nationalist experiences—ongoing historical dialogues and tensions performed under the contested sign of "indigeneity." (For an exemplary study that keeps these dialogues and tensions in view, see Mallon [2005]: "Samoan *Tatau* as Global Practice.")

It is not simply a matter of richer "historicist" description: telling it as it was or like it is. Realism has inescapable political and even prophetic dimensions, for it prefigures what does and does not have a "real" chance of making a difference. The aspirations of indigenous movements today for self-determination and sovereignty reflect an altered balance of forces, a post-1960s shift in what may, in certain circumstances, and without guarantees, be possible. Much is emerging under the sign of indigenous sovereignty, and the term's range of practical meanings is difficult to circumscribe, taking into account specific local and national contexts as well as uneven conditions of "globalization." Exercised and negotiated at different scales, sovereignty's meanings today are different from those projected at the treaty of Westphalia or imposed by Louis XIV and Napoleon. And they exceed the visions of integration and independence associated with either Wilsonian internationalism or anticolonial national liberation. Sturm's (2002) subtle exploration of the Gramscian "contradictory consciousness" that has historically made and remade an irreducibly diverse "Cherokee Nation" is a case in point. Indigenous sovereignty, in its current range of meanings, includes the "domestic dependent nation" status of Native Americans, the semi-independence of Nunavut, the national status of Vanuatu (and its transnational tax shelters), the bicultural polity emerging in Aotearoa/New Zealand, the cross-border institutions of the Saami, the federalism of New Caledonia's Matignon and Noumea Accords, the "corporate" institutions of Native Alaskans, the broad range of agreements that govern uses of Aboriginal country in Australia, and intensifying struggles around natural resources and "cultural property."

Roger Maaka and Augie Fleras explore this "proliferation of sovereignty discourses," arguing that they do not reproduce the nineteenth-century models underlying settler-colonial states. The current discourses express "patterns of belonging that accentuate a sovereignty without secession, involving models of relative yet relational autonomy in non-coercive contexts" (2000: 93, 108). Indigenous movements take advantage of interstitial possibilities, failures, and openings within national/transnational governmental structures of "graduated sovereignty" (Ong 2000). James Tully, drawing on Taiaake Alfred's trenchant Mohawk vision, sees indigenous social movements not as struggles *for* freedom (in the older sense of absolute independence, but as "struggles *of* freedom to modify the system of internal colonization from within" (Tully 2000: 58, original emphasis). Charles Hale (2002), in his Gramscian assessment of Mayan social movements, unevenly articulated with neoliberal multiculturalism, comes to a similar conclusion. Attaining formal independence does not necessarily change the situation, as the predicament of Pacific microstates struggling to reconcile cultural/political autonomy with economic (inter)dependence shows (Bensa and Wittersheim 1998). "Sovereignty," understood as a range of current practices, evokes pragmatic possibilities and structural limits. Thomas Biolsi's (2005) analysis of four distinct sovereignty claims currently made by Native Americans is a pointed reminder of this strategic complexity, as is Andrea Muehlebach's (2001) account of mobile "place-making" in struggles for self-determination and sovereignty at the United Nations.

Within each context, appeals to all-or-nothing ("ideological") sovereignty combine and alternate with negotiated ("pragmatic") sovereignty. A nonreductive assessment of the historically possible, a political/prophetic realism, recognizes this necessary alternation and tactical flexibility. Without radical visions and maximalist claims, indigenous movements risk co-optation. Without ad hoc arrangements and coalitions, where economic and military power remain overwhelmingly unequal, little can be gained in the short term. And the risk of backlash is great. One of the values, perhaps, of bringing diaspora into the complex domain of the indigenous is to import a constitutive ambivalence. Diasporic experience is necessarily both nationalist and antinationalist. Absolutist invocations of blood, land, and return coexist with the arts of conviviality, the need to make homes away from home, among different peoples. Diasporic ruptures and connections—lost homelands, partial returns, relational identities, and world-spanning networks—are fundamental components of indigenous experience today.

Part II

❖

COYOTE AS A SIMPLE MAN.
t. 9996

Coyote as a Simple Man. (Drawing by L. Frank, used courtesy of the artist.) A self-described "decolonizationist," L. Frank traces her ancestry to the Ajachmem/Tongva tribes of Southern California. She is active in organizations dedicated to the preservation and renewal of California's indigenous cultures. Her paintings and drawings have been widely exhibited, and her Coyote series from *News from Native California* is collected in *Acorn Soup,* published in 1998 by Heyday Press. Like Coyote, L. Frank sometimes writes backward.

4

❖

Ishi's Story

"Ishi's Story" could mean "the story of Ishi," recounted by a historian or some other authority who gathers together what is known with the goal of forming a coherent, definitive picture. No such perspective is available to us, however. The story is unfinished and proliferating. My title could also mean "Ishi's own story," told by Ishi, or on his behalf, a narration giving access to his feelings, his experience, his judgments. But we have only suggestive fragments and enormous gaps: a silence that calls forth more versions, images, endings. "Ishi's story," tragic and redemptive, has been told and retold, by different people with different stakes in the telling. These interpretations in changing times are the materials for my discussion.

Terror and Healing

On August 29, 1911, a "wild man," so the story goes, stumbled into civilization. He was cornered by dogs at a slaughterhouse on the outskirts of Oroville, a small town in Northern California. The man had been hiding for forty years with a dwindling remnant of his kin in the steep ravines of Mill Creek and Deer Creek, feeder streams of the Sacramento River in the Mt. Lassen foothills. His people, the "Yahi," were virtually exterminated by white settler militias in the late 1800s. Some fled north, taking refuge and intermarrying with other Indian groups around Redding and the Pit River. Those who stayed were pursued, killed, kidnapped, and starved, until only a single individual remained in Deer Creek.

The man's remarkable story has come down to us—an unfinished legacy of the Gold Rush, that epochal disaster for Native Californians. The survivor, a Yana-speaking Indian, whose personal or family names were never revealed, is known to us simply as "Ishi," a label affixed in

Figure 4.1. Ishi binding points on salmon
harpoon; this photo was used for more than
four decades on the book's cover. (Courtesy of
the Phoebe A. Hearst Museum of Anthropology
and the Regents of the University of California;
catalogue no. 15-5727.)

1911 by the anthropologist Alfred Kroeber, and made famous fifty years
later by Theodora Kroeber's great book.

Theodora Kroeber, Alfred Kroeber's second wife and widow, published *Ishi in Two Worlds* in 1961. This "biography of the last wild
Indian in America" was an instant classic, widely translated and a peren-
nial best seller for the University of California Press. The original cover
photo, reproduced in many later editions, shows Ishi, close to the ground,

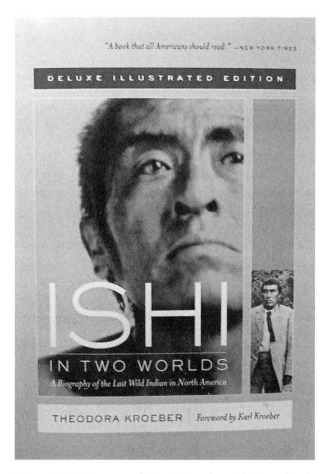

Figure 4.2. New cover design, 2004, show Ishi immediately after capture and in jacket and tie (detail of photo shown in Figure 4.4, p. 110). (Courtesy of the Phoebe A. Hearst Museum of Anthropology and the Regents of the University of California; catalogue no. 13-949.)

in his Mill Creek habitat—an image of precontact Indian life. It is a staged performance. For the photo was taken near the end of Ishi's life, after four years in San Francisco, during a return trip instigated by his anthropologist friends. Ishi's face, in partial shadow that has been intensified in the printing, suggests a primitive mask.

The 2004 edition of *Ishi in Two Worlds* includes a much-expanded

Figure 4.3. Ishi at the Oroville jail, 1911. Photographer, John H. Hogan (Courtesy of the Phoebe A. Hearst Museum of Anthropology and the Regents of the University of California; catalogue no. 15-5910.)

selection of photos showing Ishi in many garbs and poses, plus images drawn from the late nineteenth-century historical record. The cover has been redesigned to suit the changing times. All elements suggesting primitiveness are gone. Ishi is visible in a suit and tie; and the somewhat distanced "object" of an ethnographic gaze from the earlier covers is now a divided, complex "subject." Seen up close, with part of his face outside the frame, Ishi's expression is proud, troubled, ambiguous . . . The photograph, taken at the time of Ishi's capture, transmits a more defiant mood than more familiar images.

The most reproduced image of the "wild man" was taken in 1911 by a local photographer at the Oroville jail. Ishi was held there temporarily, prior to the arrival of Kroeber's assistant, Thomas Waterman, who would take the refugee to a new home in San Francisco. In the photograph, Ishi's fear and emaciation (very different from the well-fed man in the 1961 cover photo) are evident. Normally the Yahi's hair would have been long, but following custom he has burned his short, in mourning for his deceased family. The image is a powerful construct. A weird lack of background—the result of a backdrop, and perhaps of some work in the darkroom—makes the man seem completely cut off. Hovering nowhere, almost extraterrestrial, a lost soul . . . Stripped of any context, he is pure artifact, available for collection; pure victim, ready to be rescued.

Theodora Kroeber's book about "Ishi" made this name-of-convenience familiar, personal, even intimate through its absorbing account of the refugee's life in San Francisco, where he became something of a celebrity. For five years, he lived and worked at the University of California's Museum of Anthropology. There he was employed as a custodian, and on Sundays, he would cheerfully demonstrate Yahi techniques of arrowhead manufacture and archery for eager crowds. The Indian was also a willing ethnographic informant, particularly in the areas of oral tradition, technology, and language. Many remarked on his "gentlemanly" restraint, his decency and humor. Confronted with the civilization of San Francisco the Yahi sustained a mix of curiosity and reserve. He was less impressed by airplanes than by doorknobs and matches. What terrors he certainly felt (of crowds, of human bones stored at the anthropology museum), he largely kept to himself. In 1916, Ishi succumbed to the tuberculosis that was widespread at the time, and particularly dangerous to Native Californians.

Ishi's name, during his five years at the museum, would become closely intertwined with that of his friend and protector, Alfred Kroeber, a towering figure in North American anthropology and founder of the discipline at the new University of California. A relationship of respect and loyalty developed between them—a friendship conditioned by both men's sense of restraint, by Ishi's dependence on someone he called "Big Chiep," and by the demands of science. Over time, their relationship has come to be burdened with significance, and so Ishi's story is also, inescapably, Kroeber's.

Theodora Kroeber evokes Ishi's time in San Francisco with skill and compassion. While she never knew the subject of her biography, she had access to many who remembered him vividly, most notably, of course, her husband, who died just before the book's publication. She also drew on a substantial collection of photographic, acoustic, and documentary records preserved by the Berkeley anthropology museum (Jacknis 2008). While recent scholars such as Orin Starn (2003, 2004), writing from different places of hindsight, have identified factual errors and have questioned some of her emphases (as I do here), *Ishi in Two Worlds* remains crucial. It is still the source for most of what we know about Ishi's life. With a generous appreciation of human complexity and an eye for the telling detail, Theodora Kroeber, a novice author, created a masterpiece. Reading her, generations have come to know the man called "Ishi."

This knowledge is a mixture of insight and blindness. The book's compelling human portrait often makes it hard to recall the severe limits on what was actually known of this man by Theodora Kroeber's principal sources. We forget how little Yahi Alfred Kroeber and his colleagues spoke, and how rudimentary was the Yahi's English. His stories and songs, more than fifty hours preserved on wax recording cylinders, remain very partially understood—for there was no other source for Ishi's language, a dialect of the Yana group. The man's excited voice comes across the decades. He loved, apparently, to tell stories. We hear his words distantly, with only a fragmentary sense of what he was trying to say, or to whom.

Ishi's story does not end in 1916, or with its most influential retelling four decades later. His death and its aftermath are still charged with meaning for diverse California audiences. And it is increasingly significant today that the human portrait created by *Ishi in Two Worlds* was not based on the views of Native Californians. Though she knew and was friendly with California Indians Theodora Kroeber apparently did not feel the need to seek out and include native perspectives on this resonant life. The Cherokee scholar Karen Biestman notes the omission:

"Had Mrs. Kroeber consulted Natives in the region . . . she might have heard narratives of intermarriage, shared experiences, and mutual histories. Ishi's life and Yana existence are alive in the oral traditions of these people . . ." (2003: 148). Biestman goes on to recognize the value of *Ishi in Two Worlds,* given the 1950s "termination" period, a time when stereotypic cowboys and Indians populated the general culture, and complex, sympathetic images of tribal people were rare. As we will see, the historical moment has shifted. Theodora Kroeber's perspective seems more partial, and her book has become meaningful in new ways, viewed from different distances.

Ishi wouldn't talk about his family—the dead; and we have no idea why, exactly, he walked out of hiding toward Oroville where he was captured. Why did he travel south? Where was Ishi going? It has long been assumed that, lonely and exhausted, he was simply giving himself up . . . to white civilization. Oral histories of the Maidu, into whose traditional lands he was walking, come to a different conclusion.

My own recounting of Ishi's story holds off the tendency of narratives to come to closure; rather, it works to keep the gaps open. And it registers the recent claims on Ishi's behalf by Native Californians, claims that make inescapable the question of who should represent his legacy and for what purposes. This is a critical, troubling question that should not be too quickly resolved. I follow the retellings of Ishi's story: additions, critiques, and appropriations that make it meaningful for the future, not the past, of Native California. For Ishi was evidently not the "last" Indian in California, nor was he, except in a very artificial sense, a "wild" Indian.

Theodora Kroeber wrapped up Ishi's story in a humane, angry, lovely, bittersweet package. Now it's being unwrapped—by people with different stakes in the man, his poignant tale, and in his physical remains.

Under the gaze of Minerva, the Roman goddess of wisdom, a miner works near the Sacramento River. A grizzly bear rests at her feet and ships ply the river. The Sierra Nevada mountains rise in the background. Wildlife, agriculture, natural beauty, commerce, and opportunity are all represented on California's Great Seal . . . The seal was designed by Major R. S. Garnett of the U.S. Army, and adopted by the Constitutional Convention of 1849 before California became a state in June 1850.
—"The Great Seal of California," netstate.com

My engagement with Ishi's story began in the classroom, where I taught *Ishi in Two Worlds* to University of California undergraduates. My course, Constructions of the Exotic, analyzed images of "primitive" peoples produced by Western scholars, travelers, photographers, and filmmakers. Having offered the class several times, I thought I should find a text closer to home than the Melanesian and African materials I had been featuring. *Ishi in Two Worlds* was a natural choice because it revisits California's founding history, and because it is a complex portrait of an individual Indian that both exhibits and questions stereotypes. Moreover, the book raised important problems of historical perspective: it embodied liberal assumptions still held by my students, while being dated enough to make these assumptions visible. The pedagogical challenge was to affirm Theodora Kroeber's generous rendition of an exemplary life, while also bringing out her book's blind spots. We needed to recognize a history of changing appropriations of Ishi, including our own.

By juxtaposing this poignant story of the "last wild Indian in America" with works by contemporary Indian authors I hoped to make my students feel less confident about the inevitable disappearance of tribal societies. What was missing from our state's great seal, with its images of nature, commerce, mining, and classical culture? How was this vision of progress without California's Indians a self-fulfilling prophecy? Theodora Kroeber's unflinching account of terror and ethnic cleansing disrupted the pastoral landscape. With her help, we confronted the historical amnesia that supported our moral superiority when contemplating violence and genocide in distant parts of the world. Ishi's story reminded us that officially supported Indian-hunting parties, who fired into sleeping villages and spared neither women, children, nor the aged, were little more than a century old in our own Golden State. The world Ishi grew up in was not essentially different from the Congo of Conrad's *Heart of Darkness*—another book on the syllabus—where imperial invasion, extractive capitalism, and racial extermination coalesced in a kind of normalcy.

Teaching about Ishi resonated with my other research interests. A long-standing concern for the history of anthropology found much to contemplate. Thus toward the end of this essay I give particular attention to Alfred Kroeber, to the tradition he founded at the University of California, and to current prospects for a postcolonial science. Anthropology tends to be celebrated in early versions of Ishi's story and questioned, even vilified, in its more recent retellings. I offer a more dialectical view, drawing on recent reflexive, collaborative trends in a changing discipline. I also find particular support in the writings of Ursula K. Le Guin, who as the Kroebers' daughter is part of the tale's extended family. Her anthropologically inflected science fiction meditates on issues fundamental to Ishi's legacy: colonization, violence, cultural transformation, and exchange. And she has helped me think about possible futures in a postcolonial California. The many visions and revisions that populate this essay are all, ultimately, part of this open question. To confront a determinate history and think beyond it—without being frozen by denial, victimhood, or guilt—this is surely the challenge for diverse people living together, trailing specific, entangled, sometimes tragic pasts.

A great deal has been written, said, danced, sung, and filmed about Ishi during the past couple of decades. Much of this production finds a hearing in what follows. However, I limit myself almost entirely to public expressions, with occasional traces of more discreet local retellings or the oral traditions of California Indians. There are certainly voices, and deep silences, that I don't know about. In the sphere of publication four important books have recently appeared: *Ishi in Three Centuries,* edited by Clifton Kroeber and Karl Kroeber (2003); *Ishi's Brain,* by Orin Starn (2004); *Wild Men: Ishi and Kroeber in the Wilderness of Modern America,* by Douglas Cazaux Sackman (2010); and *Ishi's Untold Story in His First World,* by Richard Burrill (2011). Readers wishing to update *Ishi in Two Worlds* (still an essential starting point) can now turn, as I have, to these extensions and revisions.

The title *Ishi in Three Centuries* is already an intervention. From Theodora Kroeber's "two worlds" (a before-after sequence with inevitable resonances of innocence and loss, a Fall into "the modern world") the story shifts to a three-part history—necessarily open ended, since the third century of Ishi revisionism is just beginning. The volume brings together a broad range of recent writing: documentary sources and controversies; scholarly articles on Ishi's stone tools, essays on sound recordings and spoken language; close analyses of his image in popular culture and of one of his better-translated texts. Karl Kroeber provides a spirited defense of anthropological humanism (profitably read in counterpoint to my approach here). And space is made for contrary perspectives, notably an important critique by Nancy Scheper-Hughes. Most significantly, perhaps, *Ishi in Three Centuries* is the first publication or film about Ishi to include significant contributions from native sources.

Ishi's Brain, a very different kind of book, is subtitled *In Search of America's Last "Wild" Indian.* Part ethnography, part detective story, part personal quest, part historical revision, Orin Starn's narrative follows in detail the recent repatriation movement and especially the discovery of Ishi's brain, "lost" in storage at the Smithsonian Institution. Having played a key role in this discovery, Starn writes as an engaged anthropologist, a participant-observer, and an advocate. He is deeply informed, lucid, and fair in his judgments. My own thinking about Ishi's legacy has been strongly inflected by the events of the last decade, and Orin Starn has generously shared his research with me during this period. We attended some of the same gatherings, and I can trace many of the ideas that find expression here to our conversations or to passages in his indispensable book.

Wild Men and *Ishi's Untold Story* were published as I was finishing the present text, and so I have relied on them less than the others. But each has provided materials and insights not to be found elsewhere. Douglas Sackman is a cultural historian who provides a richly contextualized narrative of Ishi's life and times. He is particularly illuminating on contemporary issues surrounding nature and wildness, on Ishi's San Francisco explorations, and on Alfred Kroeber's complex psychological relations with his charge. Richard Burrill is a local historian, Ishi enthusiast, and indefatigable archivist of anything related to settler-Indian relations around Oroville. His self-published book is an annotated scrapbook containing important oral-historical interviews, documentary traces of all kinds, maps, evocative historic photographs, and clippings. The many voices collected here are suggestive records of cross-cultural and intertribal relations in turn-of-the-century Northern California— supplemented by Burrill's sometimes incautious extrapolations.

My own retelling depends on the postcolonial ethnographic revisions of authors such as Greg Sarris (1993, 1994), Les Field (2008), Brian Bibby (2005), and L. Frank and Kim Hogeland (2007). Each of these innovative works contributes a partial and carefully positioned view of Native California history and people today. What I have to offer in no way substitutes for their detail and intimacy. My perspective is that of an outsider, empowered and limited by distance and mobility. Joining the newly discordant polylogue about Ishi, I try to keep things interrupted and in process. Ishi has served all manner of people as a source of healing imagination, and I am not immune from his magic. The wild man's reopened story as an important sign of the times, prefiguring an emergent, if always impeded, postcolonial California. Perhaps in saying this I am reaching for a different kind of utopia (Le Guin 1989): history moving sideways, looping—syncopated, always emerging, never arriving. At the very least, multiplicity and irony make possible a critique of univocal authority, whether the assertion of a single truth comes from dominant powers or insurgent social actors. In my story of stories the forward movement of progress, revolution, and epochal change are held in suspicion. Instead of a clear historical path, we confront a bush of alternatives, a present reality of entangled relations without an available "outside" or a clearly discernible "after."

The consequence of such a commitment to complexity *in medias res* is a kind of hesitation, and distance taken: a posture of wait and see; at best, perhaps, an alert, divinatory attitude. This is the "historical" perspective I aspire to, without any guarantee of overview, objectivity, or superior sophistication. Perhaps paradoxically, I have found ironic distance to be a catalyst for transgressive hope. Forever interrupting: "What else is there?" "Not so fast . . ." (Clifford 2000). Of course ironic disengagement need not become an end in itself. Charles Hale (2006) makes a strong case for activist commitment against what he represents as postmodern cultural critique—two pathways for an academic anthropology struggling to become postcolonial. I disagree only when the contrast hardens into a zero-sum, either-or choice. The openness to contingency and multiplicity I cultivate here is neither a final resting place nor a prescription for all. It certainly does not claim an epistemologically superior "meta" perspective. It is a form of critical attentiveness not of disengagement—a necessary moment in our intellectual work of historicizing and cognitive mapping. This kind of irony can inhibit determinism and moralism, keeping us lucidly off center among all the contemporary transformations.

An Igbo proverb, quoted a quarter-century ago in *The Predicament of Culture* (Clifford 1988b) makes even more sense today: "You don't stand in one place to watch a masquerade."

> Ha, Ha. You white man . . . Ha. Ha. Ha.
> —Old Mary, from Jaime de Angulo's *Indians in Overalls*

Ishi's story braids together multiple narrative forms: pastoral fables, a tragic denouement, a survivor's tale, plots of savagism and civility, loss and reconciliation, sacrifice and healing. For almost a century it has sustained an understanding of historical fatality. But under pressure, in new conjunctures, the story is unraveling.

Figures like Ishi—"the last of his tribe," "the last wild Indian"—crop up frequently in settler-colonial histories. Wherever preexisting populations are decimated and violently displaced, the indigenizing ideology of the newcomers will sooner or later require an Ishi: iterations of *The Last of the Mohicans* or *Derzu Uzala*. The new society needs requiems for lost worlds, versions of "imperialist nostalgia" (Rosaldo 1989). However much colonial settlers claim they are entering an empty land, or a place whose inhabitants are less than human, childlike, or needing "improvement," they know, at some level, that what's happening is an invasion, a brutal conquest. For some, "exterminate all the brutes" or "the only good Indian is a dead Indian" will suffice, especially at times of insecurity, real or manufactured. But for most, the violent replacement of one people by another requires more scientific and humanistic rationales. In the nineteenth century, ideas of racial evolution and survival of the fittest justified the "necessary" replacement of one people by another. Notions of natural historical "extinction," based on an analogy with animal species, could justify brutal acts. Killing savages, or letting them die in isolated holding areas, was just helping along the inevitable (Lindqvist 1997). In a more humane mode, projects such as the "civilizing mission," religious "conversion," or civic "assimilation" all pointed toward the same end.

But these more liberal rationalizations of conquest could never be quite adequate as founding myths for a settler society, a new population sinking roots in a vacated land, aspiring to permanence. Projects of conversion and assimilation were too contradictory and uneven. At least some of the prior occupants of settler lands, spatially segregated by necessity of conquest, survived, holding on to a distinctive racial and cultural disposition. "Savages" could never really be "civilized." Assimilation would always be incomplete. A clearer break was needed, some terminal moment that could symbolically end the violence of occupation and found the settler nation. As Deborah Bird Rose (2004) argues in an illuminating discussion of settler-colonial violence and its aftermaths, a teleological, Christian, historical vision required a sharp break, or "year zero." This before-after hinge structured an inevitable progress: civilization replacing savagery, white people supplanting aboriginals. Stories like that of Ishi served a sacrificial purpose, bringing the period of conquest to a close, often in a spirit of tragic pathos. The physical death of an individual could stand for a collective birth: a historical period definitively ends, another opens, finally in the clear.

None of this is very clear now. The finality condensed in figures like Ishi cannot obscure the many deaths, transformations, struggles, negotiations, and rebirths that are part of unfinished settler-colonial histories. Tasmania's famous Truganini may or may not have been the last pure specimen of her race, but there are plenty of indigenous Tasmanians active today in land-claims and sovereignty politics. Likewise, the California Indians whose death knell tolled in the name "Ishi" are a growing presence in the state, active in linguistic and cultural renewal, expansive gaming operations, repatriation claims, and tribal recognition struggles. In California, as in many settler-colonial nations, the struggles of indigenous, "first nations," people, have become newly visible. Ishi's story no longer functions as an elegiac resolution for the state's founding violence. It takes on new meanings, messier and more ambiguous.

Ishi's story is being "taken back," in consequential ways, by Native Californians. The present essay affirms this necessary process. And it argues that what is under way can't simply be a matter of reversing a colonial relationship or returning to a true account, as if it were a question of uncovering, finally, the man's real, proper name. For no one, of any tradition, can credibly claim to know Ishi's name or very much about his subjective reality. He remains, powerfully, an enigma—or as Gerald Vizenor (1994) calls him, "Ishi Obscura." We hear the personal name "Ishi" in a veritable forest of quotation marks. Yet this very obscurity sheds a kind of light. As we will see, the changing versions of the wild man of Oroville bring us in touch with the ongoing contact histories, simultaneously wounded and inventive, of Native California.

Ishi in Two Worlds was written in the late 1950s and published in 1961, a year after Alfred Kroeber's death. While the book, in style and tone, is Theodora Kroeber's, it strongly reflects the view of her main informant. She tells us that even forty years after Ishi's death her husband found the story too painful to write. She accepted the task. *Ishi in Two Words,* although it reflects a particular, now dated, retrospective view, remains the best-documented and fullest account of Ishi. One often finds it cited as if it were a primary source (along with a later compilation of documents relevant to Ishi, Heizer and Kroeber [1979]). Having begun to write late in life, when her children had grown up, Theodora Kroeber skillfully wove together an individual's biography with California history to create an engrossing, often moving narrative. What Ishi and his people suffered is told with a restrained, but unflinching, outrage. In style the book is literary but not flowery, never sacrificing precision for sentimental effect. The details of Ishi's life in San Francisco are recorded in evocative detail, with a nice eye for incongruity. And though "prefeminist" by recent standards, Theodora Kroeber does at times gently register a distanced view of male relationships: Ishi's friendships at the museum. While she takes seriously her work as a documenter and historian, she is primarily a biographer concerned to make a violently interrupted life cohere—the portrait of a sympathetic, knowable individual. Karl Kroeber (2004), in a new foreword to his mother's book, stresses the continuing value of her project: recognizing and translating Ishi's fundamental humanity. The present essay explores the ways this fundamental human access has been produced and disrupted, made and unmade by differing social actors. Ishi is still being found and lost in translation.

Reading *Ishi in Two Worlds* today is an exercise in self-historicizing. We confront the difference between 1961 when it appeared and our own standpoint almost a half-century later. What has intervened? The sixties and their aftermaths, most importantly the various Indian revival movements: Red Power, the American Indian movement, Wounded Knee II (the 1973 standoff), and a complex tribal and pan-Indian politics that has broken the monopoly of whites speaking for Indians in a broad range of public spheres. At global scales, the political landscape has been altered by the cumulative effects of postwar decolonization—uneven and locally articulated, hemmed in by neocolonialism, but making spaces for a broad range of contestations and voices. Tribal capitalism has more recently made its appearance (development corporations in Alaska, Indian gaming in California, cultural tourism virtually everywhere). New, urban-based forms of identity politics and "indigenous" mobilizations are being pursued at regional, hemispheric, and international levels. Much has changed.

Theodora Kroeber's book is a work of the 1950s reaching back to the early years of the century and the heroic institutionalization of Boasian anthropology. But it also reflects a darker, late twentieth-century consciousness. Thomas Buckley, in an acute discussion of Alfred Kroeber and his legacy, observes:

By 1960, the year of Kroeber's death, a half-century of cataclysm suggested that his faith in progress had been misplaced. Theodora Kroeber was twenty-one years younger—a writer fully in and of the twentieth century—and she seems to have written *Ishi in Two Worlds* in part in response to what the mid-twentieth century had revealed about Western Civilization. The Nazi Holocaust in Eastern Europe, the bombing of Dresden, Hiroshima and Nagasaki, Stalin's mass murders, the collapse of empire and the end of classic colonialism after the Second World War, the Negro civil rights movement in the United States of the mid-fifties, all helped to place the history of Indian-white relations in late nineteenth-century California in a harsh new light. In the late 1950s, the evidence that a profound potential for genocide, racism, and oppression lay darkly in the very heart of Western civilization seemed irrefutable. (1996: 289)

No reader can forget Theodora Kroeber's uncompromising narrative of genocide. As Buckley emphasizes, *Ishi in Two Worlds* "confronted a wide, twentieth-century audience for the first time with some of the bare facts" of early California colonialism. Her book is very raw, very specific, on the relentless, cold-blooded extermination of California's original inhabitants, and in particular Ishi's people, the "Mill Creek Indians". After the 1860s, a diminishing tribal remnant, which included the boy Ishi, was driven into deep hiding for forty years. Ishi thus grew to maturity in a situation of unnatural isolation. (Though exactly how isolated the Mill Creeks were during this period, both from white society and from their Indian neighbors, has been questioned by recent revisionist history and archaeology, as well as by native oral traditions.) The ordeal ends with Ishi, his mother, sister, and another old man scattered by a surveying party that stumbles on their refuge, which they called "Grizzly Bear's Hiding Place," invisible up under a cliff. Ishi apparently never sees his sister and the man again. His ailing mother dies soon after, and then he is left alone. Three years later he walks south toward Oroville and the lands of the Concow Maidu.

From the wild man's first appearance in 1911 through the publication of *Ishi in Two Worlds,* this journey out of hiding would be framed as a passage from "the Stone Age" to "the modern world." The refugee's actions were interpreted as "giving himself up," a kind of suicide or acceptance of fate. In any event, once he left Mill Creek there seemed to be only one historical path he could follow. It led inexorably to the "future": white civilization and death in the anthropology museum.

However, the question of where Ishi was going depends on a more specific topography. Feeder streams of the Sacramento River such as Deer and Mill Creek ascend toward Mt. Lassen through country that is, even today, wild and difficult of access—valleys bordered by steep ridges, tangles of brush, and poison oak. In the mid-nineteenth century, Yana-speaking groups occupied this territory. Ishi's kin, those widely known as the "Mill Creek Indians" (and later by the name of their Yana dialect, "Yahi") lived a couple of valleys north of several Maidu-speaking peoples. To the west there were Wintu speakers, to the north, Atsugewi (Pit River). The Yana-speaking survivord who escaped the killings of the 1860s and 1870s joined with other language groups to the north, either the Redding (largely Wintun) or Pit River Indians. In Ishi's time, boundaries and identifications were rather fluid. The "Yahi" inhabited a tribal borderland.

To anticipate a later discussion, recent Indian retellings have questioned the assumption that Ishi was "walking into civilization," giving himself up. Maidu oral tradition asserts they were his kin too, sometimes claiming that Ishi's mother was Maidu. Bride capture, as well as voluntary marriage across linguistic borders, was not uncommon. Contemporary Maidu point to a history of peaceful contacts between the two groups, as well as recurring fights. Butte Meadows was a traditional meeting place for summer "Big Times" of trading, gambling, and socializing. Would Maidu communities have welcomed the Yahi survivor? We'll never know. (The dogs that cornered him outside Oroville emerge here as decisive historical actors.) Given the contingency of Ishi's "capture," we have, at least, to question long-accepted assumptions that the conquering civilization was his only possible destination.

Theodora Kroeber portrays Ishi's sojourn in San Francisco as the best outcome for a tragic history—a soft landing in extinction. But were there any alternatives? The option of settling the survivor with other Indian groups was apparently never seriously considered, either by the anthropologists or by Ishi. He might have lived in small rancherias to the north where some speakers of Northern Yana (a distantly intelligible dialect) had found refuge. Or he might have lived among Maidu to the south, had there been willing hosts. There he would have been isolated linguistically but recognizable as a member of a neighboring group with established links of both rivalry and exchange, and possibly (the point is contested) kinship through his mother. In a 1973 interview the Maidu artist Frank Day recalled that his father, one of the last Concow Maidu headmen, was called to the Oroville jail in hopes that he could communicate with Ishi. He failed completely. In any event, there is no guarantee that Ishi would have been well received in one of the crowded tribal enclaves into which California's native peoples had been forced by the relentless miners and settlers. Ishi might well have been treated with suspicion, viewed as a dangerous outsider. Fear of witchcraft was a fact of life in the artificial communities that brought together diverse, sometimes hostile, Indian groups. Distant kinship ties could have made some difference, but Ishi was, almost certainly, the last of the Mill Creek band. He had no known family left, at least no one he would recognize. And it is risky to project back in time a translocal "California Indian" solidarity, something that has only begun to emerge, and quite unevenly, in recent decades.

Alfred Kroeber and Thomas Waterman certainly saw in Ishi a precious, uncontaminated, specimen from an older California. They had a strong interest in keeping him near at hand, in a research setting. But they did, at least once, present him with an alternative: life in the museum or on an Indian reservation. In concrete terms, it was not much of a choice. For a devastated, starving man, a comfortable place among friendly people no doubt seemed good, far better than whatever reception he might have imagined from a white world that had sent armed men to kill his people. Today one sometimes hears comments to the effect that Ishi was "captured" by the anthropologists, held "prisoner" in the museum. In literal terms this is unfair: Ishi was generously treated, had a job, spending money, and freedom of movement. The comments may, however, express a sense that the refugee was a prisoner of drastically limited options, a narrowed freedom created by colonial violence, with an inability to imagine alternatives. Of all the choices made, more or less consciously, by Ishi or on his behalf, the one that gives most pause concerns his exposure to disease in the city and in his public roles at the museum. Would it not have been better to find him a home on a ranch, or in some healthier environment? Perhaps he might not have relished isolation in a rural setting. It is hard to disentangle Ishi's own wishes, the research interests and convenience of the scholars, and a realistic assessment of risk. Would Ishi have been less likely to contract tuberculosis outside a city or town? There was disease in the rancherias. In any event, assumptions that Ishi naturally belonged with other California Indians, that the anthropology museum could never be a "home" for him, reflect contemporary identity politics more than any real access to his feelings (Starn 2004: 263, 275–276).

All this is hindsight—questions made pertinent by the subsequent history, the nondisappearance, of California Indians. It is now possible, necessary, to imagine that things could have turned out differently. But given the concrete options as they appeared at the time, and assuming Ishi's acceptance of his circumstances, the narrative of *Ishi in Two Worlds* takes on a sense of inevitability. The effect is reinforced by the book's overall structure: a before-after story of historical destiny, divided into two parts called "Ishi the Yahi," and "Mister Ishi." The book's "two worlds" are firmly identified with past and future: the journey into modern civilization can only be a path of no return.

The book's two parts could also be called: "The Terror" and "The Healing." Both words are used repeatedly by Theodora Kroeber, and they recall Michael Taussig's analysis of New World Colonial cultures, *Shamanism, Colonialism, and the Wild Man*, which he subtitles: *A Study in Terror and Healing* (1987). The wild man myth, as critics like Roger Bartra (1994) have shown, has long accompanied European visions of "civilization." While the imagination of a savage "other" pre-dates the early modern period, it received fresh life with Europe's expansion into the New World. Taussig calls the wild man myth a "left-handed gift" to the colonized, for it justified the exploitation and extermination of uncivilized "savages," while also endowing them with an occult power, even eventually a moral superiority. Once the period of murderous pacification was complete, the surviving remnant could be romanticized, endowed with extraordinary powers—spiritual, shamanistic, close to nature. Out of defeat inspirational figures such as the famous Lakota visionary Black Elk would emerge. The savage Indian became, almost overnight, a wise Indian, a soulful Indian, a source of healing in a materialistic society. A troubled society, perhaps, but overwhelmingly powerful: Taussig never loses sight of the fact that the colonizer's receptivity to the Indian's wisdom depended on a prior history of terror, the establishment and maintenance of settler dominance.

Almost fifty years after Ishi's death, *Ishi in Two Worlds* adapts the structure of terror and healing for a liberal audience. Theodora Kroeber addresses readers familiar with the relativist Boasian anthropology made popular by writers such as Margaret Mead and Ruth Benedict. Her account of the terror preserves Ishi's "wildness" seen positively as isolation from civilization and rapport with nature, while transferring "barbarism" to the Indian killers of the late nineteenth century. She portrays Ishi as marvelously benign—his patience, good sense, humor, and generosity winning over all around him. She would later evoke the survivor's almost magical power in her epigraph to *Ishi the Last Yahi: A Documentary History* (Heizer and Kroeber 1979: v): "Howsoever one touches on Ishi, the touch rewards. It illuminates the way."

"The Terror" is gathered in Theodora Kroeber's Part One where we learn a considerable amount of California Indian history: ethnographic and linguistic details of the Yana, the Gold Rush invasion, the spread of ranches and farms, the rounding up and hunting down of Indian bands. This first part of *Ishi in Two Worlds* is a harrowing story. While recognizing some exceptions, it affixes clear responsibility for the genocide that was integral to California's Americanization during the last half of the nineteenth century. Recent research has made visible a more complex picture of frontier contacts (Starn 2003: 201–207). The "Mill Creeks" were probably a mixed group of refugees from several language groups who knew how to fight back—not exactly the culturally pure "tribelet" Alfred Kroeber called "Yahi." And the well-publicized self-image of the white vigilantes (who bragged of shooting women and children and flaunted long strings of scalps) has tended to erase other accounts of frontier reciprocity, of live and let live. Some settlers were protective of Indians. Others, genuinely afraid, went along with the killing, against their better judgment. But this less Manichean, revisionary, frontier story cannot ultimately erase the brutal, cumulative facts of expropriation and extermination. The graphically documented events chronicled in Theodora Kroeber's Part One tear the fabric of California's civil peace, touching a wound that—at least for native peoples—has never been healed.

But Part Two of *Ishi in Two Worlds* ("The Healing") almost makes us forget the terror. Its affectionate title (which sounds a bit condescending now) is "Mister Ishi."

The newly discovered public figure posed barefoot in a jacket and tie with Alfred Kroeber and Sam Batwi, the northern Yana-speaking translator who had worked with the linguist Edward Sapir. Batwi didn't get along with Ishi and was soon sent home. In the new edition of *Ishi in*

Figure 4.4. Ishi with Sam Batwi and A. L. Kroeber, 1911. (Courtesy of the Phoebe A. Hearst Museum of Anthropology and the Regents of the University of California; catalogue no. 13-944.)

Two Worlds, and in other publications, this photo would be cropped to include only Kroeber and Ishi. The translator was seen by the scientists as an acculturated, impure Indian. No further effort was made to bring Ishi together with other Yana-speakers, and Sam Batwi quickly disappeared from Ishi's story. Yet, viewed from 2013, he prefigures the Indian people who would rebury Ishi a century later and remember him as their ancestor.

At the Museum of Anthropology, Ishi demonstrated archery, made

Figure 4.5. Ishi at the Museum. (Courtesy of the Phoebe A. Hearst Museum of Anthropology and the Regents of the University of California; catalogue no. 15-6088.)

arrowheads, and constructed a "Yahi house" at the Museum of Anthropology. However, none of the images in the first, and until recently the most common, edition of *Ishi in Two Worlds* shows him doing Indian things while wearing Western clothes. In San Francisco he declined to disrobe for the camera, but once, bared his chest for a visiting photographer, who was documenting the "vanishing race" for a popular book of that title. Gerald Vizenor (1994: 126) coments:

> Ishi was never his real name, and he is not the photographs of that tribal man captured three generations ago in a slaughterhouse in Northern California. He was thin and wore a canvas shirt then, a man of natural reason, a lonesome hunter, but never the stout postiche of a wild man lost and found in the museum. Two tribal men were captured, two pronouns in a museum, one obscure and the other endured in silence. Ishi the obscura is discovered with a bare chest in photographs; the tribal man named in that simulation stared over the camera, into the distance.

Figure 4.6. Ishi by Joseph Dixon, 1913. (Courtesy
Department of Library Services, American Museum of
Natural History; catalogue no. 31704.)

Part Two of *Ishi in Two Worlds* is framed in a spirit of kindly under-
standing. The museum staff and anthropologists are consistently called
"Ishi's friends." Three stand out: Alfred Kroeber, director of the
new Museum of Anthropology ("Big Chief"); Thomas Waterman
("Wattamany"), Kroeber's junior colleague in anthropology, who was
very attached to Ishi and who regularly entertained him at home; and
Saxton Pope, a surgeon at the adjoining research hospital. "Popey" was
Ishi's personal physician, and an archery buff—a passion he shared with
Ishi on many outings together. Much could be said about these rather
different friendships, their asymmetrical investments, and (visible at
times in Theodora's gentle gaze) their masculinity—scientific reserve

alternating with boyish camaraderie. This perspective seems particularly relevant to Pope's rapport with Ishi, which was based on hunting with bow and arrow, and it infuses the restorative enjoyment felt by Alfred Kroeber, Waterman, Pope, and Pope's teenage son Saxton Jr. on a camping trip to Mill Creek that the men took with Ishi during the last healthy summer of his life.

Ishi resisted this return to his homeland. It was not a place of happy memories, and he was anxious about encountering the wandering spirits of his dead relatives. But the enthusiasm of the others and the "chiep's" authority wore him down. Once in Deer Creek, having satisfied himself that his family members had found their way along the trail of the dead, he relaxed.

The month that followed was apparently an agreeable mix of ethnographic show and tell, photo opportunities, and good clean fun: joking, swimming, and hunting. No doubt the anthropologists' interest in re-creating the old days helped sustain a nostalgic atmosphere that avoided reliving the times of hardship and killing. Ishi wore a loincloth and performed traditional activities for Kroeber's camera (although he declined to join the others in skinny-dipping). The ethnographic data produced during the trip was deep: a map of the two valleys where the Yahi roamed contained more than two hundred place-names; notebooks were filled with hundreds of plants and herbs. In Theodora Kroeber's narrative, this return trip, in space and time, was the highlight of Ishi's "brightest year":

> Going back to the old heartland in the company of the three living people who meant most to him would seem to have been an adventure akin to psychoanalysis. At first reluctant to retrace the covered tracks of childhood and painful adult experience, Ishi gave himself over to the adventure, at last wholly, and in the sharing of places and recollections succeeded in closing the gap between his former world and the present one. (1961: 216)

The healing mix of ethnography, psychology, and human bonding is made explicit. A cruel history of violence seems to be forgotten. And this no doubt reflects the experiential reflections of Ishi's companions who loved the camping trip and were, as Theodora Kroeber records, reluctant to return to "civilization." Theirs was a ludic regression that might well find a place in Philip Deloria's penetrating study, *Playing Indian* (1999), as well as in Eve Sedgwick's well-known work on

Figure 4.7.   Ishi on Deer Creek expedition.
(Courtesy of the Phoebe A. Hearst Museum of
Anthropology and the Regents of the University
of California; catalogue no. 15-5767.)

homosociality (1985). The Yahi survivor must have felt more ambivalence: "Happy as were these days, he became suddenly eager to be back
in the museum, to be *home*" (216). He rushed to break camp and was
first on the train. Would he have been eager, like his companions, to
return at the end of the summer for acorn harvesting? We will never
know. It was June 1914. In August the outbreak of war changed everything. "The four friends could not know that never again would they be
together in this carefree way: that for Ishi there was ahead but a scant
year of enjoyment of his present radiant health" (217). Ethnographic
pastoral is abruptly overwhelmed by history—the fate of all such nostal-
gias. But in Theodora Kroeber's narration, Ishi seems to have been

Figure 4.8. Juan Dolores, photo from *Ishi in Two Worlds*. (Courtesy of the Phoebe A. Hearst Museum of Anthropology and the Regents of the University of California; catalogue no. 15-5151.)

healed, his two worlds brought together. And he shares the cure with his comrades.

Juan Dolores was a different kind of friend from the museum. While only a page or two are devoted to him in Theodora Kroeber's book, he is one of the more intriguing loose threads in Ishi's story. Dolores was a

Papago (today called Tohono O'odham) from Arizona who earned his living as a teamster, managing horses on construction projects in several western states. When he could, he worked as a linguistic informant under Alfred Kroeber's sponsorship. Dolores corresponded with Kroeber from his construction jobs, raising questions about translation and the grammatical intricacies of Papago, while pressing politely for a higher rate of payment for the texts he was preparing. In one letter he expressed a yearning for his homeland. A government allotting agent had been pressing him to return home, Dolores wrote with characteristic irony: "He wants me to get married, grow corn. But how can I afford to do that . . . Anyway I'm a tramp, too attached to my freedom" (Dolores 1911). Indians routinely came and went in the San Francisco museum, and Dolores was a regular there, sometimes combining work as a museum guard with his linguistics. For a time he was Ishi's roommate, and the two developed a warm relationship, based—according to Theodora Kroeber—on a shared notion of what it meant to be a "proper Indian, a person of manners, sensibility, and dignity" (1961: 159). They made an interesting pair: Ishi, who had lived most of his life in hiding; Dolores, a multilingual traveler, something of a skeptic about everything, but with strong attachments to Papago language and tradition.

Theodora Kroeber (1961: 159) quotes a letter from Dolores to her husband that ends on a typical note:

> I see by the paper that Professor Waterman has been to see the strange Indian which has been captured somewhere in Butte Co. I suppose you are so busy that you have no time to go and see this wild Indian.
>
> I think I have to run away and hide some place in the mountains of Arizona and when you find me tell [President] Taft or somebody that they have to make a treaty with me. I think that will be the only way I can get some good place to stay the rest of my life.
> Goodbye,
> Your friend, Juan Dolores

Dolores and Ishi wandered around San Francisco—its parks, restaurants, and shops. "Indians in unexpected places" (Deloria 2004), they came into contact with Mexicanos, with Chinese, with other Indians, with people of all classes. As Theodora Kroeber observes, this offered a more cosmopolitan experience than is suggested by the familiar image of Ishi the "wild Indian" taking refuge at the museum. (On Ishi's walks in the city see also Sackman [2010: ch. 6].) Theodora Kroeber speculates, too, that the worldly Papago may have counseled the Yahi against sexual entanglements with white women (1961: 160, 221). (She knew Juan Dolores well—and guessed that he would have been speaking from experience.) In the universe of *Ishi in Two Worlds,* the friendship with Dolores opens a small window on the complexities of a changing California Indian life, in and out of cities (Sarris 1994; Ramirez 2007). Today, Dolores serves as a kind of placeholder for unanswered questions of how Ishi's Indian contemporaries—emphatically not dying primitives—might relate to his predicament.

Theodora Kroeber's account has a deft human touch. We understand Ishi's dignity and restraint, his good humor and sociability. There are views of his fastidious habits and curious perceptions (his utter fascination with a spring-loaded window shade), and his smile, so rare in the public iconography of "Indians." We also learn of Ishi's work with his scientist friends on linguistic elicitation and translation. Apparently he recognized the value of recording his language, stories, and technical skills. In these domains he was a willing informant (Jacknis 2003). In others—the history of his confinement and his family—he kept silent. On his arrival in San Francisco the refugee was asked about his time in hiding. He responded with a long, incomprehensible performance, the "Wood Duck Story," which lasted for an afternoon and into the following morning. The recitation, later repeated for recording on wax cylinders, has never been adequately translated.

Believed by the general public and scholars alike to be an emissary from the Stone Age, Ishi was a treasured ethnographic source. Communication with Kroeber and Waterman worked best in those areas of culture where physical demonstration was possible. Understanding complex beliefs or extended narratives posed major obstacles, for the anthropologists and for Ishi. This is not to say that communication was insubstantial. A good deal can be expressed and understood with relatively few words if there is patience and goodwill. But many personal ideas and feelings, as well as cultural subtleties, were inevitably lost in a shared discourse that Edward Sapir, who worked intensively with Ishi and was the interlocutor most familiar with other dialects of Yana, described as "a crude jargon composed of English, quasi-English and Yahi" (Sapir 1916: 329). Sapir's painstaking work with Ishi is the primary basis for contemporary efforts to understand his texts. Victor Golla (2003) provides an authoritative account of Ishi as a linguistic informant and of what can, with many gaps, be known of his language today.

Waterman bitterly reproached himself for allowing Sapir to overwork his charge during the summer of 1915, when the fatal tuberculosis was taking hold. An illness the preceding December, not confirmed as tuberculosis, had worried Kroeber and Waterman, intensifying their feeling that the time for productive research might be running out. Whether or not the intense summer work hastened Ishi's demise, there was certainly no element of coercion. By all accounts Ishi was an enthusiastic participant in what turned out to be the last chance to make adequate transcriptions and translations of his Yahi words. Sapir possessed a particularly good ear for Yana phonology. In their collaboration, as in the sound recordings, the informant had to be reined in. Difficult transcriptions and subtle meanings needed to be methodically checked. There was clearly something Ishi wanted to say, to give . . . To whom? To posterity? (Whose?) To science? (To his museum friends?) Perhaps, after so many years of isolation, it was simply a pleasure to be speaking Yahi for someone who, while not understanding very well, at least cared. Traditional stories were usually told during the winter, a slow season of communal gatherings. Was the museum a kind of extended winter for Ishi, a place of relative immobility, social intensity, and performance?

Ishi was, it seems, not unhappy in his new home. The Berkeley anthropologists were, of course, eager to learn whatever they could about an aboriginal culture they believed to be unaffected by the modern world. They also gave material support and genuine affection to their charge. He reciprocated, with loyalty and research cooperation. This, in any event, is how they remembered him. As one reads the surviving records from these years (of contentment? of resignation?) one can't help feeling Ishi's acceptance of his fate, and a kind of forgiveness. Early on, when offered the possibility of moving to an Indian reservation, he says he wants to stay: "I will grow old in this house, and it is here I will die" (Kroeber 1961: 218).

Perhaps he understood his museum years as a kind of afterlife. He could not have expected to survive the encounter with whites in Oroville, people he had only known as murderous. Was he embarked on a trip to "the edge of the world"—as later fictional retellings by Theodora Kroeber and James Freeman (1992) would have it? Or by following the railroad line to the city by the sea, was he already walking the trail of the dead—as imagined by the documentary film *Ishi: The Last Yahi*? Or was he on a mission to bring Indian wisdom to the white world, as many have implied, and sometimes explicitly asserted? Did he possess "trickster" capacities for survival and adaptation in new circumstances, drawn from traditional coyote myths (a speculation in the documentary, and a theme in various Indian retellings)? But maybe he was just glad to be safe at last, warm, and well fed.

In 1961 Theodora Kroeber offered a bittersweet, almost happy ending—at least a plausible best outcome for a tragic story—given the memory of terror, and the sense of an inevitable death hovering over Ishi, and his people. The man called Ishi's reported last words end the book: "You stay. I go." It was a common Yahi leave-taking. But in this context the phrase inevitably carried a broader allegorical significance: a vision of resignation, and of indigenous disappearance in California: "You stay. We go."

Readers, at least those that did not know of the persistence, ongoing struggles, and renewal of California Indian societies, could be content with this apparent closure: Ishi accepting the inevitable: death in the house of cultural understanding, looked after by his white friends.

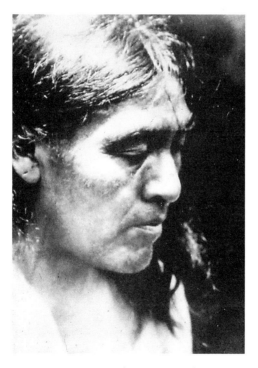

Figure 4.9. Portrait by A. L. Kroeber.
(Courtesy of the Bancroft Library, University of California, Berkeley; catalogue Ishi-Por 7.)

The image of Ishi in Figure 4.9 concludes Theodora Kroeber and Robert Heizer's 1968 Sierra Club collection of historical photographs, *Almost Ancestors: The First Californians*. It sums up a message of dignified resignation. (One sees something similar in many of Edward Curtis's famous Indian portraits from the same period.) Alfred Kroeber, who took the photo, was asked by his wife forty years later to characterize Ishi. His reply gives resignation a slightly different twist: "He was the most patient man I ever knew. I mean he had mastered the philosophy of patience, without trace either of self-pity or bitterness to dull the purity of his cheerful enduringness" (Kroeber 1961: 229). "Patience" is etymologically rooted in suffering and the endurance of pain. (Ambrose Bierce, in his *Devil's Dictionary*, defined it as "a minor form of despair, disguised as a virtue.") But whatever pain Ishi endured tends to be lost in evocations of his "cheerfulness." Theodora Kroeber's gloss on her husband's comment twice returns to this word, concluding: "His way was the way of contentment—the Middle Way, to be pursued quietly, working a little, playing a little, and surrounded by friends" (229).

Ishi in Two Worlds is not a simple book: its author worries, now and again, about its gaps and the tendency of a biography to artificially round out a life. In the prologue she compares her task to stringing scattered and disparate beads on a thread: "Surprisingly, the circle of [Ishi's] life's necklace appears whole despite its many incompletions" (n.p.). Believing that a biographer has a duty to sum up the meaning of a life, she places Ishi on a Taoist path of moderation, the "Middle Way." Yet just as she fulfills the biographer's duty, she hesitates: "The figure of Ishi stands, part of it in the sun, varicolored and idiosyncratic and achieved; part in deep shadow, darkened by the extent of our own ignorance and by its own disadvantagements. A biography should include something at least of the nature of these shadows, the unrealized potential, the promise unfulfilled . . ." (1961: 229). And she notes the violence of being reduced to a single name rather than using several as he would have in traditional social settings; she mentions Ishi's linguistic isolation, his marital and sexual deprivation, his exposure to lethal diseases.

But the shadows evoked in this paragraph quickly dissipate in a luminous conclusion. Anthropological humanism, the assumption of a "broad base . . . of pan-humanity" (1961: 230), is vindicated by this man's unique, but universal, life experience. Whether he is seen as a last emissary from the Stone Age or as someone adapting, inventively, in new circumstances, Ishi was simply, and essentially a human being, a man capable of growth, and—like everyone, within limits—of freedom. Theodora Kroeber concludes that Ishi "chose" life with his white friends; he "chose" a salary and independence rather than government wardship; "and when 'civilization' bestowed upon him the gift of tuberculosis he chose to fight it according to Popey's instructions and to accept defeat with grace, his concern being to make himself as little a burden as might be to those who cared for him" (230).

In the years since his death, California Indians have not found Ishi's "choices," as narrated here, particularly edifying. The resigned death among anthropologists, going gently into that good night—this Ishi wasn't very heroic. He was a bit too much the white man's Indian at the end: the "last of his people" image left scant room for all the real struggles for survival. And the man's supposed cultural purity made other Indians seem inauthentic. As we will see, in recent decades this view of Ishi has changed.

For its primary, non-Indian, readership, the denouement of *Ishi in Two Worlds* works to heal the terror, sewing up the wound opened in Part One. The story closes with a vision of humanely scientific friendships, an affectionate respect for this engaging, wise, giving, and ultimately forgiving Indian. We need not question this portrayal as it represents the individual feelings and motivations of Kroeber, Waterman, and Pope. But the mixture of personal affection with professional interest in a unique specimen now appears more ambiguous than Theodora Kroeber allows. There are many reasons, to question the way the book provides narrative closure to Ishi's story: an ending where human decency prevails: a good man dies well among good people.

A quite different final comment on Ishi's life breaks the spell. This alternate summation concludes *Ishi the Last Yahi: A Documentary History*, published by Robert Heizer and Theodora Kroeber in 1979. A notice from the *Chico Record* newspaper, March 28, 1916:

"Ishi," the man primeval, is dead. He could not stand the rigors of civilization; and tuberculosis, that arch-enemy of those who live in the simplicity of nature and then abandon that life, claimed him. Ishi was supposed to be the last of a tribe that flourished in California long before the white man reached these shores. He could make a fire with sticks, fashion arrowheads out of flint, and was familiar with other arts long lost to civilization. He furnished amusement and study to the savants at the University of California for a number of years, and doubtless much of ancient Indian lore was learned from him, but we do not believe he was the marvel that the professors would have the public believe. He was just a starved-out Indian from the wilds of Deer Creek who, by hiding in its fastnesses, was able to long escape the white man's pursuit. And the white man with his food and clothing and shelter finally killed the Indian just as effectually as he would have killed him with a rifle. (1979: 242)

Ishi's story does no healing here. There's nothing to redeem a pathetic life, nothing to soften the fundamental violence of Ishi's fate. And as for the good years at the museum, the *Chico Record* makes short shrift of Ishi's friends' scientific humanism.

In a new introduction to *Ishi in Two Worlds* Karl Kroeber quotes this text and notes its strategic location. He describes his mother's effort in the *Documentary History* to include "a diversity of perspectives she had judged inappropriate to her first book" (2004: xix). It may be worth pressing a bit further in historicizing the shifting emphasis. One suspects that the willingness of Robert Heizer and Theodora Kroeber to give the last word to so caustic a realism reflects the late 1970s, Wounded Knee II, the Alcatraz occupation, and a renewed sense of deep and continuing Indian-white antagonisms. Perhaps also a certain distance is taken here from Alfred Kroeber himself, a ghostly coauthor during the writing of *Ishi in Two Worlds* two decades before. Robert Heizer, Kroeber's friend and successor at Berkeley, differed from his mentor by focusing squarely on the history of violent contacts and cultural destruction in California. By 1979, resurgent tribal movements across the country had forced attention from the healing back to the terror, and to the continuing reality of inequality and racism. But it was still too early to include native voices in a "documentary history" of Ishi. Oral traditions remained mostly unheard, and native revisionism had not yet gone public. Heizer and Kroeber's collection would look different today.

There was a sour note in the humanist harmony that concludes *Ishi in Two Worlds*. Ishi fell ill with tuberculosis when Alfred Kroeber was away on sabbatical leave in Europe and New York. Kroeber stayed in close touch with the progress of the illness, and when the end suddenly loomed, he fired off a letter to E. W. Gifford, assistant director of the museum, instructing Gifford that there must in no circumstances be an autopsy or any dissection of Ishi's body. (At the research hospital, autopsies were routine.) Kroeber saw no scientific interest in the procedure, since the cause of death was perfectly clear, and, he noted, there were plenty of unstudied skeletons in the museum. In a much-quoted passage he insisted: "If there is any talk about the interests of science, say for me that science can go to hell. We propose to stand by our friends" (Kroeber 1961: 234). These were very strong words for a restrained man, a man of science. Kroeber knew, as did the others at the hospital, that Ishi was deeply shocked by the dismemberment and preservation of corpses, which he believed should be cremated and sent on their way to the land of the dead.

Kroeber's letter arrived too late. Gifford, the junior member of the team, was unable to resist pressure (led it seems by Ishi's fellow archery enthusiast, the surgeon Saxton Pope) for what would be called a "simple autopsy." Ishi's remains were then cremated, sealed in a ceramic jar, and reverently (by Christian standards) laid to rest, along with various Yahi accoutrements. The improvised collection occupied a niche at Mt. Olivet Cemetery in San Francisco for eighty years.

But it had not quite been a "simple autopsy." Buried in Gifford's apologetic report to his absent superior, as quoted by Theodora Kroeber, was the phrase "the brain was preserved." Removing brains for further study was not standard practice at the hospital, and the phrase raised a question about whether all of Ishi had been cremated. For most readers, the autopsy left a slight bad taste at the end of *Ishi in Two Worlds*. But it was largely overcome by the surrounding account of Ishi's stoicism, the genuine grief of his friends, Kroeber's impassioned letter, and the sincere, if awkward, attempt at a proper burial.

What had happened to the brain? For eight decades, no one cared. Then, in the late 1990s a group of Ishi's southern neighbors began asking questions and agitating for repatriation and reburial of his physical remains. For the first time, the anthropologists' entitlement to look after Ishi and his remains would be publicly challenged. For the Butte County Native American Cultural Committee and its chairman, Art Angle, repatriation of Indian bones was a moral responsibility. As a boy, Angle had witnessed boxes of his own family's ancestral remains carted off by state authorities during earth moving for the immense Oroville Dam that flooded large sections of Concow Maidu land along forks of the Feather River. Ishi's exile from his homeland stood for many other stories of forced removal. The exile could be made whole, Angle insisted, by returning him "where he belongs." "Ishi was a captive," he told the

Oroville Opportunity Bulletin, "from the time he was born until his death, by a society that surrounded him. The whole Yahi tribe is still in limbo and will be until Ishi's remains are repatriated to the Indian people for proper burial" (February 18, 1999: 4). Repatriation would be a form of collective healing for all Indian people in California—a remedy for histories of violence, disrespect, and dispossession.

The pressure applied by the Maidu group, making use of the local press and the *Los Angeles Times,* set in motion inquiries by Nancy Rockafellar, a researcher at the University of California, San Francisco, and Orin Starn, an anthropologist at Duke. The search is described in Starn's *Ishi's Brain.* Starn turned up letters in Berkeley's Bancroft Library recording Alfred Kroeber's decision, after his return from sabbatical, to donate Ishi's brain to the Smithsonian Institution in Washington, D.C., where the preeminent physical anthropologist of the day, Ales Hrdlicka, was amassing an important collection. (It included, we might add, the brains not only of native people from all over the world. John Wesley Powell, founder of the Bureau of American Ethnology, donated his.) Once prestigious, Hrdlicka's comparative racial science was, by the time of Ishi's death, already becoming discredited. Nothing was ever done with Kroeber's collegial gift, which ended up, carefully labeled, floating in a Delaware holding tank.

In a troubling book, *Grave Matters* (2011), Tony Platt reveals how Indian bones were collected in large numbers for over a century, by amateurs and professional academics. The desecration of burial sites was—and continues to be—a common practice, abhorred and protested by native communities. Leading figures like Franz Boas and Alfred Kroeber, who no doubt found grave robbing distasteful, nonetheless pursued the practice methodically in the name of science. Native tellers of Ishi's story have found Alfred Kroeber's decision to send the brain to the Smithsonian incomprehensible and deeply shocking. Privately and at public meetings pressing for repatriation, they asked, over and over: how could this "friend" do so barbarous a thing? And indigenous people are not the only ones to pose the question. Why didn't Kroeber, who opposed the autopsy so vehemently, at least reunite Ishi's remains? How could "Popey," probably as close to Ishi as anyone in his new home, have advocated an invasive procedure that he knew his friend found repellent? (A "simple autopsy"—as recorded in Pope's meticulous published report—involves the removal, measurement, and weighing of every single internal organ, all of which are stuffed back into the cadaver and sewed up. For a non-medical reader, the clinical detail is shocking.) Science simply had to know everything about this unique, admirable specimen of humanity.

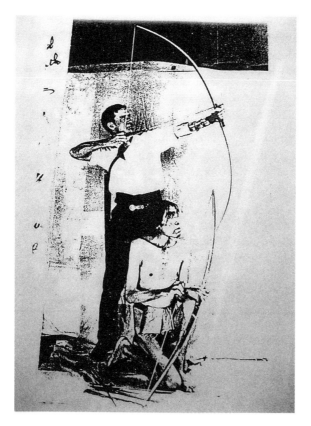

Figure 4.10. Saxton Pope with Ishi in the last days of his life, March 1916. (Courtesy Jed Riffe, Rattlesnake Productions.)

In the last weeks of Ishi's life, Saxton Pope—Ishi's physician and friend—arranged for a photograph to be taken of the two men, posing as archers. Pope stands tall, dramatically drawing his bow, full of life. Ishi crouches below him, cruelly emaciated. When the surgeon saw the developed image he regretted having coaxed his exhausted patient out of bed. Nonetheless, he included the picture in his medical summary. Alfred Kroeber, editing the report for publication, removed it. One sees why. The image is hard to look at, and it has never appeared among the many views of Ishi that have made their way into print. It stands to remind us of what could not be included in *Ishi in Two Worlds* without seriously disrupting the book's concluding mood.

His temperament was philosophical, analytical, reserved, and cheerful. He probably looked upon us as extremely smart. While we knew many things, we had no knowledge of nature, no reserve; we were all busybodies. We were, in fact, sophisticated children.
—Saxton Pope, "The Medical History of Ishi"

To have a bow break in the hand while shooting, Ishi considered a very serious omen and a portent of sickness . . . He himself had two bows shatter in his grasp, and doubtless this and several other malign influences of our civilization, in his mind, contributed as causes of his own last illness. During the declining days of his life, the one thing that brought that happy smile to his face which characterized him, was the subject of archery. A little work, feathering arrows or binding points on with sinew, gave him more pleasure than any diversion we could offer. Even when too weak to work, he liked to show me some little trick or method in making a shaft or backing a bow. To the last his heart was in the game.
—Saxton Pope, "Yahi Archery"

Various places had odors suggestive of certain animals. Ishi said that white men smelled bad, like a horse.
—Saxton Pope, "Yahi Archery"

Scientific interest, paternalism, admiration, and affection coincided in the scientists' relations with Ishi. They didn't see the contradictions that now scream at us. On balance, with a strong dose of historical relativity, I can understand Kroeber's actions with respect to Ishi's brain. It's hard to see them as barbarous, in the context of the prevailing racial and cultural assumptions of his time, and if one gives due value to a form of scientific research he believed to be progressive and antiracist. (Franz Boas, his mentor, famously disproved bad racial science using skull measurements.) Although Kroeber and Boas saw their own cultural research as historical and interpretive, they respected scientific projects such as Hrdlicka's. Kroeber no doubt thought that, if he sent Ishi's brain to the Smithsonian, something good, some contribution to knowledge, might come of the unfortunate autopsy. Personally distraught by Ishi's end (which came in the wake of his first wife's death, also from tuberculosis, and on the eve of his own midlife breakdown and temporary departure from anthropology) Kroeber may have felt there was no way, any more, to do the right thing for his friend.

Kroeber, Waterman, Pope, and Gifford did their best for Ishi, acting with generosity, given the ideological horizons of their time. But this sort of historically contextualized understanding can no longer be the final word. The humanist story of friendship and good intentions, so memorably told by *Ishi in Two Worlds*, unravels under pressure.

Ishi Redux

The survival of California Indians—part of a widespread indigenous resurgence at local, state, regional, and international levels—gives new meanings and critical twists to Ishi's story. At least three overlapping discourses are at work, reflecting a variety of native responses in changing times. The following labels are rough approximations: Ishi the emissary, Ishi the trickster-surviver, Ishi the healer.

The emissary.   Like the famous Lakota shaman Black Elk, Ishi carries a message. He represents the wisdom of a natural/spiritual/cultural world. Understood in overlapping and different ways, Ishi inspires new generations of Indian and non-Indians.

"This is the incredible story of the last hero of the Yahi tribe and how he brought to 'civilization' all the courage, faith and strength of the Yahi Way of Life." Theodora Kroeber wrote a fictionalized youth version of the Ishi story that was for many years required fourth-grade reading in California's public schools. The sentence quoted above appears on its back cover, while the front shows a gentle young brave kneeling, bow and arrows laid aside, with his outstretched palms sniffed by a rabbit. I would hear a version of this Indian hero bringing a message to the white world in a different context: a commemoration ceremony held in September 2000 near Mt. Lassen, organized by the Pit River tribe and Redding Rancheria to celebrate the return of Ishi's remains for burial somewhere in the area. (Starn [2004: 267–285] gives a full account.) Mt. Lassen has for centuries been a meeting place for aboriginal groups, including Ishi's Mill Creek band. This ceremony—which included a talk circle, a generous salmon dinner, and an evening bear dance—was open to all, paid for by tribal funds. Starn (270) wonders whether the source of these funds, casino revenues, might have pleased Ishi, given the competitive gambling games so popular among the California bands of his time.

In an upland meadow a circle of speakers testified to Ishi's meanings today: authorities from the Redding and Pit River tribes, Mickey Gemmil, Tommy George, and Barbara Murphy; elders and young people; and, toward the end, Orin Starn, Nancy Rockafellar, and the Smithsonian's Thomas Killian, non-Indians who had played important roles in the repatriation. The participants brought their own needs and desires to the ceremony, their hopes for some kind of reconciliation. Many expressed a profound sense of kinship with the Yahi, returning at last to the land and to his own people. Among the speakers was a teenager, struggling for words to say why Ishi was important to him. The answer didn't come easily. He recalled once seeing old photos of Ishi demonstrating crafts. "That was awesome." But at times he seemed to be grappling with his anger at continuing injustices. "All those bones still unburied . . ." And how to identify with this man's experience, his death in a museum? It had not been easy. The young man said he had come, finally, to understand Ishi's purpose: "He went to those people to teach them how to live off the land."

A striking poster distributed to everyone present summed up the ceremony's meaning. "Welcome Home Our Relative, Ishi. May We Never Forget Our Ancestors." Ishi's exile was finally over. A large portrait of Ishi in three-quarter profile filled the poster. It was an adaptation of Figure 4.9, above, the image I had associated with Edward Curtis's vision of American Indian defeat and resignation. On the poster the portrait was slightly changed: a feather had been added alongside Ishi's face. At first I thought the feather contributed to a more generic, "Plains Indian" profile. I later learned that eagles and eagle feathers are sacred to Indian tribes in California and beyond. The feather thus expressed a spiritual connection, and Kroeber's evocative portrait had been transformed. It was now an image of homecoming, a return to the land and to a widening network of relations.

In another renewal of Ishi's legacy, the California Indian Museum and Cultural Center in Santa Rosa recently organized a special exhibition to coincide with the centennial of his appearance in Oroville. *Ishi: A Story of Dignity, Hope and Courage,* along with a video of the same name, stressed the positive meaning of Ishi's experience for today's Native Californians. At a related conference, co-organized with the Hearst Museum at Berkeley, Earl Neconie, a Kiowa tribal activist, gave the blessing and called Ishi a "hero" (also, with a smile: "the first Native American employee of U.C."). Joseph Meyers, the Pomo activist, legal scholar, and founder of the Santa Rosa museum (invoking, perhaps, the language of tribal sovereignty politics), described Ishi as a "diplomat." The museum video's accompanying text sums up the message: "To a world of violence and destruction Ishi brought peace and kindness."

At the Santa Rosa museum, Ishi is an emissary to future generations of Indians. The exhibit, lucid and effective, was curated by Executive Director Nicole Meyers-Lim. Of interest to all ages, it is primarily directed toward school groups. Two panels filled with photographic images and explanatory texts greet the visitor: "What Is Civilization?" and "Return to Deer Creek." The former portrays Ishi as a sojourner in San Francisco, wary but engaged, and it stresses his "Yahi view of civilization." The latter panel is composed of Kroeber's photographs of Ishi in a loincloth enacting precontact life on the camping trip in his homeland. Visitors are confronted with two visions: one a critical, Indian experience of modernity, the other a memory of traditional life. Nearby, two Plexiglas cases hold artifacts on loan from the Hearst Museum. They express the same double historical vision. Three classic Pomo baskets from around 1900 occupy one case. The other contains a metal saw from Ishi's "Stone Age" hiding place, along with arrowheads made from glass bottles and a beautiful fishhook, all crafted in San Francisco. It is easy to see how these objects and images might be used to elicit questions about tradition and change from schoolchildren.

The museum's third display area focuses on "Values." Here Ishi's voice, recorded a century ago, is heard faintly—unintelligible but somehow present. Visitors are invited to open small, hinged doors, each bearing a close-up portrait of Ishi and labeled with a particular Indian value. Inside: a brief definition. I quote four, from the museum's study guide.

Courage—This value is defined by the quality of mind or spirit that allows a person to face difficult circumstances, danger or pain. Ishi demonstrated courage in many ways. He faced many difficult events, massacres, the loss of his family members, being moved from his homeland to San Francisco just to name a few.

Generosity—This value is defined by the quality of giving to others. Ishi practiced reciprocity, he shared many things with the anthropologists and others he met while living in San Francisco. He shared knowledge about his traditional skills, he shared time teaching others about his culture and he shared items he made with visitors that came to the museum.

Respect—This value is defined by a person's ability to not interfere with the rights/beliefs of others or to show consideration for the rights/beliefs of others. Ishi respected the cultural beliefs of his tribe. When sharing information with the anthropologists he kept much of his cultural and spiritual beliefs private.

Dignity—This value is defined by a person who exhibits self-respect, or shows an elevated quality of character. While living in San Francisco Ishi interpreted the world around him according to a Yahi worldview. He looked at San Francisco society in terms of what would be useful to a Yahi person. For example he was once taken to an air show in San Francisco and asked what he thought of the planes, his response was that "hawks fly better."

In the juxtaposition of "Generosity" and "Respect" the museum explains how Ishi could cooperate willingly with anthropologists while never losing his sense of who he was as a Yahi, never fully accepting their "civilization." His life, for all its extraordinary suffering, carries a crucial message for future generations seeking ways to live as Indians in a settler-colonial, capitalist modernity.

The trickster-survivor.   Perhaps more than most, Indian identities are command performances. A different strand of native revisionism recognizes that Ishi's various images—pathetic, soulful, heroic—are constructed in relations of power. Ishi's evident interest in selected aspects of urban, technological society, like the Lakota Black Elk's career as a Catholic catechist, fits uneasily with the role of traditional spokesman, emissary of indigenous or natural values. Ironic comments on Ishi's story by Indians complicate the automatic authenticity, the spiritual and human value that he has been made to incarnate—both for a dominant society and for a resurgent tribalism caught up in the strategic mobilizations of identity politics. These turnings of the tale are reminders that no single Indian identity exists: no unified "native point of view," as the anthropologists used to call it.

Ishi enjoyed a good cigar.

Gerald Vizenor, the Anishanaabe novelist, has turned repeatedly to Ishi in his cultural criticism and drama. As a professor at the University of California, Berkeley, he kept the Yahi's memory alive—a persistent irritant in the university's long relationship with the state's original inhabitants. Vizenor led a movement to rename the building that housed Ethnic Studies "Ishi Hall." He had to settle for an "Ishi Courtyard," while pointing out that this, like all names recognizing native peoples, was a substitute for other names that remain in the shadows. But, he said at the Ishi Courtyard dedication, "the shadows of tribal names and stories persist, and the shadows are our natural survivance" (quoted in Owen 2003: 379).

"Survivance" (a rare usage meaning "survivorship") is Vizenor's term for a process of existing in and out of shadows, in and out of the visibility of imposed and adopted simulations required to be legible by power, to exist within a hegemonic settler-colonial sense of the real. The ways that "Ishi" played and subverted the roles expected of him as an authentic Indian make him an adept and enigmatic hero of "post-Indian survivance" (Vizenor 1994). This is not exactly survival, the latter connoting a process of hanging on, of transmitting past life. Survivance, in Vizenor's sense, is more dynamic: the old stories and names underwrite transgressive engagements with power and with the new. Ishi in this view is a trickster who takes on the roles of simulated authenticity offered to him by his museum friends while holding other aspects of himself apart. Ishi shows up while hiding; he speaks while keeping silent. What's at stake is not a duplicitous "playing along" but an ironic acceptance of the performativity of living in an unequal, power-saturated environment. (Louis Owen [2003] offers a lucid exegesis.) Vizenor finds something of his own trickster identity, his storyteller's way of messing with reality, in a subversive, almost postmodern Ishi. Like everyone else, Vizenor makes free with "Ishi Obscura." But unlike almost everyone else, he knows what he is up to:

> Ishi is in our visions, and he persists by that [museum nickname] in our memory. We hear his exile as our own, and by his tease and natural reason we create new stories of native irony, survivance, and liberty. My stories are an expiation of our common exile in this culture of tricky giveaways. (2003: 372)

For much of Ishi's existence in white civilization he no doubt acquiesced in a command performance, under an assumed name. His new identity was a way to relate with others, to be recognized. Vizenor (1994: 134) invokes a strange, poignant anecdote recorded by Saxton Pope, here in Theodora Kroeber's words:

> A Sioux Indian once passed judgment on Ishi. It happened this way. Pope and Ishi were attending a Buffalo Bill Wild West Show, of which they both were fond. There were a number of Plains

Indians in the show. One of them, a tall, dignified man decked out
in paint and feather war bonnet, came up to Pope and Ishi. The
two Indians looked at each other in silence for several moments.
The Sioux then asked in perfect English "What tribe of Indian is
this?" Pope answered, "Yana, from Northern California." The
Sioux then gently picked up a bit of Ishi's hair, rolled it between
his fingers, looked critically into his face, and said, "He is a very
high grade of Indian." When he had gone, Pope asked Ishi what he
thought of the Sioux. "Him's big chiep," was Ishi's enthusiastic
reply. (1961: 228–229)

Whatever this authentification performance meant to the Sioux and the
Yahi then, and whatever elements of Indian humor may have been lost
on the earnest romantic, Saxton Pope, the anecdote has an inescapably
satiric effect in Vizenor's universe. Ishi and the Sioux are both "simulated Indians."

Uncovering the real "Ishi" cannot be a matter of removing a fake
mask, or discovering a shared humanity. The man exists for us under an
assumed name, invented by others. His "survivance," Vizenor writes, "is
heard in a word that means 'one of the people,' and that word became
his name."

So much the better, and he never told the anthropologists,
reporters, and curious practitioners his sacred tribal name, not
even his nicknames. The other tribal pronoun endured in silence.
He might have said, "the ghosts were generous in the silence of the
museum, and now these men pretend to know me in their name."
Trickster hermeneutics is the silence of his nicknames. "Ishi is the
absence," he might have said. (1994: 128)

Ishi's "silence" holds a place for realties that exceed the dominant
order of truth, beyond the reach of cultural relativism and anthropological translation projects. And Vizenor also invokes "tribal stories" that
mediate different realities: resourceful ways to connect and disconnect
separate worlds. He celebrates Ishi's inability to learn how to slow down
when reciting his stories for the scholars. The "informant" speaks past
his listeners, his very volubility a kind of silence. Silence is stories that
don't translate. And it is the very name, or nickname, "Ishi," papering
over an absence of other names. It is an expression of what can't be heard.
Not now, not in this history. A trace of what "he might have said . . ."

Gerald Vizenor is certainly not alone in his awareness of the inescapable ironies of tribal survivance in and through simulations—
performances both coerced and playful.

Many photographs were taken of Ishi. The images are haunting: the man
seems somehow present and absent. *Partial Recall* (Lippard 1992) collects essays by Native American artists and writers exploring the predicament of Indian histories and identities entangled with images.
Almost any one of the trenchant, poignant texts brought together by
Lucy Lippard could provide commentary on Ishi's story.

For example, Rayna Green is "transfixed" by an old photo: the confident, unflinching gazes of two Indian girls in white dresses reclining on
a Victorian couch:

> There they were, these girls surrounded by Curtis boys dripping
> dentalia and fur—the sepia kings, shot through spit and petro-
> leum jelly. Lords of the plains, Potentates of the Potlatch, the Last-
> Ofs. I take out my immediate distaste on them, but it's Curtis and
> the other pin-hole illusionists I'm after. Get a *life,* I want to say to
> them. Quit taking out your fantasies on us. Just give me one in
> overalls and a cowboy hat. Then we can get serious about what
> was happening to these people. (1992: 47)

Or Paul Chaat Smith:

> They said that Ishi was the last North American Indian untouched
> by civilization. I don't know about that, but it's clear he was really
> country and seriously out of touch with recent developments.
> We're talking major hayseed here, at least . . .
>
> One day they took Ishi on a field trip to Golden Gate Park. An
> early aviator named Henry Fowler was attempting a cross-country
> flight. You can imagine the delicious anticipation of the anthro-
> pologists. The Ishi Man vs. the Flying Machine. What would he
> make of this miracle . . . ?
>
> Ishi looked up at the plane overhead. He spoke in a tone the
> biographers would describe as one of "mild interest." "White man
> up there?"
>
> Twenty years later my grandfather would become the first
> Comanche frequent flyer. (1992: 95)

Jimmie Durham:

> Geronimo, as an Indian "photographic subject," blew out the
> windows. On his own, he reinvented the concept of photographs
> of American Indians. At least he did so as far as he could, con-
> cerning pictures of himself, which are so ubiquitous that he must
> have sought "photo opportunities" as eagerly as the photogra-
> phers. Yet even when he was "posed" by the man behind the
> camera, he seems to have destroyed the pose and created his own
> stance. In every image he looks through the camera at the viewer,
> seriously, intently, with a specific message. Geronimo uses the
> photograph to "get at" those people who imagine themselves as
> the "audience" of his struggles. He seems to be trying to see us.
> He is demanding to be seen, on his own terms. (1992: 56)

Ishi was often photographed by visitors to the anthropology museum
and, according to Theodora Kroeber, soon became expert in matters of
pose and lighting.

Jolene Rickard: "We survived by watching, listening and experiencing
life. A photograph is not going to give that firsthand experience, but it
may haunt your memory into seeking life" (1992: 110).

James Luna, a Luiseño/Diegueño artist from Southern California, became
famous with a display of himself wrapped in a towel lying in a museum.
The Artifact Piece (1987), a direct reference to Ishi the living exhibit, is
also a general comment on salvage collecting, spectatorship, and the performance of authenticity. In a room devoted to American Indians at the
Museum of Man, San Diego (and later at the Whitney Museum in New
York) Luna lay motionless on a bed of sand. Nothing prepared casual
visitors for this artifact, somehow both living and dead. Official-looking
labels were placed alongside the body, providing its personal name and
explaining scars caused by specific incidents of drinking or fighting.
Luna's personal belongings from the reservation were displayed in nearby
cases—including music (country and western, jazz, Mexican, Sex Pistols)
and poetry (Allen Ginsberg's *Howl*). An individual life evoked . . . And
this Indian artifact was listening in on the surrounding conversations.

   An Indian in a loincloth. The performance of authenticity both Luna
and Vizenor satirize can be seen in Figure 4.12, a photo from *Ishi in*

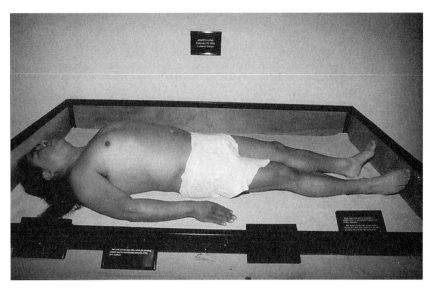

Figure 4.11. James Luna, *The Artifact Piece.* Performance/installation, The Whitney Museum, New York City, 1990. (Image courtesy of the artist. Photographer Robin Holland.)

Two Worlds that was taken on the museum-dweller's camping trip to Deer Creek. In the book's early editions, virtually all the images of Ishi were of this kind: reenactments of a former "precontact" life. If they thus represent a "simulated Indian," how should the real Ishi be portrayed? Perhaps "fully" clothed? That was, after all, his chosen style of self-presentation as soon as the cameras began to be pointed his way. Yet he consented to the camping trip's "cultural striptease," as Vizenor calls it. He even enjoyed playing Indian and apparently thought the documentation of his traditional lifeways worth doing. Some of it, however, he kept secret. His survivance, his way of living as an "Indian" in "civilization," was evidently a matter of selectively taking up new ways while refusing others, giving and holding back. Ishi was never comfortable shaking hands, avoiding this form of contact whenever possible. But he particularly appreciated pockets—which soon filled up with what Theodora Kroeber tactfully called "the usual male miscellany."

Which image delivers the real Ishi? James Luna's performance piece (1991–1992) *Take a Picture with a Real Indian* commented on this unanswerable question. Audience members were invited to choose among

Figure 4.12. Ishi making a bow. Deer Creek, May–
June 1914. Photography by Saxton Pope. (Courtesy of
the Phoebe A. Hearst Museum of Anthropology and
the Regents of the University of California; catalogue
no. 15-5798.)

three possibilities: Luna feathered in Plains Indian regalia, Luna in a polo
shirt and slacks, Luna naked in a loincloth. Two of the options were life-
sized cutout photos; one was three-dimensional and alive. However, instead
of being troubled by a choice between reductive authenticities, audiences
tended to get into the fun. Andrea Liss reports that "in recent stagings of
this piece, Luna has only been able to calm or numb the crowds by saying,
'OK, next you can take your picture with a real nigger'" (1992: 13).

   In 2002, asked to speak at the California College of the Arts in San
Francisco, I suggested that James Luna be invited at the same time to
stage a conversation. As I stood at a lectern presenting an early version

Figure 4.13. Pockets. Ishi at the University, October 1911. (Courtesy of the Phoebe A. Hearst Museum of Anthropology and the Regents of the University of California; catalogue no. 15-16827.)

of the present essay—with projected slides of Ishi on a screen behind— Luna impersonated a janitor and silently swept the stage around me.

In the discussion that followed he observed: "I am not a coyote. Coyote was not a nice guy. I am a clown." He also said: "I wasn't born in a teepee. I was born in TV . . . I am a contemporary American Indian artist."

Luna recalled his father: "Passing on the tradition of alcohol."

As an artist, he has publicly performed the most disturbing, least noble aspects of tribal life—experiences of alcoholism and intratribal violence. In 1992 he created an installation, *The Sacred Colors,* which uses the four directions of pan-Indian cosmology to create a serene group portrait of himself with three friends, men and women representing black, white, red, and yellow races of humanity. In the catalogue he offers this vision of reconciliation: "I must tell you that I am sometimes left in awe of many of our tribal ways: [their] complexity, yet profound simplicity. I was thinking about this when I thought of the sacred colors. Like the four directions, we use the colors to distinguish and balance our world" (quoted in Liss 1992: 19).

Luna considers himself a "cultural warrior," a voice for his people. On an airplane flight to participate in the 2005 Venice Biennale, he reflects on his predecessors: the Luiseño Catholic Pablo Tac, who made the trip to Italy in 1832, and his elders who brought literacy skills home from the boarding schools and who were seen to have changed. He also thinks of Ishi, the so-called last wild California Indian, "a pretty smart guy" who thought that the match was the best creation of Western culture. "Mr. Ishi," the anthropological specimen and cross-cultural observer, joins James Luna and Pablo Tac in the "stratosphere" (Luna 2011: 42, 44–45).

Identity and authenticity remain open questions in the work of James Luna, Gerald Vizenor, and the others I have just quoted. Their differently ironic sensibilities are intimately concerned with social and political processes of survival through resistance, engagement, and transformation. Irony and satire are not primarily modes of distance or critique but expressions of what Louis Owen calls "utopian desires that lie at the paradoxical heart of trickster stories" (2003: 376). Thus Indian identity, tradition, even authenticity, are not "essentialisms" to be criticized or abandoned but rather sites of ongoing interrogation where real historical relations, both ludic and deadly serious, are improvised.

Ishi, by all accounts, loved jokes.

The healer.   According to Theodora Kroeber and her sources, Ishi was "religious . . ."

> He believed according to Yana formula in the making and peopling of the world by gods and demigods, and in the *taboos* laid down by the Old Ones. He also believed in a Land of the Dead where the souls of Yana live out their shadow community existence. Christian doctrine interested him, and seemed to him for the most part reasonable and understandable. He held to the conviction that the White God would not care to have Indians in His

home, for all Loudy told him to the contrary. ["Loudy," Llewellyn Loud, was a museum employee given to Christian sermonizing.] It may have occurred to him that the souls of white men would fit poorly into a round dance of Yana dead. If so, he was too polite to say so. (1961: 224–225)

How these attitudes came to be known is not said. In any event, they express a plausible, characteristic restraint—holding on to core Yana beliefs and attachments, even while experimenting with new situations, relationships, tools, and customs. Ishi's basic attitude seems to have been a tolerant curiosity about other lifeways—an engagement that did not require abandoning his own values. This was how the anthropologists, imbued with Boasian cultural relativism, saw their charge.

His manner in and around the museum made people feel optimistic about human conviviality and the possibility of bridging deep cultural differences. His smile made them feel better about themselves. Moreover, he embodied something innocent and wise: more a "wild child" than a "wild man." Like Kaspar Hauser, or the hero of Jerzy Kosinski's *Being There,* his simple gesture or word could seem deeply meaningful.

Figure 4.14. Indian. Drawing by L. Frank. (Courtesy of the artist.)

Ishi's quiet, magical power turns up in Theodora Kroeber's biography of her husband, *Alfred Kroeber: A Personal Configuration*. Ishi does not make an appearance in the narrative until 1913, at a special moment. Henriette, Alfred Kroeber's first wife, has just died of tuberculosis. He sits frozen at his office desk, "his mind blank."

> There came to him as he sat there the silken sound of tiny particles of falling flakes of glass from the next room where someone was at work—Ishi. Kroeber went next door. A barefoot but otherwise ordinarily dressed Indian sat on a piece of canvas tarpaulin, expertly fashioning an obsidian arrowhead with a chipper made of the antler of a deer. Ishi smiled a greeting but did not stop the rapid flaking stroke; he was used to having this friend of his sit beside him, watching him at work. (1970: 80)

Flashbacks recall Ishi's arrival at the museum, the tragedy of his people, and his new relations with the anthropologists. Theodora Kroeber recalls that the devastated survivor almost immediately began to fashion artifacts "for the museum so that outside worlds would know something of his own Yana world."

> Through the few words they exchanged, through the comfortable silences between the words, [Kroeber] felt Ishi trying to help him in his own loss, to comfort him, to transmit to him something of his own Yana faith. There was much unfinished work for him and Ishi to do. There was other unfinished work in the full notebooks next door. (1970: 84)

Kroeber returns to his office to focus on Yurok grammar. Ishi had taught him the healing power of work—a Yana virtue perhaps, but also a thoroughly Christian and Victorian value. Ishi's patient ability to persevere was an inspiration to Alfred Kroeber. Whether this particular anecdote is his or his wife's extrapolation, Ishi's fundamental purpose in the narrative is clear.

Healing may be Ishi's most potent, and continuing, role. And in recent decades, California Indians have been turning the theme in new directions. Rather than representing a rupture with the past ("the last" pure

Indian), an enigmatic survivor, or a trickster escape artist, Ishi's story becomes an epitome of exile and return, loss and reconnection. For Art Angle and those involved in Ishi's repatriation, his story is unfinished; his return to his homeland will be a completion, a healing experience, not just for those with close historical connections to the Yahi but for all California Indians. Ishi's story makes new meanings, now, in diverse tribal ways.

Liz Dominguez (a member of the Chumash tribe) writing for *News from Native California* (Fall 1998) tells of being inspired by hearing Ishi's voice—tapes of his recorded songs and stories. Though she can't understand his words, there's something very powerful in the presence of his voice. She searches out similar records in the "salvage anthropology" of her own people, finding old tapes of her great-great-grandmother, collected by salvage linguists like J. P. Harrington. The heritage quest will lead her into active Chumash-language learning and singing. Liz Dominguez ends her essay: "Thank you, Ishi, your message came through."

More of Ishi's recordings are currently being translated by the linguist Leanne Hinton and her collaborators at Berkeley. The task is a formidable one, for there are no other records of Ishi's dialect than those he left—no dictionaries, grammars, or fully translated texts. But when the latest transcriptions and (partial) translations are complete, the audience will certainly be more than academic. The collections of linguistic and oral tradition made in this century by "salvage anthropologists" such as Kroeber and his followers are finding new audiences and uses, as they are repatriated by Indian activists, writers, scholars, and artists. (For example, Julian Lang [2008] provides an example of recycling Mattole linguistic materials in a conceptual art project.)

Figure 4.15 reproduces the oil painting *Ishi and Companion at Lamin Mool,* created in 1973 by the Maidu artist Frank Day. Comparing Ishi's face in this extraordinary image with its likely source, the lost soul photographed at the Oroville jail (Figure 4.3), we see how the refugee has been recoded: from despair to power, from terror to healing. And it is no longer a question of bonding with white friends in the museum. Ishi's healing power is reimagined in a context of tribal survival and empowerment.

Frank Day's magical realist renditions of precontact places, events, and myths have been influential in the emergence of California Indian art (Dobkins 2003). Day was born in 1902, the son of an important headman and a native speaker of Maidu. After years in a government boarding school and decades of travel throughout North American

Figure 4.15.   Ishi and Companion at Lamin Mool. Painting by Frank Day. Oil
on canvas, ca. 1973, 36" x 24". (Courtesy H. C. and Käthe Puffer, Pacific
Western Traders.)

Indian Country, he returned to Northern California and took up
painting. His "auto-ethnographic" (Pratt 1992) versions of Concow
Maidu tradition are mixtures of documentary realism and imaginative
invention. Dramatic canvasses depict historical events and spiritual
happenings, often together in a composite image. Day also recorded
many hours of taped commentary, storytelling, and memories. In this
way, and as the organizer (along with Wintu artist Frank LaPeña) of a
traditional dance group, Frank Day has become part of the inventive
continuity of Maidu culture. While some of his renditions and memories
are contested, and while Christianity is very much part of the process,
Day's energetic production of image, word, and dance has been seminal.
He died in 1976.

The painting depicts Ishi a few weeks before his capture, in the act of
healing a fellow Indian from a gunshot wound. Day recalled that he and
his father stumbled on this very scene in early August 1911, at a place
not far from Oroville where different Indian bands traditionally gath-

ered. Ishi is not the emaciated refugee who would be captured a month later, but rather a powerful shamanic figure. He works with an elaborate contraption for heating water without any telltale smoke: sunlight focused by a reflecting shell. The stones are heated in the water and applied to the wound. Day's is a unique image. There is no other surviving California evidence of such a doctoring technique.

While it is impossible independently to verify Frank Day's recollection, there's no doubt about the current significance of his retelling. The encounter he reports is part of Maidu oral tradition, which includes other close encounters with kinsmen/neighbors, hiding in the valleys to the north. Starn (2004: 292) recounts one such story, and Richard Burrill (2011) documents other recollections. In Frank Day's image of healing, Ishi's story is detached from the dominant history to play an inspirational role in the politics of Indian resurgence. This includes a restored connection between the Maidu and Yahi. Frank Day's memory of Ishi would be cited as evidence by the Butte County Native American Cultural Committee asserting their right to repatriate Ishi's remains.

Ishi's story has been remembered and reinterpreted in varied tribal contexts, but most of these oral sources are inaccessible to an outsider. Beverly Ortiz has generously shared with me what she knows about a performance in March 1976 at Shasta College in Redding, based on a newspaper clipping shared with her by Josephine Grant Peters (Karuk/Shasta/Abenaki). The play *Ishi* was written by Charlotte Burleson, a Redding resident, and Andrea Kelsey, a Hoopa Indian from Davis. A local newspaper quotes Vivien Hailstone (Karuk/Yurok/Member of the Hoopa Tribe), an elder and activist who plays Ishi's grandmother: "The reason I'm doing it is because it isn't just Ishi of the Yahi tribe who was the last. My heart is heavy as I do this because it's my tribe, it's all tribes—who are dying. And this being the Bicentennial, I hope that we can work together to plan the future, rather than have others plan it for us." The article continues: "Ms. Kelsey, whom Mrs. Burleson credits with achieving the accuracy and poetic quality of the play, finds the entire production unique. 'Every person in the cast, except for two who play white men, is a California Indian and that is unique,' she says. 'In other plays, you have people acting as Indians. What you get, I believe, is a loss of feeling as well as reality. Most of these people have had no acting experience at all, but I find that they don't do so much playacting as reliving'" (Ortiz personal communication [2013]). Quotations such as these offer glimpses into what Ishi's experience has meant, over the years, to California Indians as they relive past traumas and struggle to take control of their future.

There is also a dark side to Ishi's healing touch.

In a provocative "epilogue" to his long quest for Ishi, Orin Starn drives up into the mountains to the tiny town of Taylorsville, site of Greenville Rancheria, where some eighty Mountain Maidu reside. He is bringing a cassette tape containing four of the songs Ishi recorded on wax cylinders, these four sung in Maidu rather than Yahi. The dialect is, however, different from that understood by the handful of remaining Maidu speakers around Oroville. One of these suggested the songs might be in the mountain dialect, so Starn arranged for several of the remaining native speakers in Taylorsville to listen for their language in the faint, scratchy voice from almost a century ago. Imagining they would be pleased to hear the old words, even spoken by a Yahi neighbor, Starn was surprised by the reactions:

> There was a long silence once I turned off the tape. At last, Wilhelmina [Ives] said: "He shouldn't have sung those songs." It turned out that she and the others had no objection to [the first two samples] gambling songs, which they recognized as ones they'd heard as children. These were songs made up of vocables instead of real words, a kind of Indian scatting intended for the raucous fun of a gambling tournament. What bothered the five elders were the other two songs, which were doctoring songs. "He shouldn't have sung those songs," Wilhelmina repeated. "They were given by the spirit to the medicine man." Could they have been Ishi's own songs? If Ishi was a healer, as some believe, then he would have had his own songs. Wilhelmina didn't reply. It was as if she knew that the songs belonged to some mountain Maidu doctor, and yet was reluctant to say so straight out. As I had already learned, contrary to the more benign New Age view of "Indian healing," the secret casting of jealous spells was part of the doctoring of the old days. I could only guess that Wihelmina didn't want to enter into the tense, even dangerous subject of the medicine men and their power for good and evil, especially with an outsider.

After some speculation by the elders about why Ishi sang the songs—was he "hunting for his own death," or had he realized that "everything was over, there wasn't anyone else left?"—the conversation flagged.

> Was there more to the story? Unshared secrets about the meaning of the songs? It would have been rude to press further. I stayed only a bit longer before heading back down the highway." (2004: 300)

The discomfort with Ishi's doctoring songs reminded Starn of a story that had briefly surfaced in 1997: the last Yahi was really a "malevolent shaman" expelled by his group. Maybe the elders were holding something back. Or perhaps they had simply said all they knew and declined to speculate. Starn's ambiguous *denouement* among the mountain Maidu pointedly returns us to Theodora Kroeber's "deep shadow" surrounding the man called Ishi.

But the resonant figure still works its magic. Starn weaves a personal quest into his multistranded history. Among the "ranks of unfulfilled strivers and wannabes" (the many Ishi aficionados in search of something essential), Starn counts himself—"a white man who likes Indian company, a Californian stranded in North Carolina, a writer who hates to write" (2004: 294). The anthropologist, making a life, but still feeling exiled in North Carolina, finds a renewed connection with the region of his upbringing. His activist scholarship brings a new sense of involvement with Northern California's tragic, transforming history. And the trail of Ishi's story finally leads him to a one-hundred-year-old Maidu matriarch, Vera Clark McKeen, whose powerful bear hug will be "life itself" (296). In *Ishi's Brain*, Starn is "always coming home," to borrow the title of Ursula K. Le Guin's utopian ethnography of a future California (discussed at the end of this essay). Always coming home—the phrase seems to sum up the redemptive promise of Ishi's story.

Sacrificial healing makes particular sense in cultures infused with Christian values. This includes Native California where today mixed forms of Christianity and indigenous messianism, healing visions and world-renewal cycles, are active in transformed traditions. Ishi's story lives in an unfinished history composed of braided and tangled strands, Indian and white, old and new, intimate and public. For native people, the healing potential in Ishi's story has been affirmed throughout the recent repatriation process. "Bringing Ishi home" by gathering and burying his physical remains helps close a wound . . . at least for a time. And while repatriation, this time, was relatively smooth, it unfolded within the tensions, ruptures, and rearticulations that had inflected Northern California Indian societies since 1917. When Ishi came home to his people in 2000, it was to a radically altered social landscape.

When the brain was finally located at the Smithsonian, a consensus quickly formed that Ishi's dispersed remains should be returned, as Art Angle put it, "where he belongs." Museum staff, California State officials, academic scholars, and California tribes were mobilized in the process, which moved—by repatriation standards—quickly. But where, exactly, did Ishi belong? Thorny historical and political problems were raised by the need to give Ishi's remains back to his people. Who were the proper recipients? There were no "Yahi" (or Mill Creek Indians) left. The Butte County Maidu group (southern neighbors, and sometime rivals of the Mill Creeks) had initiated and led the movement for reburial. They traveled to Washington, D.C., where they performed ceremonies for the brain and began negotiations for its return. Having taken responsibility for Ishi, were they the appropriate relations?

Everyone agreed that there should be a reburial by California Indians, without interference and in accordance with their traditions. But this had also to be accomplished in accordance with repatriation laws requiring that if no immediate family can be determined then "cultural affiliation" should be the relevant criterion. A historical can of worms opens. When so much has changed, what are the crucial elements of "cultural" identity? If groups have moved and recombined what are the appropriate threads of "affiliation"? In Ishi's case, the "Yahi" were gone. Yet they were socially and historically connected to several neighboring groups, now reconstituted as "tribes." In Ishi's day, sociopolitical notions like "tribe" or "nation" did not exist: there were no reservations in California of the sort established elsewhere, no legally recognized "Indian Country." Since Ishi spoke a dialect of Yana, and since there were now people of mixed Yana blood (having lost the language for generations) in the Redding and Pit River communities to the north, perhaps these were the most appropriate groups to receive the remains. Having contacted Redding and Pit River people who remembered and valued Yana ancestry, among their other roots, the Smithsonian recognized their right of repatriation—thus anchoring "cultural affiliation" in language.

It was a cogently argued and defensible decision (Speaker 2003). But as a consequence, the Smithsonian rejected a Maidu petition based on oral traditions asserting kinship relations with the Yahi. Art Angle had publicly stated, on more than one occasion, that "Ishi was at least half Maidu." The Butte County Committee's argument also pointed to physical proximity, a local history of contacts confirmed by linguistic and archaeological evidence of mutual trade and influence (Ishi's Maidu vocabulary). Oral tradition is, of course, adaptive, often politically realigned in present circumstances. Was Frank Day's memory of the encounter at Lamin Mool part of oral tradition before it took shape in his painting sixty years after the fact? What about the improbable elements it contains? Ishi's physical vitality just weeks before he was found in a state of exhausted emaciation? The unique healing contraption? His wounded companion, nowhere else in the documentary record? A certain skepticism is inescapable. But so is the fact that oral traditions often contain historical truths invisible to the (always selective) surviving record. Ishi wouldn't speak about his deceased family or say much about their life in hiding. How would the anthropologists at the museum know whether his mother was or was not Maidu? If she was captured at a young age, she might not have spoken Maidu to her son. And given recent archaeological evidence that the "Yahi" were a more mixed band than previously thought and were in contact with those around them, Maidu stories of relations with their neighbors to the north, of leaving food for the wild ones out in the hills, of being ready to welcome Ishi in 1911, become more plausible. They can no longer be dismissed on purportedly objective or scientific grounds.

It is arguable that the whole search for Ishi's people was a kind of anachronism or misplaced concreteness. The "cultural affiliation" required by repatriation law simply cannot be traced in a single direction, given the historical rearticulation of local identities and the emergence of new scales of identification. A larger pan-Californian, or Northern California Indian, interest in Ishi was, at times, invoked by Art Angle, and new intertribal networks of identification have emerged in the identity politics of Northern California. Individuals often list two or more tribes when identifying themselves as Indians. Many of these people, with no direct Yana connections, have felt the return of Ishi's remains to be a part of a shared history. Yet older, more local processes of kinship also remain strong. In a confused, multiscaled intertribal landscape, the Smithsonian was unwilling to acknowledge broader pan-Californian "cultural affiliations" with the last Yahi. As defined in their protocols, "culture" remained local, tied to blood and language, rather than emergent, multiplex, or coalitional. The tribes of California, identified in Kroeber's time (Maidu, Yana, Wintun, etc.) had crystallized, definitively in the law and more ambiguously in native opinion. Thus repatriation by Ishi's northern kin meant, in practice, exclusion of his southern neighbors: trading partners, rivals, and perhaps family.

The Redding and Pit River people, though latecomers to the repatriation process, felt a renewed connection to their braided Yana roots and a responsibility to do the right thing for a lost ancestor. At the September 2000 ceremony in Lassen National Park, they expressed a profound commitment to the process of bringing Ishi home. There were moving testimonials, from young and old, and a powerful bear dance (a trance dance for healing). I sensed here (and also in the earlier Maidu-organized events around Oroville) a strong feeling of reconnection with a lost relative, righting a profound and still painful wrong.

There were raw feelings from the arguments over who should receive Ishi's remains, especially among the Maidu who had done so much to lead the process and were, finally, excluded from the burial. (Art Angle chose not to attend the Mt. Lassen celebration.) But there was also a widespread understanding that this was not a time for disunity. During the meetings I attended, at least, contrary claims about Ishi's affiliation were registered and left uncontradicted. The tribal actors in the process evinced mutual respect, if not close cooperation. In a real sense, the man from a tiny group of refugees in Mill and Deer Creeks had become a common ancestor. If he once symbolized the death of indigenous Californians, his return now demonstrated their vitality. Thus, Ishi's repatriation brings into view a transformative history of realignments: people forced off traditional lands, regrouping in new/old configurations: Christianities, neotraditionalisms, heritage productions, casinos, and tribal development projects.

The "tribes" of California took shape in the early years of the twentieth century. Aboriginal California had been intensely local and one of the most linguistically rich regions of the planet. Alfred Kroeber and his colleagues set out to document this extraordinary diversity, which they felt to be disappearing. The result was a map of California Indian languages: a prodigious research effort. Like all maps, it projected a specific reality. Its sharp outlines marked off languages and dialects that did not exactly match sociocultural units. Local societies were in practice socially porous, crossed by trade, kinship, multilingualism, and intertribal gatherings (Field 2008: 75). Moreover, within the territories defined by language there could be multiple dialects, some largely unintelligible to each other. In Ishi's time, people distinguished their community using the name of a local site or of a headman, rather than saying, "We are Yana" or "We are Karok." A common habit of equating language with culture oversimplifies more complex affiliations. The makers of the linguistic map knew this, and did not assume that "Yana" designated a tribe in today's cultural/political sense. The same can be said for "Maidu" or "Wintun." Since the map was completed, however, these rather fluid groupings have hardened and become institutionalized under strong pressures to function in a government-imposed politics of "tribal" recognition.

Ishi's people, the "Mill Creeks" (referring to a particular streambed and steep valley) were certainly not a tribe. "Yahi" was a dialect name recorded by Edward Sapir. How discrete was the group's existence, even in hiding from the Indian-killers? As we've seen, past and present intertribal relations in California suggest the existence of multiple affiliations. And recent research by the archaeologists Jerald Johnson and Jim Johnston has underlined the relativity of Ishi's isolation. "Grizzly Bear's Hiding Place," the last Deer Creek refuge, was filled with pilfered commodities from the white man's world. The Yahi language recorded by Kroeber and his colleagues included Spanish loan words, as well as bits from Wintu, Atsugewi, and Maidu (Starn 2003). Richard Burrill's (2011) oral histories offer further suggestions of interaction. Thus current retellings of Ishi's story, both by natives and by scholars, question his ahistorical isolation and "wildness," the "Stone Age" purity so valued by his scientific friends at the anthropology museum.

The Mill Creeks, or Yahi, were a liminal group occupying a borderland. And if contemporary discourse requires they be given a discrete "tribal" identity, it is not obvious that this should be primarily articulated with the the people who once spoke Central and Northern Yana. (I bracket, for the moment, evidence for connecting west with Wintu and northeast with Atsugewi, since these affiliations were not at issue in the repatriation process.) The sketch map drawn by Ishi on the camping trip and reproduced by Theodora Kroeber (1961: 215) shows active trails beyond Yahi country leading both north and south.

The tension between Redding/Pit River and Maidu participants in the movement to return Ishi's remains was certainly increased by the either-or test of tribal identity imposed by repatriation law and the Smithsonian's decision. Older rivalries and local histories may also have played a part. In public, however, the participants, exercising diplomatic restraint, left opposed opinions uncontested. The Yahi's return was a time for tribal unity, for wide participation in the healing process. Ishi's return, like many ongoing repatriations of native bodies in North America and elsewhere, has had a cathartic effect. I felt this at the meetings and ceremonies I attended. Space was made there for non-Indians: allies and participants in the repatriation process. Many people were moved (differently) by Ishi's homecoming.

Ishi Variations

Ishi's story has been taken back, retold, by California Indians and by other native writers and artists. It bears repeating that what I know of these changing worlds, based only on public expressions and not the many, more intimate, private exchanges, is not the whole picture. Revisionism, dialogue, and contestation are ongoing in a tangle of California histories, native and nonnative. Ishi's story continues to be a productive site for rethinking these histories. The last sections of this essay explore other retellings as signs of the changing times. I discuss two major films about Ishi, Theodora Kroeber's book for schoolchildren, debates within the Berkeley Department of Anthropology, and the science fiction/utopias of Ursula K. Le Guin. I see these revisions as part of a dialogical process that reopens imagined pasts and projects possible futures. The retellings address distinct audiences and changing frontiers of difference within the ever-receding horizon of a postcolonial society.

The term "postcolonial" is controversial. I use it with hesitation, lacking a better name for the equitable resolution of conquest's unfinished business. In the sense developed by Stuart Hall (1996) "post" cannot mean "after"—not in the sense of something beyond, or transcending colonialism. "Post" is always shadowed by "neo." As a periodizing term, it evokes an unfinished transition, not an end point, an uneven work in progress. To the extent that "postcolonial" developments seem to be subverting or moving away from long-established, hierarchical, binary structures (both of material power and of thought) it can be called utopic. But this utopia, as will appear below, needs to be thought of as a process, not an outcome. Utopia is as likely to be found veering off sideways as leaping forward through time. Le Guin:

> Copernicus told us that the earth was not the center. Darwin told
> us that man is not the center. If we listened to the anthropologists

we might hear them telling us, with appropriate indirectness, that the White West is not the center. The center of the world is a bluff on the Klamath River, a rock in Mecca, a hole in the ground in Greece, nowhere, its circumference everywhere.

Perhaps the utopist should heed this unsettling news at last. Perhaps the utopist would do well to lose the plan, throw away the map, get off the motorcycle, put on a very strange-looking hat, bark sharply three times, and trot off looking thin, yellow, and dingy across the desert and up into the digger pines. (1989: 98)

In 1992, two years after the blockbuster Hollywood film *Dances with Wolves*, Ishi reached television in a $4.2 million HBO production. *The Last of His Tribe* is a full-length movie starring Jon Voight *(Midnight Cowboy)* as Kroeber; Graham Greene *(Dances with Wolves)* as Ishi; Anne Archer *(Fatal Attraction)* as Kroeber's first wife, Henrietta; and David Ogden Stiers *(MASH)* as Saxton Pope. A publicity tagline reads: "The spirit of a great warrior can never die." This is almost certainly the first time Ishi has been called a "warrior," except perhaps in Vizenor's ironic sense: "A post-Indian warrior of survivance." Publicity images show mounted men who look suspiciously like the U.S. Cavalry from battles on the Great Plains riding down Ishi and his fleeing family. (It's interesting to imagine a cavalry charge in the brush-filled ravines of Deer Creek.) This packaging is, of course, designed to make recognizably "Indian" the story of a quiet Californian in a suit and tie.

Unlike its publicity, the film takes pains to provide verisimilitude in its period settings and costumes. A distinguished linguist, the Maidu specialist William Shipley, was engaged to provide plausible-sounding Yahi sentences for subtitled conversations between Kroeber and Ishi. Many situations from *Ishi in Two Worlds* are recognizable; others are invented. The script, by novelist Stephen Harrington, does not hesitate to make free with known facts in the service of a more gripping drama. Romanticism is fused with psychology: science confronts sentiment and repression yields to catharsis in a work best called, perhaps, "The Healing of Alfred Kroeber."

Among the HBO film's liberties, the most blatant, perhaps, is its portrayal of the anthropologist's fluency in Yahi. Everything important is translatable. At dinner with the Kroebers very soon after his arrival in

San Francisco, Ishi responds to Henrietta Kroeber's request for an
account of his travails and the fate of his family with a full and completely intelligible recitation. Of course, he had always declined to discuss these matters. There are no obscure "Wood Duck" stories.
Everything in the film turns on Kroeber's relationships with Ishi and
with his wife, who is dying of tuberculosis. Her husband, in deep denial,
refuses to confront reality. He lectures to her about her condition, and
when the emotional going gets tough, he freezes. Henrietta alternately
pleads for help and treats her husband with knowing, womanly tolerance. Voigt's Kroeber is well meaning, boyishly arrogant, and emotionally blocked. With Ishi he adopts an authoritarian, parental tone. The
wild man is his charge and his prize. He brags that he will make Ishi and
his people live forever, in a book. "Big Chiep" knows best.

He will learn otherwise. After Henrietta's death, Ishi takes over the
humanizing project. At her funeral, he observes that there is no singing:
"How can she find her way to the land of the dead unless you sing for
her?" Kroeber will not, cannot, sing. When Ishi insists, Kroeber loses his
temper. Later, in a melodramatic climax to the Deer Creek expedition,
Ishi comes on the spot where (seen in a chilling flashback) his sister was
coldly executed. He collapses to his knees, and induces Kroeber to do the
same. "Do you feel her breathing . . . Do you hear her singing? . . . What
she sing? . . . sing it!" Kroeber: "I can't." Ishi, falling apart, sobs: "Ishi . . .
last . . . Yahi!"

Back in San Francisco, Ishi wanders into a dissection room at the
hospital and discovers cadavers being cut up. He is outraged, angrily
demanding that Kroeber put a stop to the barbarity. Dead people must
remain whole and find their way to the ancestors. Kroeber refuses, stub-
bornly clinging to his authority. Then in an amusing, historically dubious
episode, Saxton Pope hires a prostitute to sleep with the lone bachelor.
In the morning Ishi is found humming happily as he polishes display
cases. When Kroeber explodes in anger, Ishi wonders: "Saldu [white
people] not do this thing?" Kroeber, ever more prudish and parental,
confronts the author of the crime. Pope acidly retorts: "For whom are
you keeping Ishi pure?" As relations with Ishi sour, the dialogue becomes
even more heavy-handed. A confused Kroeber finally asks Ishi why he is
upset. Pointing to the anthropologist's notebook, the Indian gravely
replies: "You put Ishi here. Not [pointing to his heart] here."

The denouement is predictable. Kroeber flees to a sabbatical in New
York, and Ishi sickens. Anxiously following his friend's deteriorating

condition from a distance, Kroeber discovers storage drawers filled with Indian skulls at the American Museum of Natural History. He rushes to send a telegram: "No Autopsy. Science can go to hell." There follows a genuinely disturbing shot of masked surgeons ("with great reverence in a spirit of scientific inquiry") cutting up Graham Greene. Kroeber returns to San Francisco, mute with pent-up grief. Alone in Ishi's room, holding a death mask made by Pope, he finally sings—first softly, then louder and louder, weeping and singing, in Yahi.

We cut to a final vision of Ishi, now in his homeland, striding easily along the trail of the dead. He looks strong, a heroic Indian at last, clad in skins, with bow and arrows. Ishi speaks to the camera: "I heard you singing." We see Kroeber standing just behind, relaxed and at ease.

"Are you tired?" Ishi turns. "No, I feel strong."

"Your people are waiting for you?" "Yes."

Ishi strides away toward the horizon. Kroeber: "Go to them."

"Is everybody hoppy?" This was the Yahi's favorite greeting on entering a room. Graham Greene's Ishi never smiles. If Kroeber and Pope are satirically exaggerated by Voigt and Stiers, Greene underplays his part. A sidelong glance or twitch of the eyebrow communicates bemusement, concern, puzzlement at the behavior of the white people. His mystical/emotional core emerges in the struggle with his anthropologist alter ego. And aside from the outburst of weeping for his dead sister and lost tribe, Ishi is the impassive Indian of American stereotype. Strong in his attachment to his people and his values, he knows exactly who he is. With long hair, classic features, few words . . . And he looks good in a suit.

Ultimately *The Last of His Tribe,* despite some pointed, mostly comic, moments, comes down to stereotypes and a predictable catharsis. The anthropologist is the soulless white man. The emotionally grounded child of nature puts up with Big Chiep's boy-scientist excesses and clumsy good will, in the end teaching him how to feel. This gift to a white man who knows a lot, but understands little, appears to be Ishi's real purpose on his detour through San Francisco on the way to a happy reunion with his lost family. *The Last of His Tribe* thus unites the "eco-hero" narrative with another version of the reconciliation story of cross-cultural "friendship," psychologically repackaged as a romantic struggle of reason and feeling. What any of this has to do with real individuals is, of course, highly questionable.

As a fictional exercise, the film develops the familiar themes of heroism and healing. White people, particularly the men, are often misguided, sometimes silly. Ishi is never silly. Kroeber finally accepts what the Indian has to teach. And so the anthropologist's somewhat plaintive early comment to the survivor of genocide that "not all white men are alike" turns out to be true. Reconciliation after genocide is possible. The exile's return, virile and whole, rejoining his ancestors, can be read as an allegory of contemporary repatriation movements.

> Fantasy, which creates a world, must be strictly coherent to its own terms . . . This is probably one of the reasons why fantasy is so acceptable to children, and even when frightening may give the reader reassurance: it has rules. It asserts a universe that, in some way, makes sense.
> —Ursula K. Le Guin, "Plausibility in Fantasy" (posted on her personal website)

It is revealing to compare the HBO film, a historical fiction, with Theodora Kroeber's retelling destined for schoolchildren. Both versions dramatically reshape the documented story. *Ishi: Last of His Tribe* (1964) is a novella that might best be classified as "pedagogical fantasy." It supplies a rich traditional life for the isolated Yahi, offering young readers a lesson in ethnographic cultural relativism. This retelling also supplies a female companion for the young Ishi, thinking, perhaps, that girl readers would need someone to identify with. In San Francisco the adolescent Saxton Pope Jr., who went along on the Deer Creek field trip, emerges as Ishi's devoted companion and is a major source of narrative perspective. The tale's happy ending is complete: "Ishi lived for many moons, a museum man among museum men. Death came to him as he wished—with his friends in the museum-watgurwa" (208). Ishi is mourned and buried with reverence; everyone understands that he has rejoined his family. Tuberculosis and autopsies are not, it seems, appropriate for young readers. The whole story takes on an exotic, slightly dreamy feeling. San Francisco becomes "the edge of the world." The use of Yahi names throughout reinforces the effect. By adopting the perspective of a stranger in the white world Theodora Kroeber challenges her readers to step outside their everyday reality.

The youth version reads like much contemporary young adult fantasy. (It is hard not to feel the presence of Ursula K. Le Guin, who, as we know from interviews, discussed the project extensively with her mother and was, in the early 1960s, just coming into her own as a writer of fantastic fiction.) There are obvious "coming of age" aspects to the retelling: the young Ishi receives a troubling "power dream" that tells him he will go, one day, into the world of the Saldu, where he will discover that not all white people are bad, and where he will teach them. He resists his calling, but in the latter part of the book embraces the mission, confident that it is the will of Coyote and of his family. We have already seen this idea of Ishi's mission to educate, even to save, the dominant society articulated in native contexts. Orin Starn (2004: 250–254) observes its critical, utopic potential. And in James Freeman's romantic novel *Ishi's Journey,* the last Yahi dreams very explicit instructions: "Your family wishes you to teach the Saldu what our people have learned. We want the white ones to know what they have destroyed, so they will learn that to kill the animals and the land is to kill themselves" (1992: 124).

Healer, teacher, missionary . . . Ishi's life must have had a coherent purpose. He cannot have been simply a piece of historical flotsam that washed up in a museum.

Ishi: Last of His Tribe was an instant commercial success, becoming required reading in the California schools for decades. According to Karl Kroeber (2004: xx), his mother struggled over the writing and always felt uncomfortable with the outcome. The project had in effect been forced on her by publishers who threatened to produce their own youth version of Ishi's story if she declined the task. To avoid a travesty, Theodora Kroeber made a sustained and earnest effort to bring ethnographic wisdom and cross-cultural identification to young readers. When the book is viewed as a kind of fantasy, readers like me can forgive the liberties taken in making Ishi's story more coherent and meaningful. But ultimately the tale is hard to read: sentimental with all the lucid, hard edges smoothed out. I have encountered people who, when I recommend *Ishi in Two Worlds,* think they have read it. But on further inquiry it seems they are dimly remembering something they encountered in fifth grade.

It may be worth observing that Ishi's special bond with young people is a motif recurring throughout his ramifying story. There was something irresistibly childlike about this man in his fifties: his apparent helplessness and simplicity, his hesitations and enthusiasms. Ishi was, it seems, popular with children at the museum, often giving them the arrowheads he made in public every Sunday. He willingly "played Indian" with young boys (Sackman 2010: 94–95). This complicity is central to Theodora Kroeber's pedagogical version, where Ishi remains youthful throughout the story and where Saxton Pope Jr. is a point of

identification for young white readers. This adolescent boy was memorably photographed by Alfred Kroeber on the ethnographic camping
trip, grasping Ishi's long hair in the rushing waters of Deer Creek. He
also turns up as a key narrator in Freeman's novel. With Ishi as a guide,
it's good to play Indian. A surviving tale from the time of Ishi's concealment, as relayed by Orin Starn, partakes of this desire:

> The Speegle homestead was located by Deer Creek, a mere two
> miles upstream from the last Indian hideout at Grizzly Bear's
> Hiding Place. Marse and Della Speegle and their six children did
> not intrude downstream, especially during the salmon run when
> the Indians might be by the water. For their part, the Indians lim-
> ited their pilfering from the Speegle cabin to occasional basic sup-
> plies: they never broke dishes or otherwise ransacked the cabin as
> they sometimes did in their other forays. There are still Speegle
> descendants in the Chico area, and one perhaps wishful family
> legend even has it that nine-year-old Clyde Speegle met, swam,
> and learned deer calls from Ishi about 1910. (Starn 2004: 114; see
> also Burrill 2011: 83–87)

Two years after the HBO production, an altogether different rendition of
Ishi's story appeared, *Ishi: The Last Yahi* (1994). This full-length documentary by Jed Riffe and Pamela Roberts stays close to the historical
record assembled by Robert Heizer and Theodora Kroeber. Adding some
later historical and archaeological research, it inflects the narrative for
the 1990s. The film's central theme is not Ishi's relation with Kroeber
and the other "friends" in the museum, nor is it his ecological wisdom
and spiritual message. Instead, it explores his resilience and inventive-
ness, his response to unhealed trauma, and his journey's deeply enigmatic meaning. The film reopens wounds.

Riffe and Roberts make use of period photos and film footage, newspaper clippings, vice-over narration, spoken quotations from historical
figures, contemporary landscapes, "talking heads," and a recent expedition to rediscover the last Yahi refuge, "Bear's Hiding Place." The difficulty of communication with Ishi is always in view: the lack of fluency
by either party in the dialogues at the museum, and his partially translated or untranslatable Yahi stories and songs. Ishi is literally brought up

close in a series of shots that zoom in on photographs of his face. But any feeling of intimacy quickly gives way to the mystery of an illegible gaze. Throughout the film, serious attempts to render Ishi's experience and perspective bring us closer and also produce a sense of being lost in translation. Each increase in understanding opens new questions.

One of the film's most striking tactics is to combine Ishi's faint, crackling voice from the wax cylinder recordings with grainy images of land, sky, a railroad trip . . . plunging into a dark tunnel. A voice recites translated passages from Ishi's story of the Yahi journey to the land of the dead, one of his more accessible recordings. "They climb up into the sky. They go up . . ." But giving voice to Ishi in this way does not make him more humanly present. Beneath the rather surreal visual sequences and the translated words we hear a faint, scratchy voice on the wax cylinders. The acoustic/visual collage recurs at intervals, making us aware of what we are missing in the Yahi's experience and culture. As the documentary unfolds, its historical narrative takes on a mythic dimension. Ishi's life appears as a strange path through disrupted space and time, a route leading to the Yahi afterlife . . . perhaps. At his death, emaciated from tuberculosis, Ishi is anything but heroic. There is no happy ending, no family reunion or moral resolution.

Ishi: The Last Yahi keeps the history unresolved and the wound open. In contrast to *Ishi in Two Worlds,* the 1860s massacres (told in the words of the Indian-hunters themselves) are moved toward the end of the narration. These chilling flashbacks make it harder to leave the violence safely in the past. The Cherokee scholar Rayna Green comments acidly on Ishi's status as an anthropological prize, an uncontaminated Indian. Museum visitors expect something savage and find instead "the nice man in overalls." The anthropologist Thomas Buckley sees a "different sense of self and history" in Ishi's early response to personal questions: the long, mostly incomprehensible, "Wood Duck Story." And Brian Bibby tells coyote stories around a campfire near Grizzly Bear's Hiding Place, speculating that such tales may have prepared Ishi for life in San Francisco. With Coyote, who is both foolish and wise, anything can happen: in the white world people drink cloudy liquids, they fly in airplanes . . .

The film's anticolonial message comes through strongly in its historical portrayal of Manifest Destiny and in its lack of closure with respect to a

violent, racist past. The tragic fate of the Yahi, and Ishi's deferred trip to
the land of the dead, hang unresolved over the film. Ishi is given no special mission, no wisdom to deliver to the "modern world." *The Last Yahi*
sustains ambiguity (in its portrayal of anthropology and Kroeber, for
example) and confronts its audience, primarily non-Indians, with an
indigestible past. As for the future, it contents itself with what appears as
an afterthought: a short final text acknowledging the survival of Native
Californians. Produced in the early 1990s, the film would no doubt be
different if it were made today, featuring more contemporary Indian
voices (like Jed Riffe's subsequent documentaries on repatriation and
Indian gaming). The political and cultural movements of the intervening
decades have made this presence inescapable.

Ishi: The Last Yahi was screened at a conference hosted by Art Angle
and the Maidu repatriation committee at the Oroville Travelodge on
May 12, 2000. It provoked strong emotions among many of the Indians
present. An immediate reaction found the film "one-sided" and the language it contained "hurtful." One tribal leader said that the racism of
the historical quotations describing Indians as hardly human and the
graphic images and accounts of extermination forced her to leave the
room. She said she understood why the film was made, but it was very
hard to take. Another woman confirmed the history's rawness: "This is
close to our heart. It wasn't too long ago." And, she added, there is still
an anti-Indian atmosphere in Butte County. A man from the Pit River
tribe said that the images of extermination reminded him of his own
boarding school experience from the 1930s. He described beatings,
humiliations, being forbidden to speak his language. And it's still happening, he added. People say things that hurt a lot of Indian children.
Another woman expressed anger at the government's ongoing role in
determining tribal recognition, its denial of Indian peoples' right to say
who they are. (My notes, unfortunately, don't allow me to identify individual speakers with confidence, and my quotes and paraphrases are
approximations.)

Jed Riffe, who had been filming the reactions, put his camera aside to
say that this project "was more about us Anglos than about Ishi." And
he added that for him it had been a way of "unlearning" his own Texas
upbringing.

As the discussion developed, others suggested that the film needed to
balance its bleak message, adding materials to show "progress," "our government, our tribes, our intelligence . . ." There was widespread resistance

to ending Ishi's story in tragedy, his life a dead end. Summing up (and confirming, from a different perspective, Theodora Kroeber's conclusion), a Maidu woman saw an opportunity for healing—for recognizing that "we are all human beings." Native Americans need to understand, she said, that whites are human, with particular upbringings and limits. There's still a way to go. Racism persists. The wounds are still there. She recalled her grandfather's ordeal on a notorious forced march from his homeland to the Round Valley Reservation. She told of her current work on tribal history, getting to know dispersed cousins using genealogical tools she had learned about on her travels to England. She applauded the film. "Just add something at the end. Show that it didn't end there. The conference title has it right: 'Ishi: Past, Present and Future.'"

In his closing remarks, Art Angle identified Ishi's story with the history of all Indians in California. Ishi was brilliant, he said, with his amazing patience and grace, his ability to communicate, to go from one extreme to the other. When we complete his "reunification," the healing process will begin. Ishi was certainly at least part Maidu. Angle says he knows this from the elders. But repatriation is not about separate tribes, about Ishi belonging to this or that group. Angle expresses complete confidence in the Redding and Pit River people to do the right thing in reburying the remains. Through this homecoming "we can come together in healing."

The event at Oroville made it clear that the simultaneous bleeding and healing in Ishi's story would continue—that it was a kind of progress.

A powerful image expresses this bleeding and healing. *Fringe* was created in 2008 by the Canadian First Nations artist Rebecca Belmore. A billboard installed above the Montreal office of the Cree Grand Council, the eight-by-twenty-four-foot color photograph appears from a distance as simply a seminude reclining female figure. Nearer, one sees a roughly sutured wound, traversing the woman's exposed back (Figure 4.16). It looks like dripping blood, but on closer inspection the "blood" is composed of red beads strung on white thread. A horrible gash has been closed using the traditional Anishinabe beadwork of Belmore's tradition mixed with visible white material.

An ironic reference to "odalisque" traditions of European painting, *Fringe* interrupts an aesthetic gaze, or indeed any desire to make the body

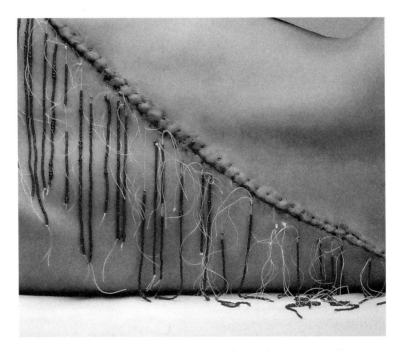

Figure 4.16.   Fringe (detail). Photo/installation by Rebecca Belmore. (Courtesy of the artist.)

whole. The damage depicted here can never be completely repaired. A terrible scar remains. But the disfigurement has now become a kind of violent beauty. And the reclining figure—whose marked skin recalls James Luna's scars in *Artifact Piece*—is very much alive. As Belmore has said,

> Some people look at this reclining figure and think that it is a cadaver, but I look at it and I don't see that. I see it as a wound that is on the mend. It wasn't self-inflicted, but nonetheless, it is bearable. She can sustain it. So it is a very simple scenario. She will get up and go on, but she will carry that mark with her. (quoted in Ritter 2008: 65)

Another roughly sutured wound concerns the University of California, Berkeley, Anthropology Department. During the spring of 1999, as the repatriation process gathered steam, the department debated a proposed public statement. They were forced to grapple seriously with the legacy of their founding ancestor, the "Big Chiep." (California Indian nicknames frequently poke fun, and the title was probably a mix of respect and humor.) Now this figure had become an overburdened symbol: Kroeber the leader and protector, Kroeber the scientist, Kroeber the friend, Kroeber the man of his time, Kroeber the betrayer. A complex individual was made to stand for liberal colonialism, for an embattled anthropology, for postcolonial reconciliation, for tragic historical contradictions. Stepping back, we can see the critique, the defense, and the healing of Alfred Kroeber within a broad historical transformation. Under pressure from the politics of indigenous revival, anthropologists and archaeologists have been feeling their way to new visions of scholarship and ethical/political engagement. This involves confronting and working through a deeply ambivalent history.

The complicity of anthropology with Western colonialism and with the apparently irreversible expansion of the global capitalist system has been frequently noted and debated. It is worth repeating a trenchant statement by Claude Lévi-Strauss:

Anthropology is not a dispassionate science like astronomy, which springs from the contemplation of things at a distance. It is the outcome of a historical process which has made the larger part of mankind subservient to the other, and during which millions of innocent human beings have had their resources plundered and their institutions and beliefs destroyed, whilst they themselves were ruthlessly killed, thrown into bondage, and contaminated by diseases they were unable to resist. Anthropology is the daughter of this era of violence: its capacity to assess more objectively the facts pertaining to the human condition reflects, on the epistemological level, a state of affairs in which one part of mankind treated the other as an object." (1966: 126)

Lévi-Strauss names a set of material and epistemological structures that have, for at least the past three centuries, determined European and North American anthropological research and claims to objectivity. "Determined" is not meant in a mechanical sense, suggesting that anthropologists have always seen the people they study as objects, or that their work necessarily takes the side of dominion. Determination is a matter of pressures and limits, historical horizons within and against which people act with constrained freedom (Williams 1977). Anthropology's changing, sometimes contradictory practices have always been historically aligned and structurally constrained. Alfred Kroeber's contradictions and his complex legacy need to be understood in this materialist but dialectical and open-ended way. As a founder of anthropological institutions in the state's new public university he both resisted and perpetuated a dominant settler-colonial system.

Theodora Kroeber, writing as her husband's biographer, pictures him as he took up his vocation:

> Kroeber stood on Parnassus with Boas, who pointed out to him the land below, its shadowed parts and its sunny places alike virgin to the ethnologist. Virgin but fleeting—this was the urgency and the poetry of Boas' message. Everywhere over the land were virgin languages, brought to their polished and idiosyncratic perfection of grammar and syntax without benefit of a single recording scratch of stylus on papyrus or stone; living languages orally learned and transmitted and about to die with their last speakers. Everywhere there were to be discovered Ways of Life, many, many ways. There were gods and created worlds unlike other gods and worlds, with extended relationships and values and ideals and dreams unlike anything known or imagined elsewhere, all soon to be forever lost—part of the human condition, part of the beautiful heartbreaking history of man. The time was late; the dark forces of invasion had almost done their ignorant work of annihilation. To the field then! With notebook and pencil, record, record, record. Rescue from historylessness all languages still living, all cultures. (1970: 51)

That intrepid men of science should naturally be the caretakers of virgin cultures in distress is, of course, a gendered vision no longer validated by historical common sense. Theodora Kroeber's gently ironic tone registers a certain distance taken from the self-appointed rescuers on the mountaintop. But she affirms the reality, and also the inevitability, of the emergency as understood by Boas and her husband. Her own story of Ishi would be infused with this same bittersweet sense of the "beautiful heartbreaking history of man."

In its time, Boasian cultural relativism—a belief that every way of life and mode of human expression was equally complex and valuable—could be a potent weapon against racial pseudoscience and evolutionist hierarchies. Its message of tolerance and understanding was significantly anticolonial, while also part of a system, a mode of liberal, often paternalistic, comprehension. In its developmental historicism, its assumption that small, "tribal" societies were destined to vanish, the Boasian project did nothing to disturb the settler-colony's self-fulfilling prophecy. While valuing other cultures, it preserved the scientist's claim to a superior, more inclusive perspective firmly located in the modern West. (Theodora Kroeber's metaphorical "Parnassus" would become literal—San Francisco's Parnassus Heights—location of the research institutions where Ishi was cared for and observed.) Yet when he opposed Ishi's autopsy Alfred Kroeber famously wrote: "Tell them science can go to hell." There were, he recognized, humane limits to scientific objectivity, the will (and right) to know. Kroeber's contradictions are good to think with.

The Berkeley Anthropology Department's discussions were triggered by the repatriation movement and by the discovery that Alfred Kroeber had, indeed, given Ishi's brain to science. A public statement, initially signed by fifteen members of the faculty, spoke of the Ishi episode as "a regrettable part of our history." The relations of Ishi and the anthropologists at the museum were, they wrote, "complex: friendships entwined with academic ambitions, resulting in considerable insensitivity to Ishi's personal and medical needs." Kroeber "failed to prevent an autopsy," and he "inexplicably" shipped the brain to Hrdlicka's collection. The text went on to address Ishi's wider symbolism in the context of anthropology's changing understanding of its relationship with colonialism. "What happened to Ishi's body, in the name of science, was a perversion of our core anthropological values . . . We are ashamed of our department's role, albeit unintentional, in the final betrayal of Ishi, a man who had already lost all that was dear to him at the hands of Western colonizers." The text concluded with a call for wide discussion of the larger issues of anthropology and its relations with historical and actual California Indian cultures.

The draft statement drew resistance from various members of the department (and at least one of the original signers expressed ambivalence about its tendency to dwell only on the negative aspects of salvage anthropology and Ishi's last years). George Foster, who had come to Berkeley in 1935 and who knew Alfred Kroeber and other actors in the drama, led a protest against the draft. He and others argued that to speak of a "betrayal" was unfair and anachronistic. In a memo, he wrote that in the circumstances of the times, Ishi was lucky to be housed at the anthropology museum. He received loyal support and state-of-the-art medical care. As for salvage anthropology, Foster recalled his own research experiences: the eagerness of the Indians he worked with to record their language and stories. The founding traditions of the department, which valued native cultures, were far from colonialist. They represented something to be proud of and required no apology.

In the ensuing discussions, many historical details were debated, a range of different opinions expressed. Nancy Scheper-Hughes, principal drafter of the original text, was convinced that the department needed publicly to turn a corner in its relations with Native Californians by confronting an ambiguous and disturbing past. Nothing short of an apology could begin to clear the air and make possible changes of practice that would lead to postcolonial cooperation and understanding. (Scheper-Hughes was influenced by her research in South Africa, whose Truth and Reconciliation Commission helped to close deep wounds.) As things heated up, *Lingua Franca*, a forum for academic controversies, picked up the story. Karl Kroeber, son of Alfred and Theodora and a distinguished professor of English and Native American literatures, wrote to the chair of the Berkeley department vehemently protesting the scapegoating of his father. He also commented on the hypocrisy of a department taking a moralistic position in this instance when it had itself all but abandoned work with Native Americans. (Notable exceptions are the collaborative California archaeology of Kent Lightfoot and Nelson Graburn's long involvement with Inuit.) In the pages of the *Los Angeles Times* (October 8, 2000), the columnist Alexander Cockburn casually included Alfred Kroeber in a sweeping condemnation of anthropologists' "depredations" as agents of colonialism and apologists for genocide. In the public eye, positions polarized: Scheper-Hughes the radical critic versus George Foster the entrenched conservative. In fact, there was a spectrum of opinions as the department debated an ambiguous legacy. The final compromise text of 1999 referred to "a troubling chapter in our history." Relations between Ishi and the anthropologists were "complex and contradictory." The first version's language was softened. Instead of "Kroeber failed to prevent an autopsy . . ." the statement now read, "Despite Kroeber's lifelong devotion to California Indians and his friendship with Ishi, he failed in his efforts to honor Ishi's wishes not to be autopsied . . ." The department strongly supported returning Ishi's remains to the care of California Indians while declining to apologize for the work of Kroeber or the assumptions of salvage anthropology. Scheper-Hughes, speaking only for the original signers, read the more critical first draft at a meeting in Sacramento where legislators were climbing on the repatriation bandwagon. Some expressed outrage at the university's apparent insensitivity (the authorities had initially appeared to be stonewalling, claimed there was no evidence of Ishi's brain being stored anywhere—evidence that was soon discovered by Orin Starn buried in Berkeley's Bancroft Library). In the months that followed, the debate died down, and repatriation moved forward. Karen Biestman aptly observes that "Ishi had . . . personalized the debate between research and human interests and challenged scientists to think and act beyond institutional boundaries." The survivor's ecological and spiritual mission to white society took a new turn. "More than any advocate, activist, lawyer, scholar, or politician who has invoked his image . . . Ishi became a catalyst for accountability and integrity" (Biestman 2003: 153). A similar sense is reflected in Nancy Scheper-Hughes's (2003) final, critically nuanced account of the controversy's significance for anthropology.

Ishi's repatriation coincided, at times awkwardly, with the centennial anniversary of the Berkeley Anthropology Department. A year-long lecture series, which included Ursula K. Le Guin and Orin Starn, culminated in a two-day event, "Alfred Kroeber and His Legacy: A Centennial Conference" (April 12–13, 2002). The event was complemented by other exhibits at the university—the Bancroft Library ("The Foundations of Anthropology in California"); the Hearst Museum ("A Century of Collection"); and the Doe Library ("In the Field," an exhibition showing Berkeley anthropologists in exotic field sites). The conference had retrospective and forward-looking aspects. At its opening session, devoted to "Historical Highlights of the Department," Karl Kroeber offered a spirited defense of anthropological "curiosity" (against postmodern cynicism) spiced with vignettes of his father's eclectic interests and sense of humor. Piero Matthey traced the friendship at Berkeley of Robert Lowie and Bronislaw Malinowski. And Nancy Rockafellar assessed the postwar contribution of George Foster to the emerging field of medical anthropology. The tone, appropriately, was celebratory—the difficult Ishi discussions nowhere in evidence. Art Angle, noted in the program as an honored guest, sat in the front row.

The next morning "distinguished alumni" of the department recalled their student years (when *was* the best time to be at Berkeley?) or described their current work. Exemplifying "Decades of Excellence," they covered an impressive range of critical topics: from religious movements in China, to development politics in post–Soviet Russia; from resistance to corporate power in U.S. journalism, to collaborative archaeology among native communities in Alaska. In the afternoon, "Anthropology and the World," organized by Laura Nader, looked beyond a focus on Berkeley anthropology to explore many current dimensions of politically engaged work.

The Berkeley Anthropology Department framed its first century as Alfred Kroeber's legacy, choosing for its publicity a virile (some said Indiana Jones–style) photo from 1912. Its present research was portrayed as forward looking and diverse (despite predictable grumbling that the canonical "four fields" had not been equitably covered). This spirit of eclecticism, and a disinclination to look back—according to Kroeber's children—was true to the founding father's spirit. In any event, Ishi's ambivalent legacy was nowhere addressed in the departmental program; and the critical issue of relations with Native Californians went undeveloped in the Hearst Museum's one-hundred-year history. Orin Starn had given a lecture in December on the Ishi repatriation and its consequences for a still-decolonizing anthropology, and that was enough.

Not quite.

During the Friday speeches, Art Angle sat quietly in the front row. As the room broke noisily into the reception, Nancy Scheper-Hughes claimed the floor and, with some difficulty, quieted the crowd. She introduced Angle, who read a prepared statement, asserting among other things that Ishi was not a wild man, was a gifted language learner, a resourceful survivor, was half Maidu, and was on his way to join his southern kin when he was captured. He ended by reminding the anthropologists of their ongoing obligations to California Indians, given all they had learned from Ishi.

As soon as Art Angle finished speaking the party hastily resumed.

A few years before the centennial, Berkeley geographer Gray Brechin published *Imperial San Francisco* with the University of California Press: a trenchant, disturbing account of mining, racial violence, water politics, and corruption in the founding of the capitalist, settler state of California. Brechin's final chapter explores the explicitly imperial visions that ani-

Figure 4.17. Hearst Museum poster, 2012. (Photograph by James Clifford.)

mated the leadership, funding, and campus design of the University of California at Berkeley around 1900. Phoebe Apperson Hearst, a passionate traveler and collector of antiquities (whose husband, George, had made an immense fortune in mining and whose son, William Randolph, would become a legendary media magnate), supported much of the university's dramatic expansion. Working with Alfred Kroeber she built the anthropology museum, a nucleus of the emerging department, where Ishi spent his last years. The patronage continues: only recently the museum, now located in Berkeley, was renamed to capture new funding from the Hearst Foundation. Accompanied by grumbling in the department, "The Lowie" became "The Hearst." On the museum's signature poster, Ishi is sandwiched between a primitive mask and an ancient Greek funeral portrait.

The juxtaposition of Ishi's image with the name Hearst opens up another level of reflection on the ambivalent history of institutionalized anthropology in California. After 1900, the modern science of man would salvage and give value to cultures that had been violently disrupted by mining and its social consequences. And significantly, a mining fortune would become the material source of the department's early flourishing. To say this is not to assert an automatic, or functional, complicity between anthropology and predatory capitalism, but rather to open a discussion of the institutional, structural constraints within and against which the humanistic work of the founders was pursued. There would be no place in the historical portion of the Berkeley department's centennial for such a discussion. No doubt it seemed inappropriate: there are times for celebration and good feelings.

Art Angle's irritating question about ongoing accountability to California Indians also found no immediate response. Today, Berkeley Anthropology shows little inclination to refocus on indigenous California. It has moved on to more global concerns. The place at Berkeley where the research traditions of Kroeber and Co. have been most positively reinvented is the Linguistics Department, founded in its modern form by Sapir's student Mary Haas. Inspired by her example, generations of students have documented vulnerable languages. William Bright and William Shipley, for example, would earn recognition as respected friends of the tribes (Karuk and Maidu) they studied and supported over many years. More recently, through the work of Leanne Hinton, Berkeley Linguistics has become involved with native activism in California around language preservation and renewal. Ishi's recorded stories are still, laboriously, being translated.

The chronically underfunded, spatially cramped, Hearst Museum has recently begun to develop cooperative relationships with California Indian groups. The history of its representation of Ishi, in artifacts and photographs, has been comprehensively discussed by Ira Jacknis (2008). In 1962, the museum presented a display of artifacts "collected" by the surveying party from the Yahi's last hiding place, along with many arrowheads, drills, and other objects made by Ishi at the museum; the display was accompanied by photographs and contemporary documents. The explanatory texts were largely drawn from Theodora Kroeber's recently published book. The immense popularity of *Ishi in Two Worlds* ensured a steady stream of visitors over the years, and throughout the 1970s and 1980s the museum was seldom without some kind of Ishi display. These generally followed Theodora Kroeber's canonical interpretation.

In the early 1990s the perspective shifted, in *Ishi and the Invention of Yahi Culture,* curated by the newly appointed historian/anthropologist, Ira Jacknis. Rather than portraying the last survivor of a lost culture, this new approach stressed adaptation and innovation: qualities of traditional California Indian cultures that were exemplified by Ishi in San Francisco. Ishi had already been making arrowheads from glass bottles while in hiding, but in the museum he fabricated beautiful, long—and ultimately dysfunctional—specimens. He also enthusiastically used glue and paints in his arrow making, as well as cotton string and other new materials. His arrowheads drew from the styles of neighboring tribes (Shackley 2000). Jacknis's perspective was inspired by anthropological theories of cultural "invention" (Wagner 1975) and by Herbert Luthin's and Leanne Hinton's interpretations of Ishi's recorded texts. In 2002, the museum took another new turn, by creating a permanent Native California Cultures gallery that "dissolve[d] the special status of Ishi and place[d] his objects into the context of the rest of California Indian material culture." This proved frustrating for visitors, sometimes from abroad, seeking to rediscover Ishi. (Jacknis 2008: 82) Ishi's iconic status was both a blessing and a burden for the Hearst Museum, given its limited display space. Jacknis aptly compares the predicament to that of singers with a "hit" song audiences must always hear, and that they omit at their peril (87).

Until now, the changing displays at the Hearst have been made without ongoing collaboration with Indian communities. Despite the goodwill of some staff members, a legacy of suspicion has developed—the result of an insular attitude and slowness to complete the collection inventories required by NAGPRA (the Native American Graves Protection and Repatriation Act of 1990). Now things are changing, and a new director, Mari Lyn Salvador, is actively building community links while establishing a Native American advisory council. When a major renovation is complete, the new Ishi exhibit will reflect Indian perspectives and ongoing cooperative relationships with California communities. Or so it is hoped. Mistrust of the university persists, fueled—as the present essay goes to press—by outrage over a play performed on campus. An avant-garde San Francisco playwright makes free with the Ishi story in ways deeply offensive to Indians in the audience. There are protests, apologies, explanations. The Internet hums . . .

In the fraught border zones of the university and indigenous resurgence, the wound called "Ishi" may never permanently close. Nor should it. However, the burial of his remains did bring a widely shared sense of relief—feelings of healing and even forgiveness. At the Mt. Lassen celebration of Ishi's homecoming the afternoon talk circle was followed by a feast, including salmon cooked on an open fire, provided by Yurok from the coast. Then by firelight another, informal, talk circle formed.

In an emotional exchange, Nancy Scheper-Hughes shared her understanding of what had gone wrong after Ishi's death. Expressing regret
as a Berkeley anthropologist, she implicated herself metaphorically as
"Kroeber's granddaughter." An older woman, a leader of the Pit River
tribe, rose to urge respect for the ancestors, Indian and white, who "had
their reasons." She then offered Scheper-Hughes's "grandfather" forgiveness "from the heart of the people." The healing of Alfred Kroeber
(that inexhaustible symbol of anthropology's tensions) was achieved.
Temporarily.

A decade later, denunciations of Berkeley Anthropology were once
again heard in Sacramento. This time a well-organized movement would
agitate for the reburial of thousands of Native American ancestral
remains: research collections held in storage under the Hearst Gymnasium
next door to Kroeber Hall and the Hearst Museum (Platt 2011: 171).

Alfred Kroeber's legacy for anthropology remains ambivalent in strong,
ongoing ways. This is particularly visible in the transformation, the
repurposing, of the "salvage" tradition.

Kroeber combined Boasian historicism with a metatheory of cultural
evolution. Cultures, which needed to be described with scrupulous
empiricism and understood relativistically, followed a linear trajectory
of growth toward ever-greater complexity and large-scale "civilizations."
In this perspective, the innovations and compromises of individuals were
relatively unimportant. And the small, "simple" societies of an older
California were ultimately destined, by structural processes of cultural
growth, to be subsumed by larger entities. The specifics of local transition were less important than the overall shape of cultural history. Thus
Kroeber focused almost exclusively on a reconstructed precontact native
culture, and showed little inclination to study the violent, but also inventive, history of culture contacts that had shaped the Indian people who
were his interlocutors. By assuming a stable anthropological "object" in
a traditional, cultural past his publications tended to make actual,
changing Indians into remnants.

Thomas Buckley, whose exemplary study of Kroeber is nourished by
fieldwork and advocacy with Northern California tribes, shows that a
less idealist history, and an attention to contemporary societies in transition, can be found in the writings of Kroeber's colleague T. T. Waterman
(Buckley 1996). We might also add, for contrast, Jaime de Angulo's wild,

poignant stories of his research among the Pit River Indians, Ishi's northern neighbors, *Indians in Overalls* (1950). Kroeber would not have considered this memoir of fieldwork to be a contribution to anthropological science, given its subjectivism and also because, as de Angulo wryly noted in a footnote, "Decent anthropologists don't associate with drunkards who go rolling in ditches with shamans" (53). In the early years of documenting California languages, Kroeber had worked with a wide range of amateurs. But a concern to professionalize anthropology during the twenties and thirties led him to distance himself from the salvage collecting of energetic eccentrics like de Angulo or J. P. Harrington (Leeds-Hurwitz 2005).

Of course Kroeber was not alone in assuming a relentless direction to history, a vision that could only view the adaptations of surviving Native Californians as degraded forms of an authenticity in terminal decline. In his monumental *Handbook of the Indians of California* (1925) he synthesized twenty years of cultural-linguistic survey work (Long 1998). This collective research remains a major resource: masses of firsthand documentary material on languages and customs preserved in the Bancroft Library at Berkeley. However, the legacy of the *Handbook* has been negative for many groups of California Indians, scattered and disorganized but now reconnecting and unable to achieve state or federal tribal recognition. The unambiguous "death sentences" (as they are sometimes called today) pronounced by Kroeber for groups who seemed to have vanished, continue to haunt their offspring who currently struggle, in a changed political climate, to live as recognized Indians (Field 1999).

The *Handbook* reflects, and to an extent freezes, the historical perspective of triumphant, late nineteenth- and early twentieth-century settler-California, a particularly depressing time for native peoples. Kroeber himself was exhausted by his two decades of intense research and institution building. In the wake of a profound midlife crisis, to which Ishi's death certainly contributed, he turned toward new topics, away from California. His was, by many accounts, a restless intellect, disinclined to retrospection, always moving on. Kroeber did not, however, abandon his original research relations. Having married the younger Theodora Kracaw, a recent widow, Kroeber spent long summers at the family's Napa Valley ranch with his children and in regular contact with visiting Indian researchers. Two family friends visited regularly: Ishi's San Francisco companion, Juan Dolores, who continued his work on

Papago, and Kroeber's long-term Yurok collaborator, Robert Spott, with whom he coauthored *Yurok Narratives* (1942). (*Yurok Myths* would appear posthumously in 1978.) In retirement, influenced by his younger Berkeley colleague Robert Heizer and by the changing times, Kroeber testified at length, as principal expert witness on behalf of Indian claimants in the California Indian Land Claims Commission hearings of the mid-1950s. In this he pioneered a new role for academic anthropologists.

The earlier "salvage" project—which nourished the court testimony, as shown by Kroeber's meticulous preparatory notes preserved in the Bancroft Library—was generating unanticipated outcomes. The work had been authorized by a sense of emergency. Many groups had to be contacted, linguistic and oral materials recorded, before crucial elders disappeared and their knowledge was lost. Kroeber conducted short-term ethnography, essentially survey work, all over California, but developed a deeper, ongoing relationship with the Yurok. Buckley provides a nuanced sense of Kroeber's reputation among members of the tribe. He unearths evidence of hostility and resistance to his research due, in part, to the legacies of conquest Kroeber declined to explore in his writing. Waterman's research in the area provides a revealing counterpoint: what Kroeber notoriously called a "little history of pitiful events," Waterman termed "white invasion."

Buckley invokes "two kinds of salvage." Kroeber's purified, precontact California reconstructions implied the nonexistence of valid contemporary cultures. The members of these very cultures, while resenting his assumptions, have nonetheless adopted many of his ideas of authenticity. In the eyes of contemporary traditionalists, native culture is defined "in the Boasian terms most tellingly introduced, in California, by Kroeber: language and music, traditional narratives, religious rituals, and material culture. Yuroks, for instance, have long used an objectified understanding of "culture" both in constructing their own accounts of the Yurok past . . . and in the continuing struggle for cultural survival that has, so far, been successful to a degree that would perhaps surprise Kroeber himself" (Buckley 1996: 293). In a second process of salvage (translation and rearticulation), the documentary collections of Kroeber and his generation "provide those most actively engaged in 'saving' their own Yurok culture with a virtual textbook, however selectively it is consulted" (293–294). Kroeber might well have viewed this partial "culture salvaged from the wreckage of modern history" as without a future. But

Buckley pointedly concludes with a quotation from "a Yurok Elder dissenting from the majority Yurok opinion of 'anthros' . . ."

> Thank God for that good Doctor Kroeber and Doctor Waterman and Gifford and those other good white doctors from Berkeley who came here to study us. If they hadn't taken an interest in us and come up here and written it all down we wouldn't know a thing today about who we really are. (294)

Kroeber's collecting was intended to contribute to the historical and scientific record of human diversity, not the survivance toolkit of twenty-first-century tribes. With pointed irony, Terri Castañeda (2002) describes how a "disappearing" salvage anthropology is itself salvaged in native-run archives and museums. New kinds of collection give life to old texts and artifacts, contributing to local histories and the emergence of inter-tribal identities.

It is hard to know whether those elders who in the early years of the century cooperated with the ethnographers and linguists in fact hoped for something like this "second life." In the wake of massive disruptions, the knowledge preserved in the white man's notebook must have seemed like a note in a bottle, a message to an unknown future. Perhaps the anthropologists' interest was a welcome affirmation—offering respect in an intercultural context that had previously shown little comprehension of their way of life. Others who resisted the intrusive "anthros" were no doubt holding on to a degree of control in the face of violent and potentially overwhelming pressures. We can't know all the specific motivations that helped and hindered salvage research. Personal relationships of trust counted for a good deal, as always. There were things to keep to oneself, and things to pass on, in the right circumstances. The feelings engaged were certainly complex and often contradictory. As Jennifer Kramer has recently argued, both giving and holding back, performing culture and keeping it secret, have been critical for the continuing, relational life of native societies in North America (Kramer 2006).

Who was Ishi addressing when he filled hundreds of wax cylinders with urgent recitations (Jacknis 2003)? And for whom did he keep other things unsaid? At the very least he enjoyed speaking Yahi and telling old, familiar stories for people who, though largely uncomprehending, at least took them seriously. Almost a century later, working with a few relatively well-recorded and translated stories Ishi told to Edward Sapir, the linguists Herbert Luthin and Leanne Hinton (2003) have come up with some very intriguing clues. In the story "Coyote Rapes His Sister" (which they compare to a Northern Yana version recorded earlier by Sam Batwi), Ishi gives unusual prominence to long, detailed recitations of daily life activities. Telling the Coyote story, he spends half the tale describing the preparation of acorns. It is almost as if the "story proper" became an appendage to a vastly expanded background—a kind of experiential, mnemonic "world." Long, intricate descriptions of everyday activities are Ishi's signature: and the linguists go so far as to say that the style is so pronounced that it makes Ishi unique in the Native American recorded canon. They argue that his idiosyncratic manner goes far beyond anything he might have produced in response to anthropologists' demands for documentary detail.

Why did Ishi speak this way? We should be wary, I think, of assuming that he was addressing an Indian "posterity." There were no longer any young listeners capable of understanding his Yahi. And Ishi could hardly have imagined the present moment in which his words have taken on the value of a recovered "heritage." He may simply have wanted things he knew and valued to somehow persist and be recognized in changing times. Luthin and Hinton suggest that the daily activities, so important to Ishi, were what kept the diminishing band of Yahi going for decades. His return to these in his storytelling was—in an emotionally rich, non-pejorative sense—nostalgic. He loved recalling these activities in an intimate, resonant language. Ishi's recollection is surely best seen not as an act of preservation, or of transmission, but as a performance in a particular here and now. Recent critical studies have focused on ethnographic and linguistic collecting as a performative social process (Sarris 1993; Dinwoodie 1999; Cruikshank 1998). In this perspective, Ishi's enthusiastic work as an informant seems less a matter of preserving traditions for the salvage "record" than of enacting them in new social contexts—a new gathering up of the self in a mode of engagement.

What sense did the past have for the refugee? Did he conceive of time in the categories of past, present, and future? Did he think historically, sharing Kroeber's sense of an ending, a feeling that his past life was now finished? Perhaps he moved in time differently, edging into a novel present with wariness and curiosity, while drawing strength and reassurance from practiced skills and old stories, from the cultural body, the *habitus,* he brought with him from Deer Creek to the place he would call "home" in San Francisco.

Ishi may have had no future, but he was going somewhere.

Utopia

What was and what may be lie, like children whose faces we cannot
see, in the arms of silence. All we ever have is here, now.
  —Ursula K. Le Guin, *Always Coming Home*

Ursula K. Le Guin, who was born in 1929, never met Ishi. And she heard
nothing of him until the mid-1950s when talk of a biography began to
surface in the family. Mother and daughter emerged as writers around
the same time and were, as the daughter put it, "age mates in the art." Le
Guin heard a lot about writing *Ishi in Two Worlds,* and she was an
important interlocutor for her mother in conceiving the version for
schoolchildren. One finds distant echoes of Ishi's story throughout Le
Guin's oeuvre—but no recognizable Ishi figure, unless one counts a wild
mountain lion who crawls into a neighbor's Napa Valley backyard to
die, as told in the short story "May's Lion" (1989).

Le Guin's oeuvre is permeated by the Native Californian stories and
voices she learned from individual Indians and ethnographic texts. She
translates and transmutes the land, creatures, and history of Northern
California. These are not, of course, her only inspirations. The daughter
of Alfred and Theodora Kroeber was brought up in a cosmopolitan environment filled with intellectual talk, books, and foreign visitors; her
work draws on folklore and popular culture, Taoism, post-sixties feminism, and environmentalism. Of course it's foolish to reduce an imaginative writer to her "sources." And there can be no question of reading her
works as *romans à clef*—for example, viewing the anthropologists and
cross-cultural interpreters that populate her fiction as avatars of her
father. Yet at broader allegorical, analytic, and meditative levels, Le
Guin often returns to knots and themes central to Ishi's world: colonial
domination and miscomprehension, the compromised but real possibilities of cross-cultural understanding, complicity and friendship at fraught
frontiers, preservation of traditions and the dynamics of change, the
communal arts of living in balance with others and in scale with the
environment.

During the Berkeley Anthropology Department's centennial celebration, in 2001, Le Guin delivered a talk that was, she said, the nearest
thing to a written "memoir" she had ever permitted herself. She wanted
to set the record straight about her father. Referring, no doubt, to the
HBO film, as well as to notions in the air during the repatriation process, she dismissed "the emotionally stunted scientist exploiting the

noble savage bit." Alfred Kroeber valued friendships with Indians, she insisted, and these were based on mutual respect and restraint. He mistrusted whites who claimed special affinities or spiritual connections. If after Ishi's death he spoke little of him it was because the grief was profound and he lacked appropriate words. Le Guin recalled her father's midlife crisis and his engagement with Freudian psychoanalysis, which also, she believed, failed to provide the language he needed.

She spoke warmly of her "Indian uncles," Juan Dolores and Robert Spott, who were long-term visitors at the Kroebers' summer place in Napa. Dolores good-naturedly allowed himself to be "exploited" by the Kroeber children: Spott, more reserved, kept them in their place. At the evening campfire, stories were told, and it seemed natural to hear Yurok spoken around the house. She remembered a milieu of freedom and social intensity, a deep feeling for place, a sense of being at "the center of the world." Le Guin's outrage at the damage done to the surrounding region in recent decades by overpopulation and agribusiness (all the "poisoned vineyards") would transform personal nostalgia into critical utopia. Her tour de force of ethnographic vision, *Always Coming Home* (1985), imagines a future Napa Valley inhabited by "a people worthy of the place," the Kesh, transformed and rerooted indigenous Californians.

Le Guin's science fiction creates imaginative thought experiments that are forms of cultural critique. *The Left Hand of Darkness*, which became an early classic of second-wave feminism, created a recognizably human world without male and female genders. While avoiding direct reference to contemporary or historical situations, much of Le Guin's work shows an acute awareness of colonial invasion, indigenous transformation, and the difficult role of anthropology betwixt and between. In her Hainish series, quasi-ethnographers, or "mobiles," moving between distant but related worlds, grapple with the simultaneous risk and necessity of cross-cultural exchange. Among these "anthropological" novels, *The Word for World Is Forest* (1976) offers perhaps the most direct meditation on critical issues in Ishi's story. It is also a direct inspiration for the global blockbuster *Avatar*—acknowledged by the film's director, James Cameron. But there are obvious differences in the way this story of indigenous victory is told, especially the lack of a redeemed white hero in Le Guin's darker version.

Written at the height of opposition to the Vietnam War, the novella is angry and explicitly political in a way untypical of its author. It portrays a lethal confrontation of different worlds, recalling the world Ishi was born into: a situation of invasion where genocidal extermination is considered simply part of the "progress" brought by technologically superior outsiders. Like California after the Gold Rush, there is no functioning, reasonable government that can be counted on to play a moderating role. In *Word for World* representatives of an emerging intergalactic League of Worlds can only ratify the outcome of a bloody conflict. Le Guin inverts the usual story of conquest, imagining a successful war of resistance. But her happy ending, as we will see, is shadowed, ambivalent. At the core of the tale two cross-cultural translators, an indigenous leader and an anthropologist, forge a friendship. The bond is real, admirable and fatal.

The heavily forested planet Asche has been invaded by two thousand men from Terra, a place that long ago wrecked its environment, destroying all the trees. Loggers and soldiers, the first arrivals, harvest timber and send it home on robot spaceships. As the story begins, a shipment of women has just been unloaded whose purpose is to reproduce, thus transforming "New Tahiti" from an extractive to a settler colony. The three million indigenous Ascheans, genetically human, have over time evolved into three-foot-tall, green-furred beings with a culture adapted to their forest world. These little people are understood to be doomed to extinction in the face of a more advanced, heavily armed society. ("Creechies" is the racist term used by the invaders, reminiscent of California's "digger" Indians, also apparently unheroic and close to the ground.) Passive and dreamy, a mixture of child and furry animal, the Ascheans pose no threat to the invaders who fly around in updated Vietnam-era helicopters armed with bombs, machine guns, and flame-throwers. Loggers defoliate and clear-cut the forests, rounding up "volunteer" laborers who are kept in "creechie pens" (against the high-minded but ineffectual regulations of a distant home government). It is a classic extractive colonial operation, reminiscent of King Leopold's Congo and many others. The Terrans are all recognizable imperial types, sexist and predatory, self-aggrandizing or, at best, "just following orders." Here Le Guin paints with a heavy satiric brush. But the expedition's anthropologist, Raj Lyubov, is more complex. He wants to understand the forest people.

The Ascheans live in a world where the line between waking and dreaming is fluid and can be manipulated. Dreaming is not limited to sleep but occurs in cycles throughout the day. Men are typically hunters or intellectuals (dedicated "dreamers"); women hunt and are political leaders. Old women have final say on important issues, their decisions informed by the male dreamers' visions. Like precontact California, there are no organized tribes or large-scale governments. Villages led by headwomen are dispersed throughout Asche's forested islands. Everything is close to the earth, lodges semisubterranean . . . Life proceeds without hierarchy or war, in social and environmental equilibrium. Population size is under control, and behavioral mechanisms have evolved to keep anger and violence, which do break out, from becoming lethal.

The Ascheans seem to be a composite of Australian Aboriginals (the "Dream Time"), and the Mbuti Pygmies of Colin Turnbull's widely read *The Forest People* (published a few years before *Word for World* was written). Other contributions may include egalitarian "gift societies" from Melanesia and elsewhere; Highland New Guinea cultures—made famous by Margaret Mead—where male and female social roles appear reversed; and of course traditional California Indian societies. But this kind of speculation only gets us so far. Le Guin characteristically reweaves bits and pieces from her wide reading into unique syntheses that can't be reduced to a list of ingredients.

Aschean culture, while it embodies the "balance" so central to Le Guin's Taoist ethical imagination, is not static or unchanging. The story of culture clash portrays two dynamic societies in struggle and synergy. Raj Lyubov finds himself in the midst of a transformative battle where neutrality is not an option. The anthropologist is caught between a vicious imperialism for which he provides a liberal alibi and an Aschean resistance movement with which he feels a growing sympathy. A "spesh" (technician or scientist), he is charged with researching and reporting on native custom without involvement in either political or military aspects of the operation. As the situation deteriorates, he struggles with this "neutrality" in ways that recall the debates about anthropology's complicity with empire that surfaced in the early 1970s, just as *Word for World* was being published.

As in much of her science fiction, Le Guin focuses on a cross-cultural friendship. Lyubov's Aschean counterpart, Selver, might have been called "an improved specimen" by Marlow in *Heart of Darkness*: a "creechie" who learns the ways of the colonists and functions as an indispensable but scorned servant. Appreciating Selver's crossover skills, Lyubov recruits him as an assistant, and the two work intensively on Aschean language and culture, exchanging perspectives on the clash of values and ontologies. The anthropologist even begins to learn how to dream consciously, guided by his friend. Selver seems content with his role as a culture broker until suddenly, in an act of suicidal revenge, he attacks one of the invaders who has just raped and killed his wife. The object of his rage, Captain Davidson, unambiguously of the "exterminate all the brutes" school, has plans for bringing "light" into the "dark" forest by cutting or burning down the entire world of the Ascheans. His visions take on apocalyptic proportions—with echoes ("thinking the unthinkable") of the 1950s Cold Warrior Herman Kahn planning for life after nuclear holocaust. Davidson, a virile warrior, is about to finish off the tiny Selver when Lyubov organizes his friend's escape into the forest. This act cements their personal loyalty, but is understood by the colonists as a betrayal. Lyubov, always a suspicious relativist, is now firmly classified "pro-creechie" (*indigènophile*, nigger-lover . . .).

Already an adept dreamer, Selver oneirically processes the terrible present and its possible futures, understanding that his world's survival requires something very new. Coco Mena, an old man and a great dreamer, recognizes that Selver is now a "god."

> This is a new time for the world: a bad time. You have gone farthest. And at the farthest, at the end of the black path, there grows a tree; there the fruit ripens; now you reach up, Selver, now you gather it. And the world changes wholly, when a man holds in his hand the fruit of that tree, whose roots are deeper than the forest. (1976: 48)

The fruit Selver has picked from Coco Mena's visionary tree is war. He will soon lead overwhelming numbers of Aschean men and women on a series of raids that mercilessly kill hundreds of Terrans, including all the females recently imported for purposes of colonization.

A couple of days before the climactic Aschean raid on the colonists' central base, Lyubov, on a fact-finding mission in a nearby forest village, encounters Selver. They reaffirm their friendship, but recognize that new forces divide them. The connection is real: Selver takes the risk of losing the raid's element of surprise by warning his friend to get out of the base on a specific night. And Lyubov does not include this information, or any mention of Selver, in his official report. Having thus misled his fellow Terrans and protected the resistance, the anthropologist has nowhere to go. He cannot, or will not, save himself. Ignoring Selver's warning, Lyubov seems as surprised as the others when the Ascheans overrun the

base, and he is killed by a falling beam in his burning house. Selver
mourns the anthropologist's death, carefully preserving all the ethnographic descriptions and texts they have produced together. These will
later be handed to representatives of the newly formed intergalactic
League of Worlds. At the novella's end, as all the surviving Terrans are
evacuated, it is confirmed that a formal decision by the league now places
"World 41" off-limits in perpetuity. Only a small scientific survey, after
five generations, will be allowed to contact the Ascheans. Selver also
learns that Raj Lyubov's ethnological reports have played a crucial role
in justifying the decision to leave his forested world undisturbed.

In *The Word for World Is Forest* a seemingly inevitable historical
momentum is stopped dead. Sheer numbers combined with visionary
leadership overcome the invaders' technological and military superiority
(lacking this time that most potent ally in the conquest of the Americas,
disease). But turning back invasion will not mean a return to the "precontact" world. Something crucial has changed. As Selver tells one of the
departing interplanetary authorities: "There is no use pretending, now,
that we do not know how to kill one another" (1976: 168). Le Guin
leaves her readers wondering if the Ascheans will sustain their peaceful,
balanced way of life. And it is far from clear whether being left alone
forever (indigenous "sovereignty" with a vengeance) is a good outcome.
There is no place for innocence in this story.

Le Guin's sense of historical interaction and change in *Word for
World* is complex. Violence is not portrayed as something simply imposed
from outside, a contaminating agent. In Aschean culture a "god" is a
"changer, a bridge between realities" (35). When Raj Lyubov first hears
the term used to describe his friend he searches the ethnographic dictionary he and Selver have compiled, finding among the definitions:
"translator." Selver, the latest in a series of Aschean "gods," men and
women, brings across a new reality from the dream time into the world
time. Lived tradition is dynamic, as the elder, Coro Mena, says: "the
world is always new, however old its roots . . ." (33). Ascheans consider
dreams and the material world equally real. But the connection between
them is obscure. A translator-god can bring one into the other, as world-
changing speech and deed. The anthropologist wonders whether in
translating/enacting a new reality—in this case calculated killing—
Selver is speaking his own language or Captain Davidson's. He cannot
know for sure. Nor can we.

It is tempting to compare the Aschean god-translator to the Indian prophets who played so important a part in Western American contact histories. Wovoka, the great Paiute dreamer who inspired the Plains sundance movement is the best known. But prophetic-dreaming religions played a role throughout Native California in the late nineteenth and twentieth centuries. Indeed, the idea of periodic "world renewal" has a deep traditional root, rearticulated as (Christian-influenced) messianism after the 1850s. Followers of Wovoka circulated in California, and dreamers (such as the twentieth-century Kashaya Pomo leaders Annie Jarvis and Essie Parrish) have been important translators of a changing tradition (Field 2008; Sarris 1993). The local histories are quite specific, and the analogy with Selver can certainly be overdrawn. Suffice it to say that a focus on dynamic traditions, empowered by dreaming and prophecy, gives a different sense of transformative authenticity than before-after narratives of the "last wild Indian" or ideologies of "acculturation." Change, even violent change, can no longer be confused with cultural death. One wonders what the scientific mission returning to Asche after five generations will find. Five generations is about the time span between the massacres of Ishi's people and the composition of *Word for World*.

Five generations after the state's founding genocide Native California is alive and different.

Ishi was not the end. He was, and still is, a translator. He brought something across from one world to another, and he was selectively curious about the new. We have seen the way his story continues to seduce, to heal, to make new meanings in changing times for diverse people. At the very least, Le Guin's parable of colonialism, contact, and change confirms this historical open-endedness. It also casts a shadow across the healing closure imagined by her mother in *Ishi in Two Worlds*, while not dismissing the desire for human reconciliation expressed there so poignantly. The anthropologist in *Word for World* is not Alfred Kroeber, but a sacrificial figure, caught in a lethal crossfire. Ishi's "friends" at the museum, working in the safe space of history's victors, were never so exposed. They didn't have to choose sides between irreconcilable antagonists. "Salvage anthropology" saw itself at a historical turning point, but after the fatal violence had done its worst. Scientific understanding could coexist happily with devotion to Ishi the survivor—a vision of cross-cultural friendship that underlies the humanist healing of *Ishi in Two Worlds*.

Le Guin wrote two decades later, at a moment when contradictions of power and knowledge had been sharpened by anticolonial movements, feminism, and, most acutely, Vietnam. In *Word for World,* while the loyalty and respect linking native and anthropologist is real, the relationship is deeply troubled. At the book's end, Selver realizes that a person like Lyubov "would understand, and yet would himself be utterly beyond understanding. For the kindest of them was as far out of touch, as unreachable, as the cruelest" (1976: 166). A harsh summation. There must surely have been times when Ishi felt this way about his doctor and archery-mate, "Popey," and about the "Big Chiep." Yet there was no way of severing the connection that had been forged. Selver: "This is why the presence of Lyubov in his mind remained painful . . ." " (166). There would be no detachment, no getting clear. Selver's intimate yet unapproachable friend stays forever in his dreams, as—in a reverse historical outcome—the patient, mysterious Ishi haunts Kroeber.

In its indirect, imaginative way, *The Word for World Is Forest* comments on *Ishi in Two Worlds.* It does so most deeply, perhaps, by unsentimentally, generously, exploring the relationship of violence and friendship. In Le Guin's parable, as we have seen, anthropological humanism emerges as both essential and impotent in situations of colonial/anticolonial antagonism. Lyubov is unable to reconcile interpersonal loyalty, political commitment, and scientific comprehension: he will not emerge unscathed with his intercultural understanding. *Word for World* shows that cross-cultural friendships, however substantial, are overridden by larger forces of structural asymmetry and conflict. While Lyubov is not Kroeber, this experience may partly explain the latter's silence about Ishi, his lack of an adequate language.

Le Guin brings us to the place of historical determination E. M. Forster memorably evoked in the final paragraphs of *A Passage to India* (1952: 322). It will be recalled that Fielding, a Briton sympathetic to Indians under the Empire, attempts to renew his old friendship with Aziz, the young Muslim doctor falsely accused of molesting an Englishwoman. As they ride amicably alongside one another, the air seems finally to have cleared. They can start fresh . . . But suddenly the horses veer apart: and all the surroundings—the temples, the jail, the palace, the birds—"in their hundred voices" seem to be saying: " 'No, not yet' " The Raj is still there.

And similarly, in settler-colonial California, a victim of genocide expires peacefully among loving friends: "You stay, I go." And a successor society understands and moves on, unencumbered by its vicious past . . . No, not yet.

And yet . . . Visions of reconciliation (always flawed and in process) abound in Ursula K. Le Guin's work. Many of her travelers between worlds are anthropologists or at least serious, relativistic participant-observers. They get involved, often for the best. A recent novel, *The Telling,* vindicates "salvage" collecting (aided by computer scanning and storage), cultural documentation portrayed not as postmortem archiving, but as central to a community's fight to sustain its oral tradition against state-mandated homogenization. Such stories, while set in faraway times and places, speak to the earthly here and now. A vision of oral archives as living and oriented to the future resonates with the contemporary recycling of salvage anthropological records by Indian activists, story-tellers, historians, and artists. *Word for World,* a tale of anticolonial victory, makes clear there can be no return to a precontact way of life. Freedom from invasion is good. Absolute separation, being left alone forever, is never a solution. In Le Guin's gently rigorous anarchism, sustainable community exists locally, but not in isolation, outside history. At the largest scale, she imagines a loose, facilitating network (not a central government) of worlds, the interstellar "Ecumene." And in narratives like *The Left Hand of Darkness,* it is contact with outside worlds that opens up nationalistic border marking and restrains chauvinism. A deeply rooted, and yet cosmopolitan, indigenous life . . .

Le Guin offers thought experiments, not political programs. Perhaps we should say hope experiments. Unrealistic. But necessary. If something like postcolonial social relations are to have any chance, we need to be able to imagine a reconciled, egalitarian future. Fredric Jameson (2005), an astute reader of Le Guin, has repeatedly argued for the necessity of utopias in a world of capitalist reification. Alternate visions are tools for thinking and feeling beyond the given, outside the "reality" that seems inevitable, natural. Utopia takes different forms: it need not refer either to a distant future or a necessary next step for everyone. The recent reopening of Ishi's story depends on the actually existing, emergent spaces of "indigenism": utopic, or perhaps heterotopic, realities (Foucault 1984). Peoples and histories assumed to be doomed are more and more visibly alive—moving forward, laterally and backwards, transgressing unilinear notions of progress (see Chapters 1 and 2). Emerging spaces of the indigenous—at once ancient and new—are composed of entangled, compromised, unexpected histories. Ishi's story would never have been reopened, his dispersed body reunited, without the embattled continuity and agency of California Indians. This "survivance" includes sweat lodges and bear dances along with installation art and gambling casinos, traditional basketry and novel writing, tribal bureaucracy and hip-hop . . . Ishi in a loincloth, Ishi in work clothes. Ishi with feathers. Ishi in a suit and tie.

His story was never just that of a man. From the moment Ishi became known he was a myth. His engaging and enigmatic "humanity"—what he managed to communicate, and what others could discover in him—was from the start allegorical—political and prophetic. How could it not be? But the determining horizon within which his story would prolif-erate has shifted. Mikhail Bakhtin's notion of the "chronotope" may be suggestive here. For a narration to unfold with a sense of coherence, it must "take place" somewhere. This spatial frame is a way to contain, to align, a temporal flux. The time/space within which Ishi's story was first told, its historical "reality," was the chronotope of the museum, a place of finality. This setting was not just the literal Museum of Anthropology in San Francisco where he lived his public life, but the "museum" (including a range of sites, like the "archive," the "monument," etc.) where valued memories and objects are gathered, rescued from a forward-rushing, linear progress that never turns back on itself. A permanent home for things worth keeping, the museum is a last destination—thus its associa-tion with immobility, death. Things in museums or archives, deposited there by history, come to stay—or so it seems.

This museum was brilliantly satirized by James Luna—a specimen that could get up and walk out. And today the chronotope no longer contains Ishi's story. Indeed, museums everywhere, under pressure from cultural property claims, repatriations, marketing, and commercializa-tion, are in flux, unstable and creative "contact zones" (Clifford 1997b; Phillips 2012). Ishi's story, we have seen, is now as much about indige-nous futures as salvaged pasts. Indeed, the whole opposition of past and future that aligned the passage of "progressive" time wavers in contexts of tribal renaissance. Time is experienced as looping, genealogical, spi-ral—the chronotope of endless homecoming.

Becoming "indigenous" after colonization, crafting traditional futures in transformed places—such processes exemplify Le Guin's nonlinear utopia. She has gathered this utopia in a work of visionary realism, the ethnography of a future society in a familiar landscape. *Always Coming Home*, her intricate portrayal of reindigenized California, is unlike anything else in her oeuvre. The Kesh, "who might be going to have lived a long, long time from now in Northern California," inhabit a valley called "Na," the Napa Valley Le Guin knows and loves from childhood. They live in a time when much, but not all, of modern industrial society and state governance has disappeared. The reasons for the collapse are hinted at, but never explained: apparently the transformation occurred through successive crises and adjustments rather than some cataclysmic event. *Always Coming Home* presents an intricate record of the world of the Kesh in a form that resembles the nineteenth-century ethnographies—ungainly collections of diverse, largely textual, data—that were the norm before more focused monographs emerged with Malinowski's generation. Le Guin's compendium brings together many sources and voices. "Raw" texts—transcribed myths, stories, language, poetry, computer printouts, and other records are combined with extended descriptions of rituals, technology, living spaces, family structure, sexual practices . . . The land, flora, and fauna of Northern California, evocatively rendered, are immediately recognizable to those familiar with the region. (How far away is this time/space?) There are individual life histories, an intriguingly constructed sample chapter from a Kesh novel, descriptions of conversations involving an ethnographer, a woman named Pandora, sometimes called "the editor." Every now and then this researcher grapples with epistemological or methodological problems in short sections called "Pandora worries . . ." The ethnographer/editor provides extended ethnological interpretations in a hundred-page section called "The Back of the Book," including a glossary for the many Kesh words sprinkled throughout. Le Guin has invented elements of a language; and, working with a composer, she supplies samples of songs and music, initially in tape cassettes, now CDs.

Readers are invited to explore this jumble of resources, guided only by curiosity and Pandora's occasional explications. An extended autobiographical narrative by a woman called Stone Telling occurs in three installments and is the only obvious element of continuity. Stone Telling recalls growing up in the valley, leaving it to live with her father in a repellant militaristic society, and then gratefully coming home with her young daughter. But this is not the place, nor is it possible, to give an adequate description of *Always Coming Home*. It is an intricate work (How, Pandora worries methodologically, can I render all the branches and shadows in this thicket of scrub oak?). A multitext, it asks for slow processing and can't be read like Le Guin's plot-driven novels. The book is overstuffed, the writing quirky, lyrical, poignant, entangling. One loses momentum and puts it aside . . . returning later, elsewhere.

Perhaps because the book is unfamiliar in form and not what her readers might expect, Le Guin has taken the uncharacteristic step of explicating her innovation elsewhere in a "theoretical" essay: "A Non-Euclidian View of California as a Cold Place to Be" (1989). After surveying several classics of the futuristic utopian tradition, she introduces a different sense of time with a Cree formula, "I go forward, look back, as the porcupine does." These words initiate storytelling: the porcupine backs into a rocky crevice and looks warily at an enemy or at the future. The admonition is to go slow, cool down (Lévi-Strauss's famous contrast of "cold" and "hot" ways of being in history is invoked). "Go backward. Turn and return."

> I am not proposing a return to the Stone Age. My intent is not reactionary, nor even conservative, but simply subversive. It seems that the utopian imagination is trapped, like capitalism and industrialism and the human population, in a one-way future consisting only of growth. All I am trying to do is figure out how to put a pig on the tracks." (85)

> Utopia has been Euclidian, it has been European, and it has been masculine. I am trying to suggest, in an evasive, distrustful, untrustworthy fashion, and as obscurely as I can, that our final loss of faith in that radiant sandcastle may enable our eyes to adjust to a dimmer light and in it perceive another kind of utopia . . . It may look very like some kind of place Coyote made after having a conversation with his own dung. (89)

A "yin" utopia, in Le Guin's Taoist vocabulary, "would be dark, wet, obscure, weak, yielding, passive, participatory, circular, cyclical, peaceful, nurturant, retreating, contracting, and cold" (90).

Le Guin's non-Euclidian utopia consists in "side trips and reversals" (1989: 95), an "interactive, rhythmic, unstable process" (91). It may, in important ways, already be here—in the belly of an increasingly dysfunctional techno-capitalist beast. Le Guin's principal sources are Taoism, feminism, and a Native California that did not die with Ishi. The Kesh live in scale with their environment, having established gender equality, population stability, and an economy of wealth-as-sharing. Their society is differentiated by skill, age, gender, "house" affiliation, personality, and so forth, but not by race or economic class. Animals are persons; rituals are keyed to natural cycles; oral transmission limits the need for archives; names change according to life stages or transforming experiences; everything is close to the earth (for example, the California Indian–style semi-subterranean community houses); altercations stop short of deadly violence; progress is imagined as "gyres"; and relations are always primary (everything already "hinged"). Individual Kesh can be quirky and difficult; but the society manages its problems, more or less well, without formal government. We discover that the Kesh have been grappling with a militaristic sect that has taken root inside their community.

Le Guin's utopia is not smooth, perfect, or finished. The phrase "always coming home" names an endless process of indigenization: a way of slowing down and going back, in order to move ahead, or sideways. There are clear affinities with native peoples' survivance since the nineteenth century: a watchful waiting, enduring in or near old places; a reinvention of traditions, of traditional futures. Who would have dreamed, in Ishi's time, that the Indian population of California would rebound to precontact levels? That tribes would be aggressively reclaiming ancestral remains from university museums? That casinos would be flourishing, with Indians a political force in the state? That intertribal "big times" in mountain meadow, pow-wows in school gyms, and Facebook would all contribute to an evolving tribalism? That native arts such as basketry, dancing, and storytelling would find a second life in heritage, performance, communication, and marketing?

Not so fast . . . We are far from utopia. Most Indians in California, as in so many other places, are poor. They still lack adequate health care, good education, and life opportunities. The exceptions, nourished by casino profits, are just that. More than a century of social trauma caused by devastating epidemics, relentless expropriation, racial intolerance and cultural prejudice, forced assimilation through missions or boarding schools—this history persists, as a determining force. (James Luna's father "passing on the tradition of alcohol . . .") Many scattered tribes now struggle, unsuccessfully, for recognition and access to even a tiny homeland (Field 1999). In the real valley of Na, industrial vineyards continue their march across the hillsides, uprooting oak communities and disrupting animal habitats.

All this is true, and more. It is never difficult to shoot down radical utopias. When we shift the focus to contemporary "reality," *Always Coming Home* looks like an elaborate exercise in wishful thinking. Jameson (1975), writing on utopian fiction, has noted its way of getting past current common sense with a strategy of "world reduction." Let's remove capitalism, the nation-state, industrial production, cars and airplanes, and see what life could be like. Le Guin does something like this, stripping away an enormous amount of "modernity"—though she keeps something like the Internet. World reduction simplifies as it clarifies. And it takes a point of view: it excludes. The Kesh world could easily become a white settler utopia: a site for New Age appropriations of native tradition, for returns to primitive authenticity, for getting closer to nature. This, when most Indians today live in cities and towns.

An indigenous California without Indians—I have heard this said about *Always Coming Home,* in a tone of dismissal.

But then I think of Gerald Vizenor's "post-Indian." And Coyote's shape-shifting that crosses up racial and cultural lines. And what about James Luna's cosmology of the four colors, a vision of conviviality here and now? In Le Guin's fictions, where people have names like Raj Lyubov, all the currently recognizable ethnicities, races, and nationalities have been scrambled.

A post-race utopia? Absolutely. Something to be suspicious of in current contexts of managed "multiculturalism—ideologies of premature reconciliation that hide realities of violent antagonism and structured inequality? Yes, to be sure. Beyond race? No, not yet.

But a tough-minded realism can lock us in the present, blinding us to other worlds, old and emerging, that already exist. We can at least search for ways of thinking and acting that keep Le Guin's "not yet" from *Word for World* in tension with the "and yet" of *Always Coming Home.* It could help us accept a different realism: the project and predicament of constantly becoming (and failing to become) postcolonial. What are the real, the really imaginable, worlds and coalitions that could lead to new forms of reciprocity and conviviality?

Ishi's story is a source of tragedy and hope, terror and healing, meaning and silence.

Becoming indigenous in new ways, in twenty-first-century California, is an urgent Indian project. There is a great deal to be sustained, reclaimed, and renewed—much to be corrected, justice to be done. But ultimately the historical processes at work—whether they appear to be

going forward, to the side, or back—will be broader and more inclusive
than the visions and projects of any one group of Californians. The many
populations of the state are not heading "home"—to New England,
Oklahoma, Mexico, China, Vietnam, Japan, Cambodia, or Iran.

The utopia of always coming home is an interactive process, not a
completed destination. Becoming indigenous together in California's
places—linked with many other global places—would have to be a long,
contradictory history.

It could never be a matter of somehow copying the Kesh. Utopias,
especially of the "yin" variety, aren't recipes. And dreams are never
innocent of power. But relearning how to live in a responsible relation
with the land, with nonhuman creatures and with available, shared
resources is hardly a project of neocolonial dominion—despite the capitalist commodification of "green" products. Sustained relationships of
multidirectional learning, remembering, and translating may yet find
ways to proceed in conditions of relative equality and mutual respect.
And the differences among peoples, Indians and others, would not necessarily disappear in a future that could merit the name postcolonial.
They could well become less absolute, less important. Let's hope so . . .
People may yet be able, like the Kesh, to change names as their life among
others twists and unfolds.

One of Ishi's stories has him exploring the new world of San Francisco
accompanied by a cosmopolitan Papago bearing the Spanish name Juan.
The wild man in the story is content to be wearing white peoples' clothes,
sleeping in their beds, eating (some) of their food . . .

What songs are playing on his iPod?

The different retellings of Ishi's story question all-or-nothing outcomes,
the inevitabilities that govern so much thinking about Westernization, or
modernization, or a triumphant American history.

Ishi's "You stay, I go" becomes: "We remain. You make room."

What became of Ishi's divided body? The brain from storage at the
Smithsonian and ashes from Mt. Olivet Cemetery in San Francisco were
placed together in a basket woven by a woman of mixed Yana ancestry
from the Redding Rancheria. The basket was buried secretly by a small
group of old and young people from the Redding and Pit River groups.
No Maidu were among them. A non-Indian, Thomas Killion, of the
Smithsonian Institution, was invited to be present.

Figure 4.18. Courtesy of the Phoebe A. Hearst
Museum of Anthropology and the Regents of the
University of California; catalogue no. 15-5414.)

Theodora Kroeber's classic, *Ishi in Two Worlds,* wasn't the last word.
It remains a moving, resonant, story—a period piece, like all our stories.
Native Californians have their own ways of telling and understanding
Ishi's life and its meanings—moving in and out of changing traditions,
tribal institutions, and all the command performances of identity. The
changing story and images of Ishi are part of this emerging future.

Ishi, the man, remains distant—however closely we listen to his
recorded voice, his partially translated stories, and his songs. His story
cannot belong to anyone, crucial though the native reclamation of his
legacy has been. Ishi's is still too richly enigmatic and productively

ambivalent to be contained. Indeed, it would be a divestment of historical responsibility by members of California's non-Indian societies if "repatriation" of Ishi were taken to mean that in going home, he had now left the white world for good—that now only his people could really understand him. If giving Ishi back means being clear of him, divested of his troubling questions, this is the wrong kind of reconciliation. "Ishi" remains a provocation, a potent silence. Around this name swirl images and echoes of entangled lives, of white and native memory, of colonization and its legacies, of historical wounds and ways to heal them.

The wild man of Oroville has, at long last, been returned to his homeland by people who recognize him as a relative. But Ishi's story won't be laid to rest.

Part III

Alutiiq kayaks approach the shore at the Tamamta Katurlluta cultural festival, Homer, Alaska, August 31, 2002. (Photo by James Clifford.)

5

Hau'ofa's Hope

In the lecture reprinted here I explore the tension of utopian and realist thinking in the career of Epeli Hau'ofa, an indigenous-cosmopolitan visionary. The tension can be felt throughout Returns: *Hau'ofa, who died in 2009, was born to Tongan missionary parents in New Guinea, where he spent his youth before attending university in Canada and earning a doctorate in anthropology at Australian National University. He settled in Fiji, where he taught for many years at the University of the Pacific and founded the Oceania Centre for Arts and Culture. A respected social scientist, Hau'ofa was also a brilliant satiric novelist. He is perhaps best known for a provocative essay of 1993, "Our Sea of Islands," which influenced a generation of Oceanian scholars and artists as well as others—such as myself— attempting to think their way out of the sterile dichotomy of "local" and "global." The essay, and a series of probing sequels, imagined the vast Pacific Ocean as a site of intense crossings and interconnections, historical and contemporary. A Eurocentric vision of tiny "islands in a distant sea" was reconceived as Oceania, a dynamic place of exchanges, of interconnected histories. This expansive regionalism, a kind of indigenous world-making, was rooted in diverse Pacific places and cultures. How these Oceanic possibilities were related to capitalist globalization and the modern world system was, as the lecture explores, a contentious issue for Hau'ofa and his colleagues. The issue has not disappeared. At the end of my remarks I turn to Alaska, providing a condensed introduction to the last two chapters of* Returns.

❖

I am grateful for the invitation to address the Association for Social Anthropology in Oceania (ASAO) as its distinguished lecturer—especially since my relation to Pacific scholarship has always been rather unprofessional, or at least spotty. I like to think of myself as an amateur—in a sense that comes through best in the French *amateur:* one who loves. Someone who cultivates a study or art from taste or attraction rather than professionally. (I pass over another meaning, more prominent in the English language dictionaries: "a person who does something more or less unskillfully.") So I address you as a nonspecialist, an amateur of the Pacific—a fellow traveler perhaps, in that vast space.

But while I may not have much new to say, for this audience, about Island Pacific societies or histories, I may be able to suggest ways that the region and some of its distinctive problems and theorists have been generative for thinking about broad issues: the nature and diversity of "indigeneity" today, scale making in various "globalizing" sociocultural processes, the inventive dynamism of "tradition," and the question of what might be called differential historicities. By that I mean ways of telling large-scale stories about where we—always a contested pronoun— have come from and are going, separately and together. Preparing this talk has made me realize how much of what I find most useful for thinking through our current utopic/dystopic moment has come from the Pacific—from a uniquely rich scholarly fusion of ethnography with history, and from inspirational scholars, writers, activists, and students— some, but not all of whom, I'll be able to mention tonight.

When I was asked to deliver this lecture I said that in the midst of a hectic academic term, I couldn't come up with something really appropriate to the Pacific, so I would need to speak from my current research on indigenous-heritage politics in Alaska. No doubt the general issues would resonate.

And then—seduced by that liquid and expansive word "Oceania" in the name ASAO—it seemed to me that my current Alaska work was, after all, in the Pacific. It's centered on people and histories on and around Kodiak Island in the Gulf of Alaska, facing south toward Hawai'i. And if Highland New Guinea can be part of Oceania, why not Kodiak— its people having lived for so long with and from the ocean: its currents, storms, and drifting, swimming creatures?

I recalled the Kodiak area's devastating twentieth-century volcanic eruptions and earthquakes along the "ring of fire." Geologically, it's a very Pacific place . . . however far north.

Others have questioned how "the Pacific" or "Oceania" got reduced to the *South* Pacific (and well before James Michener's *Tales*)—how a "tropical" region was identified where the waters could only be warm.

The ocean is both cold and warm, of course. Birds, so prominent in

Greg Dening's *Beach Crossings* (and how *he* will be missed . . .) follow the summer over vast distances from north to south and back again. You may recall how the golden plover's migrations connect Alaska with Hawai'i and the Marquesas in this vision of a Pacific history of crossings—times and places (Dening 2004).

Speaking of history: Alaska, of course, has its share of the Captain Cook epic. And its coastal tribes were important players in the intercultural political economy of the North Pacific and China, an Oceanic story brilliantly mapped by Marshall Sahlins in his 1988 essay "Cosmologies of Capitalism" (Sahlins 2000).

In the nineteenth century, how many Islanders reached Alaska on the whaling and merchant ships they crewed? And much earlier, did the Pacific navigators make it to the Aleutians? Some of you can no doubt fill me in. My knowledge of this history and of the relevant winds and currents isn't adequate.

As for currents—it's well documented that those great trees that wash out of Alaska's rivers found their ways to islands south, where some were used to make the largest of the great Hawai'ian war canoes. And in 1990, when the Polynesian Voyaging Society decided to build a new canoe, *Hawai'iloa,* entirely from traditional materials, it turned to Native Alaskan allies for large-enough logs, the koa forests of Hawai'i no longer containing adequate supplies.

World War II in the Pacific Theatre: what about the forgotten Aleutian campaigns? Southwest Alaska, Kodiak, and the Aleutians would be heavily militarized—with transformative consequences comparable to those in the Solomon Islands, Vanuatu, or New Caledonia. And today Kodiak Island hosts the largest U.S. Coast Guard base, patrolling a vast area north of Hawai'i.

There's also a missile-launching range on one of the island's southern peninsulas. It was originally destined for private satellites, but now is part of the "Star Wars" missile defense program, linking the Marshall Islands, Hawai'i, Alaska, and Vandenberg Air Force Base not far down the coast from Santa Cruz, where we are right now.

These days no one will be surprised to hear that there are Samoan communities in Anchorage, Filipinos in Kodiak, as well as plenty of north-south traffic to Alaska along the Pacific Rim from Central and South America: folks working in fisheries, service industries, and the military. This northern coast is not really a remote place in the Sea of Islands.

The Sea of Islands.   You were probably wondering when I'd get to Epeli Hau'ofa. I had planned to at least invoke his expansive vision of "Oceania" to justify discussing Kodiak/Alaska in the ASAO Distinguished Lecture. But his recent passing has returned me to those seminal writings, read afresh in a new University of Hawai'i Press edition, *We Are the Ocean* (Hau'ofa 2008). In the process, Hau'ofa has become central to the talk in a way I hadn't planned. I hope you'll see it as an appropriate tribute to a great visionary of our time. (And I might add that what I'll be saying is entirely based on his writings. I never knew Hau'ofa, as many of you did. So I hope what follows will ring, more or less, true.)

I will, after some tacking, land us in Alaska, there to encounter the same tensions that generated "Our Sea of Islands"—structure and transformation, determinism and emergence, pessimism and hope.

But allow me to continue in a personal vein for a bit more. Epeli Hau'ofa is one of three Island Pacific influences that have guided and challenged my thinking. The second is Jean-Marie Tjibaou, whom I knew in the late seventies when I was writing about Maurice Leenhardt and New Caledonia (Clifford 1982). His essays, interviews, and speeches, collected and introduced by Alban Bensa and Eric Wittershiem, have finally appeared in English (Tjibaou 2005). And Eric Waddell's intellectual biography is just out (2008).

Tjibaou and Hau'ofa shared an expansive regional vision, an alter globalization. Each in his own way was bent on reinventing the Pacific Way in new circumstances. Postindependence euphoria was gone, and they confronted the structural realities of neocolonialism and globalization, along with their possibilities. Both were committed to the renewal and transformation of local traditions, to strengthened "indigenous" spaces. And both refused to be limited by exclusivist ethnic or national politics, projecting (if the oxymoron be allowed) "indigenous-cosmopolitan" visions.

There would be lot to say, given the time, about Tjibaou and Hau'ofa: the political situations and histories of New Caledonia and Fiji and how these conditioned the manner of both Tjibaou's and Hau'ofa's thinking and activism, the Christian elements in their expansive localisms, or perhaps better, their immanent universalisms. We can only hope that their thinking—expressed in prose, poetry, fiction, speeches, and interviews—having now been collected and published, will resonate beyond Island Pacific contexts. They have a lot to say wherever small nations and societies are struggling for ways to dwell, to find breathing space in global fields of power, somehow on their own terms.

The third Pacific influence I want to mention briefly is not an individual but a network. It started with Vince Diaz, who as a student from Guam at the University of Hawai'i heard Stuart Hall give a lecture. Inspired by the vision of talking theory without losing one's soul, he applied to our PhD program at the University of California, Santa Cruz (UCSC). Teresia Teaiwa followed soon after, then Kehaulani Kauanui, April Henderson, Pam Kido, and Noleani Goodyear Kaopua. I am still processing what I learned from these students. Vince and Kehaulani organized a conference on "Native Pacific Cultural Studies on the Edge," held at Santa Cruz, which brought together a group of younger scholars who had already been meeting at conferences all over the Pacific (Diaz and Kauanui 2001). In the midst of this remarkable gathering, it dawned on me that our program, and I as an academic "advisor," had been efficiently interpellated by a dynamic social network: "simultaneously displaced and recruited," I said in my comments at the time (Clifford 2001: 484).

It was Teresia who gave me Hau'ofa's "Sea of Islands" essay not long after its first publication. In practice, scholarship doesn't so much *advance* as *get around*. Where do books and ideas flow, and where is the passage sticky, blocked? We know there are restrictive, institutional networks of publication, translation, and dissemination, as analyzed in Pascale Casanova's *The World Republic of Letters* (2005). And we know the global, post/neocolonial routes that channel younger scholars from peripheral places to powerful centers. Yet these material structures of translation, travel, and interpellation are not the only circuits.

It is necessary to pay attention not just to regulated global systems but also to contingent connections and emerging webs of influence. There was no structural reason why UCSC should have become a node in the network of an Island Pacific cultural studies scholarship in the making. It took person-to-person ties—the friendships, communications, alliances, and world-making projects of a far-flung community of younger intellectuals. Teresia Teaiwa is explicit about these processes of travel, translation, and congregation in her pointed contribution to the conference just mentioned (Teaiwa 2001a).

My immediate point, now, is that there was no reason—given my academic and intellectual connections, expectations, and areas of sanctioned ignorance—that I should have known in 1994 about the publication in Suva of *A New Oceania: Rediscovering Our Sea of Islands* (Waddell, Naidu, and Hau'ofa 1993). A collective project, this "25th anniversary publication" of the University of the South Pacific listed twenty "authors" and three "editors." *A New Oceania* gathered commentaries around Hau'ofa's famous essay (along with poems and quotations from various Pacific authors—including Tjibaou). It wasn't widely distributed or even well-glued together (my copy has now fallen apart). A truly local production, the book had to be delivered by hand.

Its arrival in Santa Cruz is an academic case of informal import-export that parallels Hau'ofa's emblematic Tongan friend shuttling between Berkeley and Fiji with coolers full of kava, T-shirts, and seafood.

"Our Sea of Islands" (1993) would be followed by three companion essays: "The Ocean in Us" (1997), "Pasts to Remember" (2000), and "Our Place Within" (2003)—all included in Hau'ofa 2008. This linked series of meditations has helped us see, and give proper weight to, all sorts of connections and crossings, old and new, heroic and mundane: travels around work, religion, adventure, family, business, and art. Hau'ofa traced movements that have built bigger spaces, dynamic connections in both space and time. These world-making, globalizing projects are enmeshed in powerful, large-scale webs of transport, labor migration, missionization, and education. They are aligned and limited by these colonial and neocolonial structures—while also using them for divergent purposes—inflecting, exceeding, passing through.

It all adds up to a utopia of sorts, which many of us share with Hau'ofa. And we do so, of course, with differing degrees of skepticism, ambivalence, pessoptimism (as Edward Said might have put it). For example, Margaret Jolly's (2001) complex and engaged critique affirms the vision's importance while bringing out its uneven relevance for distinct Pacific populations and the discrepant pressures (colonial, neocolonial, national) on past and present mobility. But whatever tensions it put on hold, Hau'ofa's hope, tempered by modesty and a self-limiting sense of humor, decisively countered a wet-blanket "realism" we're all familiar with: a historical perspective in which the capitalist world system determines and incorporates everything . . . at least in the proverbial "last analysis." Hau'ofa would claim another, more open-ended form of realism (and realism is not incompatible with vision, as Marx himself demonstrated).

Hau'ofa's writings recognize alternatives that are emergent, vernacular, and real, already happening and going somewhere—somewhere that's not easily subsumed by structural forces like modernization, global capital, or postmodernity, but that are not disconnected from them either. Hau'ofa's story loops and wanders in exploratory parallels. It makes imaginative space for worlding projects at varying scales (Connery and Wilson 2007). I think of these as "big-enough" histories, able to account for a lot, but not everything—and without guarantees of political virtue. Hau'ofa's "Oceania" project might be contrasted, for example, with a range of contemporary "indigenous" movements; with expansive, regionalizing forms of Islam and Christianity; with international feminist networks and women's organizations; with the loose alliances being forged under the aegis of NGO-led environmentalism or the World Social Forum.

Among these recognizable world-making projects we might include the extraordinary example of the Oceania Centre for Arts and Culture, tucked away in a corner of the University of the South Pacific (USP) campus in Suva, gathering, connecting, and radiating Oceanic strands of creativity and influence. A node in the proliferating circuits of contemporary indigenous art, the centre has been resolutely local and regional in scale, expansive but without a website. Its spirit is eloquently expressed in Hau'ofa's "Our Place Within" (2008). And Geoffrey White's introduction to *We Are the Ocean* gives a vivid sense of the perpetually improvised, creative, and unpretentiously radical style of the place.

Epeli Hau'ofa's vision of a New Oceania combined roots in land with routes across the sea, deep local histories with expansive social trajectories beyond every form of containment. He didn't so much escape or transcend nations, ethnicities, and the capitalist world system as find ways around and through them, energies that pointed in old/new/other directions. The vision was, and remains, profoundly hopeful. But it bears emphasizing that this isn't the utopianism of an epochal break—a revolutionary, "whole new" future, leaving behind present divisions. Hau'ofa's sense of possibility was grounded in history's multiple threads, continuities in transformation, as these are rewoven in repeated social practices. The vision extrapolated from what people were already doing— translations, articulations, performances of what had been done many times before, now engaged with new technologies, communications, social scales. It suggests a deep historical attachment: a *longue durée*, but not a return to origins or a developmental teleology. The historicity, a mix of cycles and lines, of returns and forward movements, is what Hau'ofa, in "Pasts to Remember" (2000), figures as a spiral. Reminiscent of Kamau Brathwaite's Caribbean "tidalectics" (DeLoughrey 2007), this way of conceiving history could not be trapped by the binaries of "myth" versus "history," culture versus economy, poetry versus science.

All of this is good to think with—or good to hope with.

❖

But we hope, as Marx might put it, in conditions not of our choosing.

I want to return us to the constitutive tension, embedded in a particular time and region, that generated the vision. Hau'ofa was, of course, reacting against quite specific forms of political-economic "realism" that have certainly not lost their relevance and force. More than once, even as he discovers and articulates his visionary voice, Hau'ofa reminds us of this other perspective and of the need to temper its power. He does not seek to refute or dismiss it.

At USP in the 1980s, political-economic rigor took the form of dependency theory: an account of the trap in which the so-called MIRAB nations of the Pacific were caught (MIRAB: Migration, Remittances, Aid, Bureaucracy). Their seemingly inescapable fate was belittlement. We're all familiar with Hau'ofa's alternative: his substitution of "our sea of islands" for those tiny "islands in a distant sea" (as they must appear in a Eurocentric world system). This critique of belittlement remains crucial wherever bottom-up social movements or new indigenous projects are understood to be mere epiphenomena, functionally contained by global or state structures. Hau'ofa helps us see that more is going on: dynamic and contradictory processes. (Alaska will shortly provide examples.)

The new University of Hawai'i Press edition makes Hau'ofa's key intervention and its subsequent ramifications widely available for the first time. But my gratitude is tempered somewhat by the way the new edition helps us forget the text hand-delivered from Suva to Santa Cruz, fifteen years ago. Many of you, I assume, have seen this little volume—a collage of poetry, quotations, and individual responses to Hau'ofa's seminal essay, followed by an afterword by the author (not, alas, reprinted). The lumpy ensemble gives a vivid sense of USP's first twenty-five years as a catalytic Pacific place: a site of new regional identifications and polemics.

The original edition's varied reactions to "Our Sea of Islands" show a lot of affection for a cherished colleague. But one can't help feeling throughout a sense that maybe Epeli had gone a bit soft, or off the deep end . . .

There are a lot of "yes but" replies. Yes, this is a good corrective, but really, Pacific Island societies are, in fact, small, dependent, and in the grip of relentless forces. A few quotations:

Sudesh Mishra:

> I concede Hau'ofa's point. I am moved by his enthusiasm and
> celebration of Oceania. Yet the nagging sense that real power
> radiated from metropolitan centres won't go away, and no
> matter how adaptable and mobile Oceanic peoples may be, it
> is too simplistic to say that we have more than a theoretical
> control over our destiny..." (Waddell, Naidu, and Hau'ofa
> 1993: 21–22)

The objections range from gentle dissent like this one to frontal
assault.

Joeli Veitayaki notes that Hau'ofa has for years been saying that
Pacific nations are becoming integrated in a single Australia and New
Zealand–dominated regional economy. "Now to please his students
[he]...comes up with this new perspective, which I think is mostly
superficial and unrealistic, certainly severed from the situation in the
Pacific" (Waddell, Naidu, and Hau'ofa 1993: 116). The way forward, for
Veitayaki, is to control island destinies with strengthened national sovereignties while working for development through existing international
institutions.

Vanessa Griffin agrees on the need for hopeful visions, but insists on
also confronting a darker present. Drawing on her work with Pacific
women's organizations, she juxtaposes the following to Hau'ofa's stories
of expansive Oceanic crossings:

> Read Mari Sasabe's study of women working in a Japanese can-
> ning factory in Solomon Islands: read of the early morning boat
> trip at 4 in the morning, the wait in the cold for a bus for a one
> hour bus trip to the factory, and then the hours of work, cutting
> and sluicing fish for the Japanese owned factory before the repeat
> journey home, in reverse, at night. These are islanders too, real
> islanders living on two islands away from the factory, going to it
> by boat and bus, for a lack of choice and a need for cash (Waddell,
> Naidu, and Hau'ofa 1993: 63).

Many other colleagues weigh in, with differing, ambivalent tones.

Hau'ofa's afterword, "A Beginning," anticipates his subsequent essays
and also provides a fuller sense of the historical conjuncture—the situation at USP in postcoup Fiji and throughout the region. Hau'ofa's

portrait of the university in the mid-1980s is grim. And the problem is deeper than the pervasive "despondency theory" (as Sahlins, who was in conversation with Hau'ofa at the time, would later call it).

> When I first came in 1975, the campus was abuzz with creativity and wide-ranging discussions generated by the emergence of the Pacific Way . . . By the early 1980s the lines of engagement had shifted with the increasing awareness of the neocolonial grip on our economies and polities, of the hosts of liberation struggles in the Third World, and of the intensified Reagan-led cold-war campaign against "evil empires." Neo-Marxism of the Third World variety, an even larger idea than the Pacific Way, breached our campus to join battle with our home-grown ideology. The debates, tinged eventually by racism and intolerance of opposing views, deteriorated into charges and counter-charges of "false consciousness," and into unbridled expressions of petty personal animosities. It reached a stage when death threats were issued. *It was a pity because underneath the bickering were real alternative visions of our region.* (Waddell, Naidu, and Hau'ofa 1993: 127, emphasis added)

"Real alternative visions . . ." A seminar series is organized at USP to bring into constructive dialogue the differing perspectives. It begins well, he recalls, but is almost immediately quashed in May 1987, by Fiji's military coup. "Calm immobility" follows: routinized, safe, depressing.

But Hau'ofa is beginning to nurture a different vision. It won't spring into view until 1993 when he delivers the ASAO Distinguished Lecture at the King Kamehameha Hotel in Kona, Hawai'i. Actually, he delivers a rather conventional talk there on Tongan aristocracy and democratization. But then, on his "road to Damascus," as he famously calls it— driving across the immense volcanic landscape of the Big Island to Hilo and another lecture date—Hau'ofa's vision of Pacific scale and dynamism erupts. In a white heat, he dashes off a new talk, and the rest we know: the visionary is born. This Christian/indigenous rebirth (richly developed by Rob Wilson in his book *Be Always Converting, Be Always Converted* (2009) is unforgettably narrated at the beginning of "Our Sea of Islands." Hau'ofa's essay, first delivered at Hilo, repeated in Honolulu, would be published almost immediately in the USP anniversary polylogue.

I want to shift our focus and dwell for a moment on this latter context of emergence, an origin story rooted in ideological tension rather than sublime nature or spiritual epiphany. It is the conjuncture featured in Hau'ofa's afterword—a clash, but also potential dialogue, of "real alternative visions of our region." Writing against violent assertions of Fijian nativism, Hau'ofa evokes already existing practices of coexistence and hospitality, of live and let live. He draws on his own life experiences as a multilingual, multiply located traveling native of "Oceania" to sketch counterhistories, alternatives to the coercive norms of both ethnonationalist exclusivity and economic developmentalism. He brings "culture" and "tradition" decisively into the picture—powerful, constitutive forces that, he understands, have the potential to both unite and divide. There is no way forward without them. "Any new perspective on ourselves," he writes, "must be based to a large extent on our roots. We should look into our histories and traditions, as well as into other cultures, for ideas and inspiration" (Waddell, Naidu, and Hau'ofa 1993: 128).

At USP, manifestations by students of their cultural traditions appear to many "progressives" as retrograde, dangerously divisive forms of identity politics—a critique we're very familiar with today. For Hau'ofa such an attitude suppresses a crucial resource for self-confidence and for making something different from the current reality, "which is largely a creation of imperialism."

> By deliberately omitting our changing traditions from serious discourses, especially at the School of Social and Economic Development, we tend to overlook the fact that most people are still using and adapting them as tools for survival, and, more seriously, we lose our ability to read the signs and spot quickly and early the subtle ways in which some of our leaders are manipulating them, and then scurry everywhere drumming up feeble support. I believe that we should pay a great deal more intellectual attention and commitment to our cultures than we have done, otherwise we could easily become V. S. Naipaul's mimic men and mimic women . . . (Waddell, Naidu, and Hau'ofa 1993: 129)

The invocation of Naipaul reminds us that Hau'ofa, an anthropology student in Canada, did fieldwork in Trinidad, where he found inspiration in the author's humorous and bitingly satiric early novels. And in the Caribbean he encountered another form of noncontinental region making, or "archipelagic" consciousness, as Edouard Glissant would put it. I recall that when Hau'ofa's "Sea of Islands" reached Santa Cruz in the mid-1990s I was engaged with Paul Gilroy's map/history of a "Black Atlantic," deployed against ethnic absolutism, and offering a counterhistory of capitalist, nation-state genealogies of modernity (Gilroy 1993). The two critical region- and scale-making projects reso- nated strongly across all the differences of North Atlantic and Pacific post- and neocolonial histories. (DeLoughrey [2007] explores these syn- ergies and tensions with great subtlety.)

The 1980s and 1990s, were, of course, moments of neoliberal hege- mony, of Thatcher's famous "TINA: There Is No Alternative," Fukayama's "End of History." A flexibly accumulating, expansive post-Fordist capi- talism seemed capable of restructuring, interpellating, commodifying virtually anything, anywhere. These were decades of demoralization on the Left. Dependency theory (linked, early on, with ideologies of Third World resistance) had evolved into debilitating forms of pessimism about the prospects for genuinely democratic transformations.

In 1993 how could this "Sea of Islands," stitched together from below, claim to be realistic—a project actually going somewhere in history? The twenty respondents in *A New Oceania* were seduced, but ambivalent. Surely this was just whistling in the neoliberal wind . . . And then, in the book's final pages (Waddell, Naidu, and Hau'ofa 1993: 138), came Hau'ofa's declaration of independence (he had just invoked the Kula Ring and Malinowki's Argonauts as an expansive model for Oceania): "Romantic Nonsense—So be it."

How should we understand this "So be it?" A kind of deliberate (or reckless) suspension of disbelief? Hau'ofa's earlier writings had "been there, done that" with hard-nosed political-economic realism. And now the imaginative, ironic freedom opened up by his satirical fiction—*Tales of the Tikongs* (1983), *Kisses in the Nederends* (1987)—was pulling else- where. Anyway, he knew for sure that there would be enough pessimism to go around. Henceforth, he would work the optimistic side of the street pretty much full-time.

"Romantic Nonsense?" Well, romanticism has always been an inte- gral, but often a dissonant, part of capitalist modernity. And nonsense is, after all, the trickster's principal weapon. Perhaps Hau'ofa's critical pessimism had been transmuted into a certain irony, that inimitable light touch and sense of the absurd (surely a "Pacific" style, if I may be per- mitted an essentialist moment) that cuts everything and everyone down to size.

The way forward, an Oceanic modus vivendi expressed in his subsequent essays, has proved inspiring for many of us struggling to imagine alternate ways through capitalist postmodernity. Yet the constitutive tensions that run through the USP volume have not gone away. Quite the contrary. As I reread *A New Oceania,* I'm drawn less to the conversion experience on the road to Hilo and more to that moment in 1987, the arguments at USP so abruptly shut down. Hau'ofa clearly regrets a lost opportunity to grapple together with "real alternative visions of our region"—an opportunity to inhabit, attentively, the contradictions of different historical dynamics. A dialectical realism, without transcendence.

I have come to see those tensions in the USP book as expressing fundamental, inescapable antinomies of our historical moment. We live with, work through and around them, but cannot get clear. They disrupt our renewed, never-successful attempts to align different spatiotemporal scales and projects: to join structure with process, determination with emergence, system with excess, macroeconomics with microethnography, History (capital H) with histories (final s). We operate, Stuart Hall always reminds us, on shifting, contradictory terrains. And, as Anna Tsing insists, at multiple, incongruous scales (Hall 1996; Tsing 2000).

I had conceived this lecture as a demonstration of this predicament, using the tensions and contradictions of my research on indigenous heritage projects in and around Kodiak Alaska. But thinking about Epeli Hau'ofa set me on a different tack. Those Oceanic currents . . .

My time is limited, so let me just give you a glimpse of the kinds of antinomies, and problems of representation, at issue there. I would have told two stories about the Alaska Native Claims Settlement Act of 1970 (ANCSA), an event that has profoundly inflected the course of Native histories. You may recall that this land settlement gave nearly $1 billion (back when a billion was real money) and a lot of land to Alaska Natives—a condition of building the oil pipeline from the recent discoveries in Prudhoe Bay all the way to Valdez in Prince William Sound. The prior decade had seen a growing movement of Native land claims and the formation of a pan-Alaskan alliance, The Alaska Federation of Natives. This movement hung together and eventually forced a global settlement rather than the piecemeal buyoffs that would otherwise have gotten the pipeline through. What seemed to be a big success came with a price: extinction of all other claims to land in Alaska (with allowances for traditional subsistence uses); and the land and funds were given to

Native corporations. To participate in the settlement individuals had to establish their tribal affiliations (showing at least 25 percent blood quantum) and sign up as shareholders in appropriate regional and local corporations. The idea was to give Native Alaskans a real stake in development, making them self-sufficient in the modern economy (while relieving the state of welfare obligations). Opinions on the great "social experiment" of ANCSA—the uneven performance of the corporations (despite bailouts from powerful allies like Ted Stevens) and their problematic relation to other forms of Native authority—remain, to say the least, mixed. ANCSA has been amended, and no doubt will be again. But Native corporations are now a fact of life in Alaska (and beyond, as the more successful diversify their activities from local timber and mining into areas like global telecommunications). Annual distributions to Native shareholders all over the state, supporting programs in health and social services, as well as heritage renewal projects such as the Alutiiq Museum in Kodiak, make a difference. How much and at what cost . . . ?

One story about ANCSA sees a pact with the capitalist devil and ultimately a loss of sovereignty as indigenous Alaskans are contained and subordinated by relationships they can never control. Another sees a strategic adoption of corporate structures for purposes of advancing the common good, making the best of an ambiguous new situation and exercising power at new scales. In Pacific terms, should we think of this as "development" or "develop-man," in Sahlins's (2000: 419) localized Pidgin spelling?" Was ANCSA the result of Alaska Native power flexing its muscles at a new state level—a land-claims movement holding powerful oil companies and their pipeline hostage? Or was it the flexible interpellation of Alaska's diverse and localized Native peoples into the structures of liberal governance, a managed multiculturalism?

The Native people on and around Kodiak Island were once named Aleuts or Koniags by Russian invaders, and later "Pacific Eskimos" by anthropologists. Some of them have, at times, thought of themselves as Russian. Now most call themselves "Alitiiq." Is their recent emergence as one of Alaska's publicly recognized Native peoples a product of the ANCSA moment and the proliferation of so-called identity politics in Alaska, with its selective reclamations of tradition and performances of "heritage," in new, but circumscribed, public arenas? Or is this a transformative revival, reweaving surviving elements of language, kinship, religion, subsistence, senses of place, forms of craft and art? In the latter perspective we would need to be attentive to old and new situations of performance, communication, and translation, as well as new scales of identification and diaspora.

Preceding ANCSA, what kind of historical narrative can account for the existence of Alutiiq Native religion: Russian Orthodoxy? Surely not a story of assimilation or before-after conversion, but rather a tangled tale of specific articulations, accommodations, and partial translations— a story whose fascinating details I can't get into now. Russian Orthodoxy in Alaska, as much scholarship has shown, was dramatically "indigenized," becoming a source of social distinction and relative power (Fienup-Riordan 1990; Oleksa 1992; Black 2004). You can imagine how a localized "Russian" religion, after 1867 when the Russians themselves departed and the more invasive Americans moved in, could function as a site of disarticulation from the new imperial hegemony.

Native Orthodoxy is not, however, a story of separatism, but of constrained maneuver within changing material pressures. Russia's imperial practice favored intermarriage and the creation of so-called "Creole" elites who played crucial economic, political, and religious roles in the empire. It's important to ask how Creole hierarchies transformed earlier social stratifications in the Aleutians and Kodiak, and how this accommodation has in turn been transformed by new, more explicitly capitalist "class" positions in the post-ANCSA Native corporations (Mason 2002). And is this the end of the story? Who is using whom in these transformations? Do the new elites function like capitalists elsewhere? What community obligations do the corporations substantially meet? Given the mixed results of Native corporations in Alaska—a wide range of successes and failures, and an unfinished learning curve—it's hard to say definitively.

There is simply no place of historical hindsight from which to sort out and impose a unified functional structure on these discrepant stories. It's a tangled and unfinished historical reality that I find I can't represent in a seamless way.

At one pole, familiar kinds of world-system functionalism say, in effect: "If any alternate social or cultural forces exist that do not *transform* the system, they must be *part* of the system." All differences are interpellated or called into being by power (for example, post-1960s "identity politics" is essentially a kind of managed multiculturalism allowed by, even produced by, postmodern governmental structures). This system-centered view certainly accounts for part of what's being articulated and performed in recent claims for indigenous sociocultural diversity. But it wipes away all the local histories of social negotiation and struggle, transformative continuity and place-based living, denying them any meaningful historical momentum in the contemporary moment. I find myself imagining a tangle of historicities rather than a progressively aligned common History—however "combined and uneven" its development.

At the other extreme, we're familiar with the positive, often rather self-righteous, stories of local and indigenous cultures persisting, rising from the ashes, reaching back to their pasts to fashion genuine alternatives to the "West" and its civilizing, modernizing missions. Certainly many of us have at times told some version of this story. It brings into view inventive, discrepant, social forms. It narrates entangled histories, sometimes of extreme localism, sometimes of a larger "sovereignty" politics, enacted at national, regional, or international scales. Clearly a lot is going on under the sign of "globalization." But whatever hopes (and worries) may be provoked by the interactive survival of local cultures in postmodernity, no clear, really convincing answer is provided for the materialist skeptics who ask whether this really adds up to anything important in a globalizing, capitalist world. Isn't it all basically a way to be different within an inviting, but circumscribed, set of variations, a "global system of common differences" (Wilk 1995)? If everyone gets a culture, an identity, and performative forms of recognition—well, what else is new?

My admittedly ad hoc, undertheorized solution is to always be juxtaposing histories—to always be working with more than one.

When it comes to indigenous heritage work (for example, the Alutiiq Museum in Kodiak, originally funded by *Exxon Valdez* oil spill compensation funds and now largely by ANCSA Native corporations), I can never say finally whether I'm describing a process of articulation or interpellation. Is heritage best seen as a pragmatic political recombination of existing elements in a new historical field of forces or as a command performance of identity? At worst it's an activity of self-stereotyping in terms recognizable to powerful others, at best a strategic performance translating lost and found traditions for multiple audiences, Native and non-Native. It doesn't help much to say it's always both. You tend to end up in those predictable binaries: the good news and the bad news, domination and resistance, system and subversion . . .

Yet that's where we do so often end up. Juxtaposing different stories and analytics. I see no way out of this, if by that we mean coming up with a historical totality, a unidirectional temporal representation at *any* analytic level or sociospatial scale. Incompleteness, juxtaposition, with ends unwoven and edges rough, is a more realist mode of representation than functional integration, however flexible and dynamic. How can this sense of the real be rendered in our writing and speaking, our showing and telling? I find myself offering experiments and failures, not models and successes. The antinomies at issue can't be dialectically sublated: they're constitutive tensions in a paradoxically constrained and excessive historical field of forces.

To understand this constrained openness, I rely on Raymond Williams's account of "determination" in *Marxism and Literature* (1977)—a matter of pressures and limits, not mechanical causation or before-after, "epochal" histories. We need a lot of room for complex articulations of what Williams called residual, dominant, and emergent formations. Moreover, the directionality implied by the three terms wavers when (in the spirit of both Walter Benjamin and contemporary indigenous neotraditionalism) it becomes hard to distinguish the residual from the emergent.

I hold on to the notion of an enormously powerful capitalist world system, but a nonfunctionalist system (an oxymoron, perhaps) that can't claim a global reach, either in descriptive or explanatory registers. I'm looking for a big-enough story of capitalism, understood not as a historically dynamic structure driven by its "economic" engine, but as a variegated formation always already articulated—socially, politically, culturally, and economically. I also imagine a world system that can no longer be spatialized into stable cores and peripheries, that is susceptible to deep crises and profound reconfigurations.

In the new millennium, for all the reasons we know so well, neoliberal confidence and imperial geopolitical momentum have been shaken. From the Left it becomes possible again to see around capitalism or at least to imagine its metamorphosis. A sign of the times: Immanuel Wallerstein's *Decline of American Power* (2003). The political/economic structures that sustained the modern world system for the past five hundred years are not sustainable, he argues. It can no longer reproduce itself. We are moving into a critical, perhaps prolonged, "transition" in which political/economic elements that once seemed structural will recede in importance, and more contingent "political" struggles (without guaranteed outcomes—Right, Left, or otherwise) will decide the new

political-economic arrangements. I can't go into the details of his diagnosis, which are certainly contestable. I merely note that the man who
conceptualized and described the world system is now prepared to shut
it down, or at least to imagine its radical reconfiguration.

I think we all recognize that global arrangements of power are shifting
under our feet. And while there is risk of overreaction to what may turn
out to be just another systemic, albeit quite deep, crisis, the future does
seem more open than at any other time in the post–World War II era.
What real prospects are there, now, for alternate forms of development,
of regionalism, of cultural particularity, of variegated sovereignty, of
indigenous cosmopolitan links? Is history moving in more than one
direction? What will count as "realism" in this open-ended conjuncture?
What big-enough stories? Is the present crisis, even "chaos," a source of
hope or fear? Surely both . . .

Today, Epeli Hau'ofa's utopia—based on past and present acts of connection that don't align along dominant trajectories of core and periphery,
tradition and modernity, local and global—seems more like a history
that could find space to grow. It is a hope necessarily entangled with
other, more ambivalent, scenarios and dystopias. "So be it."

6

❖

LOOKING SEVERAL WAYS

Gone are the days when cultural anthropologists could, without contradiction, present "the native point of view," when archaeologists and physical anthropologists excavated tribal remains without local permission, when linguists collected data on indigenous languages without feeling pressure to return the results in accessible form. Scholarly outsiders now find themselves barred from access to research sites, met with new or newly public suspicion. Indeed, "the anthropologist"—broadly and sometimes stereotypically defined—has become a negative alter ego in contemporary indigenous discourse, invoked as the epitome of arrogant, intrusive colonial authority. The most famous salvo is, of course, Vine Deloria's *Custer Died for Your Sins* (1969). The decolonizing critique is deepened by Linda Tuhiwai Smith (1999) and given satiric expression in the songs of Floyd Westerman ("Here Come the Anthros") and the cartoons of Phil Hughte (1994).

The history of anthropological relations with local communities includes many examples of insensitive data and artifact collection. These, combined with general assumptions of scientific authority, are understood as modes of colonial domination from the other side of a structural power imbalance, and, as histories such as David Hurst Thomas's *Skull Wars* (2000) amply document, the resentment is often justified. At the same time, the sweeping condemnations of (or jokes at the expense of) anthropologists by indigenous peoples are often combined with generous words for individuals whose work has been based on reciprocity, respect, and cooperation (see, e.g., Deloria 1997: 210; Hereniko 2000: 90). And anthropological texts are frequently reappropriated in native discourses, invoked in revivals of tradition. Indeed, the legacy of scientific research done in colonial situations is ambiguous and open ended. In Malekula, Vanuatu, A. B. Deacon's research from the 1920s is recycled in contemporary *kastom* discourses (Larcom 1982; Curtis 2003). In California, the "salvage" anthropology and linguistics of the Alfred Kroeber/Mary Haas tradition at Berkeley is an invaluable resource for tribal heritage activities. If Kroeber is currently condemned for insensitively sending Ishi's brain to the Smithsonian collection of Ales Hrdlicka or for pronouncing "death sentences" in his authoritative *Handbook of the Indians of California* (1925), on tribes now struggling for recognition, he is also gratefully remembered by Yurok elders for loyal friendships and for recording precious lore. His extensive, carefully researched court testimony in the 1950s on behalf of native claims prefigures today's advocacy roles (see Buckley 1996: 294–295; Field 1999).

This legacy presents contemporary researchers—native, nonnative, "insider," "outsider," "halfie," "diasporic"—with both obstacles and opportunities. Les Field (1999) sees an unfinished history of "complicities and collaborations." Fundamentally altered by the political mobilization of native communities, research can no longer be justified by assumptions of free scientific access and interpersonal rapport. Explicit contract agreements and negotiated reciprocities are increasingly the norm. In postindependence Vanuatu, for example, anthropology and archaeology were formally banned for a decade. Now research is permitted only when host communities agree and when the foreign researcher collaborates with a local "filwoka" doing heritage work for the Vanuatu Cultural Centre (Bolton 1999; Curtis 2003). In some contexts, anthropologists find themselves recruited for land-claims litigation, archaeologists for local heritage projects, linguists for language reclamation. In others, fieldwork is forbidden or subject to disabling restrictions. Faced with these new, politicized relations, scholars may regret a loss of "scientific freedom"—forgetting the structural power that was formerly a guarantee of free access and relative safety and ignoring the many implicit limits and accommodations that have always been part of field research. (Many scientists once felt authorized to remove human remains, without consent, from graves in native communities. If this is now beyond the professional pale, it is the result of ethical and political constraints on scientific freedom.) As native intellectuals and activists challenge academic authority, lines can harden: the current "Kennewick Man"/"Ancient One" struggle for control of an ancient skeleton is a notorious case in which unbending "native" and "scientific" positions face off in court (Thomas 2000). Even where relations are less polarized, it has become clear that local communities need to be able to say no, unambiguously, as a precondition for negotiating more equitable and respectful collaborations. In practice, the complex, unfinished colonial entanglements of anthropology and native communities are being undone and rewoven, and even the most severe indigenous critics of anthropology recognize the potential for alliances when they are based on shared resources, repositioned indigenous and academic authorities, and relations of genuine respect (Deloria 2000: xvi; Smith 1999: 15, 17; Field 1999).

This essay probes the possibilities and limits of collaborative work, focusing on a recent Native heritage exhibition in southwestern Alaska: *Looking Both Ways*. I discuss the project's contributors, conditions of production, and occasions of reception primarily through a contextualized reading of its remarkable catalogue, *Looking Both Ways: Heritage and Identity of the Alutiiq People,* edited by Aron Crowell, Amy Steffian, and Gordon Pullar (2001). I was able to view the exhibition, which was linked with a local Alutiiq cultural festival (Tamamta Katurlluta, August 31, 2002) in one of its Alaskan venues. I also discuss, more briefly, Ann Fienup-Riordan's pioneering work with Yup'ik collaborators and the recently opened Alaska Native Heritage Center in Anchorage. The goal is not a complete survey of heritage activity in the region but an evocation of changing Alaskan Native identity politics, touching on several different practices of cultural revival, translation, and alliance. Heritage is self-conscious tradition, what Fienup-Riordan calls "conscious culture" (2000: 167), performed in old and new public contexts and asserted against historical experiences of loss. It responds to demands that originate both inside and outside indigenous communities, mediating new powers and attachments: relations with the land, among local groups, with the state, and with transnational forces. In contemporary Alaska, "Native" identifications have been empowered by global and regional movements of cultural resurgence and political contestation. They have also been channeled and intensified by state policies, particularly the Alaska Native Claims Settlement Act of 1971 and its aftermath.

The Political Economy of Identity

The Alaska Native Claims Settlement Act, commonly called ANCSA, was a political compromise, articulating several different agendas: (1) land claims being pressed by a new political coalition, the Alaska Federation of Natives (AFN); (2) transnational corporations' need to build a pipeline across the state to deliver oil recently discovered in

Prudhoe Bay; and (3) the desire of state and federal governments to establish a new Native policy in the wake of the failed "termination" agenda of the 1950s and 1960s. The act awarded forty-four million acres of land and nearly $1 billion to thirteen regional Native corporations and 205 village corporations. Eligible Native shareholders had to show a 25 percent blood quantum, and participation was limited to individuals born before the date of the legislation. Unique in U.S. Native policy, ANCSA reflects the specific history of Native-government relations in Alaska, which lacks a reservation system, "Indian Country," and government trusteeship as practiced in the lower forty-eight states. It has served as a model for Inuit "self-determination" in Quebec, with ambivalent consequences similar to those in Alaska, including the emergence of a Native corporate elite (Mitchell 1996; Skinner 1997; Dombrowski 2002).

For Alaska Natives, the need for a settlement became urgent after statehood in 1958 when the federal government began to transfer lands to the new state at an accelerating rate. These lands, considered to be in the public domain, had long been accessible to Natives for critical subsistence activities. Native leaders saw that valuable resources were in danger of passing permanently out of their control, territories whose title in the past had been at least ambiguous and contestable. A land-claims movement gathered strength during the 1960s, and the discovery of oil in 1968 provided an opportunity for a systematic solution. Native leaders judged that to obtain clear title to a significant portion—in the event about 10 percent—of Alaska would be worth the price of extinguishing their claim to the rest. Without a settlement, Natives could well end up with tiny landholdings in economically undesirable areas, sharing the fate of tribes elsewhere in the United States. The AFN held firm and, after much wrangling in the U.S. Congress, concluded a deal. Something was better than nothing: ANCSA seemed a remarkably generous outcome, guaranteeing Native stewardship of important lands and resources in Alaska.

The oil companies, fearing that their access to a pipeline could be tied up in court for years, made common cause with the AFN, a potent alliance that produced an outcome that Native pressure alone could never have achieved. In Washington it seemed clear that the indeterminacy of title for most of the vast new state of Alaska needed to be cleared up if development and resource extraction were to proceed smoothly. But negotiating with Alaska Natives raised issues of governmental structure. Tribal institutions, "government-to-government" relations, federal and state stewardship responsibilities, as these existed in the lower forty-eight, were to be avoided. Moreover, the establishment of "reservations" on the U.S. model was distasteful to many Alaska Natives. ANCSA's corporate structure offered an ingenious solution. Championed by Democratic Senator Henry ("Scoop") Jackson, its liberal (we would now say neoliberal) progressive vision sought, in effect, to privatize Native lands in corporate form. It could thus avoid any strengthening or recognition of "tribal" governments in the tradition of John Collier's New Deal–era Indian Reorganization Act, while giving Alaska Natives access to economic development as investors and entrepreneurs. More than a hundred Alaska Native villages had, in fact, already achieved tribal recognition, or something close to it, from the federal government. These potentially "sovereign" political entities did not control much land, however. And ANCSA, in bypassing them, hoped to hasten the day when they would wither away. In practice, however, corporate and tribal institutions have coexisted in conflict and synergy, an ambiguous political-economic relationship.

ANCSA, in fact, left a great deal unresolved, and it soon became a site of new struggles. But in 1971 key interests—Native, governmental, petrocapitalist—found common interest in a settlement. For the oil companies, the act was a success: the Alaska pipeline was built, oil flowed. There would be problems like the *Exxon Valdez* spill and the need for compensation. But Alaska's oil and gas economy was established, and soon virtually everyone in the state, Native and non-Native, would find themselves dependent on oil. But development based on resource extraction—oil, gas, minerals, timber—was not the panacea many anticipated. Governmental hopes of creating economically independent, entrepreneurial Native communities turned out to be illusory. The idea that isolated Native villages could somehow be transformed into businesses, thus expanding employment and reducing welfare responsibilities, was an idea that made little sense in practice. As the comprehensive assessment of ANCSA'a first decade published in 1985 by the Canadian jurist Thomas Berger (1995) pointed out, village-level Native life has always depended on an economy of subsistence hunting, fishing, and gathering. Any settlement of land issues in Canada that could sustain indigenous life outside towns and cities would need to recognize the mixed economies people had been sustaining, a range of traditional and new activities with subsistence at the core. Government policy needed to strengthen subsistence, not attempt to replace it with an abstract vision of capitalist enterprise. Berger's inquiry gathered and focused many voices in a work of eloquent, critical advocacy. The villagers he listened to all over Alaska overwhelmingly affirmed the centrality of living from, and with, the land. The property allotted to village-level corporations by ANCSA was insufficient. A viable way of life required local stewardship of wide areas of land and sea, places to which Natives had long enjoyed unfettered access. Preservation of these rights for rural Natives practicing traditional subsistence had, in fact, been guaranteed in a law passed after the 1971 agreement. But the Alaska Supreme Court struck down this new legislation after determining that it was based upon unlawful favoritism. Questions of access and management are still unresolved, hotly contested by differing interests in hunting, fishing, environment, and resource management. Four decades after ANCSA the economic viability of traditional village life remains precarious.

At regional levels, ANCSA established large development corporations that controlled the lion's share of land and funding. Primarily businesses, their task was to make money and distribute income to Native shareholders. But ANCSA corporations were not understood to be simply capitalist operations like any other. Their mandate was to benefit shareholders, who were, as much as possible, members of an ethnically defined group. In principle (but very unevenly in practice), they were to employ Native Alaskans. They also had a responsibility to support health, education, and cultural renewal projects. Thus "development" was understood to be a more than narrowly economic mandate. ANCSA corporations also differed, crucially, in the nature of shareholder participation and ownership. In the original act, shares could not be sold for twenty years, after which they would become fully negotiable property. This provision introduced a fatal contradiction between the goal of preserving Native lands in perpetuity and the agendas of liberal privatization. When Berger conducted his survey, 1991 was approaching, and he encountered widespread fear that the precious resources entrusted to the corporations would soon be lost. The danger was real, and widely recognized. If the free transfer of ANCSA property were permitted, continuing poverty would force Native shareholders to sell to non-Natives. The material/spiritual foundation for indigenous life would disappear. ANCSA now looked less like a victory, a stabilization of Native lands, and more like a neoliberal form of termination by market processes. The framers of ANCSA in Washington had seen it as a way of bringing Native people into participation with the national economy, and thus over the

long term as a form of assimilation. But few were prepared to counte-
nance a rapid loss of the lands returned just two decades earlier. As a
result, the so-called "1991 amendments" were enacted, extending the
restrictions on transfers to non-Natives and partly addressing another
area of concern, the divisiveness created by the law's restriction on individuals born after 1971 from acquiring shares other than through inheritance.

ANCSA has always been hellishly complex, and its various adjustments, loopholes, and unintended consequences are sources of ongoing
adjustments and political deal making. The 1991 amendments were a
temporary fix for the original act's worst flaws, giving Native societies
breathing room for survival, and providing time for Native corporate
executives to learn how to best exploit their niche in state, national, and
transnational economies. The performance of most ANCSA corporations during the act's first decades had been uneven and sometimes disastrous. Native leaders lacked experience in business. Conflicts within and
among the different corporations led to ruinous and protracted lawsuits.
Powerful politicians like Alaska Senator Ted Stevens had to sponsor legislation to prop up failing corporations. Relatively few new jobs for
Natives had been created, and shareholder distributions were far smaller
than anticipated. Since the early nineties, and the enactment of the
amendments, some of the regional corporations have in fact begun to do
well economically. The economic picture, however, remains mixed, and
much of the success is based on moving investments out of Alaska and
into telecommunications or government contracts awarded through a
preferential policy favoring minority businesses. This has often meant
partnering with—critics would say fronting for—large business interests
with projects ranging from environmentally dubious logging to Iraq war
reconstruction. At the same time, in several corporations annual pay-
ments to shareholders have become significant, and all continue to take
seriously their mandate to underwrite community-based social and cultural programs. ANCSA remains a very mixed blessing for Native
Alaskans. Depending on whom one asks, the glass is half full or half
empty. Its defenders see a social experiment, imperfect, and very much
in process, but a crucial path for Native Alaskan participation and influence in the state and beyond. Detractors see an imposed structure that
has not delivered economic development on Native terms: an unequal,
divisive system, creating new elites and undermining the values and
institutions on which long-term Native survival depends.

The basic presuppositions of the 1971 settlement were always controversial, and ANCSA is not the only force for change in Native societies. There has never been a consensus on whether the way forward for Native Alaskans is best pursued through (economic) corporate rather than (political) "tribal" institutions. In practice both agendas are active. Many now think that tribal governments need to be strengthened, especially if village level life is to be sustained (e.g., Fienup-Riordan 1990: ch. 9). The language of "sovereignty" challenges that of "development." This means recognizing local governance structures, based on kinship, tradition, and village life, that were largely bypassed by ANCSA. It could eventually produce revisions in the law that would relocate land from regional corporations to collective ownership within tribal structures. Such a move is resisted by corporate elites in ANCSA and by those who have benefitted from the current system. Moreover, any vision of consolidating lands under (relatively) autonomous tribal governments is complicated by growing concentrations of Native people in larger towns and cities, especially Anchorage. The "settlement" remains unsettled.

ANCSA has been critically important as a structuring factor over the past four decades, but it would be a mistake to see it as determining Native futures in Alaska. The act has had diverse consequences, working with and against local traditions of governance, inflecting old and new tribal initiatives. ANCSA has been plausibly compared to a notorious earlier attempt to privatize tribal life in the name of progressive assimilation: the Dawes Plan of 1887, which at the end of the Indian wars on the Plains forcibly divided tribal lands into individual holdings (Anders 1990). Most Indians were ill prepared, and unwilling, to quickly transform themselves into yeoman farmers; material pressures soon led to sale of the allotted lands. Viewed from the top down, as governmental projects of social engineering, ANCSA and the Dawes Plan have much in common. Yet the balance of forces in the two historical conjunctures differs markedly. In the 1890s Native Americans were militarily defeated and in conditions of demographic collapse. There was no equivalent to the Alaska Federation of Natives, a key participant in the ANCSA process. The situation of Alaska Natives in the 1960s and 1970s was one of both poverty and neglect and of land claims and resurgence. New visions of sovereignty were emerging in the wider renewal of "indigenous" peoples, at state, national, circumpolar, and indeed worldwide scales. This was not the 1890s moment of defeat. Nor was it a moment of liberation. In the decades since 1970 the power of markets and media to influence social aspirations and cultural change has grown. ANCSA thus reflects a new field of forces and a politics of articulation rather than of dominance—messy, compromised, difficult to circumscribe. The Dawes Plan reduced but failed to extinguish tribal life. Will neoliberal forms of governmentality at a time of tribal resurgence, coupled with corporate identifications linked to multicultural tolerance, be more successful? (For a broader discussion of this critical, open question, see Chapter 1.)

Whatever its future, ANCSA has shaped the contemporary politics of identity in Alaska. Its explicit intent was to foster economic "development" and "self-reliance," but these terms would have different definitions in Washington, D.C., and in Native communities. Narrowly economic, individualistic visions of progress would conflict with traditions of extended kinship, communal solidarity, and the ecological reciprocities of subsistence hunting, fishing, and gathering. Heritage work, the preservation and revival of specifically indigenous values and traditions, is thus central to the struggle over how to participate in capitalist modernity on Native terms—a struggle whose outcome is far from guaranteed. ANCSA corporations have been crucial donors to the heritage projects that gained momentum in the 1980s and 1990s, including those discussed in this essay. Members of the boards of directors for both regional and village corporations have considered cultural reclamation a priority similar to health and education. Part of the broad corporate mandate, it is widely understood to be an important response to the despair and self-destructiveness that have plagued Native communities. Here, as everywhere, there is disagreement. Critics see heritage work as a palliative, draining resources and diverting attention from more urgent economic and political agendas. Moreover, a revived traditional culture can be standardized ("logoized," it is sometimes said) for corporate purposes (Dombrowski 2002; Mason 2002). This is certainly one important ideological appropriation of heritage. But as we will see, the work funded by Native corporations has multiple audiences and outcomes, not all of which are so evidently aligned with capitalist hegemony and the emergence of culturally fulfilled, normative liberal subjects.

The 1970s saw a realignment of Native identities at new scales, inflecting developments already under way and common to other postwar indigenous movements for self-determination. With the passage of ANCSA, for the first time it paid to be Native. The land-claims movements of the 1960s and the formation of the Alaska Federation of Natives made a Native politics based on pan-Alaska alliances possible. Nurtured by strengthening "circumpolar" and "Fourth World" connections, large-scale ethnic or "tribal" identifications emerged, supplementing more local village or kin-based affiliations. Heritage preservation and performance have been an integral part of these changing Native articulations. The result has been new identifications and more formally expressed notions of "culture" or "tradition," performances appropriate to changing indigenous experiences no longer exclusively rooted in village settings.

A particularly clear example is provided by the people who now call themselves "Alutiiq" (and sometimes also "Sugpiaq"), a dispersed population currently living in villages and towns on Kodiak Island, on the southern coast of the Alaska Peninsula, on the Kenai Peninsula, on Prince William Sound, and in urban Anchorage. Their uncertain status as a coherent entity in 1971 is indicated by the fact that Alutiiq are dispersed among three of the ANCSA regional corporations. Many individuals rediscovered or renewed their sense of "Native" identity in the process of ANCSA enrollment. Their collective history had been one of intense disruption and trauma: the arrival of the Russians in the late eighteenth century, bringing labor exploitation, massacres, and epidemics; U.S. colonization after 1867, with missionaries, boarding schools, and intense military presence during World War II; and devastation and displacement by a series of seismic disasters and the *Exxon Valdez* oil spill. While a great deal of local tradition had been lost or buried, there were surviving subsistence communities, kinship networks, a deep-rooted Native religion (syncretic Russian Orthodoxy), and a significant, if dwindling, number of individuals who could speak Sugt'stun, the Eskimoan language indigenous to the region. Under the impetus of the identity politics sweeping Alaska, affiliations only partially consolidated by ANCSA, people felt inspired to research, reclaim, and transmit an "Alutiiq" heritage (see Pullar 1992; Mason 2010a).

Throughout Native Alaska, innovative forms of cultural/artistic production have been devised, along with new alliances of Native and non-Native interests and new sites of performance and consumption. Today these range from regional Elders' conferences and syncretic revivals of midwinter dancing to language classes, carving and boat-building workshops, tribal museums, "native tours," and model villages for cruise-ship visitors. New cohorts of ethnically defined entrepreneurs, community leaders, and cultural brokers have emerged. Older forms of social, political, and religious authority are simultaneously recognized and transformed, selectively translated in changing situations. How these practices take hold in local contexts varies considerably, depending on demographics and ecology, the timing and force of colonial and neocolonial disruptions, possibilities and pressures for resource extraction, and ongoing struggles over subsistence rights.

Heritage, viewed nonreductively, is neither the recovery of authentic traditions and a kind of rebirth, nor a cultural palliative functioning within liberal forms of hegemony. Works like *Looking Both Ways* and the other heritage projects discussed below are necessarily compromised activities, entangled in competing interests. They need to be treated as specific coproductions in a complex social/economic/cultural conjuncture that both governs and empowers Native life. Broadly defined, heritage work includes oral-historical research, cultural evocation and explanation (exhibits, festivals, publications, films, tourist sites), language description and pedagogy, community-based archaeology, art production, marketing, and criticism. Of course, such projects are only one aspect of indigenous self-determination politics today. Heritage is not a substitute for land claims, struggles over subsistence rights, development, educational and health projects, defense of sacred sites, and repatriation of human remains or stolen artifacts, but it is closely connected to all these struggles. What counts as "tradition" is never politically neutral (Jolly 1992; Briggs 1996; Clifford 2000; Phillips and Schochet 2004), and the work of cultural retrieval, display, and performance plays a necessary role in current movements around identity and recognition. We need to keep in view multiple producers and consumers of Native heritage, stressing the constitutive processes of political *articulation,* contingent *performance,* and partial *translation.*

Heritage projects participate in a range of public spheres, acting within and between Native communities as sites of mobilization and pride, sources of intergenerational inspiration and education, ways to reconnect with the past and to say to others: "We exist," "We have deep roots here," "We are different." This kind of cultural politics is not without ambiguities and dangers (see Hewison 1987; Harvey 1990; Walsh 1992). Heritage can be a form of self-marketing, responding to the demands of a multicultural political economy that contains and manages inequalities. Sustaining local traditions does not guarantee economic and social justice, although it can strengthen the community resilience needed to resist and build effective alliances. In postindustrial contexts heritage has been criticized as a depoliticized, commodified nostalgia—ersatz tradition. While such criticisms tend to oversimplify the politics of localism, as Raphael Samuel (1994) has argued, pressures for cultural objectification and commodification are indeed often at work in contemporary heritage projects. But to conclude with a moral/political "bottom line" of objectification and commodification is to miss a great deal of the local, regional, national, and international meaning activated by heritage work.

In Chapter 1 I argued that the politics of identity and heritage are both constrained and empowered by today's more flexible forms of capitalist marketing, communication, and government. While recognizing these pressures, it is crucial to distinguish different temporalities and scales (Tsing 2000) of political articulation (local, regional, national, international), performativity (linguistic, familial, religious, pedagogic, touristic), and translation (intergenerational, cross-cultural, conservative, innovative). Global cultural and economic forces are localized and to a degree critically inflected through these processes. Indeed, the connections affirmed in Native heritage projects—with land, with Elders, with religious affiliations, with ancient, unevenly changing practices— can be substantial, not "invented" or merely simulacral. And for indigenous people, long marginalized or made to disappear, physically and ideologically, to say "We exist" in performances and publications is a powerful political act. In the past several decades, at regional and international scales, an increasing indigenous presence has been felt in many settler-colonial and national contexts. Today's indigenous movements, like earlier anticolonial mobilizations, question dichotomous, arguably Eurocentric conceptions of "cultural" versus "political" or "economic" agency. The Kanak independence leader Jean-Marie Tjibaou (1996) insisted on the practical connection between heritage affirmations and anticolonial self-determination struggles. To act politically, as Stuart Hall (1988) reminds us, people need a strong sense of who they are and where they come from. In a similar vein, Judith Butler (1998) queries recent portrayals of "merely cultural" movements as divorced from the "real politics" of structural transformation.

Of course, the conditions for "self-determination" or "sovereignty" are different a half-century after the wave of postwar national liberation movements. Under conditions of globalization, self-determination is less a matter of independence and more a practice of managing interdependence, inflecting uneven power relations, and finding room for maneuver (Clifford 2001). Subaltern strategies today are flexible and adapted to globally interconnected contexts. This is not an entirely new predicament: indigenous movements have always had to make the best of bad political-economic situations. In a neoliberal settler-colonial milieu such as contemporary Alaska—where Native groups, a political presence, control significant land and resources—basic power imbalances persist. The spaces opened for Native expansion and initiative are circumscribed, and key conditions attached to the apparently generous ANCSA settlements have been shown to serve dominant interests (Dombrowski 2002). At the same time, the social and cultural mobilizations now articulated with state and corporate multiculturalism in Alaska predate and potentially overflow the prevailing structures of government. Heritage work, to the extent that it selectively preserves and updates cultural traditions and relations to place, can be part of a social process that strengthens indigenous claims to land, resources, and autonomy—to a status beyond that of another minority or interest group. My discussion of *Looking Both Ways* makes this guarded positive claim. The long-term political and economic effects of recent Alutiiq cultural mobilizations remain to be seen, and the outcome will necessarily be compromised and uneven.

In the next section I introduce the *Looking Both Ways* project and juxtapose it with other heritage exhibitions and publications that have responded to the changing Native situation in Alaska. Having presented a range of experiences, I return to the complex question already raised of how Native presence in the post-ANCSA period should be understood historically, as an articulation of new liberal forms of government with older, transforming energies of Native resilience. I then discuss the Alutiiq project's portrayal of an emergent multiaccented identity and weigh the limits and possibilities of collaborative heritage work for anthropologists, archaeologists, and linguists forging new relationships with Native communities.

Looking Both Ways

Looking Both Ways, a sign of the changing times, draws on two decades of Native cultural revival and relations with academic researchers. Two archaeological negotiations were central to the process. In 1984 the Kodiak Area Native Association (KANA), under the new presidency of Gordon Pullar, a Native activist and educator, entered into a partnership with the archaeologist Richard Jordan to involve Native youth and Elders in an excavation in the village of Karluk. Local people were deeply moved by confronting carved wooden masks, stone tools, and spruce-root baskets from their ancestral past. One woman's face "reflected both confusion and sadness. Finally speaking, she said, 'I guess we really are Natives after all. I was always told that we were Russians'" (Pullar 1992: 183). "Russian" self-identification, rooted in the older empire's Creole social structure and Orthodox religion, had persisted for a century after 1867—a way of maintaining social distinction and not being normatively American. In a new field of ideological forces, this complex identification would be rearticulated as "Alutiiq." The Karluk project, with its Native participation and local dissemination of results, became a model for subsequent excavations in Alutiiq communities (Knecht 1994, 2001). In 1987 the Kodiak Island community of Larsen Bay petitioned for the return of ancestral bones and artifacts collected in the 1930s by the physical anthropologist Ales Hrdlicka and preserved in the Smithsonian Institution's collections. After four years of sometimes bitter struggle, the materials were returned and the skeletal remains reburied (Bray and Killion 1994). The Larsen Bay repatriation was a landmark in the wider renegotiation of relations between U.S. Indian communities and scientific institutions. It contributed directly to the Native Graves Protection and Repatriation Act (NAGPRA) of 1990, and it was a rallying point for the dispersed Native peoples on and around Kodiak Island who were coming to see themselves as custodians of a distinctive "Alutiiq" history and culture.

During the 1990s Smithsonian policy, particularly at its Arctic Studies Center, directed by William Fitzhugh, moved decisively in the direction of collaboration with indigenous communities. KANA, formed in 1966 during the period of land-claims activism, had already added a cultural heritage program animated by the archaeologist Richard Knecht. This initiative would develop during the 1990s into the Alutiiq Museum and Archaeological Repository, first directed by Knecht and now by the Alutiiq anthropologist and cultural activist Sven Haakanson Jr. By the end of the decade the museum had moved into a new facility in Kodiak, built with *Exxon Valdez* oil spill compensation funding. It has expanded rapidly and now sustains a full range of educational, community archaeology, arts, and curatorial programs. Its board of directors is composed of representatives from KANA and from eight Alutiiq village corporations, and it sponsors projects throughout the Kodiak Island area. (A fuller account, based on subsequent research, is presented in Chapter 7.)

The Alutiiq Museum board hesitated before agreeing to cosponsor *Looking Both Ways*. Memories of the Larsen Bay repatriation were fresh and suspicion of the Smithsonian still strong. The museum, struggling to establish its institutional identity, would need to be guaranteed full partnership in the project. Aron Crowell, director of the Alaska office of the Arctic Studies Center, spearheaded the effort, offering access to funds and to the Kodiak collections held in Washington, D.C. With support from museum staff, he eventually secured agreement from the board members, who saw that a well-funded traveling show on Alutiiq heritage could be a way to "put Alutiiq on the map." For the Smithsonian, collaboration with the Kodiak museum was critical to the project's success. Local networks from more than a decade of KANA-sponsored heritage work could be activated. Two Elders' planning sessions exerted a crucial influence on the shape of the project, and the Alutiiq Museum provided an appropriate Native venue for the exhibition. At the 2001 opening, four generations of an Alutiiq family cut the ribbon, and visitors who had traveled considerable distances to attend were met by a team of well-prepared youth docents who had acquired specialized knowledge of specific parts of the exhibition. As reported in the *Alutiiq Museum Bulletin,* the opening combined ceremony and celebration, with speeches, a Russian Orthodox blessing, traditional dancers, and a banquet.

The exhibition was built around artifacts lent by the Smithsonian, most of them collected by William J. Fisher, a German-born naturalist and fur trader, during the last two decades of the nineteenth century. Masks, clothing, and items of daily and ceremonial life were exhibited, along with prehistoric and historic specimens from the Alutiiq Museum's archaeological repository. While the presentation was strongly historical, enlarged color pictures of contemporary individuals (drying salmon, picking berries), video recordings, and images of modern-day villages reminded viewers of the present moment—of whose heritage this was. The exhibition themes—"Our Ancestors," "Our History," "Our Way of Living," "Our Beliefs," and "Our Family"—sustained a focus on community. The old objects, returning after a century and still linked with specific places and people, provoked emotional reactions—sadness, recognition, gratitude, kinship. Texts accompanying the artifacts included both scholarly contextualizations and quotes from Elders recorded at the planning meetings.

Works of traditional art, old and new, were juxtaposed. A breathtaking skin hat once worn by shamans and whalers, collected on the Alaska Peninsula in 1883, had been "embroidered with caribou hair, yarn, and strips of thin painted skin (probably esophagus), and further embellished with puffs of ermine and sea otter fur" (Crowell and Laktonen 2001: 169). The centrality of human-animal relations was artfully, sensuously manifested in many of the objects. Among the most impressive objects was a ground squirrel parka sewn in 1999 by Susan Malutin and Grace Harrod of Kodiak Island after studying an 1883 example from the Fisher collection in Washington, D.C. "It is made from ground squirrel pelts and accented with strips of white ermine along the seams. Mink and white caribou fur are used on the chest and sleeves. The tassels are of dyed skin, sea otter fur, and red cloth with ermine puffs" (Crowell and Lührmann 2001: 47). New workings of old traditions were integral to a processual authenticity. The exhibition also included an example of the decorated Russian Orthodox Christmas star that is paraded from house to house during midwinter rituals of visiting and gift exchange, made for the exhibition by students at St. Innocent's Academy in Kodiak. (A color photo of the young men, grinning and looking very "Russian," accompanied the three-foot star.) A mask carved by Jerry Laktonen, now a successful Native artist, commemorated the *Exxon Valdez* disaster that had forced him to quit commercial fishing and take up sculpture (see www.whaledreams.com).

The mix of objects, texts, and images signified a complex Alutiiq heritage and identity, with cultural continuity through change manifested by juxtaposed ancient, historical, and contemporary artifacts. The exhibition's explicit messages were straightforward—historically descriptive, evocative, and celebratory. The result was a coherent performance and idealization of "Alutiiq" identity. Critics have pointed out that this representation tended to minimize cultural characteristics shared with Yup'ik to the north, Unangans (Aleuts) to the west, and Tlingit to the south (Lee and Graburn 2003). In this respect the exhibit was an unambiguous exercise in ethnic assertion and boundary marking (Barth 1969). The exhibition's catalogue would offer a more complex historical picture, including more diversity of perspective, while still articulating a distinctive, living heritage. Extensive and beautifully produced, the volume contains hundreds of historical and contemporary illustrations, with detailed chapters on culture, language, and history, on archaeological research results and collaborations, on contemporary identity and subsistence practices, on spiritual life and religious traditions, on Elders' recollections and hopes. The volume's dedication quotes Mary Peterson, a Kodiak Island Elder: "To all the new generations. They will learn from this and keep it going."

The catalogue—the term hardly captures the book's scope—explores a wide range of old and new places, crafts, and social practices. Heritage is a path to the future. The late Sven Haakanson Sr., from the village of Old Harbor, inspired the project's title: "You've got to look back and find out the past, and then you go forward." Haakanson said this at an Elders' planning conference held in 1997: men and women from the Alutiiq culture area gathered to talk about the old days and ways forward: childhood experiences in the 1920s, parents and grandparents, subsistence hunting and fishing, religion and social values, elements of a transformed, transforming way of life. The catalogue contains many excerpts from this meeting, as well as testimony from Alutiiq activists, community leaders, and scholars. Native voices are juxtaposed with contributions from non-Native scholars.

Perhaps the most striking feature of *Looking Both Ways* is its multi-vocality. In the very first pages we encounter the names of fifty-one Elders who participated in the exhibition or are quoted in the book. The final chapter is composed of nine extended statements. The remaining sections are written/assembled by scholars who have worked closely with local communities. Gordon Pullar, one of the volume's editors, contributes an illuminating chapter entitled "Contemporary Alutiiq Identity" (2001). Virtually every page of the catalogue juxtaposes quotations, images, and short essays. The textual ensemble makes space for some forty individual "authors"—Native and non-Native writers of free-standing essays or sources of extended testimonies. Quotations from individual Elders are scattered throughout. No one holds the floor for very long, and the experience of reading is one of constantly shifting modes of attention, encountering specific rhetorics, voices, images, and stories, and shuttling between the archaeological past, personal memories, and present projects.

In the midst of a chapter called "*Sugucihpet*—'Our Way of Living'" (Crowell and Laktonen 2001), a page begins: "Fishing sets the pace of the subsistence year. In summer, five varieties of salmon gather in the bays or ascend rivers to spawn." The following page: "I remember in the summertime my dad would wake my sisters and me up early to go fishing." The first tells us about kinds of fish and how they are dried, smoked, and canned. The second recalls the chore of cleaning the catch while being swarmed by vicious flies (176–178). Interspersed illustrations show (1) contemporary commercial fishermen netting salmon, (2) "Iqsak—Halibut hook," from about 1899, and (3) an ivory lure in the shape of a fish, from about 600–1000 A.D., found in an archaeological site on Kodiak Island. "In *Looking Both Ways*," Aron Crowell writes, "the commitment has been to diversity of perspective, depth of inquiry, and genuine collaboration among scholars, Elders, and communities" (2001: 13). The book's five pages of acknowledgments, mentioning many institutions and an enormous number of individuals, are integral to its message. But if the general strategy is inclusive, it is not synthetic. Differences of perspective are registered and allowed to coexist. The volume's three editors represent the range of stakeholders in the project.

Crowell, director of the Alaska office of the Smithsonian's Arctic Studies Center, came to the *Looking Both Ways* project from prior work in the archaeology and postcontact history of the region (e.g., Crowell 1997) and is currently pursuing collaborative archaeology with Alutiiq communities on the Kenai Peninsula. As project director he arranged the loan of artifacts, raised grant money, and served as primary orchestrator/negotiator of the exhibition and the text. He is the author or coauthor of four chapters in the catalogue. Crowell's ability to work both as a Smithsonian insider and as a long-term field researcher enmeshed in local collaborations and reciprocities was instrumental in facilitating the project's coalition of diverse interests.

Gordon Pullar has been a leader in Alutiiq heritage projects since the early 1980s, and it was his early conversations with William Fitzhugh of the Smithsonian, followed by Crowell's presentation of artifact photos to a 1988 conference on Kodiak Island, that led to concrete plans for bringing the old Alutiiq objects to Alaska. Pullar chaired the *Looking Both Ways* advisory committee and served as political liaison to various groups and organizations. He and other Alutiiq activists and Elders whose ideas influenced the project were much more than "Native consultants" recruited after the basic vision was in place; they were active from the beginning in an evolving coalition.

The archaeologist Amy Steffian, currently deputy director of the Alutiiq Museum, works on collaborative excavations with communities on Kodiak Island. In the wake of the Larsen Bay repatriation struggle, Steffian requested and received tribal permission to resume study of the Larsen Bay sites. Her experience showed that intense local suspicion of archaeology and anthropology did not preclude research collaborations in situations where trust could be established. Moreover, the fact that the Alutiiq Museum is an "archaeological repository" institutionalizes the idea that excavated heritage can be made available for study while remaining under local control. Along with other museum staff members and community supporters, Steffian helped ensure that *Looking Both Ways* would be a broadly based gathering of people as well as an impressive collection of artifacts.

The project's success depended on bringing together Native authorities, skilled professionals, and institutional sponsors—all with different stakes in the promotion of "Alutiiq heritage." Primary financial donors included the Smithsonian Institution, the National Endowment for the Humanities, Koniag Inc., the Alutiiq Heritage Foundation, the Anchorage Museum of History and Art, and Phillips Alaska. Additional support was provided by an impressive cross section of Alaska institutions, public and private, and nearly two dozen Native regional and village corporations.

As I have suggested, the project's collaborative expression of "Alutiiq heritage and identity" reflects a moment of cultural emergence and renewal, weaving together discussions, struggles, and accommodations sustained over more than two decades. During these decades a great deal was changing. The ambiguous ANCSA innovations took hold, bringing both limiting structures and new opportunities for Native mobilization. The Larsen Bay repatriation, echoing widespread anticolonial contestations, rebalanced the collaborative dependence on academic expertise that has been integral to the ongoing Alutiiq reidentifications. *Looking Both Ways* thus belongs to a conjuncture that, while locally particular, reflects wider trends. Before delving further into the Alutiiq situation, it may be useful to look at several precursors and contrasting heritage projects: signs of the changing times.

Precursors

In 1988 William Fitzhugh and Aron Crowell edited the major Russian-American-Canadian collaboration *Crossroads of Continents: Cultures of Siberia and Alaska.* Prehistory, history, anthropology, archaeology, and art criticism came together in a richly documented and illustrated account of the transnational world of Beringia. Small Siberian and Alaskan Native groups were shown to be part of a larger, dynamic indigenous region with a deep history of interconnection and crossing that had been obscured by national projects and Cold War partitioning. The project brought together for the first time many powerful and evocative artifacts collected in the eighteenth and nineteenth centuries and preserved in Washington, D.C., St. Petersburg, New York, and Ottawa. The effect was revelatory not simply for students of cultural flows but for Native Alaskans, who rediscovered lost aspects of their tribal histories and a deep transnational context for new "indigenous" alliances. In *Looking Both Ways*, Ruth Alice Olsen Dawson, chair of the Alutiiq Heritage Foundation, recalls her encounter with the *Crossroads* exhibition at its Alaskan venue, the Anchorage Museum of History and Art:

> For the first time we saw "snow-falling" parkas made out of bird skins and decorated with puffins' beaks. We saw ceremonial masks, regalia, baskets, rattles, pictures, and drawings. The impact for me was overwhelming. The exhibit sparked the start of the first Native dance group in Kodiak in years. And instead of wearing European calicos, we wore snow-falling parkas, shook puffin-beak rattles, and wore beaded head-dresses. It was a revelation. (2001: 89)

There are no voices like Dawson's in *Crossroads of Continents,* and this may be the volume's most striking difference from *Looking Both Ways.* All the contributors to the earlier collection are non-Native academics, and the contemporary lives of Koryak, Chukchi, Yup'ik, Aleut, Tlingit, and others appear only at the very end in two surveys of current history in Russia and Alaska. Named individuals emerge in a brief final section on eighteen Alaskan Native artists. There are no photographs of living people, whereas in *Looking Both Ways* they are everywhere, mixed with historical photos and Mikhail Tikhanov's fabulous early nineteenth-century portraits (prominent in both volumes). Seven years after *Crossroads* opened, Fitzhugh and Valerie Chaussonnet of the Arctic Studies Center, recognizing the original exhibition's limited audience, designed a smaller, less cumbersome version for travel to local communities on both sides of the Bering Strait (Chaussonnet 1995). In this project images of contemporary populations are featured, along with writings and quotations by indigenous authorities.

In 1996 a major exhibition entitled *Agayuliyararput (Our Way of Making Prayer)* opened in the heart of Yup'ik country—Toksook Bay, Nelson Island. In its subsequent travel to the regional center, Bethel, and then to Anchorage, New York, Washington, D.C., and Seattle, the exhibition of Yup'ik masks reversed the itinerary of *Crossroads,* starting in venues accessible to indigenous people and moving to more distant urban "centers." Masks acquired by U.S. and European museums during the late nineteenth-century frenzy of "salvage collecting" now traveled back to their places of origin. Ann Fienup-Riordan, an anthropologist whose long-term fieldwork on Nelson Island has been part of oral-history projects sponsored by Yup'ik authorities, conceived the exhibition in dialogue with Elders. Its success depended both on this local commitment and on the cooperation of museum professionals in Alaska and in Washington, D.C., New York, Seattle, and Berlin. The exhibition catalogue, *The Living Tradition of Yup'ik Masks: Agayuliyararput (Our Way of Making Prayer)* (Fienup-Riordan 1996), is a model of richly documented collaborative scholarship and stunning visual presentation. While the anthropologist appears as its author, large sections of the text are strongly multivocal, built around quotations from Elders' recorded memories and interpretations of the masks.

In *Hunting Tradition in a Changing World,* Fienup-Riordan (2000) reflects on her changing relations with Yup'ik communities over the years. She traces an evolution from assuming scholarly "independence" toward something more like alliance anthropology and toward textual forms that manifest the collaborative nature of the work. *Hunting Tradition* moves beyond systematic quotation to intersperse among its essays seven freestanding texts written by Yupiit. Along with clustered accounts of Yup'ik Christianity and extended urban-rural networks, Fienup-Riordan provides an illuminating analysis of the mask exhibition's origins and especially of its significance in different venues (209–251). The name chosen by the Yup'ik planning committee, *Agayuliyararput,* fused old and new meanings. In the pre-Christian past *agayu* referred to performances honoring animals or persons who were providers, and it has since taken on the Christian sense of "praying." "Our Way of Making Prayer" thus articulates a process of historical translation. (It was not guaranteed that priests and conservative Christians in the local communities would approve of the renewed interest in mask making and dancing. In fact they did, with enthusiasm.) Fienup-Riordan describes how the name *Agayuliyararput,* so rich in local significance, diminished in prominence, becoming a subtitle, when the exhibition traveled beyond Yup'ik communities.

In Toksook Bay and Bethel the most important meanings of the masks centered on who had made them and where they were from. Place (rather than theme or style) was the organizing principle determined by the local steering committee. It was also decided that Yup'ik language had to

appear prominently in the exhibition's name and in the Elders' interpretations, painstakingly transcribed and translated by Marie Meade, a
Yup'ik language specialist, teacher, and traditional dancer (see Meade
2000). These vernacular materials were featured in a specially printed
bilingual catalogue that preceded the lavishly illustrated English-
language version. Available at Toksook Bay and Bethel, the "Yup'ik
catalogue" sold out quickly and was adopted in school curricula teaching
local culture and history. The exhibition opening coincided with an
already established dance festival, a gathering of hundreds of people
flown in from remote villages by light aircraft, and thus it became part
of an ongoing tradition of midwinter gatherings.

The insistence on a vernacular catalogue reflects the relative vitality
of Yup'ik language use and contrasts with the Alutiiq situation, where
English is the only viable lingua franca. For historical reasons detailed
by Fienup-Riordan (1990), Yupiit were spared the severest effects of
Russian and American invasion and resource extraction. Thus they have
been able to sustain a more robust localism and cultural continuity. At
times this has produced complex feelings of inferiority among their
neighbors to the south. Comparative judgments of cultural authenticity
are, however, complex and always dependent on historical circumstances. They cannot, in any event, be automatically deduced from
Yup'ik insistence on transmitting Elders' knowledge in a vernacular publication. A revealing contrast is provided by Julie Cruikshank's account
of Athabaskan Elders' insistence that their recorded stories and memories be published in English: "What emerged . . . was a strong commitment to extend communication in whatever forms possible, writing being
one way among many. There was also optimism—probably a result of a
history of self-confident multilingualism—that English is just one more
Native language, in fact the dominant Native language at the end of the
century" (1998: 16; for an analogous perspective see Partnow 2001b: 2).
The Yup'ik and Athabaskan linguistic and intercultural situations differ,
and transmission/translation of traditional knowledge occurs within
specific limits and possibilities.

In Anchorage, Alaska's largest urban center, where significant Native
communities live more or less permanently, the masks of *Agayuliyararput*
were understood to be part of a wider pan-Alaskan indigenous heritage.
In New York, at the National Museum of the American Indian, the
masks were contextualized less in terms of local Alaskan practices than
as contributions to great Native American art. In Washington, D.C., and

Seattle, formalist, "high art" presentations predominated. Fienup-Riordan portrays these contexts not as distortions but rather as aspects of a potential range of Yup'ik meanings in the late twentieth century. The "centering" of the exhibition—its planning and opening in Toksook Bay—reflects a crucial priority for a renewed politics of indigenous authenticity. It is not, however, the sole priority, and the local is actively defined and redefined in relationships with a variety of "outsides" and scales of belonging. A "worldwide web," in Fienup-Riordan's provocative expression (2000: 151–182), of Yup'ik kinship and culture obliges us to consider a range of overlapping performative contexts, tactical articulations, and translations: rural/urban, oral/literate, family/corporate, Alaskan/international.

Hunting Tradition concludes with a recent visit to the Berlin Ethnologisches Museum by a group of Yup'ik elders (Fienup-Riordan 2000, 2005). The discussions there were governed by Yup'ik protocols and agendas. The goal was not the return of traditional artifacts preserved in Germany. The visitors expressed gratitude for the museum's curatorship, since in the old days it was customary to destroy masks after use. They were primarily interested in the return of important stories and knowledge renewed through the encounter with the old masks, spears, and bows. What mattered was not the reified objects but what they could communicate for a Yup'ik future. Understood in this historical frame, museums, as the Elder Paul John put it, were "part of God's plan."

The Living Tradition of Yup'ik Masks (Fienup-Riordan 1996) looks both ways: to a recollected past and to a dynamic present-becoming-future. The catalogue portrays Yup'ik cultural production enmeshed in specific contact histories: colonial (Russian and American) and now post-/neocolonial (indigenous resurgence). The translated renditions of the masks' meanings and uses are not located solely or even primarily in traditional (pre-1900) contexts. The catalogue emphasizes contact histories of collecting (including aesthetic appropriation of the dramatic masks by the surrealists), periods of missionary suppression, and recent movements of revival in Catholic, Orthodox, and Moravian communities. The perspectives of different generations on rearticulated currents of spirituality and aesthetics are kept in view. The collaborative genesis of the exhibition and its local significance are stressed from the outset in a chapter titled "Our Way of Making an Exhibit." The collaborative project continues with two related publications (Fienup-Riordan 2004a, 2004b), the latter complemented by a bilingual version for local use.

It is instructive to compare *The Living Tradition of Yup'ik Masks* with an earlier Smithsonian-sponsored catalogue and exhibition devoted to similar objects and histories from the same region. *Innua: Spirit World of the Bering Sea Eskimo,* by William Fitzhugh and Susan Kaplan (1982), was an innovative project for its time. Like the later exhibition, it returned objects held in Washington museums to Alaskan venues, though not to Native homelands. Its focus was a collection of artifacts acquired in the late 1870s by Edward William Nelson in western Alaska. The narrow time period, contextualized in a broad historical/archaeological/natural frame, gave the exhibition a temporal/social specificity that separated it from more common "cultural" or "primitive art" approaches. A final section of the catalogue, "Art in Transformation," provided a glimpse of later developments: the discovery of representational ivory carving and the emergence of individual "Eskimo artists" who would develop new graphic styles and carving traditions for an expanding art market. Except for these last pages, however, contemporary populations were absent from the book. An "Eskimo" voice—unattributed quotations from recorded myths—appeared as a kind of chorus.

If *Innua* seems dated today, this is a comment less on its substantive achievements, which remain considerable, than on rapidly changing times, identifications, and power relations. The lack of visible participation by Yupiit and Inupiat in the exhibition process contrasts with the explicit collaborations described by Crowell and Fienup-Riordan. Moreover, the earlier exhibition's focus on "the Bering Sea Eskimo," including under this rubric both Yup'ik and Inupiaq, would today be ruled out by the disaggregation of "Eskimos" into Inuit, Inupiat, Yupiit, and Alutiit, an outcome of Alaskan and Canadian Native identity politics during the 1980s and 1990s. This process was significantly (though not solely) driven by the struggles surrounding ANCSA, whose politics of Native regrouping were making headway at the time *Innua* was produced. Subsequent decades would see many articulations of Fienup-Riordan's "conscious culture." The Native corporations created after 1971 offered new leadership roles and sources of funding for cultural/ heritage projects such as the Alutiiq Museum, other cultural centers, and education and language initiatives. Local, regional, and international dance/art/storytelling festivals, Native studies programs in universities (sometimes including "Elders in residence"), Native participation in resource management, teacher training programs, the growth of indigenous art markets, and cultural tourism—all these contributed to a sharply increased Native presence in Alaska public culture.

A full historical—political, social, economic, and cultural—account of the increased Native presence and heritage activity in Alaska after the 1970s is beyond my present compass. However, some further reflections on how these movements are related to the social and economic contexts created by ANCSA may be useful. The relations are intimate, partial, and overdetermined. Ramona Ellen Skinner's survey *Alaska Native Policy in the Twentieth Century* (1997) shows how a law intended to foster indigenous self-determination was also a recipe for eventual termination, limiting "Native" status to those born before 1971 and allowing eventual sales of tribal assets. Amendments to the law, while staving off the worst, only partially dealt with its fundamental problems. ANCSA, from this perspective, is a pact with the devil of corporate capitalism. By making Native assets indistinguishable from other private property, the law significantly expanded participation in the Alaskan and international economy. But this "development" came at the cost of extinguishing aboriginal title to land, creating Native capitalist elites, and forcing shortsighted, profit-motivated decisions about resource management. Kirk Dombrowski's recent discussions (2001, 2002) are particularly informative on these effects, particularly in the timber-rich south.

ANCSA's influence on the new identity politics has taken different forms in specific Native contexts, depending on resource wealth, extractive pressures from powerful corporations, and degrees of urbanization and acculturation. It is obviously important to distinguish the community-based heritage education and revival practiced by institutions like the Alutiiq Museum, the midwinter Orthodox "starring" ceremonies and Yup'ik dance festivals in Toksook Bay, pan-Alaskan institutions like the Alaska Native Heritage Center, and the Indian villages maintained for cruise-ship tourists along the South Alaska Inside Passage. In each case, one needs to ask what old and new cultural and social elements are being articulated, what audiences are being addressed by specific performances, and what are the social/linguistic relations and tradeoffs of translation. Such questions are critical for a realist understanding of a complex conjuncture.

Native resurgence in Alaska maneuvers within a constellation of forces that can be characterized as simultaneously post-sixties/neoindigenous and corporate/multicultural. Heritage projects reweave social and cultural filiations in ways that are structured by this conjuncture while also exceeding it. Multiple historical projects and possible futures are active. To say this is to hesitate in the face of more conclusive accounts of progressive incorporation in capitalist modernity. For example, Dombrowski's

(2001) ethnographically nuanced analysis reveals the abuse of cultural appeals by corporate tribalism in the Alaska panhandle. The complementary analysis of Kodiak elites by Arthur Mason (2002) takes a longer historical view, but focuses narrowly on the transformation of older hierarchies into contemporary class formations. Cultural renewal in both accounts becomes primarily a function of governmental technologies, a matter of commodified tribal symbols, tourist spectacles, or an Alaskan "identity industry." In this perspective, which importantly brings Native elites and status differences into view, the state and corporate capitalism call the shots. I argue for a less functional sense of determination in which capitalism and state power do not "produce" indigenous identities, not at least in any global or final way, but set limits and exert pressures (Williams 1977: 83–89). Struggles over indigenous practice occur, as Dombrowski rightly puts it, "within and against" Western institutions and hegemonic ideas such as "identity" and "culture."

All of the heritage work discussed here is connected to capitalism in variously configured relations of dependency, interpellation, domination, and resistance. As Marx famously said, people make history but not in circumstances of their choosing. This observation has always been brutally relevant to Native peoples' experiences of conquest, resistance, and survival. Yet Marx also affirmed that, in conditions not of their choosing, people do make history. The unexpected resurgence of Native, First Nations, and Aboriginal societies in recent decades confirms the point. And while indigenous heritage and identity movements have indeed expanded dramatically during the recent heyday of corporate liberalism, this conjuncture does not exhaust their historicity. Native cultural politics builds connections extending before and potentially after the current moment. I am inclined to see the "praxis of indigenism" (Dombrowski 2002) in Gramscian terms—as a contingent work of positional struggle, articulation, and alliance. An example of this praxis can be found a short plane ride from Kodiak Island.

Interactions: The Alaska Native Heritage Center

In Anchorage, the state's largest city, a growing indigenous presence finds expression at The Alaska Native Heritage Center. Opened in 1999 as a "gathering place" for all Alaska Native groups, the center functions as a site of cultural exchange, celebration, and education. Entirely Native-run and not dependent on academic experts, it draws its funds from a

broad range of sources—corporate (Native and non-Native), philanthropic, and touristic. All of its programs are approved by a college of
Elders representing the principal Native regions. Dialogue among indigenous peoples is promoted, and communication with visitors, a high priority, takes place on Native terms. The center sometimes enters into
contracts with non-Native scholars and facilitates collaborative projects.
For example, its staff worked with the Smithsonian's Arctic Studies
Center to produce a pedagogical video and website for *Looking Both
Ways*. Housed in a new complex on the outskirts of Anchorage, the
center maintains links with local and regional Native authorities while
cultivating "partnerships" with a broad range of sponsors.

The Alaska Native Heritage Center is not a museum focused on a collection but something more like a performance space, featuring face-to-
face encounters. Everything is designed to facilitate conversations between
different tribal Alaskans and between Natives and non-Natives. At the
door, visitors are personally greeted. The central space is a stage where
every hour dancing or storytelling is presented. In the Hall of Cultures,
visitors are encouraged to talk with Native artists and "tradition bearers"
about their work. The status of "tradition bearer" is a recent development in North American indigenous heritage contexts where new social
roles (artists, curators, translators, tour guides) have been emerging. It
denotes, loosely, individuals of deep cultural experience who are not (yet)
Elders. The latter designation depends on traditional usage and local
consensus—which may, of course, include disagreement. Tradition
bearers can include people of more or less mixed background who in
recent decades have studied and adopted Native ways, reactivating old
crafts, stories, languages, and subsistence practices. The title denotes an
explicit commitment to transmitting community values and knowledge,
to mediating between (deeply knowledgeable) Elders and (relatively igno-
rant) youth. Tradition is borne by these cultural activists into a changing
world, performed for new and diverse audiences. The translator, in Ezra
Pound's familiar phrase, "makes it new."

All of the artifacts on display are freshly made traditional pieces—
masks, drums, kayaks, parkas, boots, button blankets, headgear.
Outside, around an artificial lake, five houses represent the past lifeways
of Alaska's principal indigenous regions. Everywhere, young Native men
and women act as hosts and interpreters, actively engaging visitors.
During the summer months, tourists visit in large numbers, including
regular busloads of cruise-ship passengers—a lucrative market that the

center has successfully pursued. Workshops and gatherings support its yearly themes (for example, boat building, health and Native medicines). In winter, school visits, art demonstrations, and workshops are organized (for example, "Exxon Mobil master artist classes," in which one can learn to make Tsimshian hand drums, Alutiiq beaded headdresses, Aleut model kayaks, and other emblematic Native artifacts). The center also arranges "cultural awareness workshops" funded by Wells Fargo Bank and adapted to the needs of diverse clients such as the Girl Scouts, the FBI, the army and the air force, Covenant House, and various government agencies.

Like most Native heritage projects, the center addresses diverse audiences—local, regional, state, and international. The performances, alliances, and translations vary according to the context. For tourists and other visitors with limited time, the center provides a clear vision of Alaskan Native presence and diversity. Color-coded maps and labels identify five principal Native cultures/regions—Athabaskan Yup'ik/ Cup'ik, Inupiaq/St. Lawrence Island Yup'ik, Eyak/Tlingit/Haida/ Tsimshian, and Aleut/Alutiiq—each endowed with a stylized image or logo. The five traditional house types reinforce the taxonomy. A message of current vitality is reinforced by face-to-face contacts, especially with young people. For Alaskans of various backgrounds, specialized performances and educational events offer more sustained encounters with Native artists and tradition bearers. The program of workshops and discussions addresses Native people of all ages from many parts of Alaska, some employed at the center, others participating in particular events. Its work thus contributes to a loosely articulated Native Alaskan identification following from the widespread post-1960s indigenous revival movements and the difficult but largely successful alliances leading to the ANCSA land settlement.

Native resurgence, a complex process of continuity through transformation, involves articulation (cultural and political alliance), performance (forms of display for different "publics"), and translation (partial communication and dialogue across cultural and generational divides). All are clearly visible in a center publication that documents and celebrates one of its annual themes and summer workshops: *Qayaqs and Canoes: Native Ways of Knowing* (Steinbright and Mishler 2001). Teams of "master builders" and "apprentices" gathered at the center over a period of five months to construct eight traditional boats: two Athabaskan birch-bark canoes, four styles of kayak (Aleut, Alutiiq, and two Central

Yup'ik), a Northwest Coast dugout canoe, and a Bering Straits open skin
boat. Today, only the last-mentioned boat type is still actively made and
used; the others have entered the relatively new category of what might
be called "heritage objects"—specially valued material sites of remembrance and communication. (Such traditional objects can, of course, be
recently made as long as their connection to past models is recognizably
"authentic"—for example, the squirrel parka from *Looking Both Ways*
mentioned above.) In the primarily first-person accounts of boat building,
Elders, heritage activists, youth, and other participants in the workshop
offer perspectives on keeping the skills alive in changing times.

A range of "Native ways of knowing" come together in *Qayaqs and
Canoes:* oral transmission from experienced Elders, library and museum
research by Native and non-Native builders, and aspirations to identity
by younger apprentices. In a variety of team contexts, young family
members learn from older master builders; men learn sealskin stitching
(a traditional woman's task); women participate in kayak framing (formerly a man's job); an Aleut activist of mixed heritage (an Anchorage
police detective who has rediscovered his Native past through kayak
research and construction) teaches the art to a young man of Inupiaq
background and to a young Alutiiq woman from Kodiak Island; an
eighty-eight-year-old Athabaskan Elder works in close collaboration
with an anthropology doctoral student (originally from North Dakota)
recording traditional tools and techniques; an Alutiiq activist and tradition bearer learns kayak construction from a young New Englander
who, through research and dedicated practice, has become expert in the
craft, and they both find out about waterproof stitching from a woman
of Cup'ik ancestry now living on Kodiak Island; the Aleut and Alutiiq
groups observe the Yup'ik teams who are guided by more knowledgeable
Elders; and extended networks are activated ("Got a call from my dad in
Chignik saying he had a good tip for me on dehairing skins").

Participants recall old stories of travel and contact among different
Alaskan populations, and they see their interethnic encounters at the
center as renewing this tradition. There are repeated references to a sense
of expanded Native affiliations, the linking of different, newly related
heritages. Alutiiq participants recall listening to spoken Yup'ik and getting
the gist. Elders find ways to translate knowledge rooted in specific local
hunting and gathering practices for younger apprentices raised in more
urban conditions. The performative nature of contemporary heritage
projects is visible across a range of occasions: the public accomplishment

of painstaking crafts and the final, exuberant celebrations, dramatic launchings on Kachemak Bay with traditional dancers, Orthodox prayers, formal speeches.

Different contexts of performance—the technical demonstrations and talk that pervade the workshop, the intertribal exchanges, the public displays and celebrations, the circulation of an evocative, elegantly illustrated book—activate different audiences and situations of translation. In their commentaries, the participants recognize that tradition is being renegotiated for new situations. Young women express satisfaction at doing work formerly restricted to men. Elders adjudicate what practices are bound by rules and what can be pragmatically altered. In an atmosphere of serious fun, people work within while pushing the limits of tradition. Grace Harrod, who taught the Alutiiq team waterproof stitching, offers a humorous and far-reaching anecdote:

> I called my mom on the phone in Mekoryuk. I said, "Mom, I'm going to sew a kayak." Over the phone she just hollered, "You don't know how." So, my dad, Peter Smith, got on the phone, and I said, "Dad, I'm going to sew a kayak." He said, "It's going to sink" in Eskimo. He started laughing. I said, "Dad, it's going to be in a museum. They're going to put it in a museum when I'm done with it." He said, "Go ahead, sew it. It won't sink in a museum." (87)

One might be inclined to interpret this kayak as a "traditional" object belonging to a nostalgic, postmodern culture—a thing with meaning only as a specimen and a work of art, artificially separated from the currents of historical change (thus "unsinkable," in its museum). But this would privilege the authenticity of objects over the social processes of transmitting and transforming traditions and relationships. It would miss the multiaccented, intergenerational work, the stories, the articulations, performances, and translations that go into the kayak's reproduction. Similarly complex, open-ended social processes are active in the identity formations of those who have recently come to be known as Alutiiq.

Emergence and Articulation

The name "Alutiiq" does not appear in *Crossroads of Continents,* where the people south of the Yup'ik are primarily described as "Pacific

Eskimo," and in a more recent book Fienup-Riordan writes of a "larger family of Inuit cultures, extending from Prince William Sound on the Pacific Coast of Alaska . . . into Labrador and Greenland" (2000: 9). Significant cultural similarities link traditional life around Kodiak with societies to the north. But there are also major differences. For example, egalitarian social structure among the Yup'ik contrasts with Alutiiq hierarchy—the latter suggesting links with coastal societies to the south. In the classification "Pacific Eskimo" linguistic form overrides differences of social structure, subsistence, history, and environment. The recent self-identification as "Alutiiq" (or "Sugpiaq") declares independence from the Inuit/Inupiaq/Yup'ik cultural "family." Another longstanding term for the people represented in *Looking Both Ways* is "Aleut." This name was, through most of the twentieth century, a term of self-reference for Native/Russian Creole populations on Kodiak Island and the Alaska Peninsula. ("Alutiiq" is, in fact, an adaptation of the Russian "Aleuty" in the sound system of the indigenous language Sugt'stun.) A Russian misnomer for the chain islanders (who generally now prefer to be called Unangan), "Aleut," in its expanded usage, registers common historical experiences (Russian colonization, exploitation, massacres, religious conversion, intermarriage and Creole social status) as well as shared maritime hunting economy and coastal subsistence. Linguistically, however, the chain islanders and people of Kodiak differ markedly, and while cultural and kinship ties are still significant, there has been a strong recent tendency to distinguish "Aleut" from "Alutiiq." (Recent trends toward "Sugpiaq" strengthen the border-marking.) Tactical name changes—reflecting new articulations of resistance, separation, community affiliation, and tribal governance—are familiar and, indeed, necessary aspects of decolonizing indigenous politics. Imposed names are peeled off, old names made new.

Looking Both Ways, particularly the polyphonic catalogue, makes serious attempts to avoid freezing these processes by objectifying Alutiiqness. Its strong archaeological and historical emphases keep many tangled roots in view. For example, early explorers plausibly related the inhabitants of Kodiak Island to Greenland "Eskimos," to Siberians, to Aleutian islanders, and to "Indians" (Athabaskans and Tlingit). In their archaeological, anthropological, and historical survey of "Alutiiq culture," Aron Crowell and Sonja Lührmann (2001) provide evidence that at different moments each of these connections made sense. Later, Russian influences were strong, and the Orthodox religion would sink deep indigenous roots (Oleksa 1992). Mixed-race Creole elites both supported and indigenized colonial projects. In the late 1800s Scandinavian immigrant fishermen influenced local practices and were absorbed by kinship networks (Mishler and Mason 1996). The catalogue's historical sections offer a multivocal, nonessentialist account of a fundamentally interactive tradition. In chapters that gather together historical and archaeological evidence never before made accessible to Native communities, Crowell, Lührmann, Steffian, and Leer attempt the difficult task of telling a coherent Alutiiq story for the first time without merging past and present into a seamless "culture." Since documentary evidence, in Crowell and Lührmann's words, is "partial and imperfect at best" (30), they complement the written record with Alutiiq oral narratives.

Patricia Partnow, author of *Making History: Alutiiq/Sugpiaq Life on the Alaska Peninsula* (2001b), is the only contemporary non-Native cultural anthropologist represented in a volume that leans toward archaeological expertise. (Jeff Leer, a linguist who consults with the Alutiiq Museum and has produced Kodiak Alutiiq dictionaries, pedagogical grammars, and place-name records, also makes important contributions.) Partnow acknowledges her "mentor," the late Ignatius Kosbruk, and many Alutiiq "teachers." She has served as vice president of education at the Alaska Native Heritage Center and develops curricula on Alutiiq heritage for use in public schools. These activities indicate the kinds of commitments that make anthropological research possible in a region where only a decade ago, as Gordon Pullar recalls, "anthropologists were beginning to wear out their welcome" (2001: 78). Partnow reports her Alutiiq hosts' lack of concern with definitive origins and sharp ethnic borders. By identifying themselves as Alutiiq, she writes, "they were privileging one part of their genetic and cultural background and underplaying their Athabaskan, Russian, Scandinavian, Irish, and Yup'ik parts" (2001a: 69). Alutiiq identity is a selective rearticulation of diverse connections, a sense of continuity expressed in Elders' traditional stories, both "mythic" and "historical." (Partnow appears to confirm Julie Cruikshank's [1998] penetrating view of Athabaskan Elders' narratives less as records of a past than as reconnections of fragmented realities and reframings of current issues.) Partnow identifies five core elements of identity: (1) ties to land, (2) a shared history and continuity with the past, (3) the Alutiiq or Sugt'stun language, (4) subsistence, and (5) kinship. These are not prescriptive elements of a cultural essence, a checklist of authenticity. In today's conditions of social and spatial mobility it is seldom possible to "exemplify all five points equally. Instead, people accentuate different parts of their Alutiiqness at different times and in different places" (69). "Alutiiq" is a work in progress, a way of managing diversity and change. Each one of Partnow's five elements has undergone transformation since the Russians arrived in the late eighteenth century, and, a hundred years later, the Americans established colonial dominance. The rise and fall of fish canneries in the region, the devastating Katmai eruption of 1912, the impact of militarization during the Second World War, disrupted and reduced village communities. And new transformations would accompany the intensifying indigenous movements of the 1960s and the land settlements and corporate reorganizations of the 1970s and 1980s.

There is nothing ready-made about Alutiiqness in the chapter on contemporary Alutiiq identity written/assembled by Gordon Pullar. He begins by invoking his mother, who resolutely identified herself as Russian even though her nearest truly Russian ancestors were eight generations distant. He, by contrast, having grown up in the Cold War 1950s, had rejected this historical identity but without a clear alternative. He cites others who, at the time of ANCSA enrollment in the early 1970s, resisted pressures to identify themselves as Alutiiq—some because they felt that a Native identity would diminish a hard-won "Americanness" and others like his grandmother, who commented: "Are they trying to make an Aleut out of you?" (2001: 74).

Pullar and the Elders he cites make it clear that "Alutiiq" identification is something more than a return to an essential, continuous Native tradition. Considerable disconnecting and reconnecting was involved in the processes out of which "a new unity was forged." Clarifying fuzzy borders with near neighbors involved specific realignments and a good deal of confusion. Pullar quotes Margaret Knowles at the 1997 Elders' conference that guided *Looking Both Ways*:

> I realized that we are not the true Natives and the fact remained that we really didn't even know who we were. And that really bothered me. It angered me because I . . . well, who are we? . . . I was embarrassed when I'd be around other groups, Yup'iks, who absolutely knew who they were and where they were from, . . . and I didn't. I didn't know. And they said, "Well it depends on what anthropologist you talk to." I always believed I was Aleut

and then somebody said, "No, you're really Koniag." And, "No, you're really Pacific Eskimo," "No, you're Sugpiaq." "No, you're really more related to the Yup'ik." (2001: 81)

Pullar traces the emergence of "Alutiiq" during the 1970s as a series of reidentifications in a specific historical conjuncture, the chaotic/creative aftermath of ANCSA.

Looking Both Ways represents an unusually clear and perhaps extreme example of constitutive political articulations that are active, to varying degrees, across the spectrum of Alaskan Native identities and traditions. The Elder Roy Madsen invokes long lists of Russian and Scandinavian names, comparing Alutiiq tradition to "bits and pieces" of seaweed and twigs in swirling waters where the ocean tide meets a stream. The culture, he writes, "has been pushed, shoved, jostled and propelled from the time of our earliest ancestors to the present day." Madsen recalls the several languages he heard as a child (including Slavonic at church) and his father's familiarity with English, Danish, German, and seven Eskimo dialects. In the "tides and currents" of historical change, "the homogeneous culture of our ancestors has been transformed into the heterogeneous culture that we experience today, mixed, mingled, blended and combined with those many other cultures, retaining some of each but still with some recognizable and acknowledged aspects of the culture of our Alutiiq ancestors" (2001: 75). This sense of cultural authenticity as a process of selective mixing reflects a distinctive Creole sense of self that, in the century following Russia's withdrawal from Alaska, defined "Aleut" people in the Kodiak region. Here, in a context of indigenous identity politics, the Alutiiq ancestral tread is stressed.

Madsen's vivid image of a culture in flux and recombination imagines not a traditional "core" resisting change but rather a series of combinations of ancestral and foreign influences contributing to the adaptive survival of a Native people. The "indigenization" of Russian Orthodoxy is perhaps the most positive example (Oleksa 1992). Robert Lowie once famously described culture as "a thing of shreds and patches." Many of the contributors to *Looking Both Ways* give this conception local historical specificity. If people are devoutly Orthodox, it is because in the early years of brutal colonial exploitation a degree of safety could be found in religious conversion, which brought with it Russian citizenship. As Creole citizens in a new social structure that replaced and recombined traditional hierarchies, "Aleuts" could become important leaders and church authorities. If the Alutiiq (or Sugt'stun) language is endangered, it is because of intense disruptions and all too familiar boarding school prohibitions. If some have felt reluctant to embrace Native identity, it is because of attachment to "Russian"/Creole habits and ways of resisting American forms of religion and racial/social classification after 1867. It is also because memories of bitter events (such as Grigorii Shelikhov's massacre of Kodiak Islanders at Refuge Rock, a constitutive trauma that Pullar highlights) have led to psychic repression and a "sense of hopelessness brought on by decades of dependency on outsiders" (Pullar 2001: 76). Military defeat, enslavement and forced labor, epidemics, forced relocations, natural disasters, and continuing marginalization would be cause enough for a culture of "shreds and patches." But if indigenous memory, coming to terms with a dark history, tells and retells horror stories, it does so, in *Looking Both Ways,* to clear the way for a more hopeful future. Elders at the planning conferences insisted on this message. Pullar and many others involved with the project tell a story of struggle and renewal.

Elders remember their confusion and outrage when in 1931 Ales Hrdlicka arrived on Kodiak Island to dig up human remains for his research collections at the Smithsonian. *Looking Both Ways* contains a photograph of hundreds of boxes filled with bones awaiting reburial at a 1991 ceremony presided over by Alutiiq Elders and Orthodox priests. Pullar notes that the Larsen Bay repatriation movement "came at a time when the search for identity and cultural pride was under way on Kodiak Island. It became a symbol for tribal self-determination" (2001: 95). Here, as elsewhere in Native communities, repatriation has been a crucial process of healing and moving on. John F. C. Johnson, chairman of the Chugach Heritage Foundation, contributes an essay on the return of masks and other artifacts looted from caves in Prince William Sound. He writes: "A cultural renaissance is now sweeping across Alaska like a winter storm. Native cultural centers and spirit camps for the Native youth are being built across this great land and in record numbers" (2001: 93). Repatriation is a critical part of these heritage movements. It establishes indigenous control over cultural artifacts and thus the possibility of engaging with scientific research on something like equal terms. Repatriation is not, Johnson stresses, "the end to the thirst for knowledge, but is a new starting point in building trust and cooperation . . . Cooperation and partnership with science is important if we want to understand the full picture of human history" (92).

Ruth Dawson (2001) discusses the establishment of the Alutiiq Museum and Archaeological Repository and describes current archaeology programs that include youth internships, Elder participation, and the return of all discoveries to the community. "Children from the Kodiak schools now come to the museum to touch our past and learn about our people. The museum has helped turn around local prejudices about being Native. And the researchers now must come to Kodiak to study the collections, instead of us begging for them" (90). As Amy Steffian points out, archaeology's important role may be partly due to the fact that Alutiiq—swiftly conquered in the eighteenth century by the Russians, devastated by diseases, and for centuries participants in the capitalist world system—preserved much less "traditional" culture than other Alaskan groups (2001: 130). People concerned with their Alutiiq heritage have needed, figuratively and literally, to dig into their past to find themselves.

While this history partly explains the openness of many Alutiit to ongoing archaeological research, a shift in relations of authority and power has also been essential. Steffian suggests as much in her discussion of "partnerships in archaeology" (2001: 129–134). The self-determination achieved through the Larsen Bay repatriations altered relations with institutions such as the Smithsonian and the University of Alaska. At the same time, the growth of Native-led corporations, museums, and heritage projects has provided new sites for organizing research and disseminating results. Finally, and crucially, relations of trust and respect have been sustained over the past two decades by individual scholars working in long-term, reciprocal relations with communities. Rick Knecht, reflecting on the seminal Karluk excavation, concludes: "As archaeologists we had come to Kodiak to study Alutiiq culture but while doing so unwittingly became an inextricable part of the very culture history we had sought to understand" (2001: 134). Knecht's long activist career, first on Kodiak Island and then in the Aleutians, is a prime example of the new relations of cooperation. He worked with Pullar in KANA, served as first director of the emerging Archaeological Repository in Kodiak, and was a key player in the process of gaining *Exxon Valdez* oil spill compensation funds for the new Alutiiq Museum. By the time an Alutiiq scholar, Sven Haakanson Jr., became director of the newly built institution, Knecht had moved on to the Aleutian Islands. Amy Steffian and Patrick Saltonstall, like Knecht, veterans of the Karluk excavations, continue to work for the museum in key roles. Academically trained experts have been integral to Alutiiq heritage revival projects (Mason 2008). The relations involved have been complex and specific to individuals. Generally speaking, however, it would be a wrong to see a situation of dependency, not at least in older paternalist/colonial forms. Nor is it adequate to view experts as agents of liberal government, helping Native people become co-opted by a pro-gram of managed diversity. Entanglement and negotiation within new and unfinished structures of interdependency is a more accurate image. In the current climate, what Crowell calls the "terms of engagement" (2004) governing collaborations like *Looking Both Ways* assume mutual dependence and strategically aligned projects. For academics collabora-tion and advocacy are often the price of entry for research in indigenous societies. For Natives, obtaining credibility and authority with funding agencies and in the wider museum world requires certified experts. The relations of codependency are not static, however. Scholars like Knecht, Crowell, and Steffian work within a changing climate, an emerging field of forces. In their different ways, they negotiate the tensions and syner-gies of scholarship and politics, their pragmatic attachments to institu-tions and resources. And as we will see in Chapter 7, the Alutiiq Museum (like many other Native cultural institutions) is moving in the direction of increased control over its necessary engagements. The collaborations of *Looking Both Ways* thus reflect a moment of transition.

Heritage Relations, Changing Weather

The collaborations are not without tension. When Dawson defends archaeology, she also recognizes that "many object to archaeological research as they feel it would be better left alone. For some this may be appropriate. But for me archaeology has opened a new world. The key is that the Native people must control the research effort. Otherwise it's just another rip-off, with scientists coming in and taking instead of sharing" (2001: 89–90). Power and authority are openly at issue in the new research partnerships. For example, Pullar takes a certain distance from the version of Alutiiq anthropology, archaeology, and history pre-sented by Crowell and Lührmann:

The results of academic research are, of course, important in describing how Alutiiq people have come to view themselves today. But at the same time, the reader must decide how the various views

of Alutiiq culture and identity fit together. Listening to Alutiiq
people about how they view their own history is equally important. There are times when the indigenous viewpoint is diametri-
cally opposed to that of Western scholarship. The age-old question
"what is truth?" may be appropriate in this circumstance. The
proposition that there can be more than one truth is often over-
looked. (2001: 78)

Pullar does not object to anything specific in Crowell and Lührmann's
discussion (which weaves together academic research findings and Elders'
memories) but argues more generally that academic and Native positions
of authority need to be distinguished if new relations are to emerge. As do
many indigenous intellectuals today, Pullar urges that traditional origin
myths be given equal status alongside the findings of archaeology. The
insistence is less on agreement than on respect. He traces the emergence
on Kodiak Island of "codes of ethics" governing scientific research (prior
community permission, direct participation, sharing of results). Of
course, more than a few scholars will be reluctant to accept such limita-
tions, withdrawing to less fraught research contexts while privately—and
sometimes publicly—protesting against religious obscurantism and political censorship. Among indigenous activists a corresponding suspicion is
reinforced by painful histories of "arrogant," "intrusive," or "exploitative" scientific collecting. Indeed, Pullar's appeal for equality of indigenous "myth" and Western "science" may represent, for the moment, a
utopian vision, given histories of mutual suspicion and persistent power
imbalances (for example, the unequal struggle of oral tradition and documentary evidence in land-claims litigation). In the face of these antagonistic legacies, Looking Both Ways proposes a space in which, as Pullar
says, "the reader must decide how the various views of Alutiiq culture
and identity fit together." Crowell, in his introductory chapter, traces
changing academic practices and argues for the specificity and thus partiality of "all ways of looking at culture—from both the outside and the
inside" (2001: 8). Part genuine coalition, part respectful truce, Looking
Both Ways offers varied perspectives that need to be adjusted, weighed,
and assembled. What is proposed by all contributors to the volume is not
a take-it-or-leave-it vision of scientific versus Native truth but a pragmatic relationship: live and let live where there is opposition, and collaboration in the considerable areas of overlap.

Lines are drawn around heritage and identity but not hardened. Sven

Haakanson Jr., a recent PhD in anthropology from Harvard and currently director of the Alutiiq Museum, offers a pointed meditation on
the predicament of the "Native anthropologist." He gives no absolute
privilege to "insider" knowledge (his own academic fieldwork was among
Siberian reindeer herders) and asks why the Native anthropologist is
always, in effect, required to speak from an "emic" rather than an "etic"
position. "Is not the whole purpose of research to learn, including the
exploration of different approaches to knowing (hermeneutics)? If
Natives cannot write from *both* Native and scientific perspectives then
what is the purpose of doing anthropology?" (2001: 79, original
emphasis). Citing the examples of Knud Rasmussen (Greenlandic Inuit/
Danish), Oscar Kawagley (Yup'ik), and Alfonzo Ortiz (Tewa), Haakanson
argues that "Native approaches to the field," while not necessarily better,
"are just as valid as any others." As do many others in *Looking Both
Ways*, he recognizes differential authorities while sustaining, where possible, contexts of exchange and translation.

The Alutiiq heritage visible here is not a single thing, with sharply
defined "insides" and "outsides." In Pullar's words, it is "defined by a
mosaic of historical events and overlapping criteria" (2001: 95). Inflexible
measures of belonging such as the blood quantum required for ANCSA
enrollment in practice exclude many who cannot be sure of their exact
ancestry. *Looking Both Ways* emphasizes "kinship," including alliance
as well as blood (95–96). This relational way of being Alutiiq depends on
participation in Native life: residence in a village, Orthodox religious
practice, language use, subsistence activities, heritage revival and transmission. Alutiiqness is thus something constantly rearticulated in
changing, power-charged relations with relatives and outsiders. Indeed,
one is left with the impression that the political label "Alutiiq," although
it is becoming institutionally entrenched (with the help of projects like
Looking Both Ways), cannot be a definitive "tribal" or "national" name.
In some communities "Aleut" is still favored, and whereas "Alutiiq" suggests Pullar's historical mosaic, an alternative ethnonym, "Sugpiaq,"
evokes ties with older, pre-Russian traditions. People use more than one
term, depending on the audience and the occasion.

In *Looking Both Ways* descriptions of traditional forms of life
(archaeological and ethnographic artifacts, interspersed with Elders'
statements) evoke facets of a distinctive style: "our way of living." To call
this way of living "Alutiiq" consolidates and marks off a discrete identity.
Scholars have understood similar processes of social differentiation as

"ethnic" boundary marking (Barth 1969), the processual "invention" of culture (Wagner 1975), and "ethnogenesis" (Roosens 1989; Hill 1996). Each of these approaches captures something of what is going on. All assume that selective, creative cultural memory, border policing, and transgression are fundamental aspects of collective agency. Culture is articulated, performed, and translated, with varying degrees of power, in specific relational situations. Economic pressures and changing governmental policies are very much part of the process, and so are changing ideological contexts (for example, post-1960s cultural movements and the development of global "indigenous" politics). Components of "tradition"—oral sources, written texts, and material artifacts—are rediscovered and rewoven. Attachments to place, to changing subsistence practices, to circuits of migration and family visiting are affirmed. None of this suggests a wholly new genesis, a made-up identity, a postmodernist "simulacrum," or the rather narrowly political "invention of tradition" analyzed by Hobsbawm and Ranger (1983), with its contrast of lived custom and artificial tradition. If "authenticity" means anything here, it means "authentically remade."

I have proposed articulation, performance, and translation as components of an analytic toolkit for understanding old/new indigenous formations. Since no single vocabulary can account for all the attachments, displacements, and changes, we need to employ terms tactically and in combination. Still another dimension is suggested by a language of "diasporic" (dis)connections. In *Looking Both Ways,* Mary Jane Nielsen (2001) and Marlane Shanigan (2001) write about villages abandoned (because of economic pressure or seismic catastrophe) and express a renewed desire somehow to return. Such diasporic identifications are salient for recently dispersed urban populations living in Fienup-Riordan's tribal "worldwide web" (see Chapter 3). The *Looking Both Ways* website has received an extraordinary number of hits. Who are these visitors? Where are they? What is their relation to the traditional Alutiiq villages so prominent on the site? Unfortunately, there is no feedback or chat-room capacity that might suggest an answer. (Indigenous websites have proliferated in the past decade, performing "internal" and "external" functions of archiving, networking, and publicity.)

The multiple connections at work in *Looking Both Ways* offer a provocative context for thinking in nonabsolutist ways about heritage. Alutiiq history has been a story of intense disruptions, interactive survival, and interactive, flexible strategies for making the best of bad situations. These pragmatic responses, struggles within and against changing colonial hegemonies, can be hidden by the abstract, all-or-nothing language of "sovereignty." Alutiiq heritage and identity are most concretely understood not as past or revived "traditions" but as ongoing "historical practices" (introduced in Part One of the present book). Of course, "historical" is a term that requires translation, and in this context I find myself still grappling (see Chapter 1, and Clifford 1997a) with the words of Alutiiq Elder Barbara Shangin:

> Our people have made it through lots of storms and disasters for thousands of years. All the troubles since the Russians are like one long stretch of bad weather. Like everything else, this storm will pass over some day (quoted in Chaussonnet 1995: 15).

One might understand Shangin as positing an ancient cultural identity or tradition that is impervious to history's destructive storms. Indeed, feeling for this kind of deep continuity with a "prehistoric" past is always part of the indigenous *longue durée*. But there is surely more to the metaphor. As Craig Mishler's contribution to *Looking Both Ways,* "Kodiak Alutiiq Weather Lore" (2001), makes clear, weather in places like Kodiak Island is never something that happens to you; storms happen, and you are part of the happening. People who live exposed to winds and tides, whose everyday livelihood depends on them, have a detailed and exact knowledge of the changing weather. They know what is going on and act accordingly. Thus when Shangin says that the arrival of the Russians in the eighteenth century began a long bad spell, she is not invoking something external to Alutiiq life. History's weather, its storms and clearings, are an order that is neither "natural" nor "cultural" but, simply, given existence. Events in time occur in cyclic patterns that are both familiar and uncontrollable, recognizable and always different. From this perspective, the Russian bad weather (which brought epidemics, forced labor, Creole kinship, the Orthodox religion) and the American bad weather (missionaries, boarding schools, World War II, land claims, ANCSA, identity movements) are simply part of an unfinished indigenous history.

Collaborative Horizons

When *Looking Both Ways* opened in Kodiak it drew on the community-based heritage work of the Alutiiq Museum and Archaeological Repository. The return of traditional artifacts from the Smithsonian, albeit on loan, offered a powerful symbolic reconnection with the past. When the exhibition traveled to Homer, on the Kenai Peninsula, it was coordinated with the biannual cultural festival, Tamamta Katurlluta, celebrated by the Alutiiq villages of Nanwalek, Port Graham, and Seldovia. At Homer, kayaks (recently built in Nanwalek) arrived on the beach to be greeted by Kodiak Island dancers and a priest who delivered an Orthodox prayer. Then, at the Pratt Museum, a large potluck/pot-latch feast, featuring salmon and seal delicacies, was shared, and there were plant walks, "Eskimo Olympics" (feats of balance, tug-of-war, leg wrestling), and seal sampling (scientific dissection and data recording for subsistence monitoring). The crowd—Native Elders, activists, and youth; Homer inhabitants; museum donors and staff; visitors; and a robed priest from Nanwalek—flowed in and out of the exhibition. While the festival's "gathering of tradition" was rich, it was not all-inclusive. Many in Nanwalek did not attend. Some could not afford air travel across the bay. Others were busy with the salmon run—capturing, smoking, and drying fish. The run had recently been restored, thanks to a tribally organized spawning project in the local river and its upstream lakes. Another dimension of "heritage," perhaps. In any event, preparing and executing cultural performances requires a certain amount of leisure, time free from making a living. In traditional northern societies the long winter months offered occasions for social gatherings, exchanges, and an intense ritual life. In Nanwalek, the month surrounding the Orthodox New Year in late January is a similar period of communal intensity. Newer forms of heritage performance, taking place in museums, cultural centers, and festivals, observe a different calendar, addressing both community and "outside" audiences.

Across the bay at the Tamamta Katurlluta festival, an evening program at the Homer High School auditorium followed the afternoon feast. Alutiiq tradition was performed in several ways. Nick Tanape Sr.—a crucial Alutiiq organizer of the festival—presented Gale Parsons of the Pratt Museum with a gift in recognition of her work with local Alutiiq communities. Two dance groups, in their distinctive styles, enacted the "looking both ways" theme. A group of school-age children, the Kodiak Alutiiq Dancers, dressed in old-style snow-falling parkas and beaded headdresses, performed well-rehearsed traditional dances to a drumbeat. The mood was earnest and respectful. The evening ended with the Nanwalek Sugpiaq Dancers, exuberant performers in their teens and twenties. Their dances, newly improvised on old patterns, were inspired by *maskalataq*, syncretic masking dances performed during the Orthodox New Year with considerable room for individual invention and play. In Jeff Leer's words, "the Nanwalek Dancers purposefully use . . . knowledge [of *maskalata*] to create new dances, asking themselves what this or that movement originally represented, perhaps the surfacing of a seal or the flight of a fowl. Therefore, although the dances are newly invented, they are built around the bits and pieces of traditional Alutiiq culture that the new generation have been able to mine from the tradition bearers of the village" (2001: 219). To the twang of an electric guitar, the dancers—some in tall Dena'ina (Athabaskan) feather headdresses—mixed gestures and rhythms from Native tradition and contemporary pop or hip-hop. The effect was joyful, serious, and comic, and by the end of the evening much of the audience was gyrating on the stage. The next stop for *Looking Both Ways* was Anchorage, and at its opening celebration the Nanwalek Dancers again brought down the house.

Events and books like *Looking Both Ways* are inherently celebratory. The good news of survival and public recognition ultimately prevails over the bad news of colonialism, historical decimation, ongoing economic marginality, and cultural losses. Realities like smallpox, forced labor, contemporary alcoholism, poverty, and high suicide rates do not fit well in the redeeming vision. Selection and purification are evident in the uplifting pedagogical presentations at the Alaska Native Heritage Center. And some have criticized the Alutiiq project as "an idealized view of Alutiiq culture" (Lee and Graburn 2003: 619). *Looking Both Ways* presents a rather complex history, shadowed by Russian massacres and labor regimes. Elders regret the passing of customary skills and recall language prohibition in American boarding schools. But the overall message is, appropriately, hopeful: we (the pronoun untroubled) are still here, looking back to go forward. This, Aron Crowell reports (2004), was what Elders at the planning conferences wanted the project to stress. The positive tone is reinforced by many smiling portraits and by superb color photos of artifacts and places. A dispersed Alutiiq culture is gathered together and made present, a living heritage. Even the massacre site at Refuge Rock makes stunning Alaskan scenery.

Looking Both Ways also contains good news for its non-Native audience. As we have seen, it features a positive vision of reciprocity in academic research—primarily archaeology but also anthropology and linguistics. The project received major financial support both from

Native corporations and from national organizations—cultural, commercial, and philanthropic. Its shape, and indeed its material possibility, depended on recognized collaborative work and a broad base of participation. What sort of a model for postcolonial research practices does it offer? The question may be clarified with reference to an important essay by Ruth Phillips (2003). Drawing on her experience directing the University of British Columbia Museum of Anthropology, a pioneer in collaborative work, she poses several critical issues for community-museum projects.

Phillips distinguishes two basic models. In the "community-based" exhibition, indigenous authorities determine the selection and interpretation of materials. Museum curators function as facilitators, and a unified Native perspective is the goal. This is primarily an exhibition by and for a specific community, sometimes producing displays not sufficiently contextualized for general audiences. The second, "multivocal" model juxtaposes Native and non-Native perspectives. Different interpretations of the same objects, texts, or histories are allowed to coexist. The shared discursive space reflects a specific negotiation of authority. When the differences of perspective are too sharp, however, audiences expecting a coherent explanation can be confused. Phillips thinks of her two models as ideal types that in practice are often mixed. It is worth distinguishing them, she argues, because misunderstanding and tension can arise when participants in a project are working with incompatible expectations (2003: 163–167).

Looking Both Ways reflects a specific negotiation of agendas. The book, as we have seen, leans toward the multivocal, juxtaposing voices without seeking to express a single, coherent "Alutiiq" or "scientific" perspective. The exhibition tends toward the other model: overall, it reflects community self-images, seamlessly aligning academic (historical and archaeological) knowledge with Elders' memories and visions. (The same can be said of the website, www.mnh.si.edu/lookingbothways, which adopts an insider rhetoric—"our history," "our family," "our beliefs," etc.—featuring photos of families and local villages, juxtaposed throughout with archaeological artifacts.) The exhibition was probably most "community-based" at the times it merged with Native-directed heritage events and institutions—the opening at Kodiak and the Tamamta Katurlluta Festival at Homer. Understood as a spectrum of performances, the *Looking Both Ways* project is a specific negotiation of Phillips's two agendas.

The book, designed to be a work of historical reference and inspiration for both cultural insiders and outsiders, may well achieve something
like canonical status—for better and worse. As a collaboration, its successful mediation of potentially divisive agendas reflects, as we have
seen, a specific history of Alutiiq (re)emergence and the work of individual scholars, activists, and culture brokers to maintain reciprocity.
Taken as a whole, the project aligns oral traditions with scientific evidence, playing down discrepancies. Where this is impossible, Pullar's
"different truths" coexist.

Alliances such as *Looking Both Ways* require compromise on all sides,
patient listening, consultation, and—the key words—equality and
respect. Clearly, in situations of ongoing oppression and acute political
antagonism their resolution will seem utopic, and indeed it is utopic, or
at least strategic, in the current Alutiiq context. One may wonder who is
not included in the polyphony of *Looking Both Ways*. Is there a privileging of certain activists and spokespersons, particular Elders and tradition bearers? One occasionally glimpses the limits of this multivocality:
for example, Native opponents of archaeology are answered but not
quoted. (The resistance tends to be found among the very old, who believe
that remains should be left alone and that buried objects may have been
polluted by shamans.) Responses to the exhibition by the many Natives
who attended have been enthusiastic, but we are limited to anecdotal
accounts. Since travel to the exhibition's venues can be expensive, it is
clear that many economically marginal Alutiiq in dispersed villages
cannot have participated and may well have little interest in heritage or
tradition performed on this public scale. Thus, while recognizing the
project's remarkable inclusiveness and range of perspectives, it is important not to lose sight of the partiality and contingency of its achievement.
Through its polyphony, new positions of tribal and academic authority
are claimed; tradition is textualized for public consumption, and local
arguments and sensitive topics are inevitably glossed over.

Arthur Mason (2008) usefully draws attention to the role of outside
expertise in Native mobilizations. Drawing on Benedict Anderson's model
of nation making, he sees anthropologists, archaeologists, and linguists
supplying cultural forms for indigenous edification. Expert technologies
such as maps, censuses, and museums create spaces to be filled by an
emerging Alutiiq imagined community. In this perspective, both the
Alutiiq Museum's heritage work and ANCSA's ethnic mapping and
enrollment are modernizing functions of liberal government. By contrast,

the approach presented here stresses overlapping agendas and negotiated authorities in an open-ended historical process. During the 1970s and 1980s archaeological discoveries intensified the growing interest in an "Alutiiq" past. Following the contentious Larsen Bay repatriation process, collaborative forms of community archaeology were worked out. Professional and local interests in history and heritage found ways to coexist productively. Alutiiq renewal has indeed relied heavily on academic expertise. This was particularly true in the early decades of heritage revival. Since then, new cultural authorities have emerged. Gordon Pullar and Sven Haakanson Jr. are academically trained but not outside experts. Nor do they represent an essentialized insider perspective (Haakanson 2001). As cultural activists they remain engaged with the university, but in partial ways, and from a rearticulated Native distance. Other activists, "culture bearers," and Native "artists" bring links and expertise from the working and corporate world to the heritage agenda.

Placing *Looking Both Ways* and *Agayuliyararput (Our Way of Making Prayer)* in a wider political context, it is worth citing cautionary statements by the museum curators Aldona Jonaitis and Richard Inglis and by Ruth Phillips. Jonaitis and Inglis reflect on the limits of collaborative museum work:

> Today it is de rigeur for curators to involve [Native people]—as advisors, consultants, or co-curators—in museum representations of their culture. This is certainly an improvement over the situation in the past when a white, usually male, curator decided by himself the theme and content of an exhibition. It does not, however, solve the problems of the situation of Native peoples in the contemporary world. Museums have far more relevance to the powerful—those capable of acquiring and housing art and artifacts—than they do to the disempowered. Moreover, there is no such entity as the Native voice, one that speaks with authority for the entire community. There exist many voices, some of which speak for upholders of cultural traditions, others that address band and tribal politics, and still others that concern themselves with social issues . . . The encounter of different values, different priorities, often creates problems that can only sometimes be resolved. (1994: 159)

While the proliferation of tribal institutions such as the Alutiiq Museum complicates this equation of museums with dominant power,

Jonaitis and Inglis keep us aware of persistent inequalities and conflicting interests that can only be partially mitigated through collaboration. In a similar vein, Ruth Phillips interrogates "the role that museums play in processes of social change": "Put simply, does the growing popularity of collaborative exhibits signal a new era of social agency for museums, or does it make the museum a space where symbolic restitution is made for the injustices of the colonial era in lieu of more concrete forms of social, economic and political redress?" (2003: 158).

These assertions are not meant to discredit either collaborative heritage work or the community-based activism of tribal museums. Their authors do, however, insist on realistic expectations and the absence of guarantees. In this they reinforce the perspective of Native scholars like Vine Deloria Jr. (1997), who, while seeing new possibilities for joint projects, never loses sight of ongoing structural inequalities. Genuinely impressive works like *Looking Both Ways* need to be appreciated as fruitful, contingent coalitions rather than as performances of postcolonial virtue.

Phillips's question about the degree to which cultural celebrations may, in practice, substitute for other forms of politics does not admit of a simple answer. As I have suggested, much depends on specific political contexts and possibilities. A symptomatic critique of heritage work may see it as occupying a comfortable niche in postmodern "multicultural" hegemonies: every identity gets its exhibition, website, coffee-table book, or film.

I have argued that this view, while partly correct, misses a great deal of indigenous cultural process and politics. The old/new articulations, performances, and translations of identity are not enough to bring about structural socioeconomic change. But they reflect and to a real extent create new conditions for indigenous solidarity, activism, and participation in diverse public spheres. When they are understood as part of a wider politics of self-determination, heritage projects are open ended in their significance. To reduce the Alaska Native Heritage Center to a cultural theme park and cruise-ship destination would miss its intertribal and public education agenda, its Native youth participation, its arts programs.

Similarly, seen across their several contexts of production and reception, *Looking Both Ways* and *The Living Tradition of Yup'ik Masks* are much more than coffee-table books even if they do end up on coffee tables (and kitchen tables). The Alutiiq Museum, while open to tourists, is primarily a local cultural center whose oral history, community archaeology, language, and education projects gather and transmit a newly dynamic Alutiiq (Sugpiaq) identity. I have argued for a complex approach to the politics of tradition. Native heritage projects reach selectively into the past, opening paths to an undetermined future. They act within and against new national and transnational structures of empowerment and control. While it is too early to say what the ultimate significance of these transactions will be, it is clear that the historical weather has changed in recent decades and that indigenous cultural movements are very much part of the new climate. I have also affirmed the role played by scholars, Native and non-Native, in sustaining heritage movements. The projects reviewed here are important, hopeful coalitions. While they do not transcend longstanding inequalities or resolve struggles for cultural authority, they at least demonstrate that Natives and anthropologists, openly recognizing a fraught common history, need not paint themselves into corners.

7

❖

Second Life: The Return of the Masks

Anchorage is spread out along Cook Inlet below the magnificent snow-capped peaks of the Chugach range. Mile after mile of straight multilane boulevards made the place feel, to me, like Los Angeles, except for all the trees, pickup trucks, and mud. Anchorage is Alaska's one big city, with nearly half of the state's population of 680,000. Its inhabitants are old and new immigrants—some with origins in the Gold Rush, others lured by the recent oil and gas bonanzas, plus a steady stream of escapees from the over-civilized lower forty-eight. In addition, Filipino, Island Pacific, and Latin American migrants come in search of work. They live in trailer parks and tattered, lower-class neighborhoods like "Mountain View."

A growing number of recent arrivals are Native Alaskans. They come from all over the state, seeking jobs that are lacking in rural villages and towns, or to find education and new kinds of freedom. Many follow family networks, others land in the city because there is nowhere else to go. Some eventually return to their regional homelands. But an increasing proportion stay in Anchorage, where new contexts and styles of urban indigenous living are being invented. These often involve seasonal commuting to homelands, family visits, the sharing of subsistence foods (hunted, fished, gathered), and other symbolic tokens of "Nativeness." It is projected that by the year 2020, as much as half of the Native population of Alaska may live all or most of the time in Anchorage.

A young city, Anchorage grew rapidly as a railroad link to the Gold Country in the early twentieth century. The Second World War saw another expansion, followed by the recent boom in resource extraction. Local Dena'ina (Athabaskan) Natives, forced out of their fishing camps, embraced Russian Orthodoxy and gathered in communities further inland. Native Alaskan presence in the city is most visible today in the gleaming headquarters of the regional corporations created through the

Alaska Native Claims Settlement Act (ANCSA). Modern office suites are decorated with contemporary tribal art. An annual "Friendship Potlatch" is organized for shareholders of Cook Inlet Region, Inc. (CIRI), a multi-tribal corporation specifically created for Natives no longer connected to their places of origin. This celebratory get-together responds to new sites and scales of indigenous social life—beginning to play a wider role analogous to the pow-wow in the lower forty-eight states. Less visible gatherings occur in churches, around kitchen tables, or in conjunction with trips by family members to the Alaska Native Medical Center—a modern hospital, designed to meet Native needs, supported by ANCSA corporations and with federal funding facilitated by the late Senator Ted Stevens. (In the lobby of a new addition, alongside photos of Elders Advisory Council members, I noticed a smiling portrait of the man everyone called "Uncle Ted.") Scattered through the hospital, newly crafted heritage artifacts adorn the walls, and the gift shop is a renowned outlet for high-quality Alaska Native art.

People who may or may not—or may only sometimes—identity themselves as "Native" live among the Samoans, Latinos, and other displaced inhabitants of the Pacific Rim. Small Christian churches abound. I wondered whether anyone in their congregations had ever set foot in the downtown corporate headquarters or in the Anchorage Museum of History and Art, where artifacts of traditional Native culture are on display, and where the exhibition of Alutiiq/Sugpiaq masks whose opening I was on my way to attend would eventually travel.

A fifty-minute plane trip out into the Gulf of Alaska gets you to Kodiak Island. There are several flights a day, weather permitting, with a lot of commuting back and forth: business errands, family visits, hunting and fishing trips. The town of Kodiak, population 6,300, is Alaska's sixth "city" and its largest fishing port. The world's biggest carnivore (the famous Kodiak bear) roams the second-largest island (after Hawai'i) in the United States. There are virtually no roads. Mountainous and deeply penetrated by the ocean, much of Kodiak is a National Wildlife Refuge. Its six currently inhabited Native villages are accessible only by boat and small aircraft.

Kodiak Island Borough (the main island, nearby islands, and bands of the adjoining coast) has a population of about 14,000. Of these, 60 percent are classified in the census as white, 16 percent Asian, 15 percent Native American (Alaska Native), and the last 9 percent Pacific Islanders, other races, and those identifying as multiracial.

Figure 7.1.   View of Kodiak. (Photo by James Clifford.)

A very large U.S. Coast Guard complex just outside the town of Kodiak maintains a population of about 3,000, including families, most residing on the base. The town, as local people like to observe, is very multicultural. In addition to the whites and Natives who earn a living mostly from commercial fishing and sport hunting or fishing, Asians, Pacific Islanders, Latinos, and Europeans work in the fish-processing industry and in service jobs. SUVs and boats are everywhere in evidence, as are gorgeous mountains and inlets. Downtown, on rising land above the harbor, one finds the Holy Resurrection Orthodox Cathedral, its clapboard siding and bright-blue cupolas glistening. A few steps away: the Saint Herman Theological Seminary and a museum in the restored home of Alexander Baranov, first chief manager of the Russian-American Company. A colony of white fuel-storage tanks adds a modernist touch to the hillside. And across the street, a less picturesque, rather severely functional new structure, the "Alutiiq Center," houses offices of Afognak Native Corporation and Natives of Kodiak, Inc. On the ground floor, my destination: the Alutiiq Museum and Archaeological Repository.

Figure 7.2.   The Holy Resurrection Orthodox Cathedral, Kodiak. (Photo by
James Clifford.)

I have visited the Alutiiq Museum twice—first for a week in 2007 to
find out about its range of activities, and then for several days in May
2008 for the opening of *Giinaquq: Like a Face.* This exhibition of old
Alutiiq masks is the occasion for the present essay's reflections on cultural renewal and the "second life of heritage."

Inside the Alutiiq Museum's somewhat cramped exhibition area, the
indigenous history of Kodiak Island is narrated using maps, documents,
paintings, historic photos, and archaeological artifacts. Native tradition
is explained—ritual life, cosmology, subsistence-related seasonal activities, and communal exchanges at the Russian Orthodox New Year. A
recently built kayak fills most of a wall beneath a large, brightly colored
painting by Sugpiaq artist Alvin Amason. Museum-organized programs
fostering language revival and community archaeology are described
with texts, photos, and videos; a stuffed Kodiak bear looms in one corner.
The small gift shop features crafts and jewelry made by Sugpiaq artists,

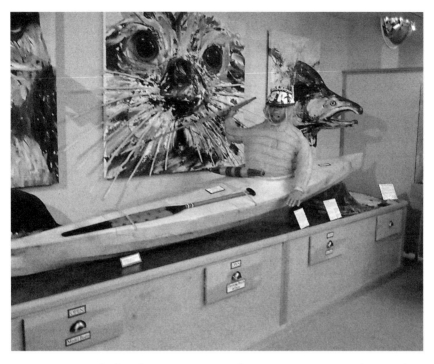

Figure 7.3.   Inside the Alutiiq Museum 1. The sea otter painting, *Chami,* is by the contemporary Alutiiq artist Alvin Amason. The kayak was framed and sewn by Bud Rozelle, Grace Harrod, and Thecla Spencer in a 1990 KANA cultural project. Paddle by artist Jerry Laktonen. (Photo by James Clifford; courtesy of the Alutiiq Museum.)

along with books and catalogues, T-shirts, caps, bags, and other branded souvenirs. A small area for temporary exhibits adjoins the main gallery. At the end of a hallway lined with several cramped offices, a door opens into the work area, a large room filled with archaeological laboratory equipment, tables, and computer workstations. In a corner: exhibit cases specially designed for transport by light airplanes, making it possible to bring collections to remote villages on the island.

The museum opened in 1995 with critical funding from the *Exxon Valdez* oil spill compensation fund. Kodiak Island waters had been fouled by the 1989 disaster, disrupting Native economies. Moreover, the cleanup itself brought secondary damage to coastal archaeological sites. By linking the disaster to an ongoing project of cultural preservation, the museum was able to qualify for compensation funding. The Kodiak Area

Figure 7.4. Inside the Alutiiq Museum 2. Video programs show archaeological excavations, and the gift shop specializes in contemporary Alutiiq art and craft. (Photo by James Clifford; courtesy of the Alutiiq Museum.)

Native Association (KANA: see Chapter 6) was already committed to heritage preservation, led by its chairman Gordon Pullar and the archaeologist/cultural activist Rick Knecht. On Kodiak, the need for a Native-administered institution to promote cultural knowledge and pride was widely felt. Archaeology had, for some time, been playing a central role in the rediscovery of Alutiiq history, and the growing collections, as well as the damaged coastal sites, needed to be managed. Eventually $1.4 million in "restoration" funding, along with contributions from regional and village Native corporations, assured the construction and initial operating budget of the Alutiiq Museum and Archaeological Repository.

Knecht initially directed the new institution, assisted by archaeologist Amy Steffian, a veteran of community-supported excavations in the village of Larsen Bay. Ultimate administrative authority was exercised by a board of directors with representatives from the participating Native

Figure 7.5. Qanqanaq—ground squirrel parka, by Susan Malutin and Grace Harrod, 1999, based on a parka from Ugashik, 1883. (Photo by James Clifford; courtesy of the Alutiiq Museum.)

corporations. And within several years an energetic Sugpiaq scholar/ activist, Sven Haakanson Jr., was recruited as executive director, a post he has filled with creativity and distinction. During my visits to Kodiak, Haakanson was my principal interlocutor, along with Amy Steffian and other patient members of the museum's staff. Of course they are not responsible for my interpretations.

Routes of Return

In addition to doing what museum directors do—raise funds, design exhibits, negotiate loans and purchases, manage collections, organize education and outreach—Sven Haakanson is an artist who makes new traditional objects such as masks, baskets, and kayaks. Masks (about which we will hear more soon) are prominently displayed in his

Figure 7.6. Sven Haakanson's workshop. (Photo by James Clifford; courtesy Sven Haakanson Jr.)

workshop. Figure 7.6 is a snapshot taken in passing and used with permission. On close inspection, the image reveals many elements of a composite Native heritage in process.

The woodworking kit in the right foreground will be familiar to hobbyists. It suggests the craft of heritage. Traditional things are fashioned with new techniques (electric drills and routers), from explicit models (photos and pencil diagrams, tacked here to the walls), understood in relation to novel cultural categories ("art," "culture," "identity"). The masks here are traditional, meaning based on nineteenth-century models. In the background we can see part of a poster from a French exhibit of Alutiiq masks: the first production of the new Musée du Quai Branly in Paris (Désveaux 2002). Through an accident of history, virtually all of the surviving old Alutiiq masks are currently in France. Reconnecting this strand of heritage thus involves travel in space as well as in time. It requires research: productive/reproductive practices of close observation, copying, inscription, photography, and standardization. Something of this can be seen in the line drawings to the right.

The presence of Russian Orthodoxy in the heritage mix is registered by a small icon pinned at the upper left. And we can just glimpse the distinctive Orthodox crosses in a mostly obscured postcard in front of the poster. The strips clamped together just below the icon are a wood outline for a Christmas ornament Haakanson was making for his daughter. The shape is based on petroglyphs from the remote western tip of the island, where he is leading a multiyear research project. The designs have become symbols of a deep, precontact Sugpiaq past, appearing as motifs in contemporary Native art, as corporate logos, and as graphics on the museum's T-shirts, bags, and caps.

Overlapping the poster from France, a surprising addition: a nineteenth-century portrait of a Maori tribal leader. The man's grandson recently visited from Aotearoa/New Zealand and stayed a while in Kodiak to teach Maori techniques of stone carving at the Alutiiq Museum. The elaborately tattooed face joins the others on the workshop wall like one more mask—and an index of today's circuits of transnational "indigeneity."

In the right background, behind some small ornamental carvings, two snapshots can be seen: pictures of Haakanson's nephew and brother-in-law hunting and fishing. In Alaska, and throughout the western United States and Canada, "subsistence rights"—hunting, fishing, and gathering—are claimed as central elements of indigenous tradition. They are also, of course, sites of tension and negotiation with the state, with non-Native hunters and fishers, and sometimes with environmentalists—all part of ongoing political struggles around land use and sovereignty.

Looking again at the whole image, we see on the left edge a map of Antarctica. Antarctica? A different circumpolar "face" of the planet? The whole world seen from another side? And that large piece of fiberboard in the middle of the picture, blocking our view? We might consider it a salutary reminder of limitation, of what can and can't be seen from this angle of vision. What follows are the observations of a visitor, who sees what is made visible, who hears what people are ready to tell.

Sven Haakanson grew up in Old Harbor, one of the remote villages on Kodiak Island. In the late eighteenth century, this settlement was the first Russian outpost on Kodiak. He told me that although his father was a respected Elder and village leader, as a teenager he learned little of his Native history. He expected, like his high school classmates, to lead a life of semiemployment, fishing commercially and guiding hunting parties. Several of his friends died young—victims of drowning and suicide. In 1981, while supporting himself as a fisherman, he found his way to a conference in Denmark where he heard a lecture by Lydia Black, the leading historian of Russian America. Why, he wondered, did I have to come halfway around the world to learn about my own history?

Haakanson then enrolled at the University of Alaska, Fairbanks, where Black was a professor—an environment where Native culture was studied and identification encouraged. He learned Russian, went on to Harvard on a fellowship for indigenous scholars, did fieldwork among Nenets reindeer herders in Siberia, and while still finishing his dissertation was named to direct the new museum in Kodiak. When I visited in 2007, he described the museum's varied programs, all contributing to a fundamental goal: to make it possible for future Alutiiq youth—whether they grow up in a village, in Kodiak, or in Anchorage—to know and take pride in their history and culture.

Haakanson's path to heritage activism differs from that of an earlier generation, local leaders who encouraged "Alutiiq" identification during the ANCSA enrollment process and who were closely involved with the new corporations. Like other younger supporters of the museum, Haakanson's Native identification took shape in a post-sixties world of indigenous identity politics. This historical context of pan-Alaskan, circumpolar, and indeed worldwide indigenous resurgence brought a sharpened awareness of colonization's destructive/transformative effects and a desire to reach back to older, precontact cultural roots. A deep history was renewed in a changing present—activities ranging from land claims and managed subsistence to revived dancing and inventive tribal "art." The recent trend away from the name "Alutiiq" in favor of "Sugpiaq" reflects a deepening of this consciousness. Alutiiq, the vernacular pronunciation of a Russian misnomer "Aleut," reflects a specific colonial history. The Creole social structure and Orthodox religion of Kodiak preserved cultural elements that would, in the 1970s, be detached and revalued under the sign of a renewed "Alutiiq" identity. Sugpiaq, an old Sugt'stun term meaning "real person" or "just like a person," reflects a strengthened sense of indigeneity. A deep, precontact heritage would prefigure a specifically Native, postcolonial future. The names Alutiiq and Sugpiaq thus denote different legacies from a history in the process of rearticulation. Today, both names and historical trajectories are commonly invoked. I use both names here, depending on context.

Haakanson's father had participated in the transition from "Russian" or "Aleut" identifications to "Alutiiq" affiliation, first in the land-title movement and then through the ANCSA process described in Chapter 6.

An influential leader of tribal institutions in Old Harbor, Sven Haakanson Sr. was a founder of KANA. Native movements throughout Alaska would be strongly inflected after 1971 by ANCSA's corporate structure, but they also drew on older sources of communal life that had persisted in subsistence sharing, kinship, and syncretic Russian Orthodoxy and Creole social structures. Aleut/Alutiiq/Sugpiaq society, as far back as is known, has included established leadership roles and economic inequality. This aspect of tradition found new expression in the corporate leadership of ANCSA development institutions. Other, more communal, elements from the past also found new outcomes in nonprofit social projects and in visions of heritage as an inclusive source of peoplehood. Working in the post-ANCSA environment, these initiatives resisted the settlement's privatized vision of the path ahead.

In Kodiak prior to the movement for Alutiiq renewal, public manifestations of heritage tended toward nostalgic evocations of a vanished Russian past. Streets were named for Russian historic figures. The Baranov Museum provided a locus for historic memory, and an annual pageant, Cry of the Wild Ram, became widely popular. The special status of Russian-identified Creoles had been undermined by the influx of new American populations. And after 1970 what was left of Creole privilege would be further displaced. Many members of the old elite, like Roy Madsen, the first Alaska Native Superior Court judge, embraced the emerging Native movement, actively encouraging "Alutiiq" identification under ANCSA. Heritage retrieval, central to this process of rearticulation, was different from commemorations of the Russian period. Native activism was revivalist not nostalgic, retrieving a past that could authorize projects in the present (Pullar 1992). In the words of Sven Haakanson Sr. (quoted in Crowell, Steffian, and Pullar 2001: 3): "You've got to look back and find out the past, and then look forward."

The first ANCSA decade brought confusion and discord, and by the early 1980s, the newly formed Native institutions in Kodiak were in disarray. A series of lawsuits over control of the local corporations virtually bankrupted several of them. In a state of paralysis, the factionalized KANA offered its presidency to an outsider, untainted by local politics. Gordon Pullar had just arrived in Kodiak to take over editorship of the Kodiak Times from his uncle Karl Armstrong, a prominent member of the older elite. Pullar (1992) recalls growing up in the Pacific Northwest where his mother, originally from Kodiak, had remained after being sent away to school by Protestant missionaries. His mother denied her Native background, resolutely claiming "Russian" identity. After her early death, Pullar became close to his uncle, who often stopped en route to Washington, D.C., on business for Koniag Inc., the regional corporation. Karl Armstrong urged his nephew to relocate in Kodiak and get involved in the land-claims movement. A sense of Alutiiq identity was awakened by these conversations, reinforced by college courses in cultural anthropology. In 1983 Pullar returned to live in Kodiak, just as his uncle was dying. Within a year he would find himself president of KANA.

An emergent "Alutiiq" society scattered across three ANCSA regions did not yet recognize itself as a coherent people. Under Pullar's leadership, KANA added heritage documentation and renewal to its social agenda— programs in archaeology, oral history, and intergenerational transmission. Stitching together a dismembered indigenous history was a way of confronting the negative legacies of two empires: Russian exploitation, diseases, and alcohol; American racism, militarism, and neglect. Pullar hoped that cultural pride and a strengthened sense of identity could be an antidote to the despair and self-destructive behavior plaguing many rural communities across Alaska. This was KANA's heritage agenda in the 1980s and 1990s. Pullar has continued to combine heritage awareness and historical research with social development work at the College of Rural Alaska in Fairbanks. And he has been an Alutiiq spokesman at United Nations–sponsored indigenous gatherings. Pullar's personal path thus represents a transition from the older Native/Creole localism of his uncle's generation to a more broadly based indigeneity: a social movement that can engage with diverse sites in Alaska and beyond.

Sven Haakanson Jr.'s route to heritage activism, while rooted in village life, is that of a new generation, inspired by both local attachments and a cosmopolitan "indigeneity." His work has taken him to Europe and Russia, to service on the boards of Alaska cultural institutions, and to recognition by the MacArthur Foundation. Under his directorship, with administrative support from Deputy Director Amy Steffian, the Alutiiq Museum and Archaeological Repository would expand its activities dramatically, becoming widely recognized as a model of its kind. Like other Native-run "museums," it is more accurately a "cultural center," sustaining a broad array of programs. Community archaeology (led by long-time staff member Patrick Saltonstall) remains a central activity, with digs organized every summer and participation open to all. Artifact collection, research, and management are ongoing, along with stewardship visits to the island's many archaeological sites and maintenance of a photographic collection and a library. A language program directed by April Laktonen Counceller, with support from linguist Jeff Leer at the University of Alaska, Fairbanks, works with the few remaining Elders fluent in Sugt'stun, organizing workshops, producing pedagogical materials, and maintaining a website. The museum brings traveling collections to remote villages and organizes themed "Alutiiq Week" activities. Artists teach grass basket weaving, carving, skin sewing, wood bending, and model kayak construction. Cultural materials are prepared for use in public schools. Long-term research investigates petroglyphs from the western tip of Kodiak Island, cryptic messages from the island's deep history. Special art demonstrations and sales, workshops, seasonal celebrations, and other social gatherings take place at the museum. Temporary exhibitions of art, craft, history, and photography are ongoing. The gift shop, an outlet for carvings and jewelry by Sugpiaq artists, is an integral component of local heritage revival.

The Alutiiq Museum, like other indigenous museums and cultural centers, addresses diverse stakeholders. It must respond to a wide, sometimes contradictory, range of desires and modes of consumption. We can review, briefly, its principal "performative" contexts, sites of political articulation and cultural translation.

The museum is intergenerational, providing situations in which traditional knowledge can be recognized and heard. Elders' specific understandings of custom, language, and history are recorded and valued. They are consulted during the planning of exhibitions like *Looking Both Ways* or *Giinaquq*. The goal is not only to create a historical archive, but also to transmit communal wisdom in new ways. Of course no one knows for sure what it will mean to be Sugpiaq in the coming decades. The museum's crucial priority of reaching contemporary youth through schools, internships, and summer programs carries no guarantees. A knowledge of history and a sense of Native pride needs to be meaningful in a contemporary cultural mix: knowing how to construct a model kayak and also a website, or wearing a fur parka and bentwood visor for a ceremonial dance but jeans and sneakers the rest of the time.

Sugpiat of different backgrounds engage with the Alutiiq Museum in different ways. Some regularly attend openings and celebrations. Others are glad of the museum's existence but rarely participate in its programs. Some only sporadically think of themselves as Native. Others find their local indigenousness primarily in the ANCSA corporations, in tribal governments, in family relations or in subsistence practices rather than in artifact collections, crafts, or activities at a cultural center. When villagers come to town, the Alutiiq Museum is not a necessary stopping place. Therefore it takes its collections to them, using modular exhibits that fit safely in small aircraft. Radio broadcasts and Internet sites are also popular. This kind of outreach aims to build Sugpiaq identification, and it is also demonstrates a "return" on the village corporations' annual contributions, support that cannot be taken for granted. The museum's imagined community is scattered, and people living in villages are just one important Sugpiat audience. For those in Anchorage and beyond it provides a symbolic center and destination, a gathering place for Native culture. Diasporic returns to the homeland, analyzed in Chapter 3, are accomplished with airplanes, the media, and the Internet.

In Kodiak, the Alutiiq Museum maintains a presence among other heritage projects: Russian (the Baranov House and Museum), maritime (celebrations of the fishing industry), and military (Fort Abercrombie, World War Two). It needs to be intelligible and attractive as a destination for tourists and a resource for public school programs. In Southcentral Alaska, the museum also participates in art-culture exchanges and collaborations involving Anchorage institutions and Alaska nonprofit agencies. It has ongoing relationships with museums in Washington, D.C., France, Russia, and Finland.

The academic world represents another set of audiences, resources, and pressures. Cultural experts—anthropologists, archaeologists, linguists, historians—have played important roles in the widespread Native heritage revival, relationships particularly salient for the Alutiiq movement. The archaeologists Richard Jordan, Rick Knecht, Amy Steffian, Patrick Saltonstall, and Aron Crowell, the linguist Jeff Leer, and the historian Lydia Black are prominent examples. These relationships have significantly determined the shape of Alutiiq/Sugpiaq cultural projects (Mason 2008), but in ways that articulate with local agendas. The balance of power, the "terms of engagement" for these collaborations have recently been shifting (Crowell 2004). As Native-administered institutions attain more autonomy, negotiated relations replace paternalist guidance. Local cultural centers are still reliant on the academic world for technical assistance, validation of research, and access to funding. Sometimes their agendas overlap productively; sometimes they conflict; sometimes collaborations achieve a way to work together while maintaining a respectful distance—a modus vivendi.

Finally, the Alutiiq Museum is responsible to its funding sources. Eight Kodiak Alutiiq organizations provide a governing structure and core operating budget: Afognak Native Corporation, Akhiok-Kaguyak Inc., Kodiak

Area Native Association (KANA), Koniag Inc., Leisnoi Inc., Natives of Kodiak Inc., Old Harbor Native Corporation, Ouzinkie Native Corporation. Currently Will Anderson, president of Koniag Inc., chairs the museum's board of directors. Ten additional members, representing KANA and the Native corporations established by ANCSA (with one at-large representative, Gordon Pullar) complete the all-Sugpiat governing body.

The Alutiiq Museum does not enjoy line-item funding from its Native corporate supporters. The budget must be negotiated annually, with variations dependent on business outcomes, changing priorities, personalities, and rivalries. Enthusiasm must be rekindled with exciting, visible projects. The museum needs to convince corporate leaders and their shareholders that it will continue to deliver a valuable service. Specific projects also rely on the usual array of grants, agencies, and businesses that support "cultural" endeavors, such as ConocoPhillips Alaska, the First Alaskans Institute, and the Alaska State Council on the Arts. Raising funds is an ever-present fact of life. The Alutiiq Museum engages in a scramble familiar to all nonprofits: creating reputation, being "innovative" in ways recognizable to funding agencies, extracting matching contributions, inspiring supporters, and pressuring the reluctant. There is the occasional windfall, such as a recent unsolicited grant of $1 million from the Rasmuson Foundation (an Alaska philanthropy that supports a wide range of projects in Alaska, from art collecting to well digging).

The museum's audiences—Elders, youth, diverse Sugpiaq constituencies from traditional villages and the big city; artists, tourists, cultural aficionados, and academics; as well as representatives from the worlds of museums, nonprofits, corporate foundations—all need somehow to be balanced and addressed in different performative contexts while sustaining the core mission and social relations of a Native community center. What is performed in this balancing act is not an abstract independence, but what I called in Chapter 3 a relative, "pragmatic sovereignty." This means acting flexibly among discordant expectations, resources, and allies. We will see such a process in the negotiations that made possible *Giinaquq: Like a Face*.

Second Life (Quasi-Theoretical Interlude)

The work of heritage renewal and reconnection responds to violent histories of colonization and capitalist expansion. For small-scale, tribal societies, the ruptures produced by military and commercial invasion, epidemics, and exile from ancestral lands have been devastating. The forced acculturations and transformations lived through by those who survived the initial shocks are relentless. We must therefore reserve a prominent place in our understanding for the kinds of powerful, tendential developments that are summarized in terms like modernity or capitalism. But what weight should be accorded to these "structural," "world-system" forces? How do they block, align, and empower cultural action? Following Raymond Williams's now classic discussion of "determination" (1977: 83–90), we can think of pressures and limits, negotiations not immutable laws: constrained possibilities rather than inevitable outcomes. Heritage, in this general perspective, is neither a recovered source of identity nor a commodified objectified product. It is something more interesting: ambivalent and hard to circumscribe.

Several works from beyond Alaska suggest an appropriate language and historical attitude. The first is an essay by Christopher Tilley, "Performing Culture in the Global Village" (1997). This account of a performance for tourists in Malekula, Vanuatu, addresses the "commodification and objectification of culture" in the revival of "ethnic lives" throughout the contemporary Third World. Tilley describes how dances long suppressed by missionaries have been revived for visitors from a nearby resort. The ceremonies, performed by men in penis sheaths and pig-tusk armbands, are scrupulous in their traditionalism, excluding all "modern" elements. An elaborate dancing ground, with a large ancestor house, smaller structures, slit gongs, sculptures, and rings of ancestral stones, has been constructed at a site convenient for the visitors. Tilley describes a performance, highlighting the entrepreneurial energy of the chief who orchestrates the event, and his self-conscious explanations of the rituals. He also notes the ambivalent participation of women in the proceeding, the fact that the participants in this ceremony are all Christians normally seen in shorts and T-shirts, and the opinion of others on the island that the whole show is an invention to attract tourist dollars.

Against these and other common presumptions of inauthenticity, Tilley marshals an array of arguments. In Melanesia, "invented" tradition is cultural life, a process of "continual creativity, diffusion and change in which it is often the combination of different elements, drawn from outside the ethnic group, and being combined and reinvented inside it in new forms, that creates cultural distinctiveness, not their simple presence or absence" (83). In this perspective, tourists (and anthropologists) are integral to ethnic self-definition and local "development." Cultural objectification, exchange, and reflexivity are normal moments in the unfinished relations of social and cultural life (Miller 1987; Kramer 2006). Conclusions about power cannot be read off in advance of the ethnographic/historical details. What appears as exploitation or pandering may contain the seeds of something else. Tilley sees the opening up of new roles for women in the revived ceremonies. And indeed, heritage collection and revaluation in Vanuatu (the innovative work of *kastom*) has offered new opportunities for female development (Bolton 2003). And once the dancing on Malekula starts again, it keeps on inventing:

> The culture displayed [by the islanders] is thoroughly mediated by performing it to tourists, and this is indeed its origin, but it is in no sense determined by the expectations of such an audience. It contains the warp and weft of an imagined community which, once woven, has the potential of being spun again in a different way, and by so doing, providing community empowerment. Through constructing this past they are better able to talk about themselves to themselves and secure a place in the global future. (Tilley 1997: 85)

Tilley encourages us to see heritage performances not as ends but as moments in a historical process, a process—it bears repeating—without assured outcomes.

In Chapter 6 we saw something similar in Ann Fienup-Riordan's conception of "conscious culture." Better than "heritage" with its retrospective bias, the phrase suggests a tactical, reflexive form of cultural performance and self-awareness (Fienup-Riordan 2000: 167). Barbara Kirshenblatt-Gimblett's incisive book on tourism and heritage, *Destination Culture* (1998), provides another provocative formulation: "the second life of heritage." What kind of second, or successor, life could this be? Kirshenblatt-Gimblett opens up conceptual, and political, space: "Heritage is not lost and found, stolen and reclaimed . . . heritage produces something new in the present that has recourse to the past" (149). Her perspective suspends value judgments and authenticity claims, allowing us to focus on specific processes of transmission: how elements from the past are being made and remade in specific relational contexts.

A very stimulating exploration of this "second life" can be found in Jeffrey Shandler's *Adventures in Yiddishland* (2006), which introduces the notion of a "postvernacular language and culture." Yiddish, the native speech of Ashkenazic Jews, was, of course, eliminated by the Nazis as a community vernacular in Eastern Europe; in Israel it was suppressed in favor of Hebrew; and elsewhere, except in certain Orthodox communities, it is disappearing as a language of everyday interaction. But Yiddish nonetheless enjoys a second life in extensive and lively performances and institutions, in new media and social settings, and in self-aware expressions of diasporic Jewishness. Shandler argues that postvernacular languages are performative—their significance inhering as much in the very fact that they are being used as in the content of their utterance. Moreover, for Shandler, "post" does not presume a secondary status. Rather, it evokes a new kind of cultural flourishing:

> Postvernacularity can be a liberating concept, prompting possibilities of language use other than the vernacular model of full fluency in the indigenous mother tongue. Thus postvernacularity has important implications for the interrelation of language, culture, and identity—indeed for the notion of what might constitute a "speech community." (23)

A perspective like Shandler's clears the air when we consider the Native language preservation and revival projects currently undertaken in places like the Alutiiq Museum. In the absence of monolingual, or robustly bilingual, contexts of everyday use, heritage languages are being recorded, archived, and learned as second languages. Shandler's perspective helps us appreciate, not so much "native languages" as what might be called "languages of nativeness." The approach suspends normative ideas of cultural wholeness or organic speech communities, weighing instead the importance of selectively rearticulated cultural and linguistic forms, performances adapted to changing interactive situations. (For example, rather elaborate invocations of genealogy and place now routinely introduce indigenous events in Canada, the United States, Aotearoa/New Zealand, and Australia.) "Languages of nativeness" have their own symbolic as well as communicative functions. And it makes little sense to compare them with speech that was widely used decades ago and is now recalled by only a handful of Elders. Postvernacular languages find a second life in complexly multilingual worlds, in the expanding public spheres of indigenous renewal and heritage activism. This, at least, is their potential. Much depends on the overall vitality of cultural renewal and the ways that the new language use is integrated—as a kind of cultural performance art—with effective communal rituals and political mobilizations. In this general vein see also James McClosky (2008) on

"Irish as a world language" and Barbara Meek's (2012) ethnography of language revitalization in an Athabaskan community.

Native communities today represent a spectrum of language uses, from vernacular to postvernacular, and with specific mixtures. Yup'ik, for example, continues to be fluently spoken in everyday contexts, often in combination with English. Alutiiq/Sugt'stun is unlikely to ever reclaim that function, and Sugpiaq culture is closer to the postvernacular end of the spectrum. This situation is far from unique among indigenous communities today who reconstruct their heritage from diverse, often fragmentary, sources, including online archives and social networks. "Second life" comes with no guarantees. It is subject to powerful pressures and is historically open ended. Yet something real, a reweaving of old and new, is happening, something our holistic concepts of culture, identity, and historical development are ill equipped to recognize.

Returning the Masks

The masks in Sven Haakanson's heritage workshop are examples of this rearticulated tradition. During the past few decades, mask carving has found a new vitality in Native Alaska. All along the coast, stretching south into Canada, artists and carvers are making masks as symbols of clan or tribal continuity and power. Their productions are used in ritual life, in potlatches among the southern tribes, and in midwinter gatherings further north. The new artifacts are also made for sale in art galleries, for display in museums and cultural centers, and as objects of social exchange and gift giving. Masks modeled on traditional designs— newly carved creations we might call "heritage objects"—have multiple functions: they may be used in traditional ceremonies, in dance performances at festivals, or in craft classes for children or adults. The same individuals who carve masks for ceremonial use may also produce "tribal art" for markets where prices can be high if the work is good and the carver well known.

Masks, which feature striking human and animal forms and can conveniently be hung on walls, make very good works of art. As such they circulate in established systems of collecting and valuation. They also represent recovered tradition in communities where government suppression of rituals like the potlatch had forced masked dancing to go underground or sometimes to cease entirely for several generations. That situation changed dramatically after the 1970s, during the general revival, and public recognition, of indigenous cultural life. Potlatches in southern Alaska are now common and again spectacular—featuring new masks, dance performances, orations, and exchanges.

North of the Alutiiq, in the Kuskokwim and Yukon deltas, Yup'ik heritage is also being actively performed. The old midwinter gatherings— family visits, exchanges, storytelling—again feature masks and dancing. Once forbidden, today they enjoy the blessing of priests and pastors imbued with various Christian forms of cultural pluralism (Fienup-Riordan 1996). In the 1920s and 1930s the surrealists were inspired by master-pieces of so-called primitive art. Yup'ik masks, along with the instantly recognizable carvings of the "Northwest Coast" tribes of southern Alaska, have long been prominent in European art and ethnography col-lections. But Alutiiq people have not enjoyed a similar visibility, and they have sometimes struggled with a sense of confused identity and cultural inferiority compared to their neighbors. Their experience of disruption and loss was, in fact, especially severe. The Russians arrived early, vio-lently subduing a tenacious resistance and imposing a draconian forced-labor regime in their quest for furs. Sheer survival would require major accommodations by inhabitants of the Aleutian chain and the Kodiak Archipelago—adoption of Russian language, religion, and social forms. Throughout the nineteenth century, epidemics devastated local communi-ties. And after 1867, a new imperial ruler, the United States, brought fresh missionaries, boarding schools, and (especially during World War II) a major military presence. Twentieth-century natural disasters—volcanic eruptions, a tidal wave, displaced traditional communities. So did the *Exxon Valdez* oil spill. As the post-1960s indigenous revivals gathered momentum, many people with indigenous roots in the Kodiak region remained uncertain whether they should consider themselves Russian, American, Aleut, or Eskimo (Pullar 2001). And as the new "Alutiiq" iden-tity took hold in the 1970s the need for a widely recognizable Native heri-tage became more critical. There were ongoing social continuities at local, familial levels, but few spectacular symbols of Alutiiq culture or art.

Masked dancing had once been a central part of traditional life. But by the late nineteenth century, in the wake of epidemics, physical dis-placements, and Christian prohibitions, the practice largely ceased. (Masquerades, allied with the Russian New Year festivities, did continue in villages on Kodiak Island and the Kenai Peninsula.) Moreover, it had been customary to burn masks after use, or else to let them slowly decay in secret caves. By 1900 the spectacular old masks were gone.

During the 1980s and 1990s cultural revivals featured traditional dance forms, particularly in youth groups. Crafts like kayak building, basket making, sewing animal skin parkas, and making bentwood hats and beaded headdresses were actively cultivated. At that time, several Sugpiaq artists began to carve masks, both creative works of art for sale and heritage objects closely inspired by traditional forms. But the lack of good models posed a serious problem. With a limited number of poor-quality images available, there was no way to study the old carving techniques up close. A few nineteenth-century examples survived in distant museums—Washington D.C., St. Petersburg, and, it was rumored, somewhere in Europe.

Perry Eaton, who grew up in Kodiak and pursued a successful career in Anchorage working with Native corporations and in rural development, recalls his dissatisfaction with the simple 25 percent blood quantum required for ANCSA enrollment. Was this all it meant to be "Native"? He yearned for a more substantial attachment, a more ethnic or cultural mark of identity. A skilled photographer, he would turn to art, eventually becoming a master carver and teacher. In the early 1970s, on one of his business trips to Washington, D.C., Eaton visited the Smithsonian to view the Kodiak masks collected in 1872 by William Dall. While he felt "validated" to find his tradition in so prestigious a place, what he encountered "was less than exciting visually: two small 8" x 5" bird-like carvings that had had their feathers and appendages broken off. In my heart I had wanted to find 'OUR ART!' Something significant. Something spectacular. Something to rival coastal Indian art. Something that defined me and the Island" (Eaton 2009: 284).

Meanwhile Lydia Black had interested one of her graduate students, Dominique Desson, in a little-known collection of Kodiak artifacts held by the municipal museum of Boulogne-sur-Mer, a small French city on the English Channel. With the completion of Desson's dissertation in 1995 and a presentation of her research in Kodiak, things began to change. The masks in France turned out to be the richest collection, by far, of nineteenth-century Alutiiq masks anywhere. Sven Haakanson and other aspiring carvers were inspired by the dramatic images that began to become available. An important thread to a lost Kodiak history now looped through a distant museum.

Helen Simeonoff, who had recently given up an unsatisfying job with the warrants division of the Anchorage Police Department to try to live from her landscape and wildlife paintings, attended Desson's presentation in Kodiak. The experience was transformative. Overwhelmed by the images she saw, Simeonoff saved for six years to pay for a personal visit to the collection—the first Sugpiaq to encounter the masks in more than a century. She discovered that a beaded headdress and many of the painted masks had originated in her mother's home of Afognak. On her return she showed photos and sketches to anyone who would look, inspiring Perry Eaton to make his own personal pilgrimage. Sven Haakanson Jr. began stopping in the English Channel fishing port on his way to and from conferences in Europe. In Paris, the Musée du Quai Branly, then under construction, organized an anticipatory exhibition, "Kodiak, Alaska" (Désveaux 2002). The extraordinary collection of Kodiak artifacts was emerging from obscurity. Haakanson was convinced that the masks must sooner or later be seen in Kodiak.

How had they found their way to France? In 1871 Alphonse Pinart, a nineteen-year-old Frenchman from a wealthy business family, spent a year exploring the Aleutian Islands, the Bering Sea coast, and the Kodiak Archipelago. A student of historical linguistics, he was seeking evidence for a prehistoric migration from Asia into the Americas. Pinart traveled mostly by kayak, with Aleutian guides, over dangerous seas. His scientific curiosity was broad based, and he returned with extensive notes on ethnographic as well as linguistic topics. He also brought back a remarkable collection: diverse objects with extensive documentation. Where possible, he recorded the songs and dances associated with the seventy masks he acquired. Pinart wintered in Kodiak and visited several villages of the region. How, exactly, he acquired his collection remains mysterious. Some of the oldest and largest were, it seems, removed from a cave where they had been left to decay. The smaller masks, with the original paint more or less intact, were probably made at his request by a traditional carver, perhaps to accompany a legend or song he had previously collected. Some, with the backs not carved, seem to be models, either for the artist's use or for the visitor's.

The Alaska Pinart visited had little formal colonial government, either Russian (departing) or American (arriving). A young Frenchman, he had no coercive apparatus at his disposal and was dependent on local help. The indigenous society was reeling from severe demographic shocks, social disruptions, and religious changes. The old ways seemed doomed, and people were willing to part with traditional things, especially for reasonable payment. All evidence suggests that the young scholar/adventurer respected and valued the individuals and cultures he

Figure 7.7.   Chumliiq (First One). Mask from the
Pinart Collection. (Collection du Château-Musée de
Boulogne-sur-Mer; copyright Philippe Beurtheret.)

encountered, and that he understood his salvage project to be authorized
by the historical inevitability of loss.

Returning to France, Pinart exhibited his collection in Paris and then
donated it to the Château Musée in Boulogne-sur-Mer, his home region.
There it survived two world wars, largely forgotten by experts. However,
the collection, if poorly understood, was a source of local pride, and
when Sven Haakanson began to explore the possibility of a loan to the
Alutiiq Museum he ran into a stone wall. Sending masks to a distant,
Native-run museum in Alaska was out of the question. At the Château
Musée, people were polite but suspicious. A scientific *patrimoine*
belonging to the city and the nation had to be protected. The growing

repatriation movement in the United States and Canada, supported by
new laws, was on their minds. If this newly valuable collection left
France, would it return? Haakanson's assurances and charm were not
enough. Nor could an educational exhibition on current Sugpiaq life
with a gift mask sculpted by Perry Eaton open the way. At one point the
Château Musée's director offered to loan a single mask. Haakanson,
patient and persistent, hoped that he could eventually break down prejudices and build trust. He acquired two crucial allies. Sarah Froning, an
American living in France who had written a thesis on museum issues
and knew the scene, heard him speak at a conference in Belgium. She
became an unpaid advisor on tactics, translating and drafting documents. And in 2005 a generational shift at the Château Musée brought
Anne-Claire Laronde to the post of director. Laronde's view of the
museum was less guarded, more engaged with wider networks and
trends. She saw in Haakanson's request not a threat but an opportunity.
And as knowledge deepened about the masks' contemporary significance
in Kodiak, a policy of sharing seemed the only ethical way forward.
Political leaders in Boulogne-sur-Mer would need convincing, however.
The museum and its collections were city property.

Haakanson then conceived a visit to France that would decisively
alter the climate of opinion. In 2006, nine Sugpiaq artists accompanied
him to the Château Musée for several days of intense study in the Pinart
collection. In return for their passage, each of the artists agreed to carve
a "danceable mask" for the Alutiiq Museum's growing collection and
to participate as teachers in its village outreach program. During the
visit, whatever prejudices about Alaska Natives might have been har-
bored in Boulogne-sur-Mer were quickly dispelled. The visitors inter-
acted with local leaders. Armed with cameras and notebooks, they
were intensely serious researchers. Some of them, like Perry Eaton and
the photographer Will Anderson, looked like (and were, in fact) corporate executives. The others, of varying ages and style, were far from
exotic or threatening.

And it no doubt made an impression on the hosts to see their visitors
so visibly moved—speechless and weeping—in the presence of the masks.
The sheer size of the oldest works, their boldness of design and depth of
carving, were astonishing. This was a scale and presence that photographs could not capture. The artists' responses, gathered in *Two
Journeys* (Koniag Inc. 2008), were at once technical—intense observations of the masks' construction—and emotional.

Carol Chernoff:

What struck me most was the mastery of the art, the carvings themselves, knowing they had primitive tools, and they still made these beautiful masks. The other was the sheer size of the masks—they were much larger than I realized. The size was amazing, and then when you got close to them, the mastery of the carvings, the details and workmanship put into each mask. They were so absolutely beautiful. The Alutiiq pieces I had seen until then never showed the high level of artistry. It still leaves me speechless. (2008: 40)

Gary Knagin:

I wasn't expecting that feeling I got. It was as if there was a presence there. It totally floored me. I was not ready for it. It sent chills down my spine. Something was there. I can't explain it. (2008: 71)

Lena Amason-Berns:

When we all walked into the room where so many Kodiak dance masks were laid out on tables, I think the feelings of awe, of joy, of loss were so overwhelming that we all cried together. (2008: 70)

Doug Inga:

I was walking up the stairs to the museum. Everyone was so solemn. I was very excited and just started hollering and yelping with excitement. But I got to the door of the exhibit room, and I couldn't go in. For me to be in the presence . . . it was hard because I knew our people had touched them . . . When I did go in, I was home. (2008: 68)

Alfred Naumoff:

I learned a lot about design and shapes. The cone-shaped pointed head. It took me several months to carve a mask after seeing the cone-shaped head. Usually, I picture in my head what a piece will look like finished. This one just kind of happened . . . If you see the carvings with your own eyes, you don't stop until you've finished with your hands." (2008: 74)

Figure 7.8. Giinasinaq (Big Face). Mask from the Pinart Collection. (Collection du Château-Musée de Boulogne-sur-Mer; copyright Philippe Beurtheret.)

An agreement with the museum and city to loan half of the collection quickly followed the artists' visit. Funding would need to be raised, and there were further technical hurdles, especially the delicate task of providing evidence for skeptical French authorities that no Alutiiq corporation or village would demand permanent repatriation. In the absence of an organized Alutiiq "tribe" it was impossible to provide a legally watertight contract. But good-faith guarantees were collected from the principal authorities, and the personal trust—built by Haakanson over the years and consolidated with the artists' visit—eventually prevailed. Throughout the process, Sugpiaq reactions to the masks, emotional and complex, never failed to include gratitude to Pinart and to the Château Musée. The visitors from Kodiak learned that during the Second World War, museum staff heroically moved the collections multiple times to

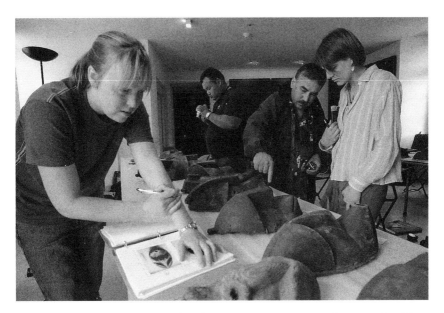

Figure 7.9. Sugpiaq artists at the Château Musée. L-r: Lena Amason, Speridon Simeonoff, Alfred Naumoff, and translator/facilitator Sarah Froning. (Photo by Will Anderson; used by permission.)

avoid the intense bombing of Boulogne-sur-Mer. The artists and Haakanson understood that without Pinart and the French museum, there would exist only a small handful of specimens from this major carving tradition. And these masks, they believed, were what the Alutiiq renaissance was missing: a cultural baseline and an iconic art form.

During April 2007, half of the Pinart Collection's masks arrived in Kodiak. A group of Elders gathered in the Alutiiq Museum workroom to witness the opening of the crates. Participants recall a moment of great intensity—laughter, tears, relief, and apprehension—as the ancestral masks, bearing renewed spiritual power, emerged.

The public opening six weeks later coincided with Kodiak's annual Crab Fest weekend. The town was packed and the mood celebratory. The night before the formal opening, I attended a banquet that filled the cavernous hall of the Elks Club. Father Michael Oleksa, for many years the Orthodox priest of Old Harbor, and the author of a remarkable book on indigenized Russian Orthodoxy in Alaska (1992), delivered the benediction. Songs were sung by many of the participants in

Figure 7.10.   Sugpiaq carver Doug Inga at the Château Musée. (Photo by Will Anderson; used by permission.)

Sugt'stun, English, and Slavonic. Youth dancers from Old Harbor performed, followed by comments from Sven Haakanson Jr., Museum Board Chairman Will Anderson, and Château Musée Director Anne-Claire Laronde. A card on the table thanked the project sponsors: an array of Native corporations, museums, Alaska philanthropies, the local housing authority, businesses, and the Army National Guard, plus many individual donors. The next morning a crowd gathered outside the museum, where more Alutiiq dancers, including *Imamsuat,* a group based in Anchorage, performed in traditional parkas, beaded headdresses, and bentwood visors. A mask inspired by the Pinart collection was danced (Figure 7.11).

After the ribbon was cut, people circulated through the exhibit. The thirty-five masks sent from France filled the small temporary exhibit space. As I encountered people I knew from the museum and from other Alaska cultural institutions, I wondered who, exactly, composed the rest of the crowd. What was the range of their reactions? Who was deeply affected by the masks' return; who was merely curious? Were there Native people who didn't care enough to attend? And what about those

Figure 7.11. Dancers from the group *Imamsuat* (People of the Sea) at the opening ceremony of *Giinaquq: Like a Face.* (Photo by James Clifford.)

who couldn't afford the plane trip to Kodiak? It wasn't an occasion for systematic questioning. Sven Haakanson Jr., in his public remarks, called the Pinart collection a "baseline," a foundation on which a renewed Sugpiaq culture could build. And Helen Simeonoff said that the masks "put us on the map." Among the many people at the exhibition, I recall particularly two. An older woman was interviewed for Anchorage radio and asked about the uncrating of the masks. What was her first reaction? "Fear"—she explained that as a girl she had been told not to touch the dangerous old things the archaeologists were digging up. They still had power. She added simply: "It was very emotional." Later I spoke with a long-haired young man who pulled out of his knapsack a hefty block of wood. "My first mask." He seemed proud and a bit sheepish, telling me that he had been working on it for a couple of years and that it was still not done.

Wandering among the masks, I kept returning to *Unnuyayuk (Night Traveler)*: two flat pieces of wood-pinned together, one side painted black, the other red, a sharp edge dividing them (Figure 7.12). On the red side in low relief a face is carved. Sinew and fiber to which feathers were once attached form a ring around the almost circular mask. I was probably attracted by the ensemble's "modernist" abstraction, an almost violent, structural bifurcation. The text that accompanied it, newly translated from Pinart's notes, was mysterious and haunting.

SONG.

Unnuyayuk
Qai-ciin ikayuqa, qai-ciin ulurakllua?
ugwini pitarkirnaya'amken.
Agellrianga llam iluakun; ikayuma kat'um tayatannga.
Aciqallrianga llilerwiatnum gui.

Night Traveler
Why is it my helper spirit, why is it you are apprehensive of me on the seal rocks?
I will bring you game to be caught.
I went through the inside of the universe; my helper, that one made me afraid.
I went down where they are motioning.

LEGEND.

They say that during a trip this mask looked at the devil and half of its face was burnt by the sight.

DANCE.

He enters the qasgiq [ceremonial house], goes to the left corner and, his back to the audience, he dances on his knees during the first part of the song. When the second song starts, he gets up with his back still turned, goes to the center and jumps and bounces before disappearing.

Leaving the museum, I wandered down to the boat harbor where the Crab Fest was in full swing. The festival, celebrating its fiftieth anniversary, originated during the now defunct King Crab boom of the 1950s

Figure 7.12.   Unnuyauk (Night Traveler). Mask from
the Pinart Collection. (Collection du Château-Musée
de Boulogne-sur-Mer; copyright Philippe Beurtheret.)

and 1960s, years when Kodiak fisherman could make real money supplying restaurants all over the world. The festival crowd was large and
diverse, people of all ages wandering among the many food stalls—
hamburgers from St. Mary's parish, tamales and pupusas from the Iglesia
Crstiana Protección y Poder, meat skewers from River of Life Christian
Fellowship, corn dogs and cheese sticks from the American Legion, and
other fare from Peking Second Floor Restaurant, Sushi Etc., Mommy's
Heart Barbecue on a Stick" . . . Environmental groups and government
agencies mounted poster displays; the NRA showed guns. A restored
1958 Chevy sedan was raffled off.

Up the hill at the Baranov Museum, home of Russian America's first
governor, visitors were contemplating historic tools and artifacts, a
reconstructed nineteenth-century living room, an old *baidarka* (kayak),
and of course a stuffed Kodiak bear. Visitors could also discover work

by contemporary Sugpiaq artists and a superb collection of intricately woven Native grass baskets. A wall panel was devoted to "Benny" Benson: born in Chignik, a village on the Alaska Peninsula, the son of an "Aleut" mother and a Swedish father, Benson, in 1927, designed the Alaska territorial (and later state) flag. A nearby photo commemorates Franklin Delano Roosevelt's visit to the heavily militarized Kodiak Island in 1944. As I wandered through the museum, it seemed to me that Russian, Native, and American histories were inextricably mixed. The museum gift shop featured nesting Russian dolls, many of them smiling Alaska Native women.

Three Catalogues

The Sugpiaq masks have returned to a changed world, to new uses and interpretations. Three books published in the new millenium supply meaningful contexts. The first recovers the masks' precontact traditions, focusing primarily on the nineteenth century. The second sees them as travelers, in colonial and postcolonial worlds. The third adopts the perspective of contemporary Sugpiaq renewal. There are complicating elements in each, but these are the primary emphases. *Kodiak, Alaska,* the very substantial publication from the 2002 French exhibition, offers handsome color images of the Pinart collection along with scholarly essays, historical, ethnological, and curatorial (Désveaux 2002). *Two Journeys,* a "photographic companion" made for the opening of *Giinaquq: Like a Face,* evokes Pinart's 1871 expedition to Kodiak and the reverse journey of the Sugpiaq artists to Boulogne-sur-Mer in 2006 (Koniag Inc. 2008). The third, a fully developed catalogue, appeared a year later: *Giinaquq: Like a Face/Comme un Visage: Sugpiaq Masks of the Kodiak Archipelago* (Haakanson and Steffian 2009a). It presents the masks from diverse perspectives, with a particular emphasis on their role in contemporary art and cultural practice.

Kodiak, Alaska documents the history of Pinart's collection and provides a descriptive catalogue *raisonné.* It also offers important scholarly reflections, historical and anthropological, on the meanings of the masks in an older Sugpiaq culture and within a wider spectrum of Native Alaskan masking traditions. Overall, the view is distanced and retrospective. The principal exception is a short essay by Sven Haakanson Jr. evoking the reemergence of Sugpiaq culture: Elders' memories and archaeological research leading to a revival of dancing and carving.

Figure 7.13.   Temciyusqaq (Skeptical One). Mask
from the Pinart Collection. (Collection du Château-
Musée de Boulogne-sur-Mer; Photo by Will Anderson;
courtesy of the Chateau Musée de Boulogne-sur-Mer.)

Haakanson evokes his childhood in Old Harbor—vaguely aware of
masks, but being told that they were part of a shamanistic religion and
should be left alone. He hints at the persistence of a more positive sense
of masking among older Orthodox Sugpiat. But he could only learn the
power of masks as living beings by carving them himself.

Ethnohistorian Félix Torres supplies a rapid account of Pinart's career
and of the historical "turning point" for Aleutian and Kodiak societies—the transition from Russian to U.S. rule—that marked the moment
of his visit in 1871. Torres also supplies a lucid analysis of "recomposed
identities" (Aleuts, Sugpiaq, Chugach, and Alitiiq) over the past century.
Throughout the volume, "Sugpiaq" designates a cultural tradition that

privileges pre-Russian roots. "Alutiiq," in Torres's view, denotes a relatively recent identity. Haakanson uses both names, Sugpiaq and Alitiiq, sometimes in the same sentence. The catalogue provides glimpses of the changes currently under way around Kodiak Island while staying focused on the past. Haakanson supplies a photograph of a Pinart collection replica being danced. It is the sole image of a contemporary Kodiak person, artifact, or scene in the lavishly illustrated catalogue.

Essays by Dominique Desson and Rosa Liapounova (from the St. Petersburg Museum of Anthropology) supply valuable details from Pinart's research notes and from the observations of nineteenth-century Russian travelers. Sugpiaq masking, like the better-known traditions of Yup'ik to the north, had a propitiatory function, encouraging land and sea creatures to "give" themselves to hunters. But masking could also honor ancestors, accompany initiations, and take satiric forms with roles for both men and women. Unlike other cultural forms, masking could occur in summer as well as winter. The nineteenth-century Russian visitors described a kind of theatrical "play," what Emmanuel Désveaux calls "an authentic theatre of the world," characterized by "an extraordinary creative freedom" (2002: 106–107).

Désveaux, who organized the exhibition, provides the catalogue's analytic centerpiece, a complex argument that accounts for the uniqueness of Alutiiq artistic tradition. Why don't the masks look like those of the Yup'ik or the Northwest Coast tribes? Drawing on Lévi-Strauss's *Mythologiques* (1971) and *The Way of the Masks* (1999), Désveaux sees cultural differences as inversions and transformations in a regional series. The Kodiak region is a specific crossroads within a larger, relational matrix. This ingenious reconstruction of a precontact intercultural landscape has little to say about how these structures have engaged with historical influences such as Russian Orthodoxy, capitalism, or indigenous revival. But the chapter portrays a dynamic tradition, raising the question of what new transformations can be expressed through this productive language of forms. Désveaux distinguishes the secret practices of whaling (a form of shamanism) from the more public activities of masking (a kind of "theatre)" (2002: 116). The distinction helps to account for the latter's remarkable freedom and invention, and also for the masks' customary destruction. Désveaux's interpretation perhaps draws an overly sharp line between sacred and profane functions. But the stress on performative flexibility is certainly relevant to an ongoing process of heritage and to the second life of masking. Old Sugpiaq masks have new things to say.

Two Journeys: A Companion to the Giinaquq: Like a Face Exhibition (2008) lists "Koniag Inc." as its author. Will Anderson, current president of the regional corporation and one of the Sugpiaq visitors to Boulogne-sur-Mer, writes a foreword. The preface is co-authored by the directors of the collaborating museums, Sven Haakanson and Anne-Claire Laronde. But in a real sense the "authors" of the text are the ten artists whose experience anchors the book. Photographs taken by Anderson illustrate the thirty-five masks that traveled to Kodiak. And his large, evocative images show the artists working at the Château Musée. They study the masks close up; they cradle and discuss them. Quotations throughout the book, some of which were cited in the previous section, recall the experience. There are brief accounts of Pinart's voyage and of the two museums' collaboration. But the inspirational experience of reconnecting with a lost culture is the book's central message. *Two Journeys* is extraordinary in its sense of visual and subjective closeness, its attempt to communicate experiential intensity.

The volume's other major message is its affirmation of a transnational alliance. Haakanson and Laronde write that the exhibition "illustrates how the residents of two small fishing communities on nearly opposite sides of the world . . . joined forces to shed light on each other's pasts and in so doing are creating a brighter future." For the French, they add, the Pinart story is one of heroic scientific endeavor, preserving an endangered legacy that now becomes a "gift the French share with Alutiiqs." And "for the Alutiiq People, the Pinart collection represents ancestral knowledge . . . Studying the collection is like being an apprentice to an Alutiiq master" (2008: 3). The collection thus becomes a testimony to the spirit and tenacity of both peoples. The masks are still here only because of the French "unwavering commitment" to preserving a patrimony. And the revival of a culture with renewed stakes in the collection is evidence of Native resilience in the face of relentless colonization. The two small museums are proud of their linked histories and reciprocal collaboration. Public comments at the exhibition opening revealed a particular satisfaction that their work together, a kind of alter globalization, did not rely on networks controlled by major cultural institutions such as the Quai Branly in Paris or the Smithsonian in Washington and Anchorage.

Giinaquq: Like a Face/Comme un visage (2009a) appeared a year after the exhibition opened in Kodiak. Its bilingual text and a chapter by Anne-Claire Laronde on Pinart maintain the project's importance for both French and Alaskan histories. However, the work's principal orientation is toward Sugpiaq cultural renewal. A planning conference of Elders and cultural activists established important issues of policy and purpose. The photographic documentation at the core of the volume is the work of active artists and mask carvers, Perry Eaton, Sven Haakanson, and Will Anderson. It aims to provide a practical resource for new cultural work.

One is struck by the consistent use of "Sugpiaq" throughout. This clarifies a confusion of names and identifications. "Alutiiq," linked to the Russian name "Aleut," was institutionalized during the ANCSA enrollment process. "Sugpiaq" now evokes a distance taken from this moment, making imaginative space for a cultural tradition with roots prior to, and potentially after, colonization and capitalism. A tradition prior to the Russians is emphasised. This tilt toward "Sugpiaq" does not, however, reflect a concern for precontact culture similar to the retrospection organizing *Kodiak Alaska*. *Giinaquq* is quite different in audience and function from the French catalogue. It explicitly "looks both ways," to the past and the future simultaneously. Moreover, the preference for Sugpiat does not involve an ideological purification of Native tradition on and around Kodiak Island, separating its Russian components from an authentic, older root.

In the catalogue's longest chapter, Gordon Pullar reconstructs the world Pinart encountered in 1871. Beginning from the specific situation of cultural crisis and political transition that accompanied the replacement of Russian by U.S. rule, the chapter surveys a century of Sugpiaq/Russian/American contacts, accommodations, and disasters, quoting frequently from contemporary sources. Pullar portrays "a society under stress" (2009: 59), a fragile equilibrium and indigenized "Russian" social structure shaken by the transition to U.S. rule. Mask carving was disappearing, and in this period of disorder, Pinart was able to acquire what were probably the last traditional specimens. Pullar concludes: "Had Pinart not visited Kodiak Island, the Sugpiat of today would have far less information to go on in reconstructing their culture and history from this time period. It is clear that the Kodiak Island Sugpiat continue to be very grateful that a visionary nineteen-year-old from France visited their homeland more than 135 years ago" (60). The indigenous future thus depends on, as it reworks, a colonial past.

"Sugpiaq" as used in *Giinaquq: Like a Face/Comme un visage* denotes a restored tradition, transformed through successive crises, recollected from surviving shards, and going somewhere today. In Chapter 1, I called this process of connecting pasts and futures a "historical practice. Here it is driven by current creative energies and is reflected in the catalogue's core, a photographic documentation of all seventy-seven masks held in France (including seven at the Musée du Quai Branly in Paris). The intent is "intentionally technical" (Haakanson and Steffian 2009b: 84). The catalogue is conceived as a practical tool. Unlike previous photographic presentations, which adopted an aesthetic approach, stressing the masks' formal properties as seen from the front, Haakanson and his sculptor colleagues wanted images that would show each mask from multiple angles, including the back. The older Sugpiaq masks in the collection are distinctive in their large size and dramatic carving (some as much as six inches deep). Only a side view can do this justice. And for those interested in the technical details of carving and construction, an interior perspective, a view from behind, is essential. The catalogue supplies several shots of each mask and establishes their physical scale with images of individuals holding and wearing them. The masks are still aesthetically striking, but the close-up formalism of earlier volumes is avoided. The catalogue's seventy-seven-page photographic section was conceived by experienced mask carvers who wanted to provide usable models. Soon after the exhibition left Kodiak for Anchorage, an intensive carving workshop, "Future Masters," was held at the Alutiiq Museum.

Lost and Found in Translation

Like its images, the catalogue's documentation is oriented toward heritage renewal, offering accessible fragments from the Sugpiaq past for contemporary mask making and dancing. Translations of Pinart's handwritten notes (originally in French, English, Russian, Latin, and Sugt'stun) were revised for the *Giinaquq* project by Sven Haakanson and Linguist Jeff Leer, who worked closely with three fluent Sugt'stun-speaking Elders: Nick Alokli, Mary Haakanson, and Florence Pestrikoff. Some formerly obscure terms were cleared up (others, no longer in use today, remain inaccessible). Punctuation and line breaks were added. If the "Night Traveler" song reads like a poem, it is revealing to compare it with Pinart's word-for-word rendition in French, translated from field notes that were, of course, themselves translations (Désveaux 2002: 56). *Giinaquq's* versions have now been multiply revised to the satisfaction of Native speakers, an indigenous anthropologist, and the best academic

authority on the language. These recovered, "original" meanings resonate with meanings in the present. For example, as explained in the
Giinaquq catalogue, the new translation of the Alutiiq word *ikayuqa*
"significantly changes the meaning of the song in which [it] appears and
the interpretation of that song today" (Haakanson and Steffian 2009a:
179). The word was rendered in Pinart's field notes with the Russian
word *d'yavol*, meaning "devil." In his French word-for-word version,
Pinart chose the French *esprit*, "spirit." The new version chose the more
accurate, and today more palatable, "helper spirit." But perhaps something powerful, fearful, disappeared with "devil."

"Devil" is certainly not adequate. And a "helper" spirit makes the
French *esprit* less abstract, suggesting a specific relationship of actors,
human and nonhuman. However, "helper" and "spirit" don't transmit
any sense of danger. In Native American traditions, the beings in question are not always friendly and need careful management. Is the new
version a more direct translation of the "original" texts? Yes and no.
Pinart's Russian and French are bypassed and the original Alutiiq language given priority. Certainly, the new translators have a better grasp
of the language than Pinart. But who translated for him? And why was
the Russian word "devil" chosen? In any event, no one has direct or
intuitive access to what the practical usages of *ikayuqa* were before
Russian Orthodoxy and all the historical disruptions intervened. Not
contemporary Elders, whose knowledge of Sugpiaq tradition is mediated by these transformations and rearticulations. Not the linguists
and anthropologists who interpret based on partial recorded sources.
Not the archeologists who are limited by equally fragmentary material
evidence.

"Helper spirit" is not the original meaning of *ikayuq*. It is a transformation of that meaning in a disrupted and dynamic indigenous history.
It becomes meaningful for an Alutiiq/Sugpiaq heritage that is taking its
distance from Orthodox "devils," a heritage that now makes sense in
cities and across oceans. The masks return. They find fresh meanings in
a changed world. And so does *ikayuq*.

To say this is not to assert, in a spirit of critique, that the new translations are merely "political." The Alutiiq Museum's scrupulousness, its
respect for both scholarly and traditional ways of knowing, is impressive. But the goal is not strict fidelity to a (fragmented) past. Translation
is change. All the masks displayed in Kodiak and presented in the exhi-

bition catalogue carry individual names. Some names, like "Night Traveler," were originally recorded by Pinart. But others, missing in his notes, have been added by contemporary Sugpiaq Elders. As Haakanson and Steffian explain, the mask's new names "helped to reunite them with the Kodiak Sugpiaq community and to breathe new life into sentient objects that have been asleep for more than a century" (2009b: 83). It is said of translation, "*tradittore/traduttore.*" Translation is betrayal. It is also said that to translate something is to "make it new." Both sayings apply to the second life of heritage.

On the catalogue's dedication page two important Elders and a Russian-American historian are honored. "In memory of Larry Matfay, 1907–1998, Sven David Haakanson Sr., 1934–2002, Dr. Lydia T. Black, 1925–2007. Thank you for helping to keep the Sugiaq culture alive." Below their names a color photo bears the caption: "Phyllis Clough dances a memorial mask carved by Perry Eaton in honor of her late father Sven Haakanson, Sr." The mask, large, elaborately painted, and adorned with feathers, resembles others in the Pinart collection. Phyllis Clough, wearing a red anorak and jeans, dances on her knees, arms spread wide.

Memorial masking was an active part of Sugpiaq tradition in the nineteenth century. It evidently has a future. One wonders which other aspects of the former way of life will be renewed in the ongoing "selective tradition" (Williams 1977: 117). Whaling and shamanistic activities from the past are unlikely to be restored, at least not in as direct a way as masking. The masks' traditional hunting functions, facilitating a life-giving circulation of animal spirits, could well find renewal in connection with contemporary subsistence practices and ecological visions. The more "theatrical," humorous, and satiric aspects of Sugpiaq dancing never entirely disappeared but persisted in some village midwinter Russian New Year festivals. These practices feed directly into contemporary heritage performances (for example, the Nanwalek Dancers discussed in Chapter 6). It remains to be seen which traditional functions will be reworked in a revived Sugpiaq tradition, engaged with new performative styles, audiences, and markets.

As the lost and found masks of the Pinart Collection return to Kodiak, physically and virtually, they function simultaneously as objects of historical and anthropological knowledge, as occasions for museum contemplation or sacred veneration, and as practical tools, for use now.

Interpellation and/or Articulation
(Theoretical Interlude)

The masks find their "second life" in many overlapping contexts: in the world of indigenous identity politics where groups such as Alutiit/Sugpiat achieve distinction through iconic cultural symbols; in the proliferating world of "tribal art," where the masks provide models for new creations that can be sold to collectors or acquired by museums; in communal and personal contexts that value "heritage objects" derived from traditional forms; in Native crafts taught in schools and museum workshops; in public and private ceremonies where new versions of the masks are danced, accompanied by stories and songs; in tourist venues where the old forms become simplified performances or stylized motifs for jewelry, clothing, and other souvenirs sold to visitors. How these different areas of cultural production and consumption are kept in balance—and what constitutes a proper balance—is a matter for community discussion, argument, social experiment, and negotiation.

The Alutiiq Museum and its ongoing projects respond to a particular history of cultural destruction, change, and renewal. The history of the Kodiak Archipelago differs, in important ways, from that of the Yup'ik to the north and the Tlingit to the south. The early, overwhelming impact of the Russians and the later, militarized presence of the Americans have no equivalent except among the Unangan (Aleutian Islanders). Yet precisely because of the severity of cultural disruption in Sugpiaq communities, their heritage renewal poses with special clarity questions of general importance for indigenous survival and transformation today. Asking these questions returns us to some of the comparative and theoretical issues raised at the beginning of this book. How can a "realist" perspective deal simultaneously with structural determination, political contingency, cultural transformation, and emergence?

In the big picture of an evolving capitalist "world system" (Wallerstein 1976, 2003) or "cultural dominant" (Jameson 1984) how important is indigenous history making and heritage reclamation? Posing the issue in this way invites hard questions. For example: in contexts like Alaska, isn't Native resurgence, even "sovereignty," a matter of sustaining minor differences—comfort zones within larger systems of managed diversity and the marketing of place (Harvey 1990)? Culture can, of course, be a commodity not essentially different from oil, gas, or timber. In the end, don't inspirational projects such as *Giinaquq: Like a Face* simply empower people to be fulfilled subjects in a multicultural market or per-formance space of identities? And perhaps more disturbingly: how much do these cultural activities really change persistent realities of economic inequality and social exclusion (Dombrowski 2001, 2002)? Such ques-tions trouble all discussions of heritage work and identity-based political claims. They are not easily answered. Nor should they be. Economic and political constraints continuously empower and limit social and cultural initiatives of the sort I have been tracking in and around Kodiak.

But for all their apparent realism, the hard, "materialist," questions of political economy miss a great deal of lived reality. Structural power is only one kind of power, and assertions of its determining force often mask a desire for totality. The ultimate goal may be to subsume multi-scaled, uneven, and unfinished historical processes within a single devel-opmental, explanatory system. But no such totalizing system exists, nor has it ever existed. In Chapter 1, I argued that "Western" visions such as this are ethnocentric projections of an expansive region that was extremely powerful for several centuries, but never globally hegemonic. Assuming a more complex, less determined, global landscape, we can see the restorative and forward-looking practices of indigenous activism as implicated in colonial and neocolonial (capitalist) structures, but not ultimately determined by them. This is a realist claim supported by the inventive survival of peoples long condemned to death by teleological visions of history. But it is also a wager on the future. The flourishing of relatively autonomous indigenous ways of life is anything but assured. And we simply cannot know what difference these embattled sites of exception (Native "sovereignties") will make in an interconnected world.

In Kodiak, and throughout Alaska, the politics of identity and the economics of resource extraction cannot be separated. "Alutiiq" identi-fications were powerfully encouraged after 1971 by the opportunity to share in the benefits of ANCSA, a settlement driven by the need to build an oil pipeline. And the Kodiak Museum and Archaeological Repository was built with core funding from the *Exxon Valdez* oil spill compensa-tion fund. One way to conceive of these connections in theoretical terms would be to say that powerful state and capitalist structures "interpel-lated," called out, the new identities and forms of heritage mobilization. Louis Althusser's famous parable of interpellation imagines a person "hailed" by a policeman: "Hey you." The person turns and is consti-tuted as a subject of the law (Althusser 1972). In psychologically more complex versions of the model, desire plays a part. Hailed to a social role, one feels completed, recognized, and empowered as a responsible citizen, an educated person, a creative artist, someone with "rights." Interpellation is not simply coercive: it is energizing and fulfilling. It enables and organizes diverse forms of belonging within cultural, social, and economic systems. In this perspective, being "Native" is a way of participating, finding fulfillment, in a regulated diversity.

The theoretical metaphor of interpellation is a reminder that what we wish to be, what makes us feel authentic and completed, are social performances significantly structured by power. We adopt available roles, rising to occasions that are not of our choosing. What is involved, for example, in becoming a Native "artist"? What forms of aesthetic production, of exchange and commodification, are inescapable? Or consider the command performances required of nonprofit organizations like the Alutiiq Museum by their funding sources. How do these powers align and limit what can be accomplished? Questions such as these, while important, tend to discover what they already know: the efficacy of power is given in advance. Seeing people as interpellated "subjects" simplifies agency, which can be ambivalent, and tactical.

When the subject turns to the policeman (how could she not?) does she make available her whole self? What is revealed, what held back? Are there any crossed fingers behind the back? And is there a mask, a special name or "face" for dealing with the powers that be? Colonized people—and they are not the only ones—have always sustained multiple subjectivities for dealing with different occasions of recognition and attempted control. In the case of Alutiiq interpellation under ANCSA, the processes of identification and reidentification were never simply a matter of being called out by power. Did people choose to be "Alutiiq" because the state made it advantageous to do so? What other recovered memories, family traditions, historical momentums, and political strategies were active? Movements to secure Native title were already under way in the Kodiak region, as elsewhere in Alaska, prior to the land settlement. And the 1960s saw the widespread beginnings of what has become a major indigenous cultural revival. Alutiiq/Sugpiat identifications, while encouraged by ANCSA, preceded and have always exceeded the act's corporate agenda.

To grasp this historical complexity, we need to sustain conceptual space for clashing and combining cultural and political agencies. I have found it useful to keep "articulation," a different theoretical metaphor, in tension with "interpellation." If interpellation provides a way to think about being solicited, convoked, called into social existence by power, articulation keeps us attuned to historical processes of connection and disconnection, making space for a performative politics. Tactical, relational forms of agency are emphasized. As explained in Chapter 2, the concept of articulation presumes powerful, but contingent, social, cultural, and economic links, alliances, and negotiations. In this perspective, ANCSA was a conjunctural linkage of multiple stakeholders, social projects, economic interests, and historical momentums. In a transformative process, new corporate structures for Native identification and organization were established. These structures would become a major part, but only a part, of post-sixties Native resurgence. And the changes are ongoing. Neither ANCSA nor neoliberalism has achieved a final form. Indigenous modes of "development" (social and cultural as well as economic) are likewise works in progress, not always congruent with market logics.

Articulation denotes real and consequential connections, but relations that are partial and not inevitable or ultimately determined. Articulation always presumes the possibility of disarticulation (the fingers crossed, the aspects of life kept separate from dominant power) and rearticulation (current movements away from ANCSA corporatism toward sovereign forms of "tribal" governance). In this perspective, the shifting terms "Alutiiq" and "Sugpiaq" denote, not completed identities, but ongoing processes of reidentification. Articulation provides a way to think about material dependency and entanglement without assuming cultural homogenization or eventual subsumption by capitalism. Articulation is worldly historical practice, in tension always with forces of interpellation.

This theoretical disposition helps us grasp a complex series of historical transformations specific to Sugpiaq/Alutiiq experience. At issue is a linked chain of social hierarchies: precontact indigenous, Russian Creole, and contemporary capitalist. Sugpiaq society has long been stratified, its inherited wealth and leadership roles more reminiscent of Northwest Coast Indians than the more egalitarian Yu'pik to the north (Clark 1984). The eighteenth-century Russian conquest violently rearticulated (detached and reattached) indigenous social structures as it selectively incorporated the people of Kodiak (then called "Aleuts" or "Koniags") in its extractive, commercial fur operation. The Russian empire, always short of ethnic Russians, was staffed by mixed-race Creoles. Intermarriage and recruitment of local leaders was encouraged.

Native agency also played a role in the reformation of traditional social structures. To survive in desperate conditions of military defeat, forced labor, and demographic disruption, people converted to Orthodoxy and trained in Russia to assume economic, political, and religious roles in the new order (Black 2004). After the Russians departed in 1867, and well into the twentieth century, Creole elites clung to their sense of distinction as they confronted an American binary racial regime that lumped them with other "primitive" Natives. Their increasingly anachronistic Russian identification finally found a positive way to reconstitute itself in the American system. Creole elites discovered a new sense of distinction as "Alutiiq" in the post-ANCSA world. Instead of distinguishing themselves from lower-status Natives, they now activated the indigenous thread in their mixed heritage, assuming leadership positions in the new corporations. In this new status they encouraged the revitalization of Alutiiq/Sugpiaq heritage and cultural pride in forms recognizable both to a growing indigenous public sphere in Alaska and to a liberal, multicultural America. The work of heritage thus provided ideological legitimacy for the new institutions and their leaders. But the nature of leadership (as we saw with younger activists like Pullar and Haakanson) was changing, and the contexts in which identity needed to be performed were multiplying.

The nature of the historical links between Sugpiaq social structure, Creole elites, modern corporate leadership, and indigenous cultural assertions can be differently interpreted, reflecting the explanatory weight given to interpellation or articulation. One narrative, forcefully argued by Arthur Mason (2002, 2010b), construes Creole hierarchies as direct precursors of class privileges, and heritage revival as symbolic capital, adapted for an American corporate modernity. A different genealogical perspective sees Creole social and cultural formations as hybrid relays in a history of Alutiiq/Sugpiaq continuity. In this view (Oleksa 1990, 1992; Pullar 2009), the mixed-race colonial social structure and its syncretic Orthodox religion transformed and selectively preserved older Sugpiaq life-ways. (Indeed, Father Oleksa argues very forcefully that this indigenization has fulfilled, renewed, the Orthodox project.) Gordon Pullar's recent treatment of nineteenth-century Creole society recognizes its hierarchical structure and the distinction between Creole elites and low-status Natives. But his narrative also traces a Sugpiaq history that survives through the nineteenth century into the twentieth, a genealogical community that would eventually reintegrate many members of Mason's Creole cohort. Pullar's historical work is focused on the nineteenth century, but he brings the story forward in a revealing note. During ANCSA enrollment most Creoles could meet the Native blood requirement:

> But [they] had been referring to themselves as Russians for many years in an attempt to maintain their elevated social status and to escape job and other forms of discrimination commonly practiced against Natives. Thus, when they were accepted under ANCSA many of those who had always claimed their "Nativeness" did not believe it was fair that people who had been referring to themselves as Russians should be eligible to share in the benefits. The phrase "He was never a Native until 1971" and the designation "land claims Native" became popular when referring to those who had not openly identified as Native prior to ANCSA. As time went on, however, many of the Creoles distinguished themselves in Native leadership positions and are widely accepted today as legitimate members of the Sugpiat community. (Pullar 2009: 213)

Creoles, in this account, earn their rediscovered identity: they appear as actors in a Native, not a capitalist, genealogy.

The two genealogies are interested, entangled, and unfinished. Neither Sugpiaq (ethnic) nor capitalist (class) interpellation provides a stable, functional outcome. Native identities and capitalist projects both flourish in contemporary national and transnational contexts. They do so in alliance and tension, in processes of articulation and disarticulation. Mason's work brings the reality of structural inequality into discussions of contemporary indigeneity (see also Dombrowski 2001). This is an important contribution. Too often, assumptions that Native people are naturally, or inherently, egalitarian have led to confusion and accusations of bad faith. (How dare Indians profit from gambling casinos! How can a successful businessman also be a respected Native artist or Elder?) Mason also interrupts any assumption that Alutiiq/Sugpiaq identity is predetermined, a latency waiting to be rediscovered. However, as an account of Alutiiq/Sugpiaq heritage revival in the 1960s and 1970s, his analysis, with its sharp focus on a single-leadership generation, is limiting. Many other historical actors contributed to the resurgence. And as we have seen, successive generations of activists and artists would draw from different backgrounds and networks—local, diasporic, and

transnational. Mason's narrow sociological account is usefully complemented by ethnographically richer portrayals of Sugpiaq life. Patricia
Partnow's (2001b) oral-historical research on the Alaska Peninsula and
Mishler's (2003) multiyear study of Old Harbor and Ouzinkie are good
sources for a broader sense of old and new—Sugpiaq and Russian/
American—components of a composite, articulated, tradition. The role
of Elders, kinship, and oral traditions in sustaining community life
comes more clearly into view. And in the historical research of Sonja
Luehrmann (2008) the social activity of women, agents of articulation
across hierarchies and families, becomes apparent.

Entangled Agencies

Articulation and/or interpellation. A historical realism that can live
with this tension helps us understand, without simplification, three areas
that have been critical to the work of the Alutiiq Museum: funding, art
production, and the making of alliances.

Funding. Since the Alutiiq Museum was enabled by oil money, it might
be tempting to see an essential dependence on corporate capitalism. However, analysis of funding needs to go beyond guilt by association. Exxon
did not, in any significant sense, create or "call out" a project that was
already under way in KANA's heritage renewal work. And the original
funding has not directed the museum's subsequent course. Institutions
like the Alutiiq Museum are, of course, dependent on their material (social,
political, economic) sources, and these are quite diverse: Native development corporations and nonprofits, philanthropic foundations, government
cultural agencies, local civic and business groups, individual donors.
Projects are always packaged with funding sources and institutional partners in mind. Sometimes the availability of specifically targeted funds
solicits a new project (interpellation) that can be linked with a prior
agenda (articulation). Researchers are, of course, accustomed to making
their projects recognizable to granting agencies. Obviously, the overall
climate of available support, the need to collaborate and compete, con-
strains what the museum can do. But in the Alutiiq/Sugpiaq projects
with which I am familiar there is little evidence of censorship or direct
control by funding agencies. Reliance on external sources is double-edged.
On the one hand, it narrows options; on the other it forces the museum
to stay engaged with its constituencies, responding to their concerns.
     To criticize funding dependency presumes a possible independence.

This is an abstraction. Nonprofits maneuver in force fields of power. A more realistic, and politically salient, analysis would trace of how interdependencies are managed. Funding is an opportunistic articulation of different agendas. How are the terms of engagement structured? What has been given up, and what future possibilities are enabled by present trade-offs and compromises?

Art production.   The Sugpiat who visited Boulogne-sur-Mer identify themselves as "artists"—painters, sculptors, wood workers, jewelry makers, basket weavers. They make objects that are, in differing ways, expressions of a contemporary Native tradition. In a thoughtful essay, one of their number, Perry Eaton, explores his developing relationship with Sugpiaq masks. He begins with the summer of 1958 when he had returned to Kodiak from his home in Seattle to fish for salmon with his father. While working on the nets he overheard a friend of his father mention the recent "devil dancing" in Karluk village—blackened faces, drumming and "jump[ing] around." It all seemed rather mysterious: the masks were gone, but masking persisted, more or less out of sight. Eaton would pursue a successful career with Native corporations and a pipeline construction company, in rural development, and as first president and CEO of the Alaska Native Heritage Center. He sustained an interest in photography: "I have always been an artist." By the 1990s, inspired by Desson's thesis, Helen Simeonoff's advocacy, and the example of other "artists from the island," Jacob Simeonoff, Doug Inga, and Jerry Laktonen, Eaton turned to mask carving.

While making his first Sugpiaq mask, he focused on how it "could be attached to the face and allow movement for a dance."

> This naturally led to the philosophical question "Why are you making this mask? To hang on the wall or to dance?" It was at that moment that I decided to be a mask maker and not an "artist" in the Western sense . . . That takes nothing away from an artist, and in fact I have done several pieces of art using the masks as a base but I don't consider them masks in the true sense. For me an Alutiiq mask must have the capacity to be danced." (Eaton 2009: 286)

Eaton makes cogent proposals about how the Pinart masks (including the very largest) were once worn and danced, proposals based on a close study of their interior structure.

For a carver, all sides of the mask are equally interesting. But in an art context, it would be strange (except as a Dada gesture) to hang a mask with its face to the wall. Eaton clearly feels a strong distinction of roles. Yet throughout the essay he calls Sugpiaq carvers "artists." And in a concluding comment on the Pinart collection, he writes: "Taken as a whole, on the most elementary level, what the masks represent is sculpture of a very distinctive and highly stylized nature, representing the unique art form of the Kodiak people" (2009: 293). The masks are, and are not, art. Eaton's apparent inconsistency makes room for the varied roles that masks play in Sugpiaq life today. A traditional mask, old or newly carved, is always both a communal artifact intimately connected to dance, story, and song, and an artistic icon, a marker of identity in the wider performative spaces of art, identity, and the market.

To be an artist means participating in worlds of consumption, meeting the expectations of collectors, tourists, galleries, and museums. In this sense, the identity "artist" is a process of interpellation. However there is more to being a Native artist. Tribal art is, virtually everywhere, from Vancouver to the Australian Outback, an integral part of indigenous social and cultural resurgence. In practice, being a Native artist involves connecting discrepant worlds in contingent ways. The status "artist" is thus a site of articulations and translations, lived differently in specific intercultural force fields. Helen Simeonoff painted landscapes and cats—also compositions inspired by the Pinart Collection. Lena Amason-Berns inventively extends the formal structure of the masks into sculptures designed to hang on walls. Alfred Naumoff builds kayaks, both reduced models and full-size versions, according to traditional specifications. Native artists make art for sale: they also produce finely crafted heritage valuables and ceremonial accoutrements. Where does art stop and living tradition begin in this spectrum of social, economic, and cultural projects?

"Artists" like Perry Eaton, or Sven Haakanson in his workshop, often make careful copies of old models. But we should pause for a moment on the word "copy." Its opposite, "original," is accorded primary value in familiar systems of authentification. A copy is secondary, of lesser value. But in Sugpiaq practice, and indeed in many other indigenous traditions, making a copy renews what is most real, substantial, and, we might plausibly say, authentic, in a material object. Traditionally, masks were destroyed after use. What "mattered" were the stories and songs associated with the masks—also the dances and reciprocal exchanges active in each performance. A new version of a Pinart mask is, in this ontology, as important, perhaps even more important, than an old version immobilized in a collection. The Sugpiaq visitors to Boulogne-sur-Mer, intensely observing, measuring, touching, sketching, and photographing, were accomplishing more than just cultural documentation or art making.

"Art," like "culture," is a process of recruitment into given roles, and simultaneously an expansion and subversion of these roles. If we cannot decide whether the visibility of Sugpiaq artists today is a story of interpellation or articulation, co-optation or subversion, so be it. In his study of contemporary indigenous art and colonial culture Nicholas Thomas traces a power-charged history of exchanges, what he acutely calls an "awkward if not antagonistic intimacy" (1999: 281). And a growing number of critical works sensitively explore the negotiated worlds of contemporary "tribal art" (Phillips 1998, 2012; Meyers 2002; Townsend-Gault 2004; Kramer 2006; Morphy 2008; Ostrowitz 2009). The differing claims of tradition and invention, collective process and personal ambition, communal and individual property, are always sites of tension. A nonreductive understanding makes space for awkwardness, contradiction, and the unexpected, searching for a perspective that holds off premature celebration or critique.

When assessing a project like *Giinaquq: Like a Face,* one can always portray it as simply completing a heritage portfolio for proper indigenous subjects. After all, an explicit goal of the undertaking was to manifest symbolic capital, to present the masks as artistic achievements, icons of Sugpiaq distinction among more recognizable Native Alaskan neighbors. The masks' return also signaled the (relative) independence of the Alutiiq Museum from the Smithsonian and the Anchorage Museum of History and Art. Several external audiences were certainly in play. At the same time, the exhibition accomplished intimate social and cultural work. The emotion felt by the travelers to Boulogne-sur-Mer was deep, potentially transformative, as was the excitement in Kodiak when the masks returned. This was not just another traveling exhibit, but a restorative connection across time and space. A homecoming and a beginning.

Alliance making. The Alutiiq Museum forged opportunistic and flexible relations with the Château Musée. The return of the masks was a kind of repatriation, but not of an absolute kind. The masks now belong to a reciprocal process of ongoing exchanges. It would certainly have been possible to take a hard line on "cultural property." Alphonse Pinart was an avid and efficient collector. He had no ethical qualms about appropriating old masks from a secret whalers' cave in the name of science. His otherwise detailed research notes are silent on exactly how he acquired the now priceless artifacts. But there appears to be little inclination in Kodiak to portray him as an exploitative colonial collector and to demand the return of stolen property. After all, Pinart was young and relatively powerless. The ethnological and linguistic documentation attached to the objects he gathered was, for the time, scrupulous and respectful. He arrived at the last moment it was possible to find the old masks. He wasn't responsible for their disappearance in the wake of invasion and enslavement, epidemics, missionaries, and all the rest. In this case, "salvage collecting," whatever its motivations, turned out to be a very good thing.

Sugpiaq people today, at least when writing and speaking publicly, praise Pinart and the custodians of their treasures at the Château Musée. No doubt statements of this kind can be diplomatic, necessary for building trust and securing the masks' loan. But it is also possible that this generous attitude to a cultural resource held in a distant city prefigures an alliance we might be prepared to call "postcolonial." Future travels for the Pinart masks are now being planned. In Boulogne-sur-Mer, Sugpiaq artists are conducting carving and kayak-building workshops, while the Château Musée develops an acquisition program for contemporary Native Alaskan art. Travel, Internet links, and new technologies of representation can make objects "live," producing new cultural meanings, in two places at once. One should not exaggerate the possibilities, but they are real. World-making engagements linking two peripheral places are an alternative globalization "from below"—or perhaps, "at the edge" of larger national/transnational structures. Indeed, the confidence with which Sugpiat have felt able to appreciate the French contributions to their ongoing tradition derives from a cultural dynamism that finds inventive ways to connect with the distant masks through artistic, technological, and museological practices. Ownership of heritage, in this context, is not an all-or-nothing proposition.

As the two museums develop reciprocal relations, long-term loans are being arranged that will bring masks to Kodiak on a rotating basis. Repatriation is reimagined as a process of sharing. Conceptions of "patrimony" and "cultural property" loosen. Entrenched museum traditions of custodianship become more interactive, as the strands of unfinished histories are rewoven. The vision is not utopian. Elsewhere, movements in this direction are already under way. Ruth Phillips (2012) provides an authoritative discussion of the changing landscape. A few signs of the times: the Smithsonian's Arctic Studies Center in Alaska recently opened an exhibition space for long-term loans of Alaskan Native materials now stored in Washington—a facility at the Anchorage Museum specifically designed to accommodate visits by Elders and study by artists. At the University of British Columbia Museum of Anthropology in Vancouver, the recent reinstallation of its pioneering "visible storage" gallery has involved extensive consultation with First Nations communities and planning for new modes of access. At the National Museum of Ethnology, Osaka, Japan, collecting practices actively encourage the making of new traditional objects by Native artists and apprentices, thus contributing—in curator Kenji Yoshita's words—not to the preservation of cultural heritage "in an unchanged condition," but rather to "safeguarding, or ensuring [its] dynamism" (2008: 5). The partnership being developed in Kodiak and Boulogne-sur-Mer is, of course, complicated by its international structure. But this also makes it particularly significant, as two communities not linked by a national/colonial legacy come together to make possible new journeys: alliances, performances, and translations.

There will certainly be further exchanges, the arrival in Kodiak of more ancestral visitors. Discussions are underway with the Kunstkamera Museum in St. Petersburg, older of the oldest and richest Sugpiaq collection. Old masks, tools, baskets, drums, rattles, and gutskin jackets may continue their historical "journey" in new contexts of material and virtual repatriation. This second life extends into an unknown indigenous future through the many copies they inspire and the stories they renew in carving workshops, in village outreach programs, and in the wider worlds of tribal art. We have seen the masks' versatile connectivity in various performative settings. They undergo a process of translation from ritual artifacts and "satiric" theatre, to heritage treasures and artworks, and back to ritual performances or ludic improvisations. The masks embody cultural power—songs, dances, stories, exchanges—whose reach is both constrained and open ended.

A renewed Native heritage can be performed for multiple audiences within and outside the indigenous imagined community. Also within the self. One is not "Alutiiq" (or any identity) all the time. Contemporary Native people negotiate an uneven landscape of attachments to place and ancestors, from villages to towns and cities, where so many live today. How do objects, people, foods, symbols circulate at these new scales of communication and alliance? What powers direct or block the circulation? Who is interpellated by heritage? Who resists? When the Pinart masks return to Kodiak, who feels they must see them? Who is too busy working or can't afford the plane trip? And what will the several dozen young people who danced in costume outside the Alutiiq Museum to welcome the masks home make of the experience?

Links

The morning after *Giinaquq: Like a Face* opened in Kodiak, I drove out of town on the island's longest road with Anne-Claire Laronde (director of the Château Musée) and Martine Chenet (a Frenchwoman who has sunk roots in Kodiak and runs a coffee/luncheon establishment renowned for its pastries). We drove through the gigantic U.S. Coast Guard base, an installation that patrols a vast arc of the North Pacific Ocean. Forty miles further on, the road ended at the Kodiak Launch Center on the island's southern coast.

This aerospace complex calls itself "The Other Cape." Originally built for commercial satellites (with investment participation by Alutiiq tribal corporations) it has become an integral part of the U.S. missile defense system, firing test rockets toward the Marshall Islands and Vandenberg Air Force Base in California. Entry to the site was restricted. From our picnic beside the empty road we could see radar dishes and tall storage structures in the distance.

As we enjoyed a wonderful French lunch, I thought about connectivity. The travels of a young linguist/ethnographer in 1871 had linked Kodiak Island to France. In 2008 museums from two small fishing cities were forging an alliance.

I remembered a poster I had seen on the wall of the Alutiiq Museum's storage area. It featured a mixed-media artwork titled *Otter Girl* by Lena Amason-Berns, one of the Sugpiaq artists who had traveled to the Château Musée in 2006. Beneath the words "We Are All Connected," a painted portrait of a sea otter is set against a watery-blue background. Above the otter a fish swims, and attached around these central images is a ring of stylized seabirds painted on small plaques, with bright beads and feathers above. The composition, a face inside a decorated ring, is a modern translation of an old Sugpiaq mask design. The occasion for the poster was recorded at the bottom:

Figure 7.14. Kodiak Launch Site. (Photo by James Clifford.)

KODIAK KENAI FIBER LINK PROJECT COMPLETION
KODIAK KENAI CABLE COMPANY, LLC
AN OLD HARBOR & OUZINKIE COMPANY
JANUARY 2007

Old Harbor Native Corporation, with collaboration from Ouzinkie Native Corporation and the launch-site administration, had recently invested in fiber-optic communications. The cable project, addressing a growing need for high-speed links, now connects the Alaska mainland with Kodiak City, the coast guard base, and the aerospace facility. Considered essential for the launch site's participation in the missile defense system, the new link also permits remotely guided emergency surgery at the Kodiak hospital.

Lena Amason-Berns lives in Old Harbor, where she leads a dance revival group and pursues Alutiiq language research (activities also supported by the Old Harbor Native Corporation). Her evocative artworks are now being acquired by museum collections. Amason-Berns, who has worked in commercial salmon fishing and knows aquatic animals, makes

Figure 7.15. Poster: *Otter Girl.* Mixed media by
Lena Amason-Berns. (Used by permission.)

assemblages that are cross-species conversations. Her art expresses a
cultural and ecological vision. "We Are All Connected." The poster was
produced by the Old Harbor Corporation. It evokes a nexus of projects
and ongoing histories: indigenous renewal, Native arts, fiber-optic links,
and business opportunities. How to understand this tangle of different
histories, separately and together? The U.S. Strategic Defense Initiative
enjoys improved connectivity, joining local, regional, and global worlds;
so does the Alutiiq Museum.

❖

EPILOGUE

Our people have made it through lots of storms and disasters for thousands of years. All the troubles since the Russians are like one long
stretch of bad weather. Like everything else, this storm will pass over
some day.

—Barbara Shangin, Alutiiq Elder, Chignik Lake, 1987

The quotation concludes a two-page essay, "Alutiiq," in *Crossroads
Alaska: Native Cultures of Alaska and Siberia* (Chaussonnet 1995: 15).
Barbara Shangin's words brought me up short when I first encountered
them more than a decade ago, and I have written about them repeatedly
(Clifford 1997a, Chapters 1 and 6 in this volume). What would it mean,
I kept asking, to understand them as a realist historical statement? Not
wishful thinking, or a way of sustaining morale, or a kind of resigned
patience. Could this be a serious and credible description of what was
and is happening? The answer has not turned out to be straightforward,
and it has drawn me into complexities of translation around concepts
such as "history," the "real," "tradition," and the "future." The question
posed by these words, spoken in a remote village on the Alaska Peninsula,
has stayed with me. I have tried to take seriously Shangin's view of historical possibility, not just as a story of indigenous survival, but as a way
of living in modernity, and a way through to something else. How could
such a vision be realistic, in a world of industrializing nation-states and
global capitalism? *Returns* has offered not so much an answer as a deepening of the question.

On and off, I wondered about Barbara Shangin. Was she still living?
What life experiences and cultural knowledge went into her statement?
Who was she talking to? Her words had, by now, become iconic, the
vision of an Elder, representative of an indigenous way of thinking historically. But what had gotten lost in translation? What language was

315

she using? I asked around, when I could. But my contacts were from
Kodiak and Anchorage. The Alaska Peninsula is a different part of what
has only recently been mapped as "Alutiiq" cultural territory. The pen-
insula, a border zone, shares contact histories with Unangan (formerly
Aleut) people to the west and Yup'ik to the north. It is not easy to get to
Chignik Lake from Kodiak.

The name Shangin turned up in the index of Patricia Partnow's excellent ethnography, *Making History: Alutiiq/Sugpiaq Life on the Alaska
Peninsula* (2001b). Barbara Shangin was the grandmother of one of
Partnow's Alutiiq interlocutors. And at Chignik Lake everyone called
her "Old Gramma." Partnow writes that "she was known as a healer,
midwife, and excellent cook. She spoke little English, but passed on
much information to her grandchildren before her death in the 1970s"
(11). Shangin was no longer alive at the time of the ethnographer's visits
in the 1980s and 1990s. She left a tape of reminiscences in Sugt'stun that
remains untranslated and that does not, to the best of Patricia Partnow's
recollection, contain the words I was interested in. When I pressed for
more information Partnow kindly went through her field notes to glean
what she could.

Barbara Gregory was born about 1896 and grew up in Katmai, on
the southern coast of the Alaska Peninsula. After the major eruption of
Mt. Katmai in 1912, which obliterated the village, she and her family
relocated to Perryville. She remembered wearing long dresses and sitting
with her bare feet dangling into the smoke hole of the ceremonial house
(quasqiq) as people danced below. Barbara married Elia Shangin and
had five children before his untimely death. Later she was pressured by
the local chief to marry an influential shaman, Wasco Sanook, whose
wife had died. But she had little affection for her new husband: they had
no children and she kept the name Shangin. In 1952 she joined her
daughter in Chignik Lake, where she lived for the remainder of her life,
bringing up her grandchildren after their mother's death.

This much I was able to learn, from a distance. Barbara Shangin had
lived through a lot. A native Sugt'stun speaker, knowledgeable in the old
ways, "Old Gramma" was no doubt listened to with respect and affection at Chignik Lake. She clearly embodied traditional authority. The
text that reached me in California was attributed to an "Elder." I began
to wonder about this status. The words could have been said around a
kitchen table. What was added by making them the pronouncement of
an Elder? Her comment had now become indigenous wisdom, knowl-

edge that could be significant in new ways, making sense in distant places. Knowing a little about Barbara Shangin made me curious about what she actually said, and how her words had been transformed into a pithy quotation summing up an article on Alutiiq heritage.

In their textual form the words invited interpretation; they resonated. I, at least, had no hesitation assimilating them to the ideas of multiple, braided histories and historical realism that I was in the process of working out. Extending the metaphor of changing "weather," I proposed a kind of historical ecology in which impacts like those of the Russians and the Americans were understood to be simply part of the recurring good and bad patterns of history, something one lives through, not something one resists or leaves behind (see Chapter 6). The Russians and what followed were all part of an ongoing and unfinished Alutiiq history. But what if the vision of coming into the clear after a period of storms expressed a sense of radical hope, of starting over, finally free of all the "troubles"? My historical "realism" of sociocultural process—of entangled articulations, performances, and translations—left little space for new beginnings and epochal shifts. Maybe I had explained away the obvious. What if Barbara Shangin's words were really about starting fresh? Or even going back? The Russians did leave Alaska rather suddenly, after all. Why not the other invaders? My historical realism made such possibilities unthinkable.

I found I didn't want to know too much about the origin of Barbara Shangin's words, perhaps as a way of protecting my use of them as a paradigm of Native historical thinking—the expression of an indigenous *longue durée*. But eventually I got around to contacting the article's authors, Gordon Pullar and Richard Knecht. Working together in the Kodiak Area Native Association (KANA), the two men had played a central role in the heritage renewals of the 1980s and 1990s. It was natural that the editor of *Crossroads Alaska* should turn to them for a short introduction to the "Alutiiq," one of the seven Alaskan Native groups, along with six from Russian Siberia, featured in the volume. Pullar and Knecht emphasized the "catastrophic" effects of more than two centuries of contact. A hopeful ending was needed. In Barbara Shangin's words they found a Native voice that could express Alutiiq/Sugpiaq survival and the culture's renewed sense of control over its destiny.

Both authors responded helpfully to my questions. It emerged that Rick Knecht, on a visit to the Alaska Peninsula in 1988, had heard people say words to the effect that the coming of the white people was like a passing storm. His principal guide, Ronnie Lind, affirmed that he had heard this from his grandmother, Barbara Shangin.

Knecht ended one of his e-mails to me with the following reflections on Native historical vision in Alaska, beginning with the quotation's reference to "all the troubles since the Russians." It wasn't exactly what he had heard people saying in Chignik.

> As I recall it the reference was not to "troubles" but to whites themselves. The Chignik Lake story is the only one that I ever heard that predicts that white folk will be gone someday (Alaska should be so lucky). A more common "long-view" of history you hear when talking to Natives in rural Alaska is that the coming of the whites and all their technology was something long foretold by shamans and so on. Televisions and airplanes in particular were long foretold. This summer in [the Yup'ik town] Quinhagak I heard a new twist on this in that the little people (who appear now and again to people throughout the circumpolar world) used to appear to their ancestors wearing 20th century clothing and even sitting on tiny versions of 4-wheelers when confronting their 19th century ancestors, because little people have the ability to travel back and forth through time. But if prophesies exist, they don't seem to address what the end-game will be, or if this slow-motion train wreck of contact will continue forever. Or maybe people are just too polite to bring that up.

Knecht concluded that, whether or not the words were originally spoken by Barbara Shangin, they were "a pithy observation that made sense to people that heard it." So something meaningful was preserved in the subsequent transcriptions and transmissions, a core that could be reframed in a heritage publication, and that provoked speculations, such as mine on the idioms of historical narration and epistemology. The indigenous long view, it seems, could be expressed in narratives of changing weather, stories of time travel by little folk, or prophecies by traditional shamans.

Barbara Shangin means something different to me now. Knowing a little about her—just a little—I find that her name no longer simply symbolizes cultural authority, enunciated by a Native Elder. She is now a reminder of how indigenous knowledge is disseminated through translation and interpretation across times, places, generations, and cultures. What falls away and is added in the process?

Barbara Shangin, Chignik Lake's "Old Gramma," probably said something like the words that would eventually make sense to me. But it was in a language I'll never understand, in situations about which I can only guess. The words were remembered, repeated, inscribed, translated, condensed, and rewritten. They would become meaningful to her descendants reclaiming their Alutiiq/Sugpiaq heritage. And they would make sense to an academic intellectual in California looking for an enlarged sense of historical possibility. This was not what Barbara Shangin meant. And yet . . .

Her name now signifies all the things I can never know about Native Alaska. And her words repeat the unanswerable question of indigenous futures (what could possibly follow so much bad weather?), a question, and a hope, that comes through in spite of everything.

References

Active, John. 2000. "Yup'iks in the City." In *Hunting Tradition in a Changing World: Yup'ik Lives in Alaska Today,* ed. Ann Fienup-Riordan. New Brunswick, NJ: Rutgers University Press. 169–182.

Adorno, Theodor. 1974. *Minima Moralia: Reflections on Damaged Life.* Frankfurt: Surkamp Verlag.

Althusser, Louis. 1972. "Ideology and Ideological State Apparatuses." In *Lenin and Philosophy and Other Essays.* New York: Monthly Review Press. 127–186.

Anders, Gary. 1990. "The Alaska Native Experience with the Alaska Native Claims Settlement Act." In *The Struggle for the Land,* ed. Paul A. Olson. Lincoln: University of Nebraska Press. 126–145.

Anderson, Benedict. 1983. *Imagined Communities: Reflections on the Origin and Spread of Nationalism.* London: Verso.

———. 1998. "Long Distance Nationalism." In *The Spectre of Comparisons: Nationalism, Southeast Asia, and the World.* London: Verso. 58–74.

Anderson, Mark. 2009. *Black and Indigenous: Garifuna Activism and Consumer Culture in Honduras.* Minneapolis: University of Minnesota Press.

Ang, Ien. 2001. *On Not Speaking Chinese: Living between Asia and the West.* London: Routledge.

Appadurai, Arjun. 1990. "Disjuncture and Difference in the Global Cultural Economy." *Public Culture* 2 (2): 1–24.

Appiah, Kwame Anthony. 1998. "Cosmopolitan Patriots." In *Cosmopolitics: Thinking and Feeling Beyond the Nation,* ed. Pheng Cheah and Bruce Robbins. Minneapolis: University of Minnesota Press. 91–114.

Barker, John, ed. 1990. *Christianity in Oceania: Ethnographic Perspectives.* ASAO Monograph 12. Lanham, MD: University Press of America.

Barth, Fredrik, ed. 1969. *Ethnic Groups and Boundaries: The Social Organization of Cultural Difference.* Boston: Little, Brown.

Bartra, Roger. 1994. *Wild Men in the Looking Glass: The Mythic Origins of European Otherness.* Ann Arbor: University of Michigan Press.

Baviskar, Amita. 2007. "Indian Indigeneities: Adivasi Engagements with Hindu Nationalism in India." In *Indigenous Experience Today,* ed. Marisol de la Cadena and Orin Starn. Oxford: Berg. 275–303.

321

Benjamin, Walter. 1968. "Theses on the Philosophy of History." In *Illuminations,* ed. Hannah Arendt. New York: Schocken Books. 253–265.

Bensa, Alban. 1995. *Chroniques Kanak: L'etnologie en marche.* Paris: Ethnies-Documents.

——. 2000. *Ethnologie et Architecture: Le Centre Culturel Tjibaou.* Paris: Société Nouvelle Adam Biro.

Bensa, Alban, and Eric Wittersheim. 1998. "Nationalism and Interdependence: The Political Thought of Jean-Marie Tjibaou." *The Contemporary Pacific* 10 (2): 369–391.

Berger, Thomas. (1985) 1995. *Village Journey: The Report of the Alaska Native Review Commission.* New York: Farrar, Straus and Giroux.

Bibby, Brian. 2005. *Deeper Than Gold: A Guide to Indian Life in the Sierra Foothills.* Berkeley: Heyday Books.

Biestman, Karen. 2003. "Ishi and the University." In *Ishi in Three Centuries,* ed. Karl Kroeber and Clifton Kroeber. Lincoln: University of Nebraska Press. 146–155.

Biolsi, Thomas. 2005. "Imagined Geographies: Sovereignty, Indigenous Space, and American Indian Struggles." *American Ethnologist* 32 (2): 239–259.

Black, Lydia. 2004. *Russians in Alaska, 1732–1867.* Fairbanks: University of Alaska Press.

Blaut, J. M. 1993. *The Colonizer's Model of the World: Geographical Diffusionism and Eurocentric History.* New York: Guilford Press.

Bolton, Lissant, ed. 1999. "Fieldwork, Fieldworkers: Developments in Vanuatu Research." Special issue, *Oceania* 60.

——. 2003. *Unfolding the Moon: Enacting Women's Kastom in Vanuatu.* Honolulu: University of Hawai'i Press.

Bonnemaison, Joel. 1994. *The Tree and the Canoe: History and Ethnography of Tanna,* trans. Josée Pénot-Demetry. Honolulu: University of Hawai'i Press.

Brah, Avtar. 1996. *Cartographies of Diaspora: Contesting Identities.* London: Routledge.

Bray, Tamara, and Thomas Killion, eds. 1994. *Reckoning with the Dead: The Larsen Bay Repatriation and the Smithsonian Institution.* Washington, DC: Smithsonian Institution Press.

Brecher, Jeremy, Tim Costello, and Brendan Smith. 2000. *Globalization from Below.* Boston: South End Press.

Brechin, Gray. 1999. *Imperial San Francisco.* Berkeley: University of California Press.

Briggs, Charles. 1996. "The Politics of Discursive Authority in Research on the 'Invention of Tradition.'" *Cultural Anthropology* 11 (4): 435–469.

Brown, Michael. 2003. *Who Owns Native Culture?* Cambridge, MA: Harvard University Press.

Buck, Elizabeth. 1993. *Paradise Remade: The Politics of Culture and History in Hawai'i.* Philadelphia: Temple University Press.

Buckley, Thomas. 1996. "The Little History of Pitiful Events: The Epistemological and Moral Contexts of Kroeber's California Ethnology." *History of Anthropology* 8: 257–297.

Burrill, Richard. 2011. *Ishi's Untold Story in His First World*. Red Bluff, CA: Anthro Company.

Butler, Judith. 1998. "Merely Cultural." *New Left Review* 228: 33–44.

Calloway, Colin. 1990. *The Western Abenakis of Vermont, 1600–1800: War, Migration, and the Survival of an Indian People*. Norman: University of Oklahoma Press.

Carrier, James, ed. 1992. *History and Tradition in Melanesian Anthropology*. Berkeley: University of California Press.

Casanova, Pascale. 2005. *The World Republic of Letters*. Cambridge, MA: Harvard University Press.

Castañeda, Terri. 2002. "Salvaging the Anthropologist-Other at California's Tribal College." *American Indian Quarterly* 26 (2): 308–319.

Cattelino, Jessica. 2008. *High Stakes: Florida Seminole Gaming and Sovereignty*. Durham, NC: Duke University Press.

———. 2009. "Fungibility: Florida Seminole Casino Dividends and the Fiscal Politics of Indigeneity." *American Anthropologist* 111 (2): 190–200.

Chakrabarty, Dipesh. 2000. *Provincializing Europe: Postcolonial Thought and Historical Difference*. Princeton, NJ: Princeton University Press.

Chapman, Murray. 1978. "On the Cross-Cultural Study of Circulation." *International Migration Review* 12: 559–569.

———. 1991. "Island Movement and Sociopolitical Change: Metaphors of Misunderstanding." *Population and Development Review* 17: 263–292.

Chappell, David. 1997. *Double Ghosts: Oceanian Voyagers on Euroamerican Ships*. Armonk, NY: M. E. Sharpe.

Chaussonnet, Valerie. 1995. *Crossroads Alaska: Native Cultures of Alaska and Siberia*. Washington, DC: Arctic Studies Center, Smithsonian Institution.

Childs, John Brown. 1993. "Towards Transcommunality: The Highest Stage of Multiculturalism." *Social Justice* 20 (1): 35–51.

———. 1998. "Transcommunality: From the Politics of Conversion to the Ethics of Respect in the Context of Cultural Diversity—Learning from Native American Philosophies." *Social Justice* 25 (4): 143–169.

Chow, Rey. 2002. *The Protestant Ethnic and the Spirit of Capitalism*. New York: Columbia University Press.

Christen, Kimberly. 2004. "Properly Warumungu: Indigenous Future-Making in a Remote Australian Town." PhD diss., History of Consciousness Department, University of California, Santa Cruz.

———. 2005. "Gone Digital: Aboriginal Remix in the Cultural Commons." *International Journal of Cultural Property* 12: 315–344.

———. 2008. *Aboriginal Business: Alliances on a Remote Australian Town*. Santa Fe: School of American Research Press.

Clark, Anna. 1995. *The Battle of the Breeches: Gender and the Making of the British Working Class*. Berkeley: University of California Press.

Clark, Donald. 1984. "Pacific Eskimo: Historical Ethnography." In *Handbook of North American Indians*. Vol. 5, ed. William Sturtevant. Washington, DC: Smithsonian Institution. 195–197.

Clifford, James. 1982. *Person and Myth: Maurice Leenhardt in the Melanesian World*. Berkeley: University of California Press.

———. 1986. "Introduction: Partial Truths." In *Writing Culture: The Poetics and Politics of Ethnography,* ed. James Clifford and George Marcus. Berkeley: University of California Press. 1–26.

———. 1988a. "Identity in Mashpee." In *The Predicament of Culture*. Cambridge, MA: Harvard University Press. 277–346.

———. 1988b. *The Predicament of Culture*. Cambridge, MA: Harvard University Press.

———. 1994. "Diasporas." *Cultural Anthropology* 9 (3): 302–338. Reprinted in *Routes* (1997). Cambridge, MA: Harvard University Press. 244–278.

———. 1997a. "Fort Ross Meditation." In *Routes: Travel and Translation in the Late Twentieth Century*. Cambridge, MA: Harvard University Press. 299–348.

———. 1997b. *Routes: Travel and Translation in the Late Twentieth Century*. Cambridge, MA: Harvard University Press.

———. 2000. "Taking Identity Politics Seriously: 'The Contradictory, Stony Ground . . . '" In *Without Guarantees: In Honor of Stuart Hall,* ed. Paul Gilroy, Lawrence Grossberg, and Angela McRobbie. London: Verso. 94–112.

———. 2001. "Indigenous Articulations." *The Contemporary Pacific* 13 (2): 468–490.

———. 2002. "Post-Neo Colonial Situations: Notes on Historical Realism Today." In *Literatura e viagens pós-coloniais (ACT, No. 6),* ed. Helena Carvalhão Buescu and Manuela Reibeiro Sanches. Lisbon: Edições Colibri. 9–32.

———. 2004a. "Looking Several Ways: Anthropology and Native Heritage in Alaska." *Current Anthropology* 45 (1): 5–23.

———. 2004b. "Traditional Futures." In *Questions of Tradition,* ed. Mark Phillips and Gordon Schochet. Toronto: University of Toronto Press. 152–168.

———. 2005. "Rearticulating Anthropology." In *Unwrapping the Sacred Bundle: Reflections on the Disciplining of Anthropology,* ed. Daniel Segal and Sylvia Yanagisako. Durham, NC: Duke University Press. 24–48.

———. 2007. "Varieties of Indigenous Experience: Diasporas, Homelands, Sovereignties." In *Indigenous Experience Today,* ed. Marisol de la Cadena and Orin Starn. Oxford: Berg. 197–224.

———. 2009. "Hau'ofa's Hope." *Oceania* 79: 238–249.

Cohen, Robin. 1997. *Global Diasporas: An Introduction*. London: University College London Press.

Comaroff, John, and Jean Comaroff. 2009. *Ethnicity, Inc.* Chicago: University of Chicago Press.

Conklin, Beth. 1997. "Body Paint, Feathers, and VCRs: Aesthetics and Authenticity in Amazonian Activism." *American Ethnologist* 24 (4): 711–737.

Connery, Christopher. 1994. "Pacific Rim Discourse: The U.S. Global Imaginary in the Late Cold War Years." *Boundary 2* 21 (2): 30–56.

Connery, Christopher, and Rob Wilson, eds. 2007. *The Worlding Project: Doing Cultural Studies in the Era of Globalization*. Santa Cruz, CA: New Pacific Press.

Cooper, Frederick. 2001. "What Is the Concept of Globalization Good For? An African Historian's Perspective." *African Affairs* 100 (399): 189–213.

Crowell, Aron. 1997. *Archaeology and the Capitalist World System: A Study from Russian America*. New York: Plenum Press.

———. 2001. "Looking Both Ways." In *Looking Both Ways: Heritage and Identity of the Alutiiq People*, ed. Aron Crowell, Amy Steffian, and Gordon Pullar. Fairbanks: University of Alaska Press: 3–19.

———. 2004. "Terms of Engagement: The Collaborative Representation of Alutiiq Identity." *Etudes/Inuit/Studies* 28 (1): 9–35.

Crowell, Aron, and April Laktonen. 2001. "*Sugucihpet*—'Our Way of Living.'" In *Looking Both Ways: Heritage and Identity of the Alutiiq People*, ed. Aron Crowell, Amy Steffian, and Gordon Pullar. Fairbanks: University of Alaska Press. 137–187.

Crowell, Aron, and Sonja Lührmann. 2001. "Alutiiq Culture: Views from Archaeology, Anthropology, and History." In *Looking Both Ways: Heritage and Identity of the Alutiiq People*, ed. Aron Crowell, Amy Steffian, and Gordon Pullar. Fairbanks: University of Alaska Press. 21–30.

Crowell, Aron, Amy Steffian, and Gordon Pullar, eds. 2001. *Looking Both Ways: Heritage and Identity of the Alutiiq People*. Fairbanks: University of Alaska Press.

Cruikshank, Julie. 1998. *The Social Life of Stories: Narrative and Knowledge in the Yukon Territory*. Lincoln: University of Nebraska Press.

Curtis, Tim. 2003. "Talking about Place: Identities, Histories, and Powers among the Na'hai Speakers of Malekula (Vanuatu)." PhD diss., Research School of Pacific and Asian Studies, Australian National University, Canberra, Australia.

Darnell, Regna. 1998. "Rethinking the Concepts of Band and Tribe, Community and Nation: An Accordion Model of Nomadic Native American Social Organization." In *Papers of the Twenty-Ninth Algonquian Conference/ Actes du congres des Algonquinistes*. Winnipeg: University of Manitoba. 90–105.

Dawson, Ruth Alice Olsen. 2001. "Bridging Traditions and Science." In *Looking Both Ways: Heritage and Identity of the Alutiiq People*, ed. Aron Crowell, Amy Steffian, and Gordon Pullar. Fairbanks: University of Alaska Press. 89.

de Angulo, Jaime. 1950. *Indians in Overalls*. San Francisco: City Lights Books.

de Certeau, Michel. 1984. *The Practice of Everyday Life*. Berkeley: University of California Press.

de la Cadena, Marisol. 2000. *Indigenous Mestizos: The Politics of Race and Culture in Cuzco, 1919–1991*. Durham, NC: Duke University Press.

de la Cadena, Marisol, and Orin Starn, eds. 2007. *Indigenous Experience Today*. Oxford: Berg.

Deloria, Philip. 1999. *Playing Indian*. New Haven, CT: Yale University Press.

———. 2004. *Indians in Unexpected Places.* Lawrence: University of Kansas Press.

Deloria, Vine, Jr. 1969. *Custer Died for Your Sins: An Indian Manifesto.* New York: Macmillan.

———. 1997. "Conclusion: Anthros, Indians, and Planetary Reality." In *Indians and Anthropologists: Vine Deloria and the Critique of Anthropology,* ed. Thomas Biolsi and Larry Zimmerman. Tucson: University of Arizona Press. 209–221.

———. 2000. Foreword to *Skull Wars: Kennewick Man, Archaeology, and the Battle for Native American Identity,* by David Hurst Thomas. New York: Basic Books. xiii–xvi.

DeLoughrey, Elizabeth. 2007. *Routes and Roots: Navigating Caribbean and Pacific Island Literatures.* Honolulu: University of Hawai'i Press.

Dening, Greg. 1980. *Islands and Beaches: Discourse on a Silent Land, Marquesas, 1774–1880.* Honolulu: University Press of Hawaii.

———. 2004. *Beach Crossings: Voyaging across Times, Cultures, and Self.* Philadelphia: University of Pennsylvania Press.

Désveaux, Emmanuel, ed. 2002. *Kodiak, Alaska: Les masques de la collection Alphonse Pinart.* Paris: Adam Biro.

Diaz, Vicente. 1993. "Pious Sites: Chamorro Culture at the Crossroads of Spanish Catholicism and American Liberalism." In *Cultures of United States Imperialism,* ed. Amy Kaplan and Donald Pease. Durham, NC: Duke University Press. 312–339.

———. 1994. "Simply Chamorro: Telling Tales of Demise and Survival in Guam. *The Contemporary Pacific* 6 (1). 29–58.

Diaz, Vicente M., and J. Kehaulani Kauanui, eds. 2001. *Native Pacific Cultural Studies on the Edge.* Special issue, *The Contemporary Pacific* 13 (2): 315–507.

Dinwoodie, David. 1999. "Textuality and the 'Voices' of Informants: The Case of Edward Sapir's 1929 Navajo Field School." *Anthropological Linguistics* 41 (2): 165–192.

Dobkins, Rebecca. 2003. "The Healer: Maidu Artist Frank Day's Vision of Ishi." In *Ishi in Three Centuries,* ed. Karl Kroeber and Clifton Kroeber. Lincoln: University of Nebraska Press. 388–393.

Dolores, Juan. 1911. Letter to A. L. Kroeber, May 4, 1911. Bancroft Library, CU-23, Box 11. UCB Department of Anthropology.

Dombrowski, Kirk. 2001. *Against Culture: Development, Politics, and Religion in Indian Alaska.* Lincoln: University of Nebraska Press.

———. 2002. "The Praxis of Indigenism and Alaska Native Timber Politics." *American Anthropologist* 104: 1062–1073.

Dominguez, Virginia. 1994. "Invoking Culture: The Messy Side of 'Cultural Politics.'" In *Eloquent Obsessions: Writing Cultural Criticism,* ed. Marianna Torgovnick. Durham, NC: Duke University Press. 237–259.

Durham, Jimmie. 1992. "Geronimo!" In *Partial Recall: Photos of Native North Americans,* ed. Lucy Lippard. New York: New Press. 55–58.

Eaton, Perry. 2009. "Kodiak Masks: A Personal Odyssey." In *The Alaska Native Reader: History, Culture, Politics*, ed. Maria Shaa Tláa Williams. Durham, NC: Duke University Press. 283–293.

Englund, Harri. 2006. *Prisoners of Freedom: Human Rights and the African Poor*. Berkeley: University of California Press.

Errington, Frederick, and Deborah Gewertz. 1991. *Articulating Change in the "Last Unknown."* Boulder, CO: Westview Press.

Fabian, Johannes. 1983. *Time and the Other: How Anthropology Makes Its Object*. New York: Columbia University Press.

Ferguson, James. 2006. *Global Shadows: Africa in the Neoliberal World Order*. Durham, NC: Duke University Press.

Field, Les. 1999. "Complicities and Collaborations: Anthropologists and the 'Unacknowledged Tribes' of California." *Current Anthropology* 40: 193–209.

———. 2008. *Abalone Tales: Collaborative Explorations of Sovereignty and Identity in Native California*. Durham, NC: Duke University Press.

Fienup-Riordan, Ann. 1990. *Eskimo Essays: Yup'ik Lives and How We See Them*. New Brunswick, NJ: Rutgers University Press.

———. 1996. *The Living Tradition of Yup'ik Masks: Agayuliyararput (Our Way of Making Prayer)*. Seattle: University of Washington Press.

———. 2000. *Hunting Tradition in a Changing World: Yup'ik Lives in Alaska Today*. New Brunswick, NJ: Rutgers University Press.

———. 2004a. *Wise Words of the Yup'ik People: We Talk to You Because We Love You*. Lincoln: University of Nebraska Press.

———. 2004b. *Yup'ik Voices in a German Museum: Fieldwork Turned on Its Head*. Seattle: University of Washington Press.

———. 2005. *Yup'ik Elders at the Ethnologisches Museum Berlin: Fieldwork Turned on Its Head*. Seattle: University of Washington Press in association with Calista Elders Council.

Finney, Ben. 1994. *Voyage of Discovery: A Cultural Odyssey through Polynesia*. Berkeley: University of California Press.

Firth, Stewart. 2000. "Decolonization." In *Remembrance of Pacific Pasts: An Invitation to Remake History*, ed. Robert Borofsky. Honolulu: University of Hawai'i Press. 324–332.

Fischer, Edward, and R. McKenna Brown, eds. 1996. *Maya Cultural Activism in Guatemala*. Austin: University of Texas Press.

Fitzhugh, William, and Aron Crowell, eds. 1988. *Crossroads of Continents: Cultures of Siberia and Alaska*. Washington, DC: Smithsonian Institution.

Fitzhugh, William, and Susan Kaplan. 1982. *Innua: Spirit World of the Bering Sea Eskimo*. Washington, DC: Smithsonian Institution Press.

Flores, William, and Rina Benmayor, eds. 1997. *Latino Cultural Citizenship: Claiming Identity, Space, and Rights*. Boston: Beacon Press.

Forster, E. M. (1926) 1952. *A Passage to India*. New York: Harcourt, Brace and World.

Forte, Maximillian. 2006. *Indigenous Resurgence in the Contemporary Caribbean*. New York: Peter Lang.

Foucault, Michel. 1977. "Nietzsche, Genealogy, History." In *Language, Counter-Memory, Practice: Selected Essays and Interviews*. Ithaca, NY: Cornell University Press. 139–164.

———. 1984. "Des espaces autres" (conférence au Cercle d'études architecturales, 14 mars 1967). *Architecture, Mouvement, Continuité* 5: 46–49.

Frank, L., and Kim Hogeland. 2007. *First Families: A Photographic History of California Indians*. Berkeley: Heyday Books.

Freeman, James. 1992. *Ishi's Journey: From the Center to the Edge of the World*. Happy Camp, CA: Naturegraph.

Friedman, Jonathan. 1990. "Being in the World: Globalization and Localization." In *Global Culture: Nationalism, Globalization and Modernity*, ed. Mike Featherstone. London: Sage. 311–328.

———. 1993. "Will the Real Hawaiian Please Stand: Anthropologists and Natives in the Global Struggle for Identity." *Bijdragen: Journal of the Royal Institute of Linguistics and Anthropology* 149: 738–767.

———. 1994. *Cultural Identity and Global Process*. London: Sage.

———. 2007. "Indigeneity: Anthropological Notes on a Historical Variable." In *Indigenous Peoples: The Challenge of Indigeneity, Self-Determination and Knowledge*, ed. Henry Minde. Delft: Eburon Academic. 29–48.

Fujikane, Candace, and Jonathan Okamura, eds. 2000. *Whose Vision? Asian Settler Colonialism in Hawai'i*. Special issue, *Amerasia Journal* 26 (2).

Gegeo, David Welchman. 1998. "Indigenous Knowledge and Empowerment: Rural Development Examined from Within." *The Contemporary Pacific* 10 (2): 289–315.

———. 2001. "Cultural Rupture and Indigeneity: The Challenge of (Re)visioning 'Place' in the Pacific." *The Contemporary Pacific* 13 (2): 491–508.

Geschiere, Peter. 2009. *The Perils of Belonging: Autochthony, Citizenship, and Exclusion in Africa and Europe*. Chicago: University of Chicago Press.

Ghere, David. 1993. "The 'Disappearance' of the Abenaki in Western Maine: Political Organization and Ethnocentric Assumptions." *American Indian Quarterly* 17: 193–207.

Giddens, Anthony. 1990. *The Consequences of Modernity*. Cambridge: Polity Press.

Gidwani, Vinay, and Kalyanakrishnan Sivaramakrishnan. 2003. "Circular Migration and the Spaces of Cultural Assertion." *Annals of the Association of American Geographers* 93 (1): 186–213.

Gilroy, Paul. 1993. *The Black Atlantic: Modernity and Double Consciousness*. Cambridge, MA: Harvard University Press.

———. 1996. "British Cultural Studies and the Pitfalls of Identity." In *Black British Cultural Studies*, ed. Houston Baker, Manthia Diawara, and Ruth Lindeborg. Chicago: University of Chicago Press. 223–239.

Gladney, Drew. 1996. "Relational Alterity: Constructing Dungan (Hui), Uygur, and Kazakh Identities across China, Central Asia and Turkey." *History and Anthropology* 9 (4): 445–477.

Glick-Schiller, Nina. 1995. "From Immigrant to Transmigrant: Theorizing Transnational Migration." *Anthropological Quarterly* 68 (1): 48–63.

Glissant, Edouard. 1992. *Caribbean Discourse: Selected Essays*. Charlottesville: University of Virginia Press.

Golla, Victor. 2003. "Ishi's Language." In *Ishi in Three Centuries,* ed. Karl Kroeber and Clifton Kroeber. Lincoln: University of Nebraska Press. 208–227.

Gossen, Gary. 1999. "Indians Inside and Outside of the Mexican National Idea: A Case Study of the Modern Diaspora of San Juan Chamula." In *Telling Maya Tales: Tzotzil Identities in Modern Mexico*. London: Routledge. 189–208.

Graburn, Nelson. 1998. "Weirs in the River of Time: The Development of Historical Consciousness among Canadian Inuit." *Museum Anthropology* 22 (1): 18–32.

Green, Rayna. 1992. "Rosebuds of the Plateau: Frank Matsura and the Fainting Couch Aesthetic." In *Partial Recall: Photographs of Native North Americans,* ed. Lucy Lippard. New York: New Press. 47–54.

Griffin, Vanessa. 1993. "Putting Our Minds to Alternatives." In *A New Oceania: Rediscovering Our Sea of Islands,* ed. Eric Waddell, Vijay Naidu, and Epeli Hau'ofa. Suva, Fuji: School of Social and Economic Development, University of the South Pacific. 56–65.

Gupta, Akhil, and James Ferguson. 1992. "Beyond 'Culture': Space, Identity, and the Politics of Difference." *Cultural Anthropology* 7 (1): 1–23.

———, eds. 1997a. *Anthropological Locations: Boundaries and Grounds of a Field Science*. Berkeley: University of California Press.

———, eds. 1997b. *Culture, Power, Place: Explorations in Critical Anthropology*. Durham, NC: Duke University Press.

Haakanson, Sven. 2001 "Can There Be Such a Thing as a Native Anthropologist?" In *Looking Both Ways: Heritage and Identity of the Alutiiq People,* ed. Aron Crowell, Amy Steffian, and Gordon Pullar. Fairbanks: University of Alaska Press. 79.

Haakanson, Sven, and Anne-Claire Laronde. 2008. Preface to *Two Journeys: A Companion to the Giinaquq: Like a Face Exhibition,* by Koniag Inc. Kodiak, AK: Alutiiq Museum. 3–4.

Haakanson, Sven, and Amy Steffian, eds. 2009a. *Giinaquq: Like a Face/Comme un visage: Sugpiaq Masks of the Kodiak Archipelago*. Fairbanks: University of Alaska Press.

———, eds. 2009b. "Sugpiaq Masks from the Kodiak Archipelago." In *Giinaquq: Like a Face/Comme un visage: Sugpiaq Masks of the Kodiak Archipelago*. Fairbanks: University of Alaska Press: 79–84.

Hale, Charles. 2002. "Does Multiculturalism Menace? Governance, Cultural Rights and the Politics of Identity in Guatemala." *Journal of Latin American Studies* 34: 485–524.

———. 2005. "Neoliberal Multiculturalism: The Remaking of Cultural Rights and Racial Dominance in Latin America. *PoLAR: Political and Legal Anthropology Review* 28 (1): 10–28.

———. 2006. Más que un Indio/*More than an Indian: Racial Ambivalence and Neoliberal Multiculturalism in Guatemala*. Santa Fe, NM: School of American Research Press.

330 REFERENCES

Hall, Stuart. 1986a. "Gramsci's Relevance for the Study of Race and Ethnicity." *Journal of Communication Inquiry* 10 (2): 5–27.

———. 1986b. "On Postmodernism and Articulation: An Interview with Stuart Hall." *Journal of Communication Inquiry* 10 (2): 131–150.

———. 1988. "New Ethnicities." In *Black Film, British Cinema*, ed. Kobena Mercer. BFI/ICA Document 7. London: Institue of Contemporary Arts. 27–31.

———. 1989. "Then and Now: A Re-evaluation of the New Left." In *Out of Apathy: Voices of the New Left Thirty Years On*, ed. Robin Archer. Oxford University Socialist Group. London: Verso. 143–170.

———. 1990. "Cultural Identity and Diaspora." In *Identity, Community, Culture, Difference*, ed. Jonathan Rutherford. London: Lawrence and Wishart. 222–237.

———. 1996. "When Was the Post-Colonial? Thinking at the Limit." In *The Post-Colonial Question*, ed. Iain Chambers and Lidia Curti. London: Routledge. 242–260.

———. 1998. "Subjects in History: Making Diasporic Identities." In *The House That Race Built*, ed. Whneema Lubiano. New York: Vintage. 289–300.

Hamelin, Christine. 2000. "Les gens de Nouméa. Mutations et permanences en milieu urbain." In *En pays Kanak*, ed. Alban Bensa and Isabelle Leblic. Paris: Editions de la Laison des Sciences de l'homme. 339–354.

Hamilton, Carolyn. 1998. *Terrific Majesty: The Powers of Shaka Zulu and the Limits of Historical Invention*. Cambridge, MA: Harvard University Press.

Handler, Richard. 1988. *Nationalism and the Politics of Culture in Quebec*. Madison: University of Wisconsin Press.

Handler, Richard, and Eric Gable. 1997. *The New History in an Old Museum: Creating the Past at Colonial Williamsburg*. Durham, NC: Duke University Press.

Handler, Richard, and Jocelyn Linnekin. 1984. "Tradition, Genuine or Spurious." *The Journal of American Folklore* 97 (385): 273–290.

Hanson, Allan. 1989. "The Making of the Maori: Cultural Invention and Its Logic. *American Anthropologist* 91: 890–902.

Haraway, Donna. 1988. "Situated Knowledges: The Science Question in Feminism and the Privilege of Partial Perspective." *Feminist Studies* 14 (1): 167–181.

———. 1997. *Modest_Witness@Second_Millenium*. New York: Routledge.

Harmon, Alexandra. 1998. *Indians in the Making: Ethnic Relations and Indian Identities around Puget Sound*. Berkeley: University of California Press.

Harvey, David. 1990. *The Condition of Postmodernity*. Oxford: Blackwell.

———. 2000. *Spaces of Hope*. Berkeley: University of California Press.

Hau'ofa, Epeli. 1983. *Tales of the Tikongs*. Auckland: Longman Paul.

———. 1987. Kisses in the Nederends. Auckland: Penguin.

———. 1993. "Our Sea of Islands." In *A New Oceania: Rediscovering Our Sea of Islands*, ed. Eric Waddell, Vijay Naidu, and Epeli Hau'ofa. Suva, Fuji: School of Social and Economic Development, University of the South Pacific. 2–19.

———. 2000. "Pasts to Remember." In *Remembrance of Pacific Pasts: An Invitation to Remake History,* ed. Robert Borofsky. Honolulu: University of Hawai'i Press. 453–472.

———. 2008. *We Are the Ocean: Selected Works.* Honolulu: University of Hawai'i Press.

Heizer, Robert, and Theodora Kroeber, eds. 1979. *Ishi the Last Yahi: A Documentary History.* Berkeley: University of California Press.

Helu, 'I. F. 1999. *Critical Essays: Cultural Perspectives from the South Seas.* Canberra: Journal of Pacific History, Australian National University Press.

Hereniko, Vilsoni. 1995. *Woven Gods: Female Clowns and Power in Rotuma.* Honolulu: University of Hawai'i Press.

———. 2000. "Indigenous Knowledge and Academic Imperialism." In *Remembrance of Pacific Pasts: An Invitation to Remake History,* ed. Robert Borofsky. Honolulu: University of Hawai'i Press. 78–91.

Hernández Castillo, Rosalva Aida. 1997. "Between Hope and Adversity: The Struggle of Organized Women in Chiapas since the Zapatista Rebellion." *Journal of Latin American Anthropology* 3 (1): 102–120.

———. 2001. *Histories and Stories from Chiapas: Border Identities in Southern Mexico.* Austin: University of Texas Press.

Hewison, Robert. 1987. *The Heritage Industry.* London: Methuen.

Hill, Jonathan, ed. 1996. *History, Power, and Identity: Ethnogenesis in the Americas, 1492–1992.* Iowa City: University of Iowa Press.

Hobsbawm, Eric, and Terence Ranger, eds. 1983. *The Invention of Tradition.* Cambridge: Cambridge University Press.

Hodder, Ian. 1991. "Interpretive Archaeology and Its Role." *American Antiquity* 56: 7–18.

———. 1999. *The Archaeological Process.* Oxford: Blackwell.

Hoggart, Richard. 1957. *The Uses of Literacy: Changing Patterns in English Mass Culture.* Fair Lawn, NJ: Essential Books.

Hughte, Phillip. 1994. *A Zuni Artist Looks at Frank Hamilton Cushing: Cartoons by Phil Hughte.* Zuni, NM: A:shiwi Museum and Heritage Center.

Ignatieff, Michael. 1993. *Blood and Belonging: Journeys into the New Nationalism.* New York: Farrar, Straus and Giroux.

Ingold, Tim. 2007. *Lines: A Brief History.* London: Routledge.

Ivy, Marilyn. 1995. *Discourses of the Vanishing: Modernity, Phantasm, Japan.* Chicago: University of Chicago Press.

Jacknis, Ira. 2003. "Yahi Culture in the Wax Museum: Ishi's Sound Recordings." In *Ishi in Three Centuries,* ed. Karl Kroeber and Clifton Kroeber. Lincoln: University of Nebraska Press. 235–274.

———. 2008. "'The Last Wild Indian in North America': Changing Museum Representations of Ishi." In *Museums and Difference,* ed. Daniel J. Sherman. Bloomington: Indiana University Press. 60–96.

Jaimes, M. Annette, and George Noriega. 1988. "History in the Making: How Academia Manufactures the 'Truth' about Native American Traditions." *Bloomsbury Review* 4 (5): 24–26.

James, Allison, Jenny Hockey, and Andrew Dawson, eds. 1997. *After Writing Culture: Epistemology and Praxis in Contemporary Anthropology*. London: Routledge.

Jameson, Fredric. 1975. "World Reduction in Le Guin: The Emergence of Utopian Narrative." *Science Fiction Studies* 2 (3): 1–11.

———. 1984. "Postmodernism, or the Cultural Logic of Late Capitalism." *New Left Review* 146: 53–97.

———. 2005. *Archaeologies of the Future: The Desire Called Utopia and Other Essays*. London: Verso.

Johnson, John F. C. 2001. "Repatriation and the Chugach Alaska People." In *Looking Both Ways: Heritage and Identity of the Alutiiq People,* ed. Aron Crowell, Amy Steffian, and Gordon Pullar. Fairbanks: University of Alaska Press. 92–93.

Jolly, Margaret. 1992. "Specters of Inauthenticity." *The Contemporary Pacific* 4 (1): 49–72.

———. 1994. *Women of the Place:* Kastom, *Colonialism and Gender in Vanuatu*. Chur, Switzerland: Harwood Academic Publishers.

———. 2001. "On the Edge? Deserts, Oceans, Islands." *The Contemporary Pacific* 13 (2): 417–466.

Jolly, Margaret, and Nicholas Thomas, eds. 1992. "The Politics of Tradition in the Pacific." Special issue, *Oceania* 62 (4).

Jonaitis, Aldona, and Richard Inglis. 1994. "Power, History, and Authenticity: The Mowachaht Whalers' Washing Shrine." In *Eloquent Obsessions: Writing Cultural Criticism,* ed. Marianna Torgovnick. Durham, NC: Duke University Press. 157–184.

Kame'eleihiwa, Lilikala. 1992. *Native Land and Foreign Desires: Pehea Lⱦ E Pono Ai? (How Shall We Live in Harmony?)*. Honolulu, HI: Bishop Museum Press.

Kastoriano, Riva. 2003. "Diaspora, Transnationalism and the State." Paper presented at La Notion de Diaspora conference, Maison des Sciences de l'Homme, Poitiers, May 16.

Kauanui, Kehaulani. 1999. "Off-Island Hawaiians 'Making' Ourselves at 'Home': A (Gendered) Contradiction in Terms?" *Women's International Forum* 21 (6): 681–693.

———. 2008. *Hawaiian Blood: Colonialism and the Politics of Sovereignty and Indigeneity*. Durham, NC: Duke University Press.

Keesing, Roger. 1991. "Reply to Trask." *The Contemporary Pacific* 3 (1): 169–171.

———. 1996. "Class, Culture, Custom." In *Melanesian Modernities,* ed. Jonathan Friedman and James Carrier. Lund, Sweden: Lund University Press. 162–182.

Keesing, Roger, and Robert Tonkinson, eds. 1982. "Reinventing Traditional Culture: The Politics of Kastom in Island Melanesia." Special issue, *Mankind* 13 (4).

Kirshenblatt-Gimblett, Barbara. 1998. *Destination Culture: Tourism, Museums, and Heritage*. Berkeley: University of California Press.

Knecht, Richard. 1994. "Archaeology and Alutiiq Cultural Identity on Kodiak Island." *Society for American Archaeology Bulletin* 12 (5): 8–10.

———. 2001. "The Karluk Archaeological Project and the Changing Cultural Landscape of Kodiak Island." In *Looking Both Ways: Heritage and Identity of the Alutiiq People,* ed. Aron Crowell, Amy Steffian, and Gordon Pullar. Fairbanks: University of Alaska Press. 134.

Koniag Inc. 2008. *Two Journeys: A Companion to the Giinaquq: Like a Face Exhibition.* Kodiak, AK: Alutiiq Museum.

Kramer, Jennifer. 2006. *Switchbacks: Art, Ownership, and Nuxalk National Identity.* Vancouver: University of British Columbia Press.

Kroeber, A. L. 1925. *Handbook of the Indians of California.* Bureau of American Ethnology Bulletin 78. Washington, DC: U.S. Government Printing Office.

Kroeber, Karl. 2003. "The Humanity of Ishi." In *Ishi in Three Centuries,* ed. Karl Kroeber and Clifton Kroeber. Lincoln: University of Nebraska Press. 132–145.

———. 2004. Foreword to *Ishi in Two Worlds,* by Theodora Kroeber. Deluxe illustrated ed. Berkeley: University of California Press. xi–xxii.

Kroeber, Karl, and Clifton Kroeber, eds. 2003. *Ishi in Three Centuries.* Lincoln: University of Nebraska Press.

Kroeber, Theodora. 1961. *Ishi in Two Worlds: A Biography of the Last Wild Indian in North America.* Berkeley: University of California Press.

———. 1964. *Ishi: Last of His Tribe.* New York: Houghton Mifflin.

———. 1970. *Alfred Kroeber: A Personal Configuration.* Berkeley: University of California Press.

———. 2004. *Ishi in Two Worlds.* Deluxe illustrated ed. Berkeley: University of California Press.

Kroeber, Theodora, and Robert Heizer, eds. 1968. *Almost Ancestors: The First Californians.* San Francisco: Sierra Club Books.

Kuhn, Thomas. 1962. *The Structure of Scientific Revolutions.* Chicago: University of Chicago Press.

Kuper, Adam. 2003. "The Return of the Native." *Cultural Anthropology* 44 (3): 389–402.

Laclau, Ernesto, and Chantal Mouffe. 1985. *Hegemony and Socialist Strategy: Towards a Radical Democratic Politics.* London: Verso.

Lambert, Michael. 2002. *Longing for Exile: Migration and the Making of a Translocal Community in Senegal, West Africa.* Portsmouth, NH: Heinemann.

Lang, Julian. 2008. "Reflections on the Iridescent One." In Les Field, *Abalone Tales: Collaborative Explorations of Sovereignty and Identity in Native California.* Durham, NC: Duke University Press. 84–106.

Larcom, Joan. 1982. "The Invention of Convention." *Mankind* 13 (4): 330–337.

Lear, Jonathan. 2006. *Radical Hope: Ethics in the Face of Cultural Devastation.* Cambridge, MA: Harvard University Press.

Lee, Molly, and Nelson Graburn. 2003. "Reconfiguring Kodiak: The Past and the Present in the Present." *American Anthropologist* 105 (3): 613–620.

Leeds-Hurwitz, Wendy. 2005. *Rolling in Ditches with Shamans: Jaime de Angulo and the Professionalization of American Anthropology*. Lincoln: University of Nebraska Press.

Leer, Jeff. 2001. "The Dance Continues." In *Looking Both Ways: Heritage and Identity of the Alutiiq People,* ed. Aron Crowell, Amy Steffian, and Gordon Pullar. Fairbanks: University of Alaska Press. 219.

Le Guin, Ursula. 1976. *The Word for World Is Forest*. New York: Berkeley Medallion.

———. 1985. *Always Coming Home*. Berkeley: University of California Press.

———. 1989. "A Non-Euclidian View of California as a Cold Place to Be." In *Dancing at the Edge of the World*. New York: Grove Press. 80–100.

Levi-Bruhl, Lucien. 1923. *Primitive Mentality*. Charleston, SC: Nabu Press.

Lévi-Strauss, Claude. 1955. *Tristes Tropiques*. Paris: Plon-Terre Humaine.

———. 1966. "Anthropology: Its Achievement and Future." *Current Anthropology* 7: 124–127.

———. 1971. *Mythologiques*. New York: Omnibus Press.

———. 1999. *The Way of the Masks*. Vancouver: University of British Columbia Press.

Lévi-Strauss, Claude, and Didier Eribon. 1991. *Conversations with Claude Lévi-Strauss,* trans. Paula Wissing. Chicago: University of Chicago Press.

Levitt, Peggy. 2001. *The Transnational Villagers*. Berkeley: University of California Press.

Lilley, Ian. 2004. "Diaspora and Identity in Archaeology: Moving beyond the Black Atlantic." In *A Companion to Social Archaeology,* ed. Lynn Meskell and Robert Preucel. Oxford: Blackwell. 287–312.

———. 2006. *Journal of Social Archaeology* 6 (1): 28–47.

Lindqvist, Sven. 1997. *"Exterminate All the Brutes": One Man's Odyssey into the Heart of Darkness and the Origins of European Genocide*. New York: New Press.

Linnekin, Jocelyn. 1991. "Cultural Invention and the Dilemma of Authenticity." *American Anthropologist* 93: 446–449.

Linnekin, Jocelyn, and Lin Poyer, eds. 1990. *Cultural Identity and Ethnicity in the Pacific*. Honolulu: University of Hawai'i Press.

Lippard, Lucy, ed. 1992. *Partial Recall: Photographs of Native North Americans*. New York: New Press.

Lipsitz, George. 1998. *The Possessive Investment in Whiteness: How White People Profit from Identity Politics*. Philadelphia: Temple University Press.

Liss, Andrea. 1992. "The Art of James Luna: Postmodernism with Pathos." In *James Luna: Actions and Reactions,* ed. Rolando Castellón. Santa Cruz, CA: Mary Porter Sesnon Art Gallery. 7–20.

Long, Frederick. 1998. "'The Kingdom Must Come Soon': The Role of A. L. Kroeber and the Hearst Survey in Shaping California Anthropology, 1901–1920." MA thesis, Department of History, Simon Fraser University.

Luehrmann, Sonja. 2008. *Alutiiq Villages under Russian and U.S. Rule*. Fairbanks: University of Alaska Press.

Luna, James. 2011. "Fasten Your Seat Belts, Prepare for Landing." In *Lisbeth Haas, Pablo Tac, Indigenous Scholar*. Berkeley: University of California Press. 41–45.

Luthin, Herbert, and Leanne Hinton. 2003. In *Ishi in Three Centuries*, eds. Karl Kroeber and Clifton Kroeber. Lincoln: University of Nebraska Press. 318–354.

Maaka, Roger, and Augie Fleras. 2000. "Engaging with Indigeneity: Tino Rangatiratanga in Aotearoa." In *Political Theory and the Rights of Indigenous Peoples*, ed. Duncan Ivison, Paul Patton, and Will Sanders. Cambridge: Cambridge University Press. 89–111.

MacCannell, Dean. 1992. *Empty Meeting Grounds: The Tourist Papers*. London: Routledge.

Madsen, Roy. 2001. "Tides and Ties of Our Culture." In *Looking Both Ways: Heritage and Identity of the Alutiiq People*, ed. Aron Crowell, Amy Steffian, and Gordon Pullar. Fairbanks: University of Alaska Press. 75.

Mallon, Sean. 2005. "Samoan *Tatau* as Global Practice." In *Tattoo: Bodies, Art and Exchange in the Pacific and the West*, ed. Nicolas Thomas, Anna Cole, and Bronwen Douglas. London: Reaktion Books. 145–170.

Mamdani, Mahmood. 2002. *When Victims Become Killers: Colonialism, Nativism and the Genocide in Rwanda*. Princeton, NJ: Princeton University Press.

Mason, Arthur. 2002. "The Rise of an Alaska Native Bourgeoisie." *Études/Inuit/Studies* 26 (2): 5–23.

———. 2008. "Vanguard Heritage Practice and the Import of Expertise." *Etudes/Inuit/Studies* 32 (2): 107–125.

———. 2010a. "Of Enlightenment and Alaska Early Moderns." *Identities: Global Studies in Culture and Power* 17: 411–429.

———. 2010b. "Whither the Historicities of Alutiiq Heritage Work Are Drifting." In *Indigenous Cosmopolitans: Transnational and Transcultural Indigeneity in the Twenty-First Century*, ed. Maximilian Forte. Frankfurt am Main: Peter Lang. 77–96.

Massey, Doreen. 1994. *Space, Place, and Gender*. Minneapolis: University of Minnesota Press.

McClosky, James. 2008. "Irish as a World Language." In *Why Irish?*, ed. Brian Ó Conchubhar and Breandán Ó Buachalla. Dublin and Syracuse: Arlen House and Syracuse University Press. 2–17.

Meade, Marie. 2000. "Speaking with Elders." In *Hunting Tradition in a Changing World: Yup'ik Lives in Alaska Today*, ed. Ann Fienup-Riordan. New Brunswick, NJ: Rutgers University Press. 246–252.

Meek, Barbara. 2012. *We Are Our Language: An Ethnography of Language Revitalization in a Northern Athabaskan Community*. Tucson: University of Arizona Press.

Merlan, Francesca. 1997. "Fighting over Country: Four Commonplaces." In *Fighting over Country: Anthropological Perspectives*. CAEPR Research Monograph, no. 12. Canberra: Centre for Aboriginal Economic Policy Research, Australian National University. 4–15.

———. 1998. *Caging the Rainbow: Places, Politics, and Aborigines in a North Australian Town*. Honolulu: University of Hawai'i Press.

Meyers, Fred. 2002. *Painting Culture: The Making of an Aboriginal High Art*. Durham NC: Duke University Press.

Miller, Daniel. 1987. *Material Culture and Mass Consumption*. Oxford: Blackwell.

———. 1994. *Modernity: An Ethnographic Approach*. Oxford: Oxford University Press.

———. 1995a. "Consumption and Commodities." *Annual Review of Anthropology* 24: 141–161.

———. 1995b. "Introduction: Anthropology, Modernity and Consumption." In *Worlds Apart: Modernity through the Prism of the Local*. London: Routledge. 1–23.

———, ed. 1995c. *Worlds Apart: Modernity through the Prism of the Local*. London: Routledge.

Mintz, Sidney. 1966. "The Caribbean as a Socio-Cultural Area." *Cahiers d'Histoire Mondiale* 9: 912–937.

Mishler, Craig, and Rachel Mason. 1996. "Alutiiq Vikings: Kinship and Fishing in Old Harbor, Alaska." *Human Organization* 55 (3): 263–269.

Mishler, Craig. 2001. "Kodiak Alutiiq Weather Lore." In *Looking Both Ways: Heritage and Identity of the Alutiiq People*, ed. Aron Crowell, Amy Steffian, and Gordon Pullar. Fairbanks: University of Alaska Press. 150–151.

———. 2003. *Black Ducks and Salmon Bellies: An Ethnography of Old Harbor and Ouzinkie, Alaska*. Virginia Beach, VA: Donning.

Mishra, Vijay. 1996a. "(B)ordering Naipaul: Indenture History and Diasporic Poetics." *Diaspora* 5 (2): 189–237.

———. 1996b. "The Diasporic Imaginary: Theorizing the Indian Diaspora." *Textual Practice* 10 (3): 421–447.

Mitchell, Joseph. 1960. "Mohawks in High Steel." In *Apologies to the Iroquois*, ed. Edmund Wilson. New York: Vintage. 3–38.

Mitchell, Marybelle. 1996. *From Talking Chiefs to a Native Corporate Elite: The Birth of Class and Nationalism among Canadian Inuit*. Montreal: McGill-Queen's University Press.

Molisa, Grace Mera. 1987. *Colonized People: Poems*. Port Vila: Black Stone Press.

Morphy, Howard. 2008. *Becoming Art: Exploring Cross-Cultural Categories*. Sydney: University of New South Wales Press.

Muehlebach, Andrea. 2001. "'Making Place' at the United Nations: Indigenous Cultural Politics at the U.N. Working Group on Indigenous Populations." *Cultural Anthropology* 16 (3): 415–448.

Nabokov, Peter. 2002. *A Forest of Time: American Indian Ways of History*. Cambridge: Cambridge University Press.

Naepels, Michel. 2000. "Partir à Nouméa. Remarques sur les migrants originaires de la region aijë." In *En pays Kanak*, ed. Alban Bensa and Isabelle Leblic. Paris: Editions de la Maison des Sciences de l'Homme. 355–365.

Nelson, Diane. 1999. *A Finger in the Wound: Body Politics in Quincentennial Guatemala*. Berkeley: University of California Press.

Newman, John Henry. 1920. *An Essay on the Development of Christian Doctrine*. New York: Longmans, Green.

Nielsen, Mary Jane. 2001. "The Spirits Are Still There: Memories of Katmai Country." In *Looking Both Ways: Heritage and Identity of the Alutiiq People*, ed. Aron Crowell, Amy Steffian, and Gordon Pullar. Fairbanks: University of Alaska Press. 84.

Niezen, Ronald. 2003. *The Origins of Indigenism: Human Rights and the Politics of Identity*. Berkeley: University of California Press.

Nora, Pierre, ed. 1984. *Les lieux de mémoire*. 3 vols. Paris: Gallimard.

Nyamnjoh, Francis. 2007. "From Bounded to Flexible Citizenship: Lessons from Africa." *Citizenship Studies* 11 (1): 73–82.

Oleksa, Michael. 1990. "The Creoles and Their Contributions to the Development of Alaska." In *Russian America: The Forgotten Frontier*, ed. Barbara Sweetland and Redmond J. Barnett. Tacoma: Washington State Historical Society. 185–195.

———. 1992. *Orthodox Alaska: A Theology of Mission*. Crestwood, NY: St. Vladimir's Seminary Press.

Ong, Aihwa. 1999. *Flexible Citizenship: The Cultural Logics of Transnationality*. Durham, NC: Duke University Press.

———. 2000. "Graduated Sovereignty in South-East Asia." *Theory, Culture and Society* 17 (4): 55–75.

———. 2006. *Neoliberalism as Exception: Mutations of Citizenship and Sovereignty*. Durham, NC: Duke University Press.

Ong, Aiwah, and Stephen Collier. 2005. *Global Assemblages: Technology, Politics, and Ethics as Anthropological Problems*. Oxford: Blackwell.

Ong, Aiwah, and Donald Nonini, eds. 1997. *Ungrounded Empires: The Cultural Politics of Modern Chinese Transnationalism*. New York: Routledge.

Ortiz, Beverley. 2013. Personal communication. Excerpt from an unattributed newspaper clipping, probably March 1976, preserved in a scrapbook by the late Josephine Peters (Karuk).

Ortner, Sherry. 1998. "Identities: The Hidden Life of Class." *Journal of Anthropological Research* 54 (1): 1–17.

Ostrowitz, Judith. 2009. *Interventions: Native American Art for Far-Flung Territories*. Seattle: University of Washington Press.

Otto, Ton, and Nils Bubandt, eds. 2010. *Experiments in Holism: Theory and Practice in Contemporary Anthropology*. Oxford: Blackwell.

Owen, Louis. 2003. "Native Sovereignty and the Tricky Mirror: Gerald Vizenor's 'Ishi and the Wood Ducks.'" In *Ishi in Three Centuries*, ed. Karl Kroeber and Clifton Kroeber. Lincoln: University of Nebraska Press. 373–387.

Partnow, Patricia. 2001a. "Alutiiq Identity." In *Looking Both Ways: Heritage and Identity of the Alutiiq People*, ed. Aron Crowell, Amy Steffian, and Gordon Pullar. Fairbanks: University of Alaska Press. 68–69.

———. 2001b. *Making History: Alutiiq/Sugpiaq Life on the Alaska Peninsula*. Fairbanks: University of Alaska Press.

Peel, J. D. Y. 1978. "Olajú: A Yoruba Concept of Development." *Journal of Development Studies* 14: 139–165.

Peters, Kurt. 1995. "Santa Fe Indian Camp, House 21, Richmond California: Persistence of Identity among Laguna Pueblo Railroad Laborers, 1945–1982." *American Indian Culture and Research Journal* 19 (3): 33–70.

Phillips, Mark. 2004. Introduction to *Questions of Tradition*, ed. Mark Phillips and Gordon Schochet. Toronto: University of Toronto Press. 3–29.

Phillips, Mark, and Gordon Schochet, eds. 2004. *Questions of Tradition*. Toronto: University of Toronto Press.

Phillips, Ruth. 1998. *Trading Identities: The Souvenir in Native North American Art from the Northeast, 1700–1900*. Seattle: University of Washington Press.

———. 2003. "Introduction: Community Collaboration in Exhibitions: Toward a Dialogic Paradigm." In *Museums and Source Communities*, ed. Laura Peers and Alison Brown. London: Routledge. 155–170.

———. 2012. *Museum Pieces: Toward the Indigenization of Canadian Museums*. Montreal and Kingston: McGill and Queens University Press.

Platt, Tony. 2011. *Grave Matters: Excavating California's Buried Past*. Berkeley: Heyday Books.

Piot, Charles. 1999. *Remotely Global: Village Modernity in West Africa*. Durham, NC: Duke University Press.

Pope, Saxton. 1918. "Yahi Archery." *University of California Publications in American Archaeology and Ethnology* 12 (2): 103–182.

———. 1920. "The Medical History of Ishi." *University of California Publications in American Archaeology and Ethnology* 13 (5): 175–213.

Povinelli, Elizabeth. 2002. *The Cunning of Recognition: Indigenous Alterities and the Making of Australian Multiculturalism*. Durham, NC: Duke University Press.

Pratt, Mary Louise. 1992. *Imperial Eyes: Travel Writing and Transculturation*. New York: Routledge.

Pred, Alan, and Michael Watts. 1992. *Reworking Modernity: Capitalisms and Symbolic Discontent*. New Brunswick, NJ: Rutgers University Press.

Price, Richard. 1998. *The Convict and the Colonel*. Boston: Beacon Press.

Pullar, Gordon. 1992. "Ethnic Identity, Cultural Pride, and Generations of Baggage: A Personal Experience." *Arctic Anthropology* 29: 182–191.

———. 2001. "Contemporary Alutiiq Identity." In *Looking Both Ways: Heritage and Identity of the Alutiiq People*, ed. Aron Crowell, Amy Steffian, and Gordon Pullar. Fairbanks: University of Alaska Press. 73–98.

———. 2009. "Historical Ethnography of Nineteenth-Century Kodiak Villages." In *Giinaquq: Like a Face/Comme un visage: Sugpiaq Masks of the Kodiak Archipelago*, ed. Sven Haakanson and Amy Steffian. Fairbanks: University of Alaska Press: 41–79.

Pullar, Gordon, and Richard A. Knecht. 1995. "Alutiiq." In *Crossroads Alaska: Native Cultures of Alaska and Siberia*, ed. Valerie Chaussonnet. Washington, DC: Arctic Studies Center, National Museum of Natural History, Smithsonian Institution Press. 14–15.

Rabasa, José. 2010. *Without History: Subaltern Studies, The Zapatista Insurgency, and the Specter of History.* Pittsburgh: University of Pittsburgh Press.

Rafael, Vicente. 1989. "Imagination and Imagery: Filipino Nationalism in the 19th Century." *Inscriptions* 5: 25–48.

Ramirez, Renya. 2007. *Native Hubs: Culture, Community, and Belonging in Silicon Valley and Beyond.* Durham, NC: Duke University Press.

Ramos, Alcida. 1998. *Indigenism: Ethnic Politics in Brazil.* Madison: University of Wisconsin Press.

Reagon, Bernice Johnson. 1983. "Coalition Politics: Turning the Century." In *Homegirls: A Black Feminist Anthology,* ed. Barbara Smith. New York: Kitchen Table Press. 356–368.

Rickard, Jolene. 1992. "Cew Ete Haw I Tih: The Bird That Carries Language Back to Another." In *Partial Recall: Photographs of Native North Americans,* ed. Lucy Lippard. New York: New Press. 105–112.

Rigsby, Bruce. 1995. "Tribes, Diaspora People and the Vitality of Law and Custom: Some Comments." In *Anthropology in the Native Title Era: Proceedings of a Workshop,* ed. Jim Fingleton and Julie Finlayson. Canberra: Australian Institute of Aboriginal and Torres Straits Islander Studies. 25–27.

Ritter, Kathleen. 2008. "The Reclining Figure and Other Provocations." In *Rebecca Belmore: Rising to the Occasion,* ed. Daina Augaitis and Kathleen Ritter. Vancouver: Vancouver Art Gallery. 53–65.

Roosens, Eugeen. 1989. *Creating Ethnicity: The Process of Ethnogenesis.* London: Sage Press.

Rosaldo, Renato. 1980. *Ilongot Headhunting, 1883–1974: A Study in Society and History.* Stanford: Stanford University Press.

———. 1989. *Culture and Truth: The Remaking of Social Analysis.* Boston: Beacon.

Rose, Deborah Bird. 2004. *Reports from a Wild Country: Ethics for Decolonization.* Sydney: University of New South Wales Press.

Rouse, Roger. 1991. "Mexican Migration and the Social Space of Postmodernism." *Diaspora* 1 (1): 8–23.

Rumsey, Alan, and James Weiner, eds. 2001. *Emplaced Myth: Space, Narrative, and Knowledge in Aboriginal Australia and Papua New Guinea.* Honolulu: University of Hawai'i Press.

Ryan, Stephen. 1996. "'The Voice of Sanity Getting Hoarse'? Destructive Processes in Violent Ethnic Conflict." In *The Politics of Difference: Ethnic Premises in a World of Power,* ed. Edwin Wilmsen and Patrick McAllister. Chicago: University of Chicago Press. 144–161.

Sackman, Douglas Cazaux. 2010. *Wild Men: Ishi and Kroeber in the Wilderness of Modern America.* Oxford: Oxford University Press.

Sahlins, Marshall. 1981. *Historical and Mythical Realities: Structure in the Early History of the Sandwich Islands Kingdom.* Ann Arbor: University of Michigan Press.

———. 1985. *Islands of History.* Chicago: University of Chicago Press.

———. 1993. "Cery Cery Fuckabede." *American Ethnologist* 20: 848–867.

———. 1994. "Goodbye to Tristes Tropes: Ethnography in the Context of Modern World History." In *Assessing Cultural Anthropology,* ed. Robert Borofsky. New York: McGraw-Hill Press. 377–394.

———. 1995. *How "Natives" Think: About Captain Cook, For Example.* Chicago: University of Chicago Press.

———. 1999. "What Is Anthropological Enlightenment? Some Lessons of the Twentieth Century." *Annual Review of Anthropology* 28. i–xxii.

———. 2000. "Cosmologies of Capitalism: The Trans-Pacific Sector of 'The World System.'" In *Culture in Practice: Selected Essays.* New York: Zone Books. 415–469.

Said, Edward. 1983. *The World, the Text, and the Critic.* Cambridge, MA: Harvard University Press.

Samuel, Raphael. 1994. *Theatres of Memory.* Vol. 1, *Past and Present in Contemporary* Culture. London: Verso.

Sangari, Kum Kum. 2002. *The Politics of the Possible: Essays on Gender, History, Narratives, Colonial English.* London: Anthem Press.

Sapir, Edward. 1916. "Terms of Relationship and the Levirate." *American Anthropologist* 16 (3): 327–337.

Sarris, Greg. 1993. *Keeping Slug Woman Alive: A Holistic Approach to American Indian* Texts. Berkeley: University of California Press.

———. 1994. *Mabel McKay: Weaving the Dream.* Berkeley: University of California Press.

Sassen, Saskia. 1991. *The Global City: New York, London, Tokyo.* Princeton, NJ: Princeton University Press.

Scheper-Hughes, Nancy. 2003 "Ishi's Brain, Ishi's Ashes: Reflections on Anthropology and Genocide." In *Ishi in Three Centuries,* ed. Karl Kroeber and Clifton Kroeber. Lincoln: University of Nebraska Press. 99–131.

Sedgwick, Eve. 1985. *Between Men: English Literature and Male Homosocial Desire.* New York: Columbia University Press.

Shackley, M. Steven. 2000. "The Stone Tool Technology of Ishi and the Yana of North Central California: Inferences for Hunter-Gatherer Cultural Identity in Historic California." *American Anthropologist* 104 (4): 693–712.

Shandler, Jeffrey. 2006. *Adventures in Yiddishland: Postvernacular Language and Culture.* Berkeley: University of California Press.

Shanigan, Marlane. 2001. "Kanatak Tribal Council." In *Looking Both Ways: Heritage and Identity of the Alutiiq People,* ed. Aron Crowell, Amy Steffian, and Gordon Pullar. Fairbanks: University of Alaska Press. 86.

Sharp, John. 1996. "Ethnogenesis and Ethnic Mobilization: A Comparative Perspective on a South African Dilemma." In *The Politics of Difference: Ethnic Premises in a World of Power,* ed. Edwin Wilmsen and Patrick McAllister. Chicago: University of Chicago Press. 85–103.

Shorter, David. 2009. *We Will Dance Our Truth: Yaqui History in Yoeme Performances.* Lincoln: University of Nebraska Press.

Sissons, Jeffrey. 2005. *First Peoples: Indigenous Cultures and Their Futures.* London: Reaktion Books.

Skinner, Ramona. 1997. *Alaska Native Policy in the Twentieth Century.* New York: Garland.

Slack, Jennifer Daryl. 1996. "The Theory and Method of Articulation in Cultural Studies." In *Stuart Hall: Critical Dialogues in Cultural Studies,* ed. David Morley and Kian-Hsing Chen. London: Routledge. 112–129.

Slobin, Mark. 1998. "Scanning a Subculture: Introduction to Klezmerology." *Judaism* 47 (1): 3–5.

Small, Cathy. 1997. *From Tongan Villages to the American Suburbs.* Ithaca, NY: Cornell University Press.

Smith, Benjamin Richard. 2000. " 'Local' and 'Diaspora' Connections to Country and Kin in Central Cape York Peninsula." In *Land, Rights, Laws: Issues of Native Title.* Vol. 2, no. 6, ed. Jessica Weir. Canberra: Australian Institute of Aboriginal and Torres Straits Islander Studies. 1–8.

Smith, Linda Tuhiwai. 1999. *Decolonizing Methodologies: Research and Indigenous Peoples.* London: Zed Books.

Smith, Paul Chaat. 1992. "Every Picture Tells a Story." In *Partial Recall: Photographs of Native North Americans,* ed. Lucy Lippard. New York: New Press. 95–100.

———. 2009. *Everything You Know about Indians Is Wrong.* Minneapolis: University of Minnesota Press.

Speaker, Stuart. 2003. "Repatriating the Remains of Ishi: Smithsonian Institution Report and Recommendation." In *Ishi in Three Centuries,* ed. Karl Kroeber and Clifton Kroeber. Lincoln: University of Nebraska Press. 73–86.

Spicer, Edward. 1980. *The Yaquis: A Cultural History.* Tucson: University of Arizona Press.

———. 1982. "The Nations of a State." *Boundary 2* 19 (3): 26–48.

Starn, Orin. 2003. "Ishi's Spanish Words." In *Ishi in Three Centuries,* ed. Karl Kroeber and Clifton Kroeber. Lincoln: University of Nebraska Press. 201–207.

———. 2004. *Ishi's Brain: In Search of America's Last "Wild" Indian.* New York: Norton.

Steffian, Amy. 2001. "Cu'milalhet—'Our Ancestors.' " In *Looking Both Ways: Heritage and Identity of the Alutiiq People,* ed. Aron Crowell, Amy Steffian, and Gordon Pullar. Fairbanks: University of Alaska Press. 99–135.

Steinbright, Jan, and Clark James Mishler. 2001. *Qayaqs and Canoes: Native Ways of Knowing.* Anchorage: Alaska Native Heritage Center.

Stephen, Lynn. 2002. *Zapata Lives! Histories and Cultural Politics in Southern Mexico.* Berkeley: University of California Press.

Stewart, Kathleen. 1996. *A Space on the Side of the Road: Cultural Politics in an "Other" America.* Princeton, NJ: Princeton University Press.

Strang, Veronica. 2000. "Showing and Telling: Australian Land Rights and Material Moralities." *Journal of Material Culture* 5 (3): 275–299.

Sturm, Circe. 2002. *Blood Politics: Race, Culture and Identity in the Cherokee Nation of Oklahoma.* Berkeley: University of California Press.

———. 2011. *Becoming Indian: The Struggle over Cherokee Identity in the Twenty-First Century.* Santa Fe: School of American Research Press.

Sullivan, Paul. 1989. *Unfinished Conversations: Mayas and Foreigners between Two Wars*. New York: Knopf.

Sutton, Peter. 1988. "Myth as History, History as Myth." In *Being Black: Aboriginal Cultures in "Settled" Australia*, ed. Ian Keen. Canberra: Aboriginal Studies Press. 251–268.

Swain, Tony. 1993. *A Place for Strangers: Towards a History of Australian Aboriginal Being*. Cambridge: Cambridge University Press.

Taussig, Michael. 1987. *Shamanism, Colonialism, and the Wild Man: A Study in Terror and Healing*. Chicago: University of Chicago Press.

Teaiwa, Teresia 2001a. "Lo(o)sing the Edge." *The Contemporary Pacific* 13 (2): 343–357.

———. 2001b. "Militarism, Tourism, and the Native: Articulations in Oceania." PhD diss., History of Consciousness Department, University of California, Santa Cruz.

Thaman, Konai Helu. 1985. "The Defining Distance: People, Places, and Worldview." *Pacific Viewpoint* 26 (1): 106–115.

Thomas, David Hurst. 2000. *Skull Wars: Kennewick Man, Archaeology, and the Battle for Native American Identity*. New York: Basic Books.

Thomas, Nicholas. 1992. "Substantivization and Anthropological Discourse: The Transformation of Practices and Institutions in Neo-Traditional Pacific Societies." In *History and Tradition in Melanesian Anthropology*, ed. James Carrier. Berkeley: University of California Press. 64–85.

———. 1997. *In Oceania: Visions, Artifacts, Histories*. Durham, NC: Duke University Press.

———. 1999. *Possessions: Indigenous Art/Colonial Culture*. London: Thames and Hudson.

Thompson, E. P. 1963. *The Making of the English Working Class*. London: Verso.

Tilley, Christopher. 1997. "Performing Culture in the Global Village." *Critique of Anthropology* 17 (1): 67–89.

Tjibaou, Jean-Marie. 1996. *La présence Kanak*. Paris: Editions Odile Jacob.

———. 2005. *Kanaky*, trans. Helen Fraser and John Trotter. Canberra: ANU/Pandanus Books. Translation of Tjibaou 1996.

Townsend-Gault, Charlotte. 2004. "Struggles with Aboriginality/Modernity." In *Bill Reid and Beyond: Expanding on Modern Native Art*. Seattle: University of Washington Press. 225–244.

Trask, Haunani-Kay. 1991. "Natives and Anthropologists: The Colonial Struggle." *The Contemporary Pacific* 3: 159–177.

Tsing, Anna Lowenhaupt. 1993. *The Realm of the Diamond Queen: Marginality in an Out-of-the-Way Place*. Princeton, NJ: Princeton University Press.

———. 1999. "Notes on Culture and Natural Resource Management." Berkeley Workshop on Environmental Politics, Working Paper WP99-4, University of California, Berkeley.

———. 2000. "The Global Situation." *Cultural Anthropology* 15 (3): 327–360.

———. 2005. *Friction: An Ethnography of Global Connection*. Princeton, NJ: Princeton University Press.

———. 2007. "Indigenous Voice." In *Indigenous Experience Today,* ed. Marisol de la Cadena and Orin Starn. Oxford: Berg. 33–68.

———. 2009. "Supply Chains and the Human Condition." *Rethinking Marxism* 21 (2): 148–176.

Tully, James. 2000. "The Struggles of Indigenous Peoples for and of Freedom." In *Political Theory and the Rights of Indigenous Peoples,* ed. Duncan Ivison, Paul Patton, and Will Sanders. Cambridge: Cambridge University Press. 36–59.

Turner, Terence. 1991. "Representing, Resisting, Rethinking: Historical Transformations of Kayapo Culture and Anthropological Consciousness." In *Colonial Situations: Essays on the Contextualization of Ethnographic Knowledge.* History of Anthropology 7, ed. George Stocking. Madison: University of Wisconsin Press. 285–313.

———. 1992. "Defiant Images: The Kayapo Appropriation of Video." *Anthropology Today* 8 (6): 5–16.

Vizenor, Gerald. 1994. "Ishi Obscura." In *Manifest Manners: Postindian Warriors of Survivance.* Middletown, CT: Wesleyan University Press. 126–137.

———. 2003. "Mister Ishi: Analogies of Exile, Deliverance, and Liberty." In *Ishi in Three Centuries,* ed. Karl Kroeber and Clifton Kroeber. Lincoln: University of Nebraska Press. 363–372.

Waddell, Eric. 2008. *Jean-Marie Tjibaou, Kanak Witness to the World: An Intellectual Biography.* Honolulu: University of Hawai'i Press.

Waddell, Eric, Vijay Naidu, and Epeli Hau'ofa, eds. 1993. *A New Oceania: Rediscovering Our Sea of Islands.* Suva, Fiji: School of Social and Economic Development, University of the South Pacific.

Wagner, Roy. 1975. *The Invention of Culture.* Chicago: University of Chicago Press.

———. 1979. "The Talk of Koriki: A Daribi Contact Cult." *Social Research* 46: 140–165.

Wallerstein, Immanuel. 1976. *The Modern World System: Capitalist Agriculture and the Origins of the European World-Economy in the Sixteenth Century.* New York: Academic Press.

———. 2003. *The Decline of American Power.* New York: New Press.

Walsh, Kevin. 1992. *The Representation of the Past: Museums and Heritage in the Post-Modern World.* London: Routledge.

Wang, Q. Edward, and Franz Fillafer, eds. 2007. *The Many Faces of Clio: Cross-Cultural Approaches to Historiography.* New York: Berghahn.

Warren, Kay. 1992. "Transforming Memories and Histories: The Meanings of Ethnic Resurgence for Mayan Indians." In *Americas: New Interpretive Essays,* ed. Alfred Stepan. Oxford: Oxford University Press. 189–219.

———. 1996. "Reading History as Resistance: Maya Public Intellectuals in Guatemala." In *Maya Cultural Activism in Guatemala,* ed. Edward Fischer and R. McKenna Brown. Austin: University of Texas Press. 98–106.

———. 1999. *Indigenous Movements and Their Critics: Pan-Maya Activism in Guatemala.* Princeton, NJ: Princeton University Press.

Watson, James. 1997. *Golden Arches East: McDonald's in East Asia*. Stanford: Stanford University Press.

Weiner, James. 2002. "Diaspora, Materialism, Tradition: Anthropological Issues in the Recent High Court Appeal of the Yorta Yorta." In *Land, Rights, Laws: Issues of Native Title*. Vol. 2, no. 18, ed. Jessica Weir. Canberra: Australian Institute of Aboriginal and Torres Straits Islander Studies. 1–12.

White, Geoffrey. 1991. *Identity through History: Living Stories in a Solomon Island Society*. Cambridge, MA: Cambridge University Press.

White, Hayden. 1987. *The Content of the Form: Narrative Discourse and Historical Representation*. Baltimore: Johns Hopkins University Press.

White, Richard. 1991. *The Middle Ground*. Cambridge: Cambridge University Press.

Wilk, Richard. 1995. "Learning to be Local in Belize: Global Systems of Common Difference." In *Worlds Apart: Modernity through the Prism of the Local*, ed. Daniel Miller. London: Routledge. 110–133.

Williams, Raymond. 1958. *Culture and Society: 1780–1950*. New York: Harper and Row.

———. 1977. *Marxism and Literature*. Oxford: Oxford University Press.

Wilson, Rob. 2009. *Be Always Converting, Be Always Converted: An American Poetics*. Cambridge, MA: Harvard University Press.

Wittersheim, Eric. 1999. "Les Chemins de l'anthenticité: Les anthropologies et la renaissance mélanésienne." *L'Homme* 151: 181–206.

Yoshita, Kenji. 2008. Introduction to *Preserving the Cultural Heritage of Africa: Crisis or Renaissance?*, ed. Kenji Yoshita and John Mack. Woodbridge, Suffolk: James Curry. 1–9.

Sources

The Prologue incorporates material published under the title "Feeling Historical" in *Cultural Anthropology* 27 (3) (August 2012): 417–426.

Chapter 1 is published for the first time in this volume.

Chapter 2 was originally delivered at the symposium "Native Pacific Cultural Studies at the Edge," 11–12 February 2000. It was published in Clifford 2001.

Chapter 3 was presented in 2005 at a conference organized by Marisol de la Cadena and Orin Starn for the Wenner-Gren Foundation, "Indigenous Experience Today." It was published in a book of the same name (de la Cadena and Starn 2007: 197–224).

Chapter 4, almost entirely new, incorporates several pages from "Response to Orin Starn," *Cultural Anthropology* 26 (2) (May 2011): 218–224.

Chapter 5 is based on a lecture delivered in 2009 and published the same year in *Oceania* 79: 238–249.

Portions of *Chapter 6* first appeared in *Current Anthropology* 45 (1) (February 2004): 5–30. It has been expanded for this volume, partly in response to the critical comments that accompanied the original publication.

Chapter 7 incorporates portions of a lecture delivered on June 26, 2010, at Minpaku: The National Museum of Ethnology, Osaka, Japan. The talk was published in 2011, with discussants' comments, in the museum *Bulletin* 35 (4): 713–743.

The Epilogue is published for the first time in this volume.

ACKNOWLEDGMENTS

A list of names cannot do justice to the generosity of those who helped me with this project. I trust they are aware, at a more personal level, of my gratitude.

Some intellectual influences have been pervasive: Hayden White, Donna Haraway, Stuart Hall, Ursula K. Le Guin, Marshall Sahlins, Anna Lowenhaupt Tsing, Paul Chaat Smith, and the late Epeli Hau'ofa.

I owe a continuing debt to Richard Sieburth, Anna Cancogni, Jean Jamin, Michel Leiris, and Jean-Marie Tjibaou, whose friendship and exemplary work were germinal for a project that now spans nearly four decades.

Over these years, my doctoral students in the History of Consciousness Department and other programs at the University of California, Santa Cruz, have challenged and inspired me. Countless advising sessions, seminar discussions and dissertations are woven into *Returns*.

Gail Hershatter, historian and colleague extraordinaire, has kept me on track in recent years. As writing partners we read and criticized each other's projects, and she has had a hand in every section of this book.

My wife, Judith Aissen, has assisted in countless ways as an interlocutor and critic. She is a constant source of loving support and an intellectual model in her own scholarship.

At Harvard University Press, I am grateful to Lindsay Waters for intellectual stimulation and unwavering support for the trilogy of which *Returns* is a part. His editorial assistant, Shanshan Wang, was a source of efficiency and good humor. At UCSC, Alexander Keller Hirsch provided research assistance and much stimulating conversation. The book's scrupulous copy editor, Anne Sussman, saved me from innumerable errors.

The following individuals offered good exchanges, criticism, or material support. Of course their assistance does not necessarily imply agreement with my conclusions.

Part One. On indigenous resurgence and contemporary cultural politics: Mark Anderson, Gopal Balakrishnan, Lissant Bolton, Alexis Bunten, Kimberly Christen, Julie Cruikshank, Vicente Diaz, Guillermo Delgado-P, Barbara Epstein, Steven Feld, Nelson Graburn, Richard Handler, Ulla Haselstein, April Henderson, Margaret Jolly, Noelani Goodyear Kaopua, J. Kehaulani Kauanui, Jennifer Kramer, Yoshinobu Ota, Ruth Phillips, Ralph Regenvanu, Patricia Shaw, Anthony Shelton, David Delgado Shorter, Kim Tallbear, Teresia Teaiwa, Nicholas Thomas, Charlotte Townsend-Gault.

Part Two. Among those with whom I discussed Ishi and California Indian history I particularly thank Orin Starn. Also: the late William Bright, Leanne Hinton, Ira Jacknis, Christiaan Klieger, the late Karl Kroeber, Beverley Ortiz, and Jed Riffe.

Part Three. My most important guides in Alaska have been Aron Crowell, Sven Haakanson Jr., Ann Fienup-Riordan, and Amy Steffian. I gratefully acknowledge their generosity and inspiring work. For pertinent information, useful critiques, and help with resources I also thank: Kirk Dombrowski, Richard Knecht, Anne-Claire Laronde, Arthur Mason, Patricia Partnow, Gordon Pullar, and the always helpful staff at the Alutiiq Museum and Archaeological Repository in Kodiak.

This project was generously supported by a Guggenheim Fellowship, the Stanford Humanities Center, a Tokyo I-House Ushiba Fellowship, and by grants from the UCSC Faculty Committee on Research.

INDEX

Abenaki Indians, 72

Acculturation/assimilation, 7, 102, 219, 220, 276

Active, John, 82

Adorno, Theodor: on the whole, 41

Afognak Native Corp., 274–275

Africa, 14, 15, 38, 58, 81

Afro-Caribbeans, 21

Agayuliyaraput exhibition, 232–236, 258

Aida, Rosalva, 36

Ainu, 15, 23

Akhiok-Kaguyak Inc., 274–275

Alaska: Afognak, 282; Aleutians, 197, 209, 248; Anchorage, 79–80, 81, 82, 197, 215, 220, 222, 234, 238–239, 255, 261, 274; Bering Straits, 241; Bethel, 233; Chignik Lake, 316, 318, 319; Gold Rush, 261; and Hawai'i, 196, 197–198; Homer, 254–255, 256; Inside Passage, 237; Kachemak Bay, 242; Katmai eruption, 245, 316; Kenai Peninsula, 230, 254; Kodiak Island, 4, 41, 196, 197–198, 207, 208–209, 210, 222, 225–231, 241, 243, 247, 248, 250, 253, 254, 256, 262–267, 271–272, 280, 281–282, 292, 301; Kuskokwim delta, 80, 280; Larsen Bay, 226–227, 230, 231, 247, 248, 258, 266; Nanwalek, 254; Native land claims in, 78–79, 207, 215, 216–217, 220, 221–222, 245, 250, 270, 272, 302, 305, 313; Native-led corporations in, 208, 209, 216, 217–219, 221,

222, 231, 245, 248, 256, 262, 271, 273, 274–275, 303, 304, 312, 314; Nelson Island, 77, 80, 232–235, 237; oil pipeline in, 207–208, 215–216, 217, 301; Prince William Sound, 222, 243, 247; Prudhoe Bay, 207, 216; State Council on the Arts, 275; Supreme Court, 218; Toksook Bay, 232, 233, 234, 235, 237; Valdez, 207; Yukon delta, 280

Alaska Federation of Natives (AFN), 215–216, 220, 221

Alaska Native Claims Settlement Act (ANCSA), 19, 78–79, 82, 207–209, 215–222, 225, 236, 240, 246; and Alutiit/Sugpiat, 208, 210, 222, 251, 253, 257, 270–271, 272, 275, 296, 301, 302, 305; and capitalism, 237; enrollment requirements, 208, 216, 281, 305; native-led corporations created by, 208, 209, 216, 217–219, 221, 222, 231, 245, 248, 262, 271, 273, 274–275, 303, 304

Alaska Native Heritage Center, 215, 237, 238–242, 244, 255, 259, 307

Alaska Native Medical Center (ANMC), 80, 262

Alcatraz occupation, 19, 122

Aleuts, 240, 241, 243, 245–247, 251, 271, 293, 303, 316

Alokli, Nick, 297

Althusser, Louis, 47; on interpellation, 301